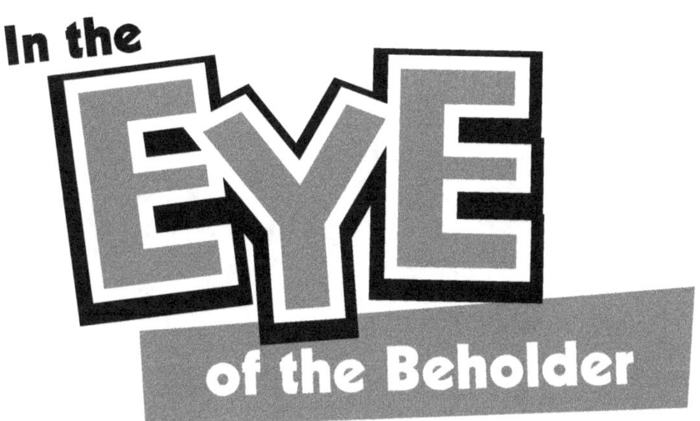

A Collection of Bol's Eye Cartoons
by Shaun Boland

For more information, visit www.bolseye.com.

ISBN: 978-0-615-40696-1

Thank You

I can't begin to thank those who have helped make this book possible without first giving thanks to the Lord. Without God, this book would not exist. Through Him I have come to believe that nothing is impossible with faith and perseverance.

To my parents, Ron and Gloria: thank you for always being supportive of my creative ventures. Your love and encouragement gave me reason to believe that I could accomplish anything that I set my mind to.

To my family and friends: thank you for your unwavering support over the years. Whether you proudly wore a Bol's Eye T-shirt in public, told a friend about the website and fan e-mail list, or gave your candid feedback, you were instrumental to the growth of Bol's Eye.

To the newspaper editors who printed my cartoons: thank you for the opportunity to share my humor with so many readers. My sincerest appreciation goes to Sue Shank, Paula Varner, Chip Minemyer, Chad Mearns, Brian Whipkey, Bob Christian and Cindy Marone. Thank you for supporting my cartoon, even during tough economic times.

And, to the readers: my deepest gratitude goes to you for welcoming my art. You are the reason that I draw Bol's Eye.

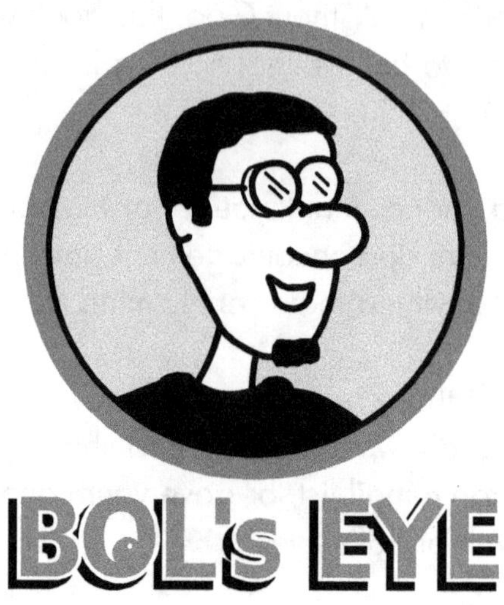
BOL's EYE

A Little Imagination

I've always had a desire to create things. When I was a child, no household item was ever safe from my wild ideas: rubber bands, building blocks, clothes pins, cardboard, hot glue–everything was fair game in my quest to build. My works of art would appear regularly on the floor and like clockwork my mother would ask me to move them so that she could vacuum. My father had his own carpentry workshop, and it didn't take long for it to become my favorite place to create. Clothes pins and cardboard were quickly replaced by wood, nails, bolts and metal.

And while I was jumping between new interests and new creations, I was always drawing. It was the one thing that I never stopped doing. If I wasn't making funnies for the elementary school newspaper, I was sketching my favorite sports players or recreating my favorite cartoon characters from TV.

In high school I sketched even more frequently, filling my notebooks with cartoons and flipbook animations. Little did I know that after graduation I wouldn't draw another cartoon for nearly seven years. My focus shifted to my college education and from it grew a strong desire to become a better artist. I knew that the knowledge and skills that I would develop in school would open doors for me in the future–and they did.

In 2003, while working at a classified ad publication, I made the decision to return to cartooning. I hit the drawing table, developed a unique style, and finally emerged with my new creation–Bol's Eye. With my cartoons in hand, I approached the manager of the paper and asked if she would run them. She approved, and in 2004 the first Bol's Eye cartoon appeared in print.

Since then, Bol's Eye has been seen in many more publications. I am excited and grateful for the opportunity to share those cartoons with you in this collection. So, without further ado, I proudly present the first-ever Bol's Eye gallery book.

– Shaun Boland

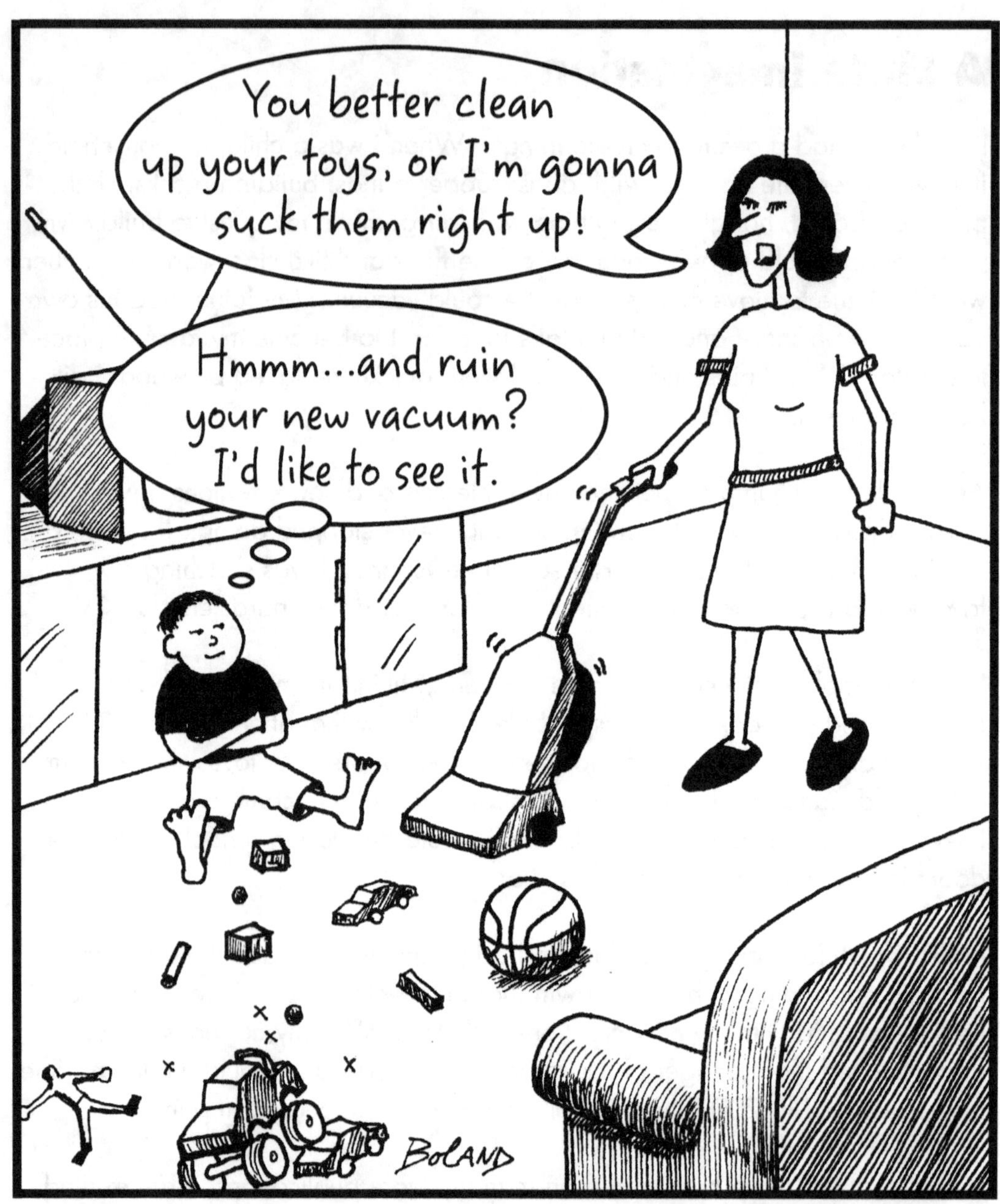

With an uncanny ability to sense a bluff, Billy went on to become a professional card player.

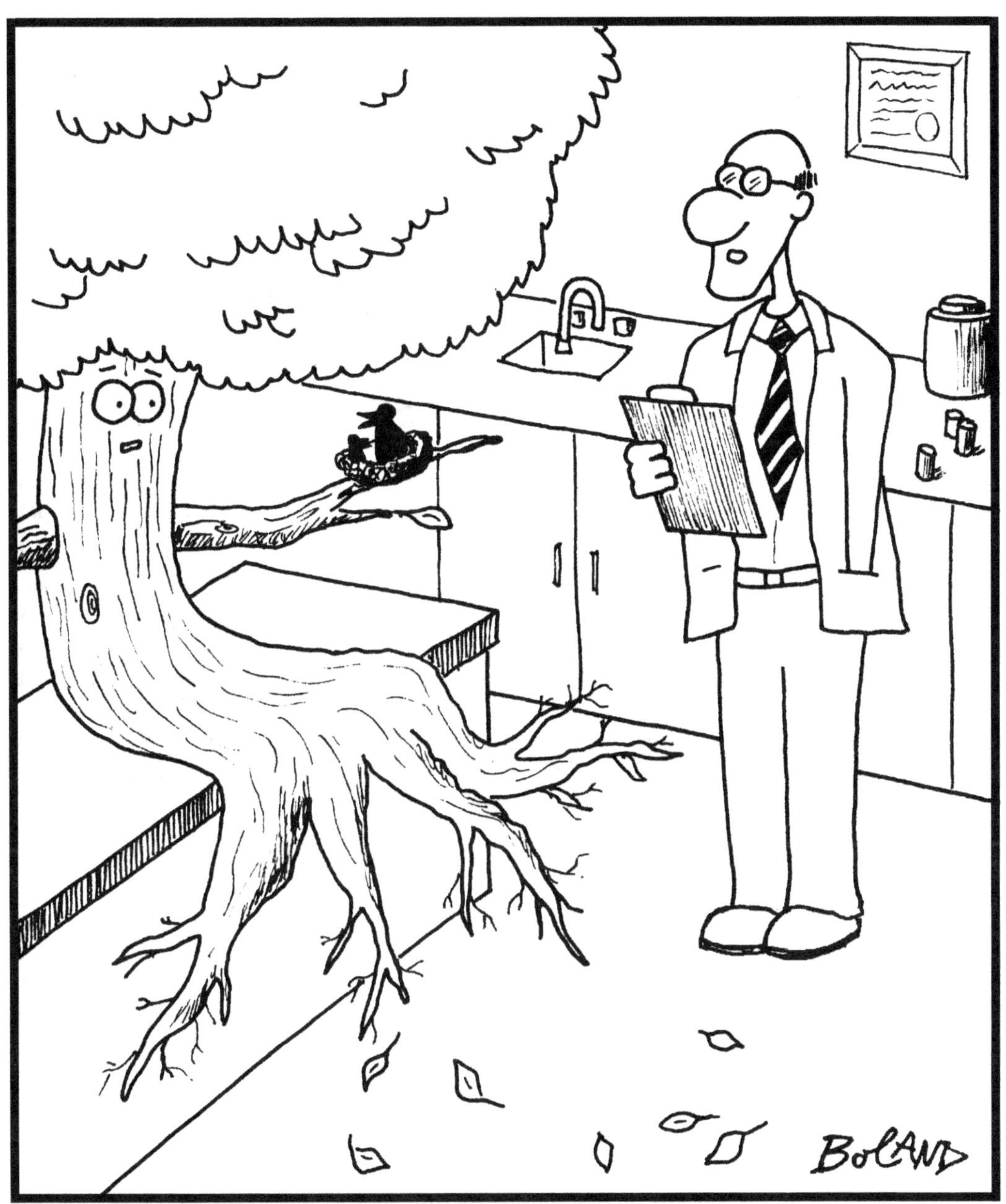

"OK..It says here that you've been feeling dehydrated lately. Well, let's see if we can get to the root of this problem."

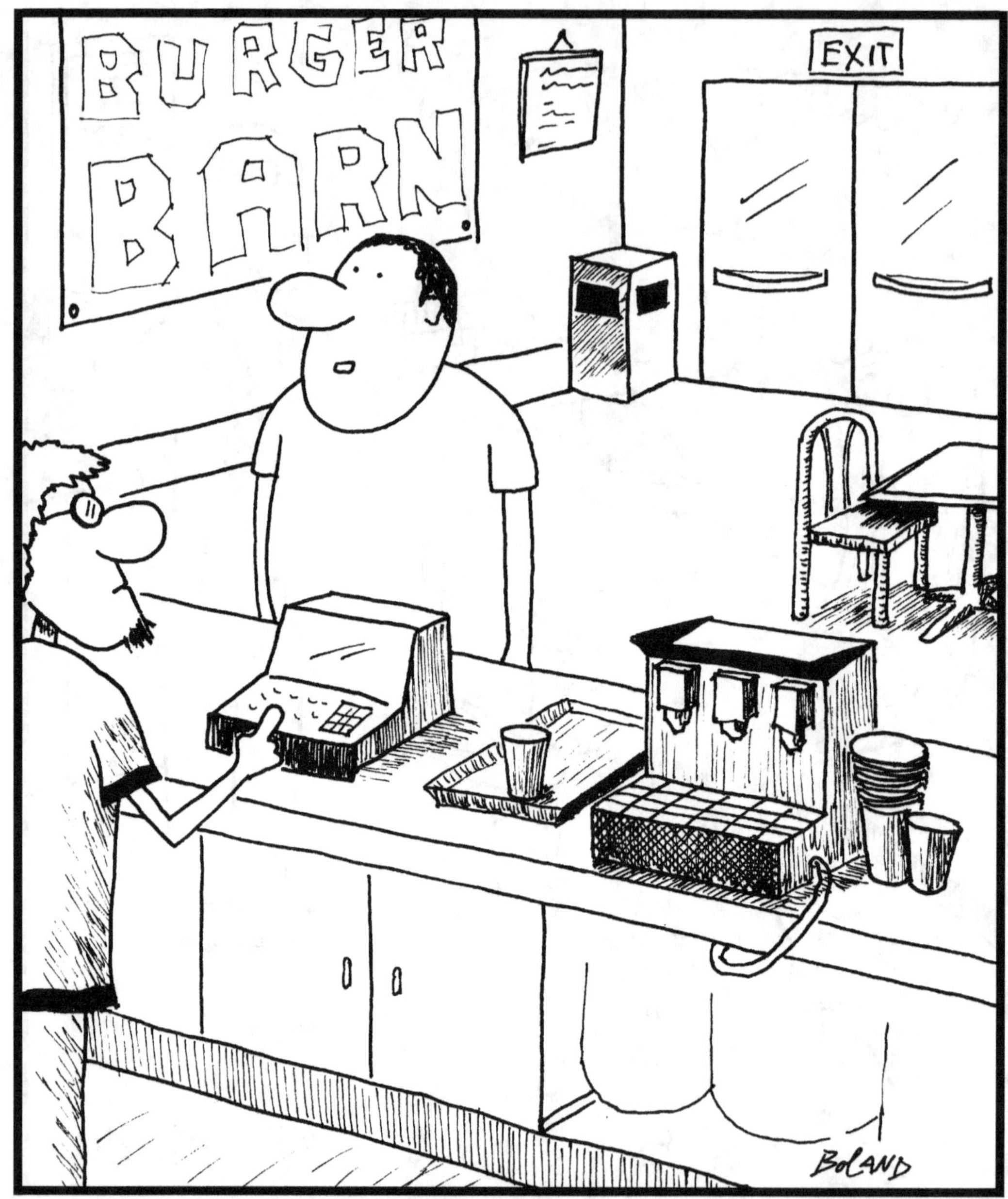

"...two triple cheeseburgers, three orders of deep fried onion rings, two hot fudge sundaes... Oh, and a salad. I'm trying to watch my weight."

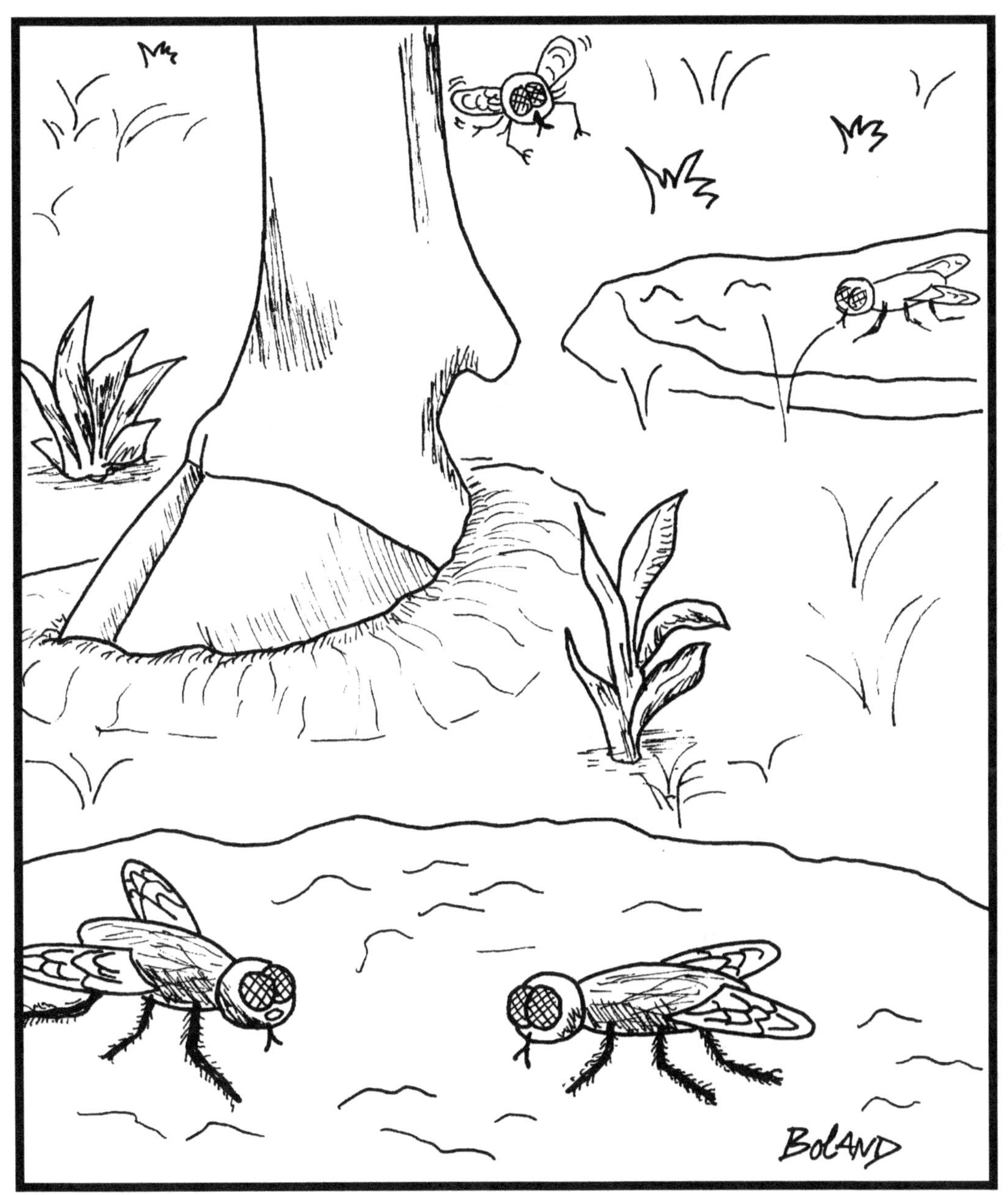

"Once again my dinner is cold and tastes like crap.........Just the way I like it."

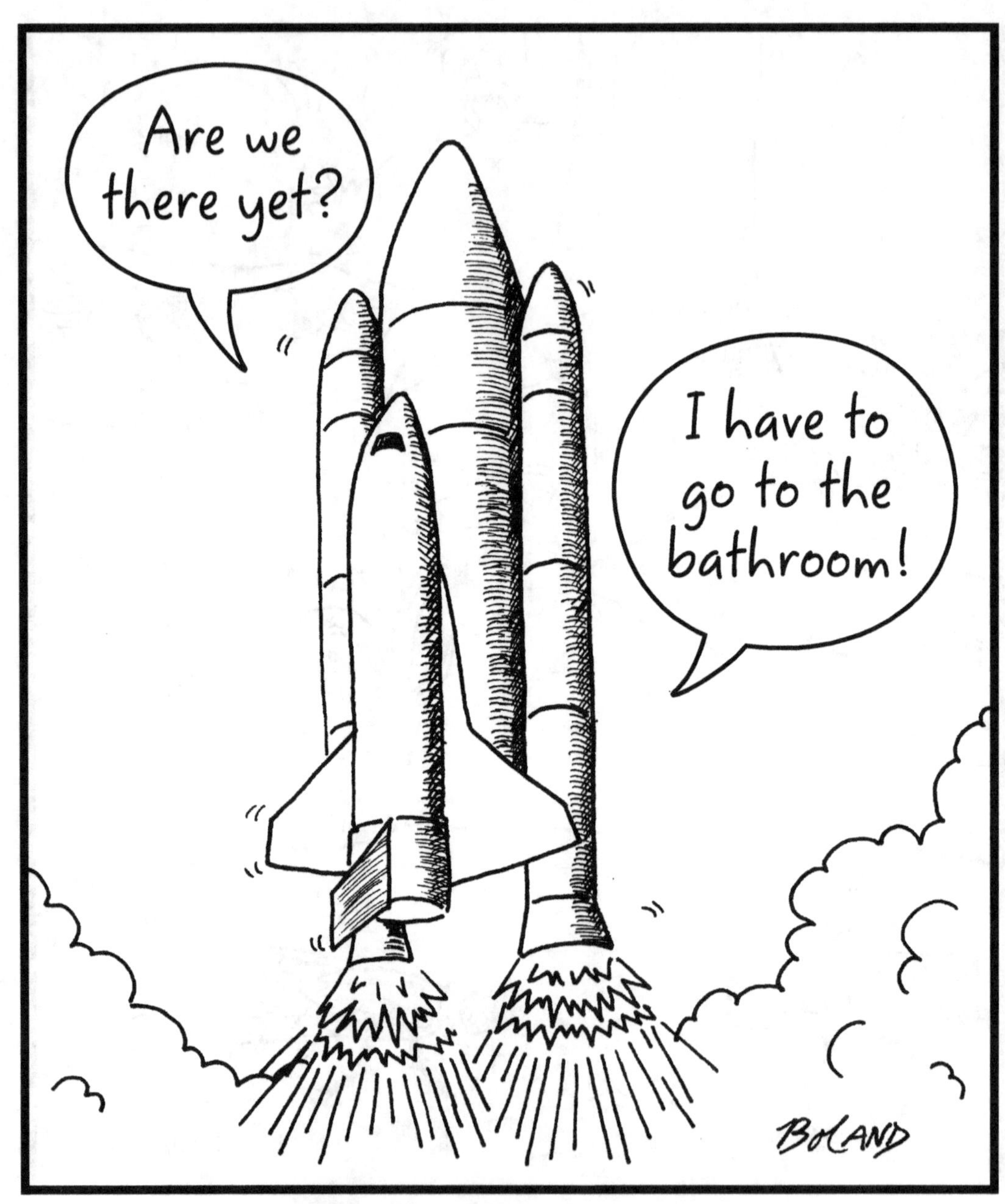

NASA's ill-conceived Take Your Kids to Work Day

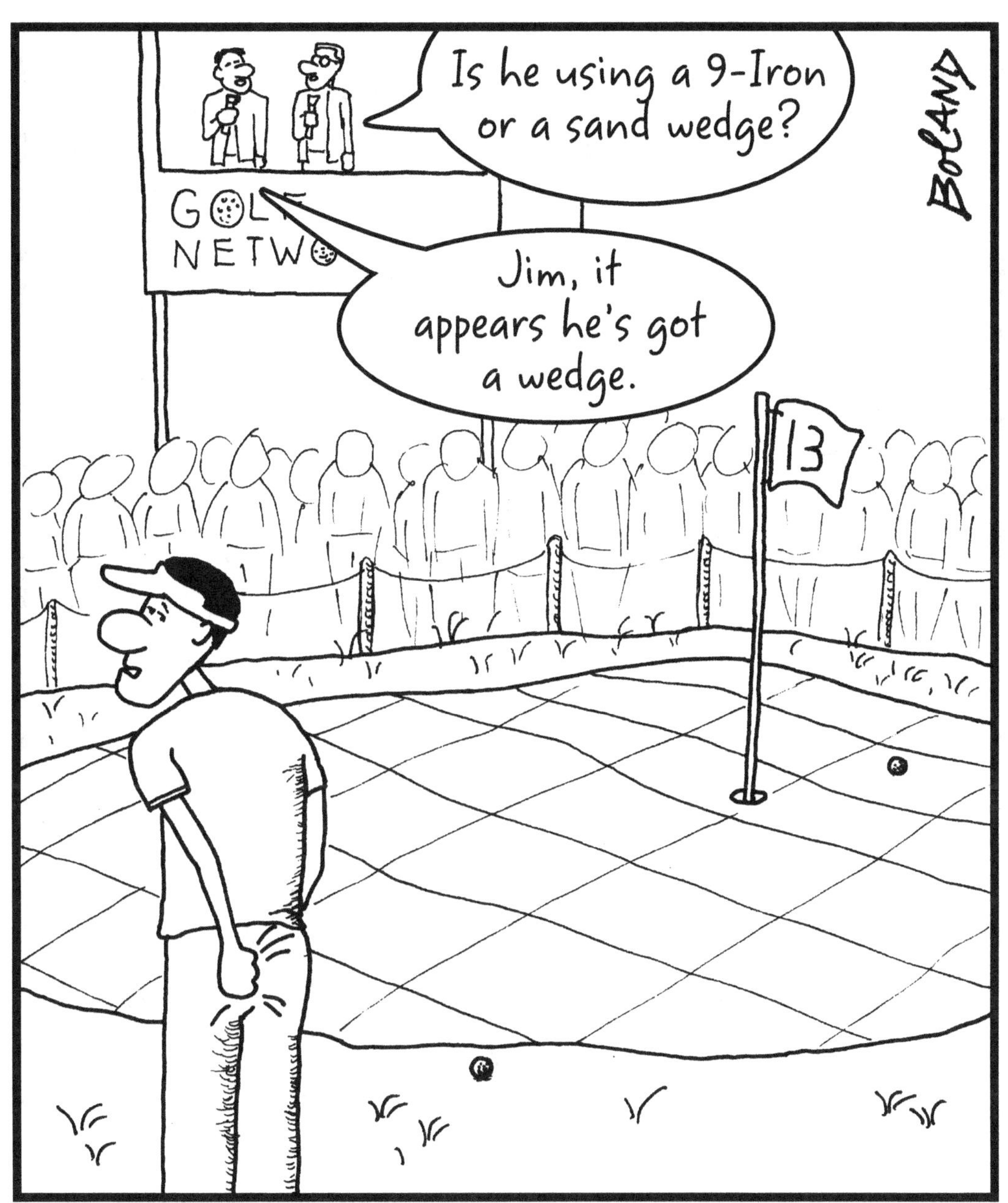
Is he using a 9-Iron or a sand wedge?
Jim, it appears he's got a wedge.
BOLAND
13

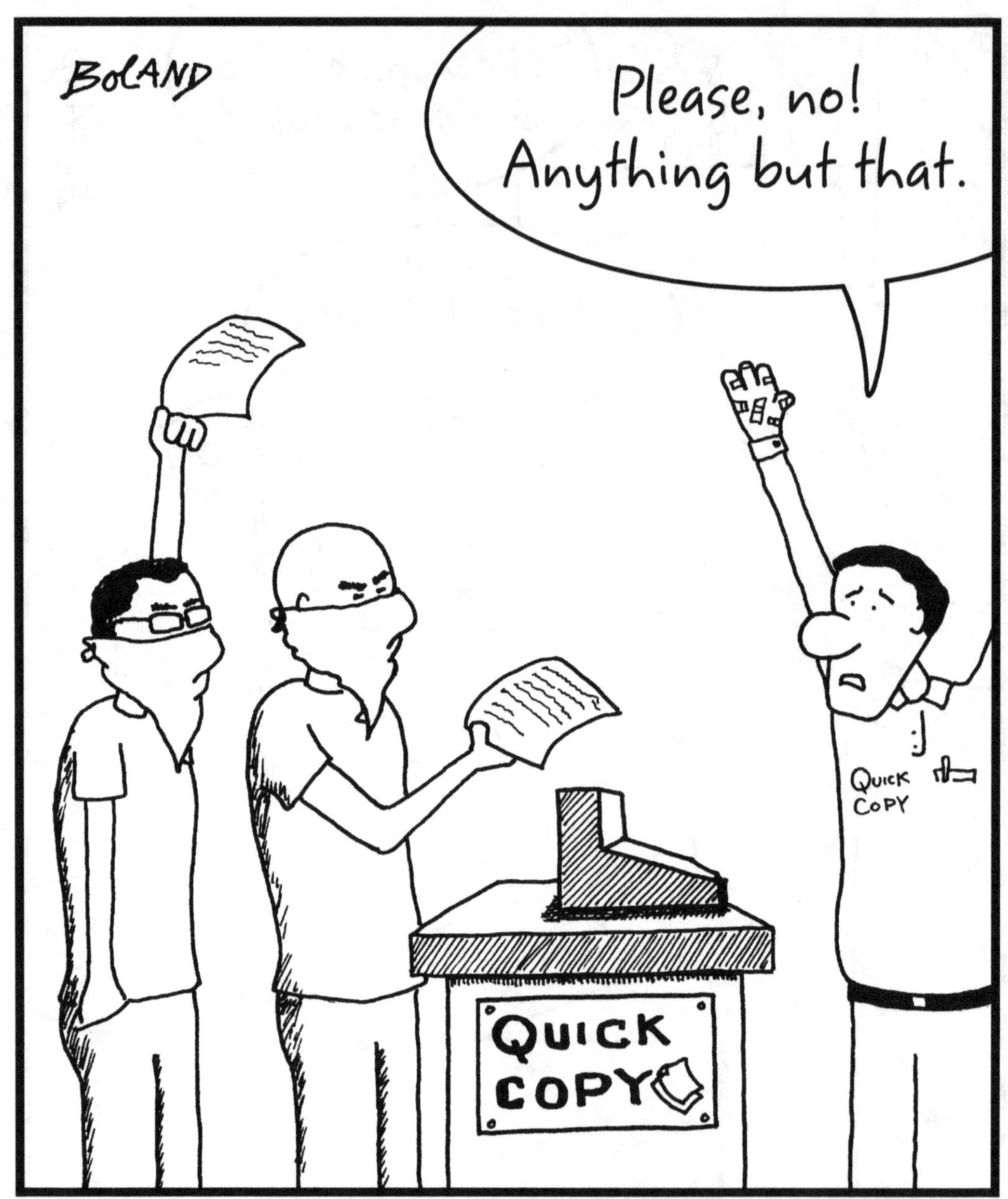

Another fiendish heist perpetrated by the ruthless Papercut Bandits

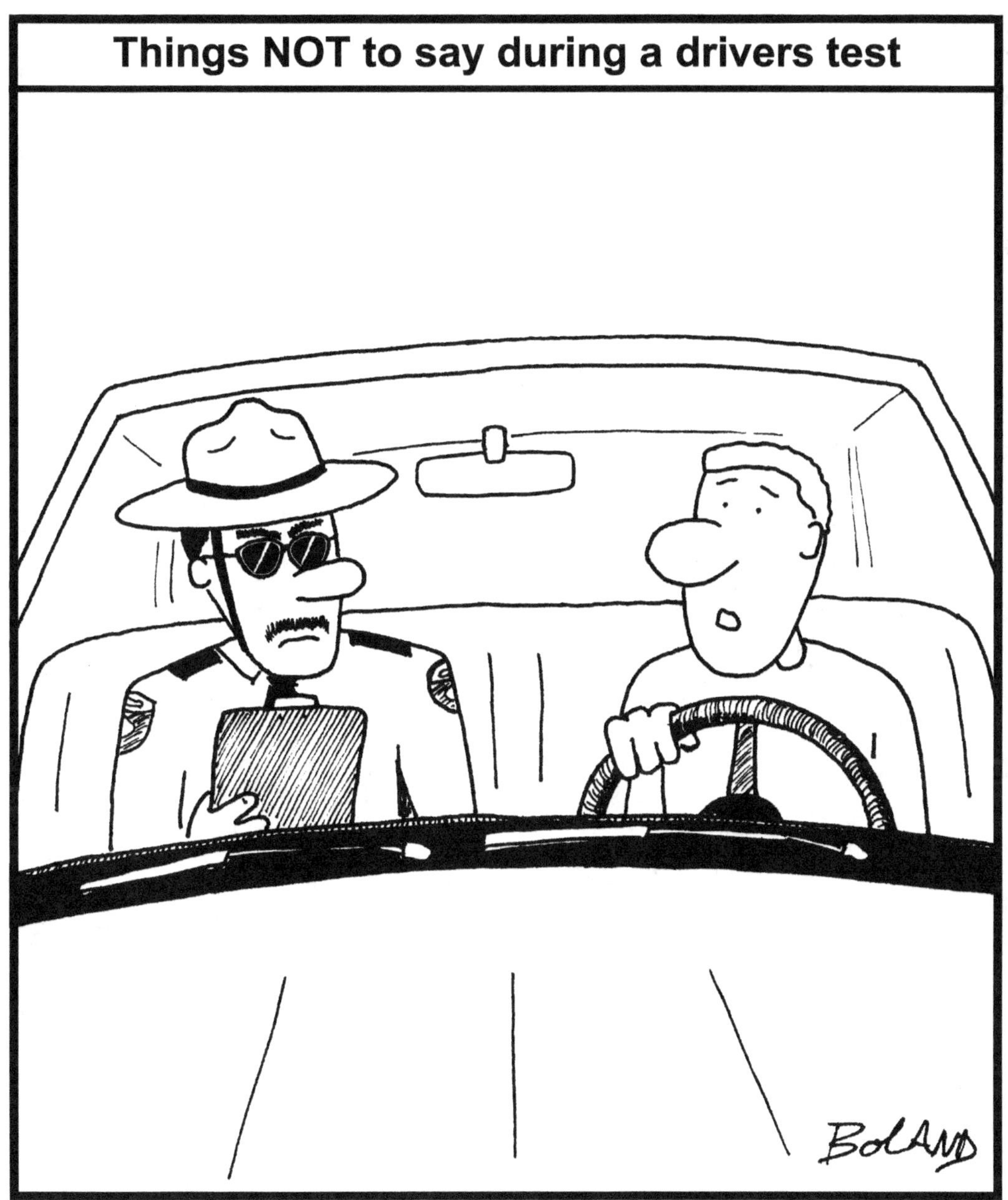

"Are you a real cop, or one of those rent-a-cops?"

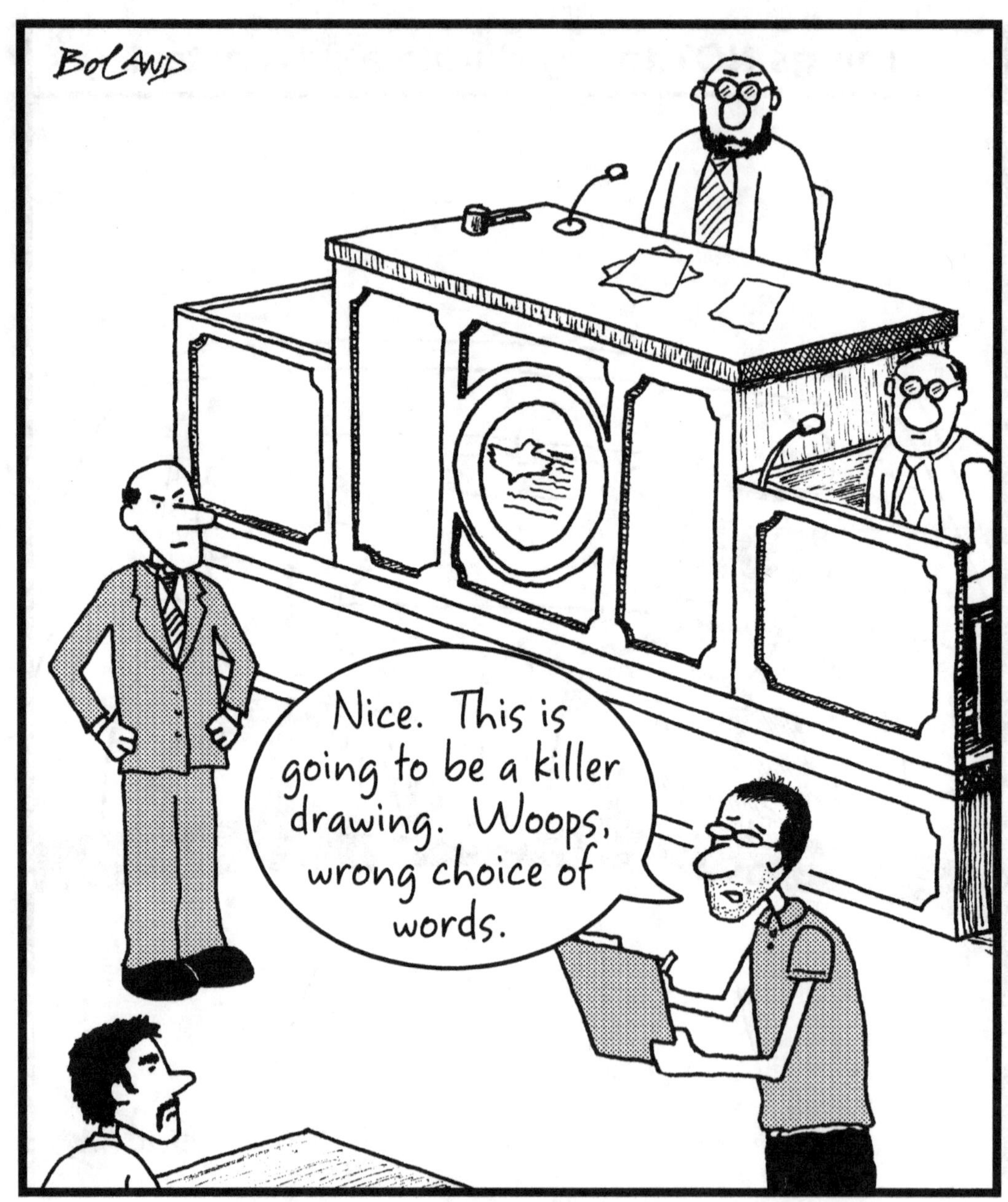

Mike's short-lived career as a courtroom sketch artist

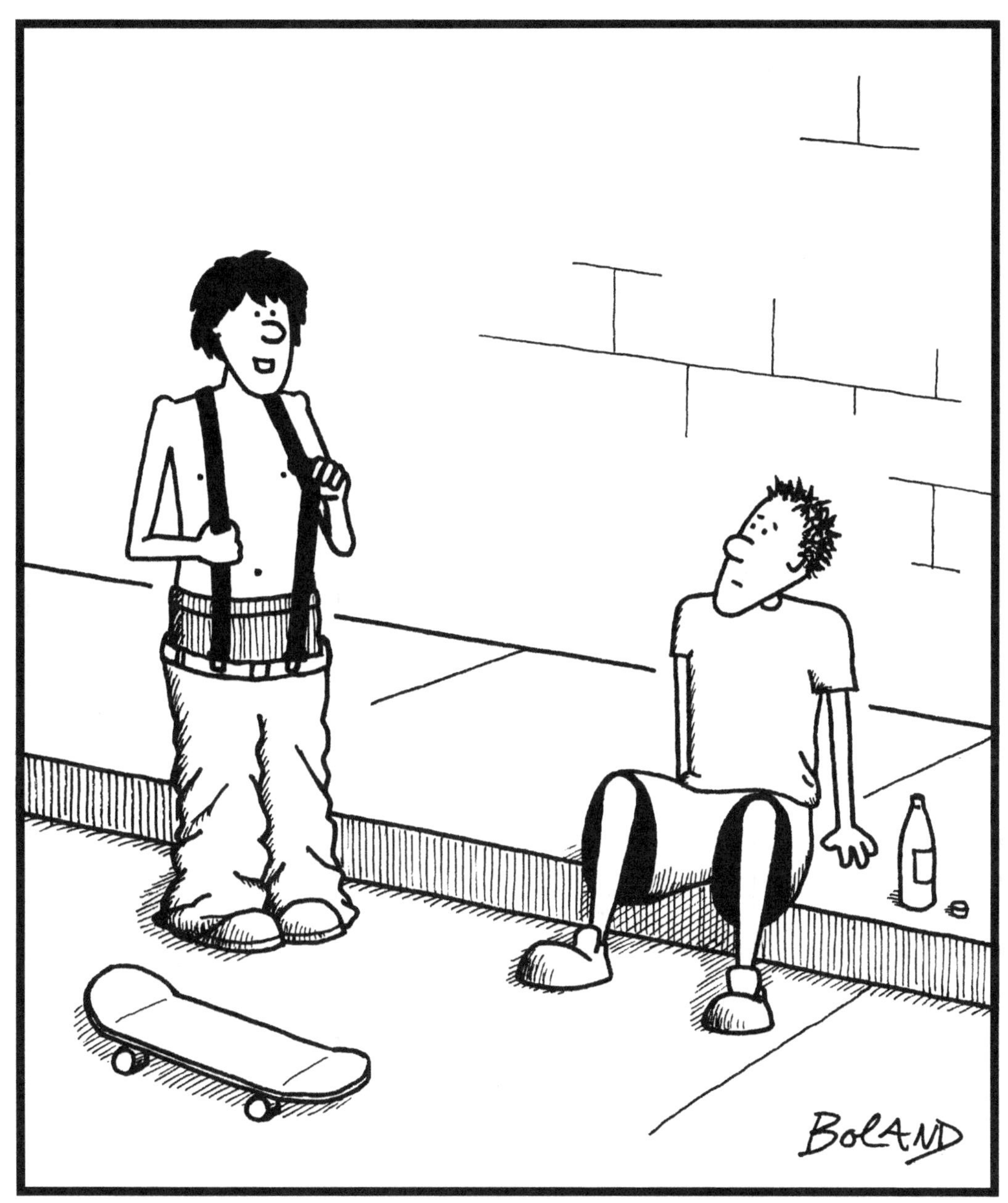

"My mom said I was too skinny to wear baggy pants like the cool kids. Well, look who's cool now."

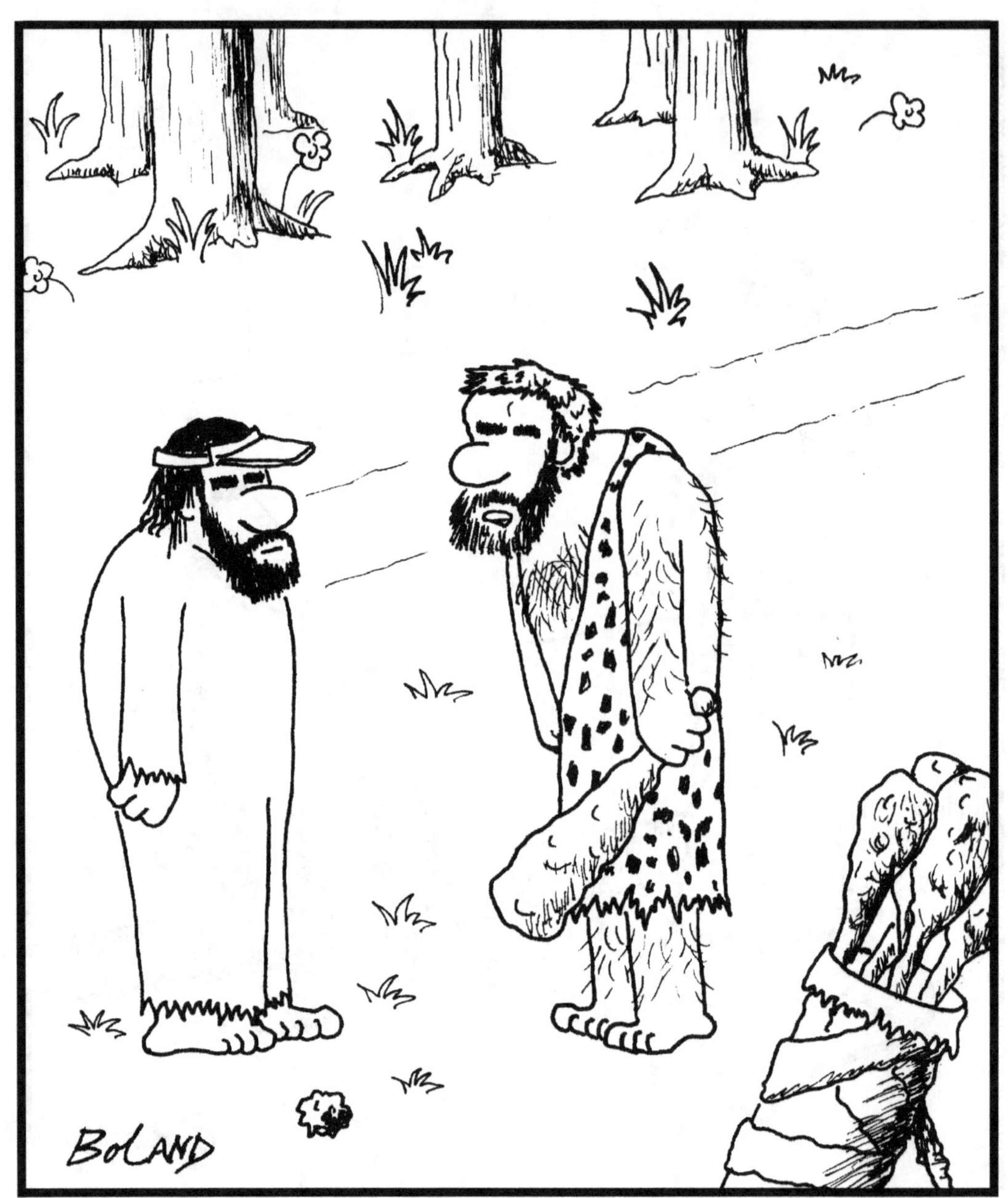

“What club me use?”

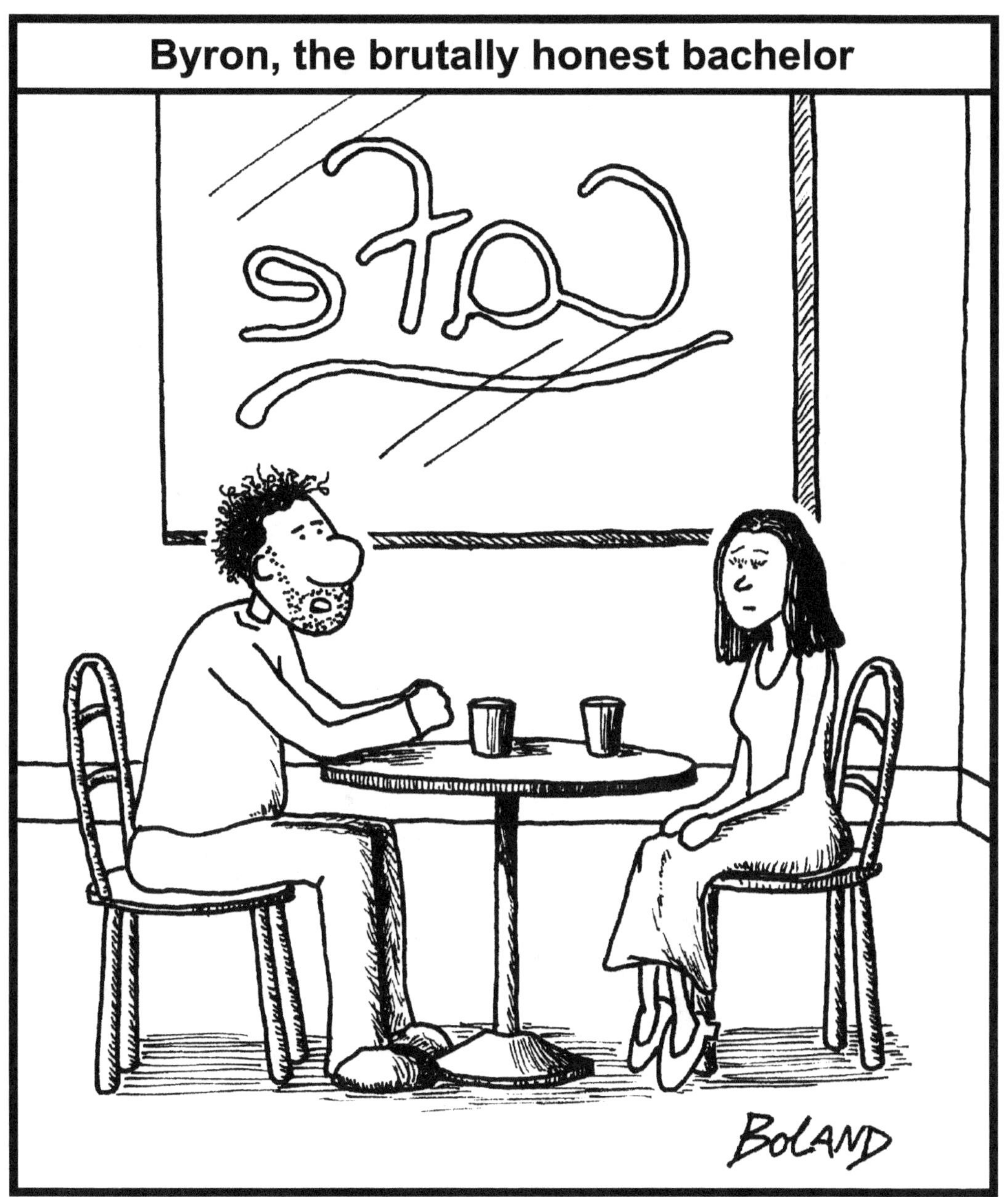

Byron, the brutally honest bachelor

"Actually, this isn't my real hair. I had it transplanted from my back."

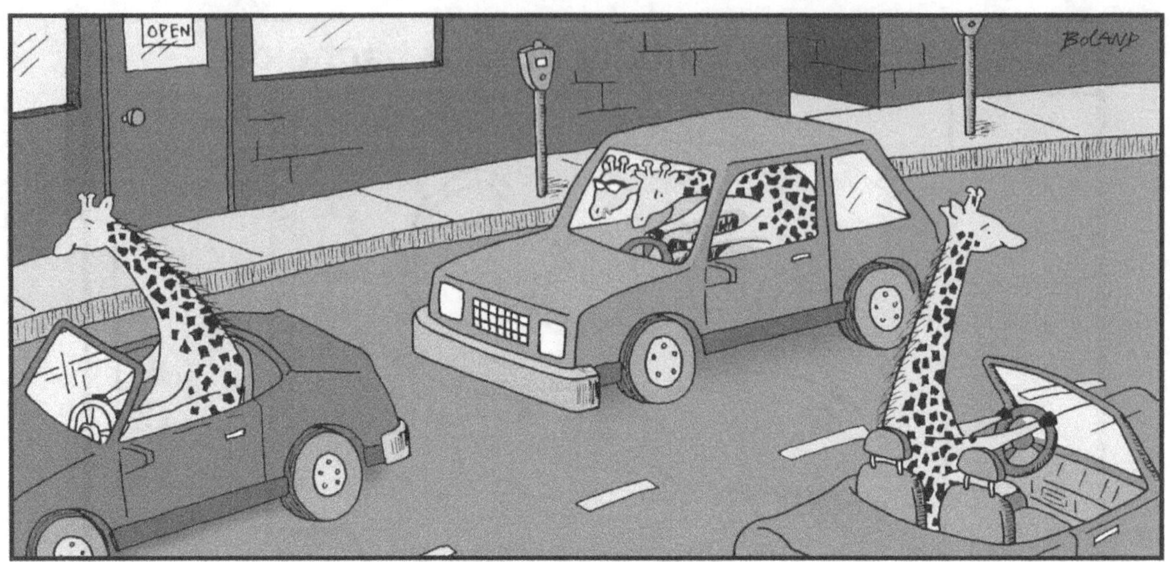

"Real smart, Frank. Real smart. Only you would buy a car online without seeing it first."

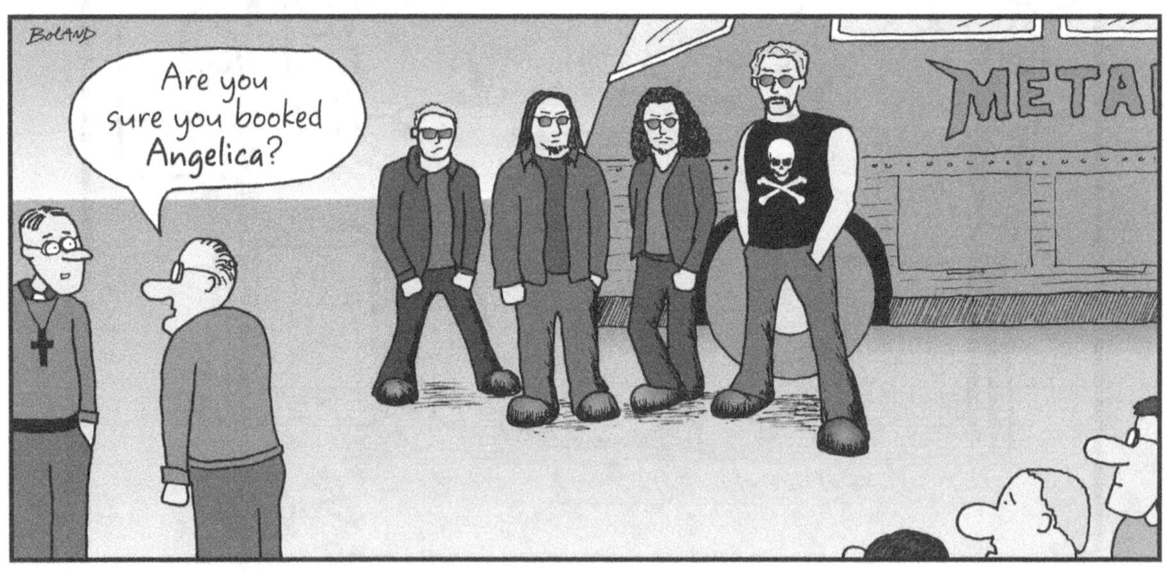

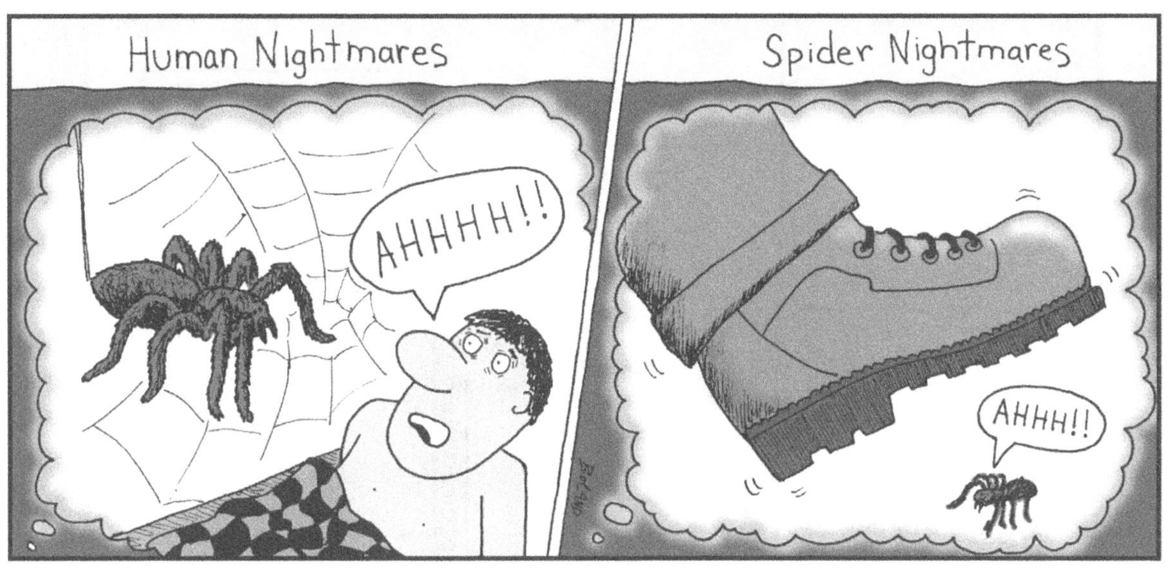
Human Nightmares
AHHHH!!
Spider Nightmares
AHHH!!

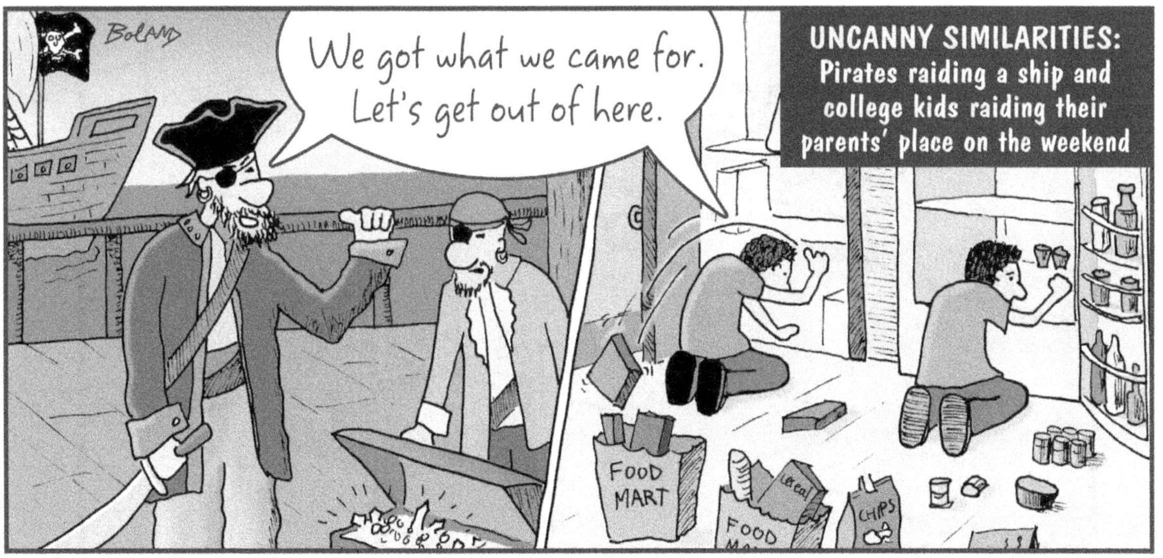
We got what we came for. Let's get out of here.
UNCANNY SIMILARITIES:
Pirates raiding a ship and college kids raiding their parents' place on the weekend
FOOD MART
CHIPS

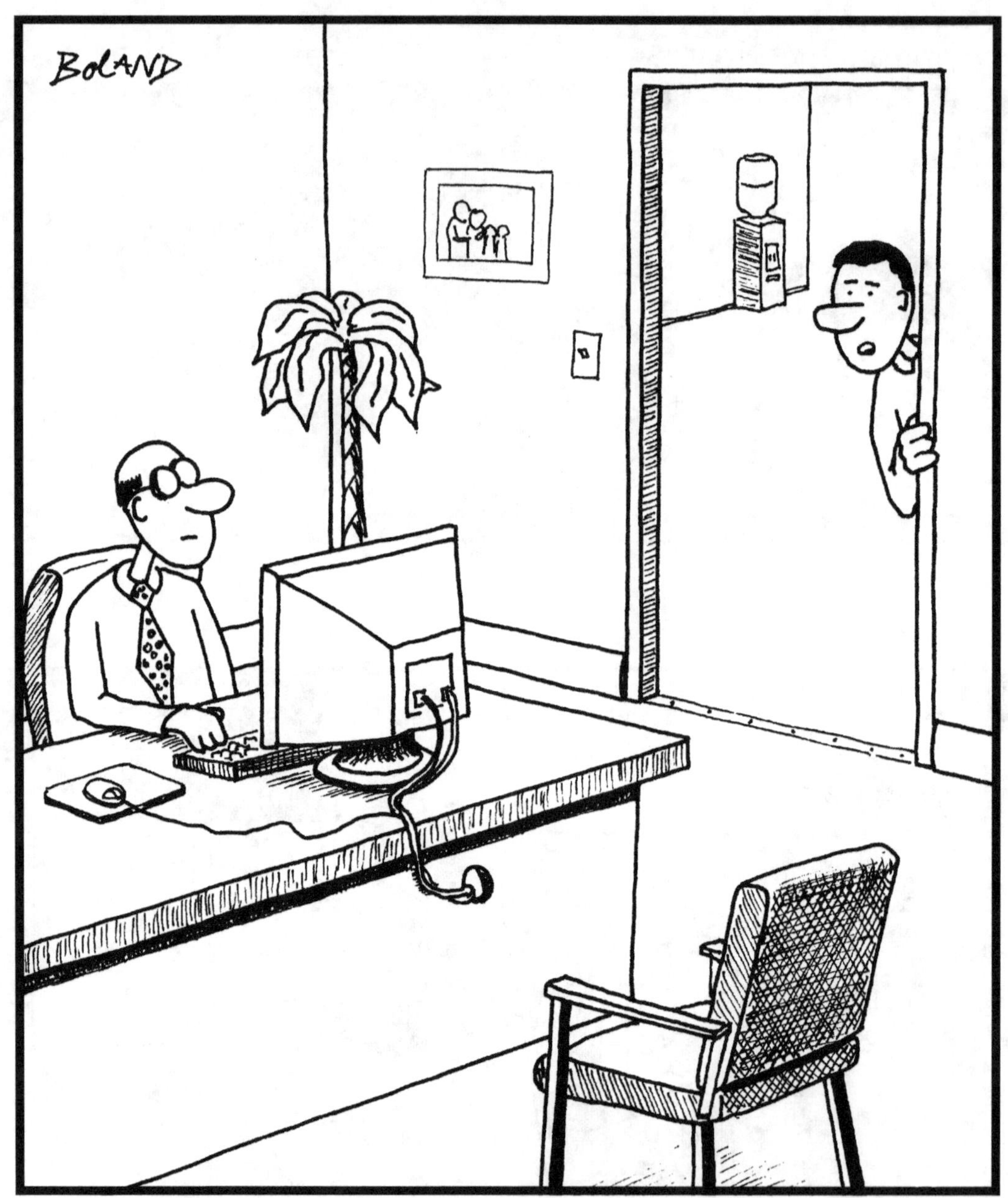

"The boss is giving a presentation on independent problem solving this afternoon...but, first he needs you to turn on his computer."

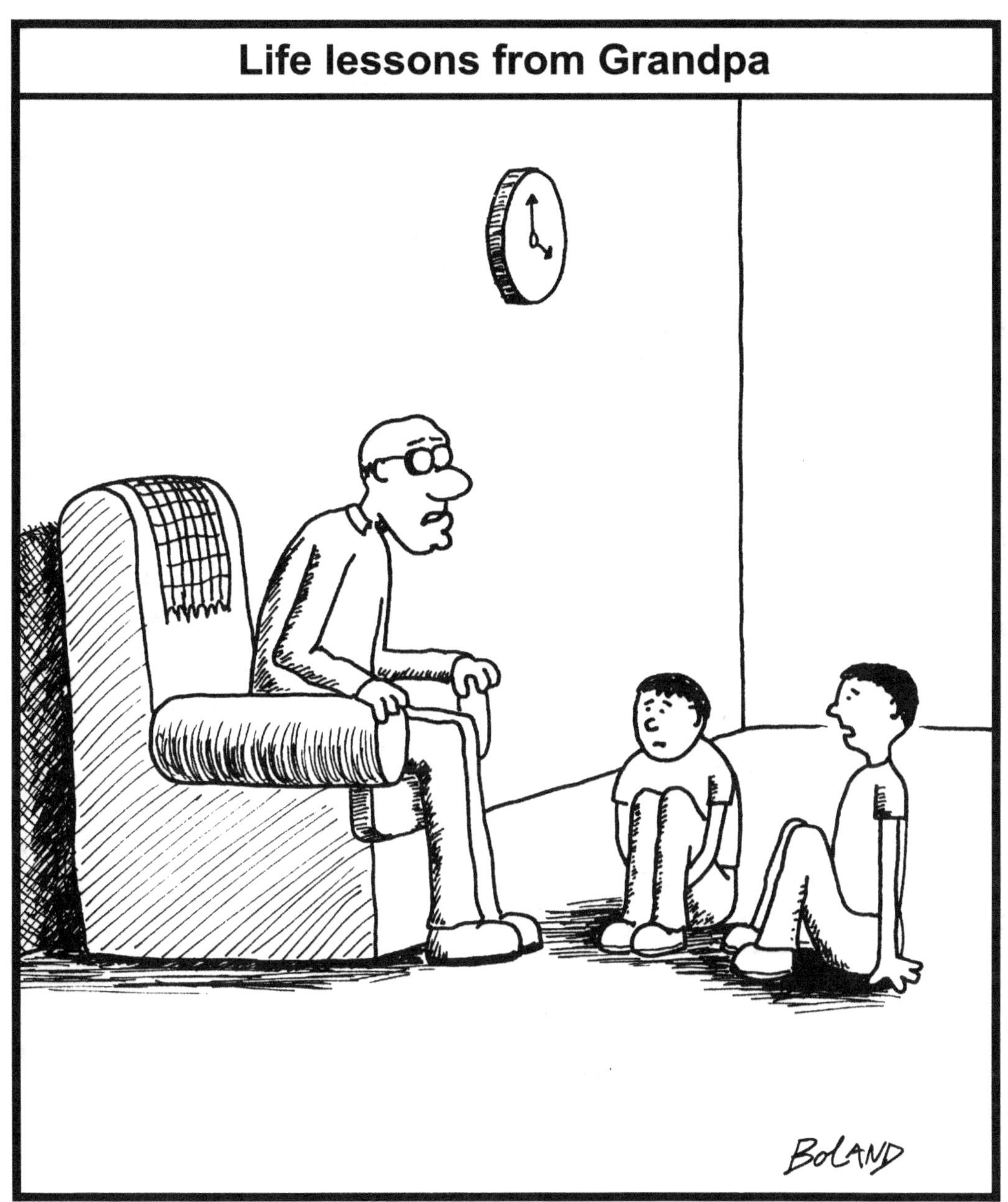

"...and that, kids, is how I got stuck to an outhouse seat in the middle of winter. Who wants to see Grandpa's scar?"

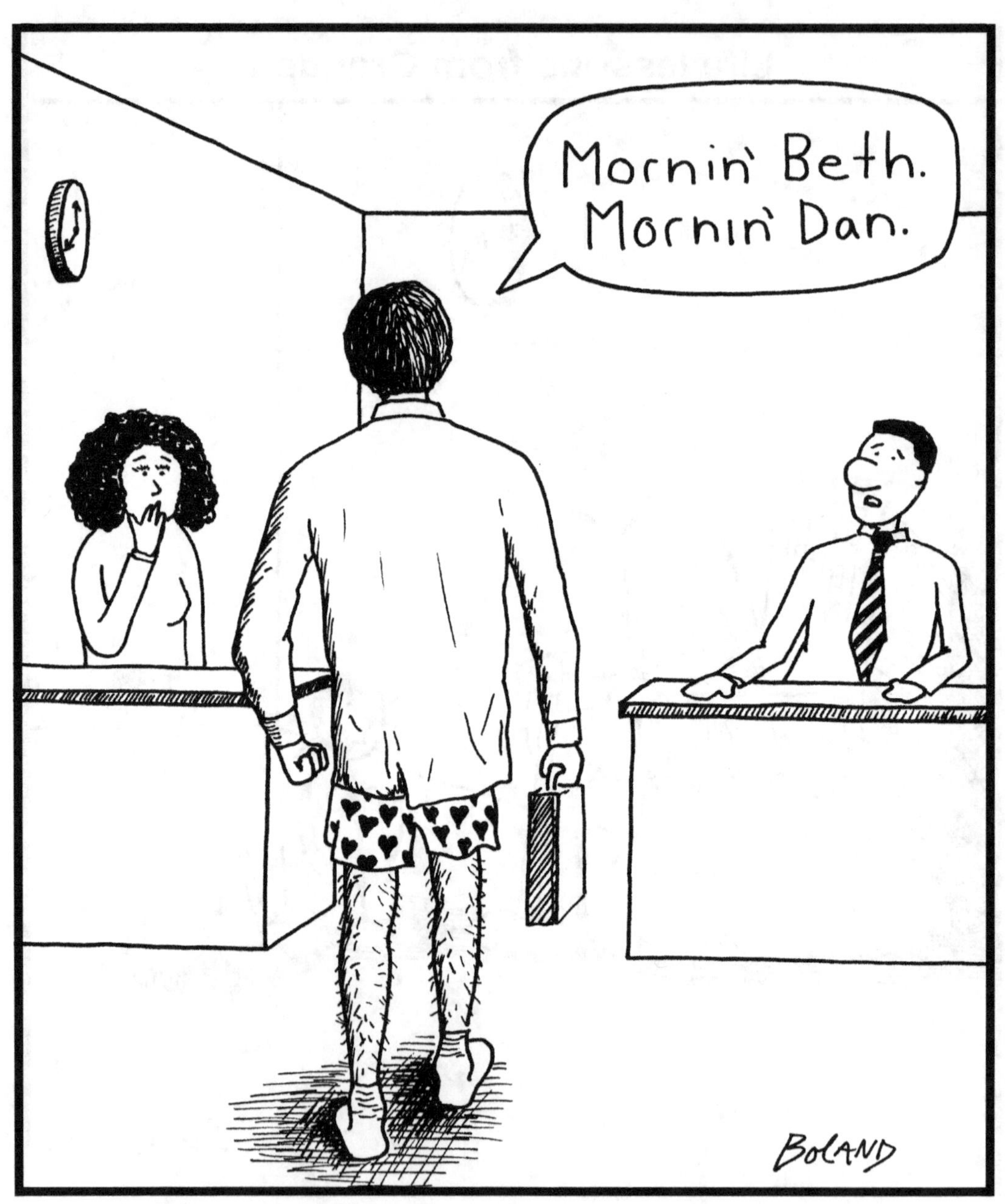

Matt takes casual fridays a little too far.

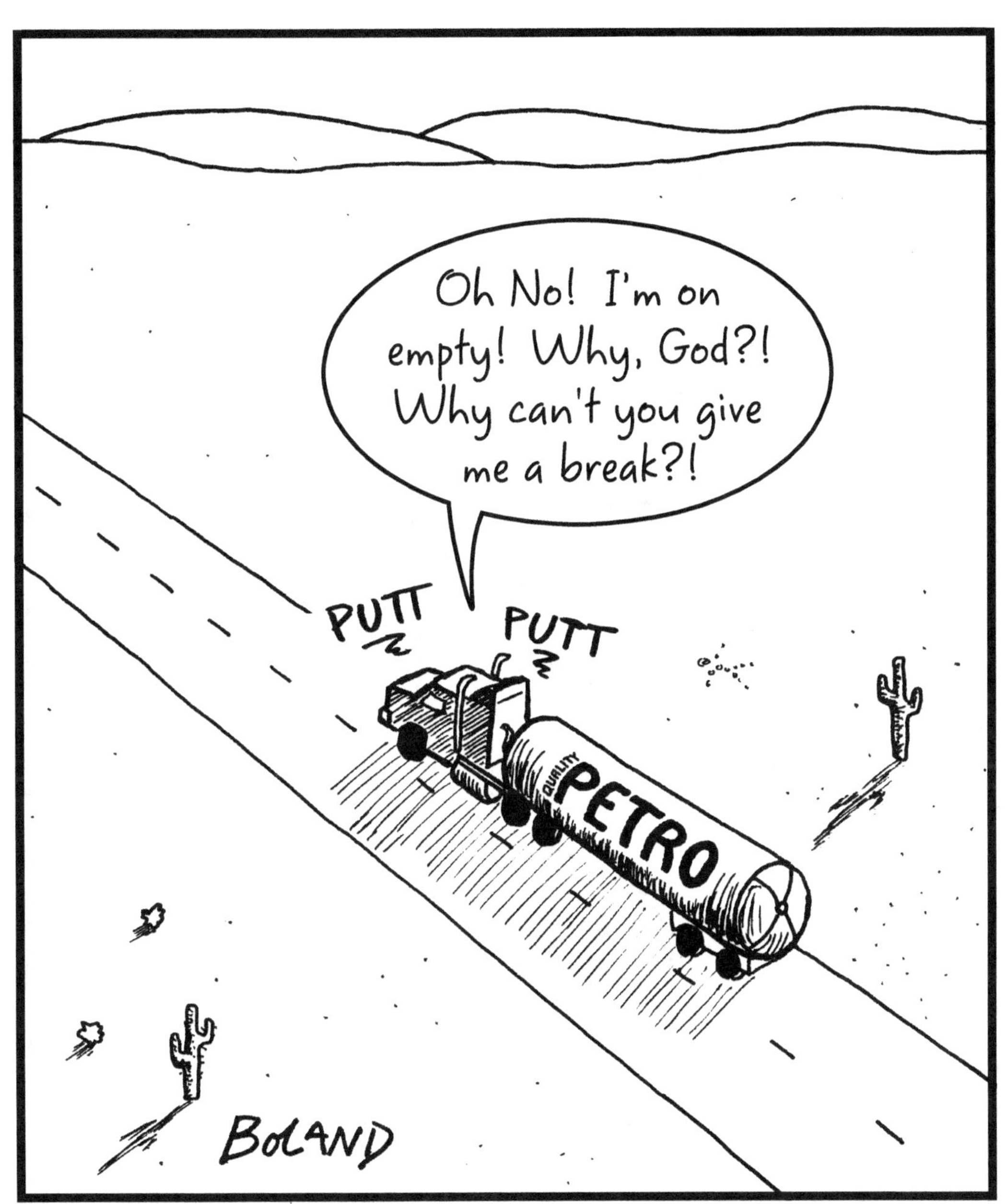
Oh No! I'm on empty! Why, God?! Why can't you give me a break?!
PUTT
PUTT
QUALITY PETRO
BOLAND

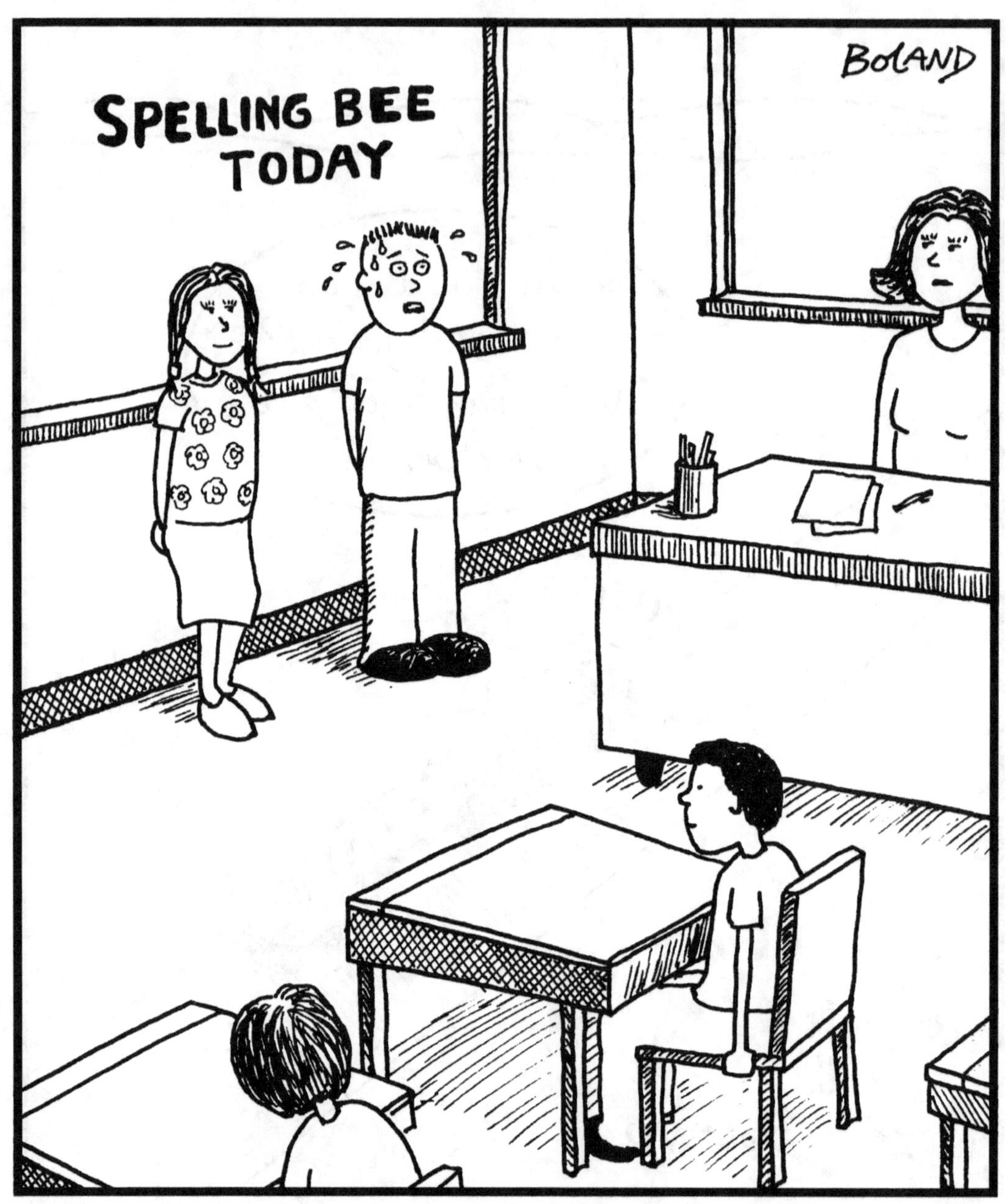

This was it – one last word. Timmy froze as he envisioned his impending future: crazed fans, unrelenting autograph requests, intrusive reporters. He knew he wasn't ready to be a star, but failure simply wasn't an option.

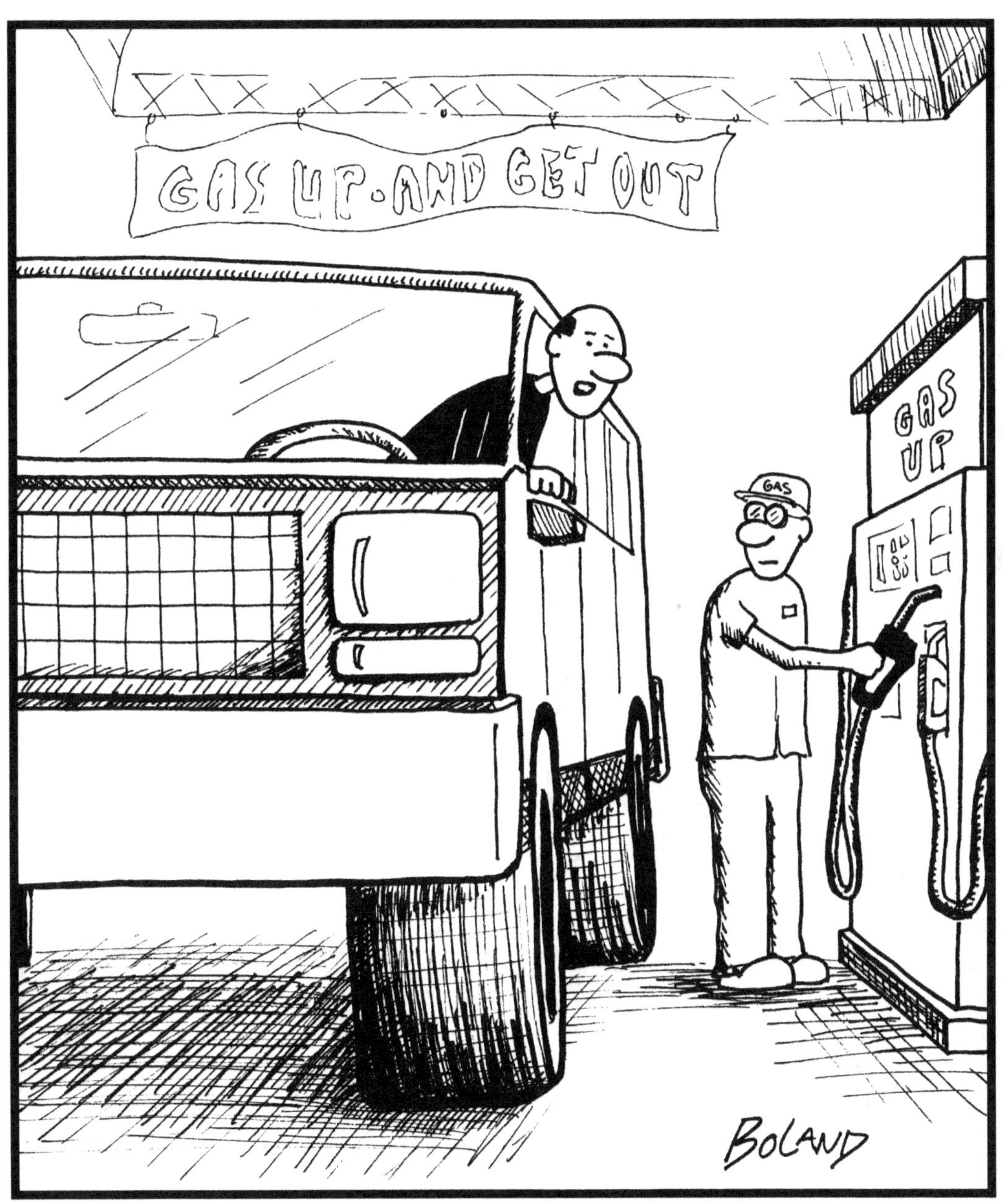

"Twelve miles to the next station, you say? Hmm... Do you happen to sell gas cans by chance?"

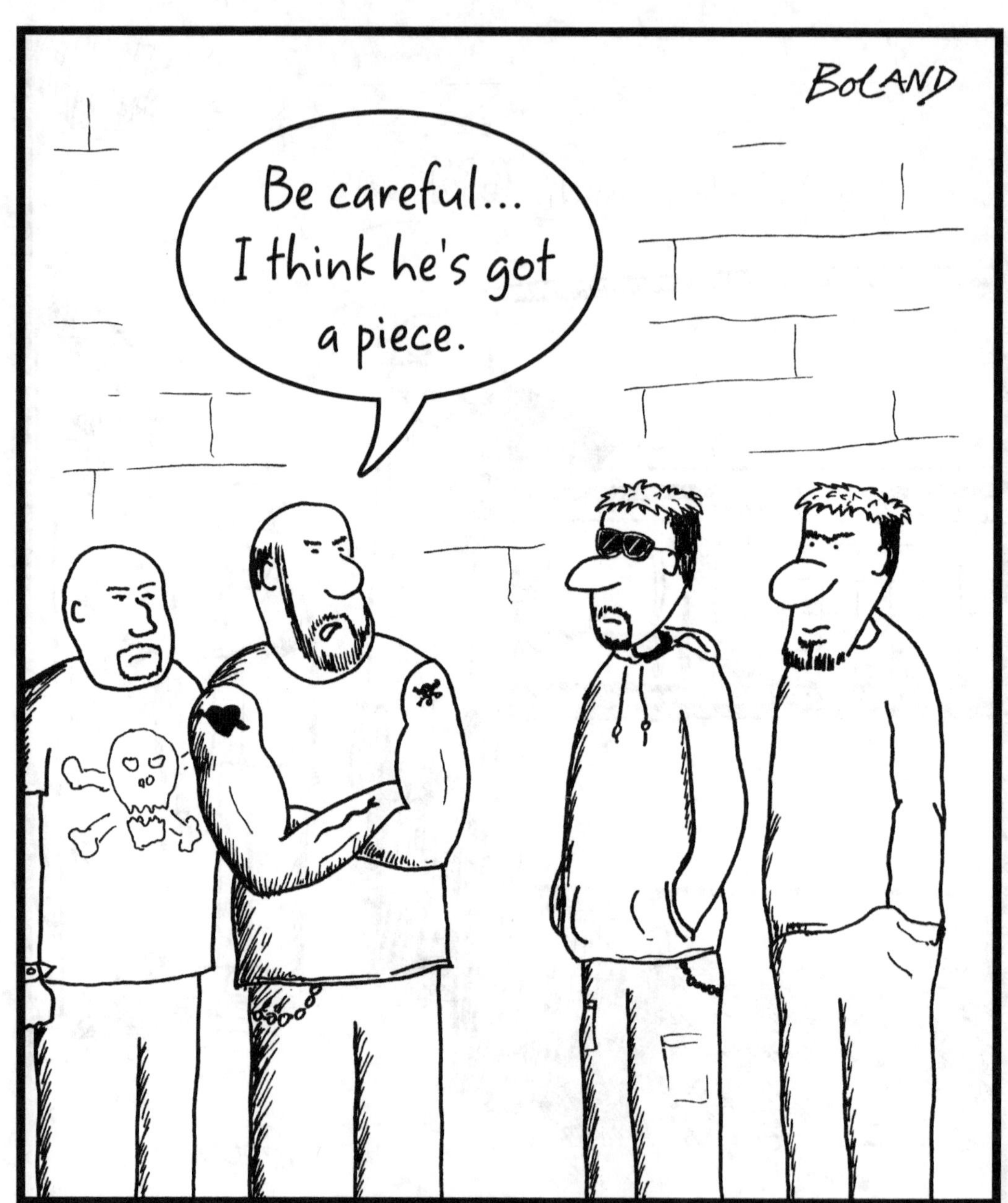

Hair club gangs

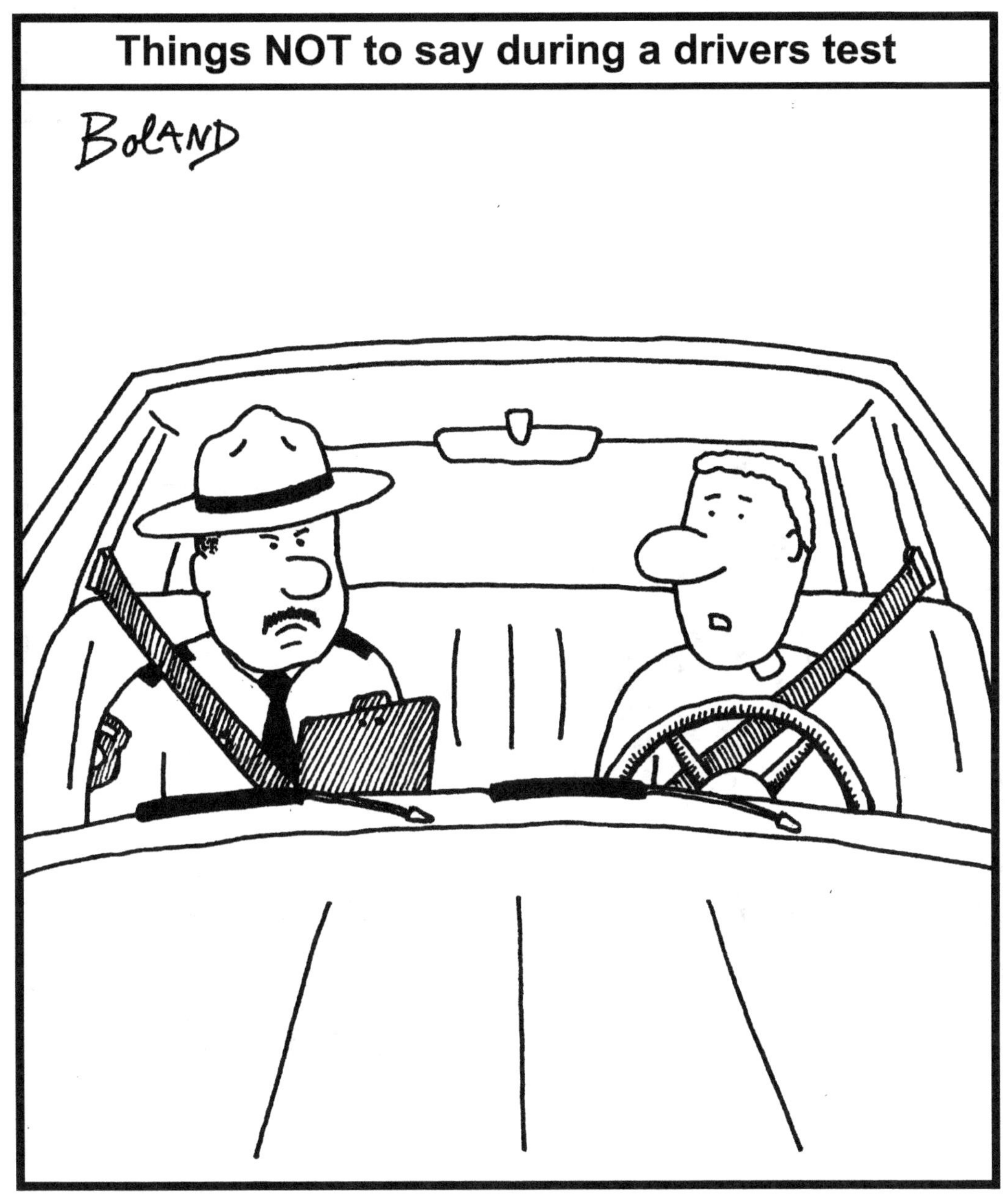

"So, are we gonna get some donuts now or after the test?"

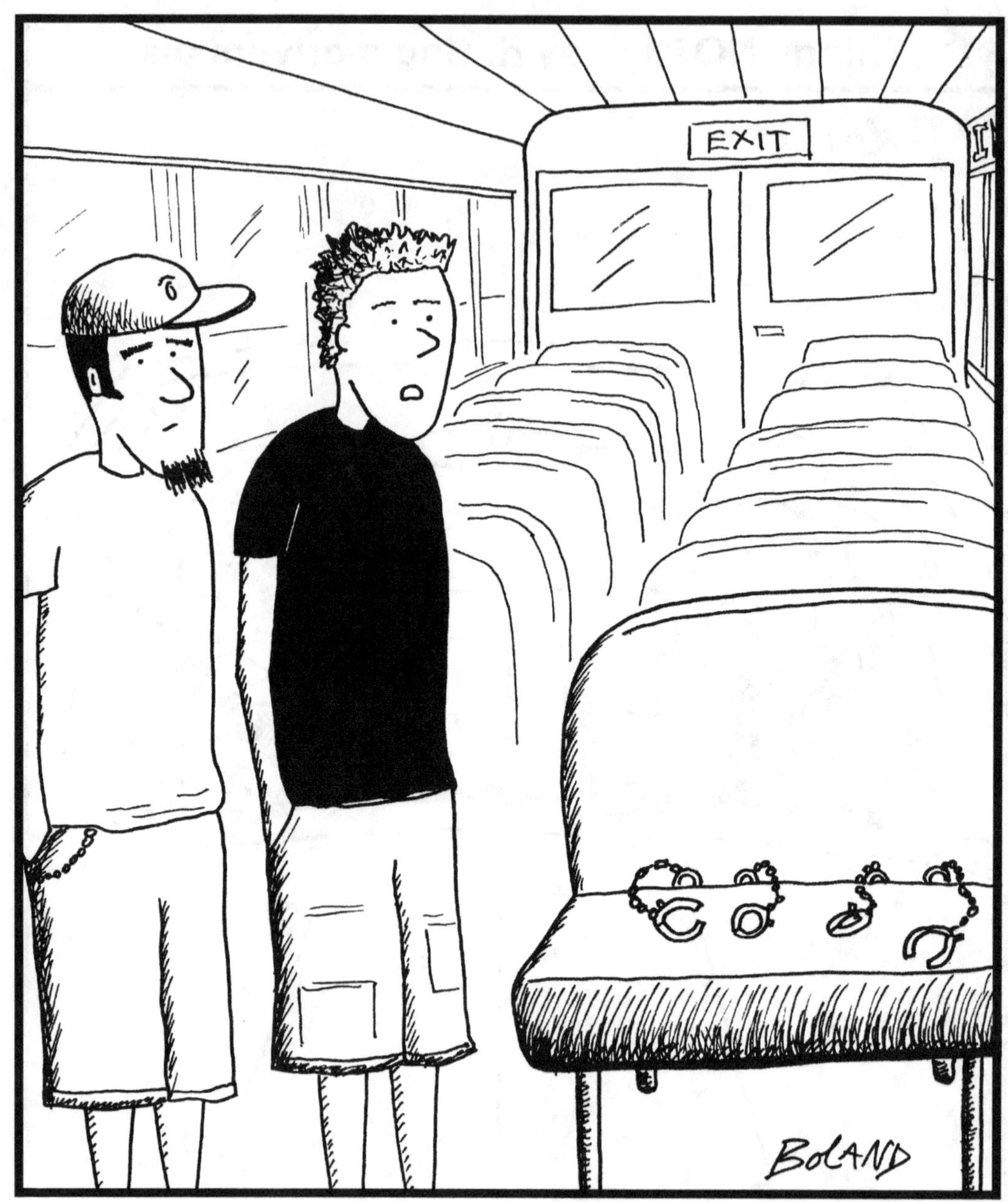

"So, these are the new 'safety restraints'."

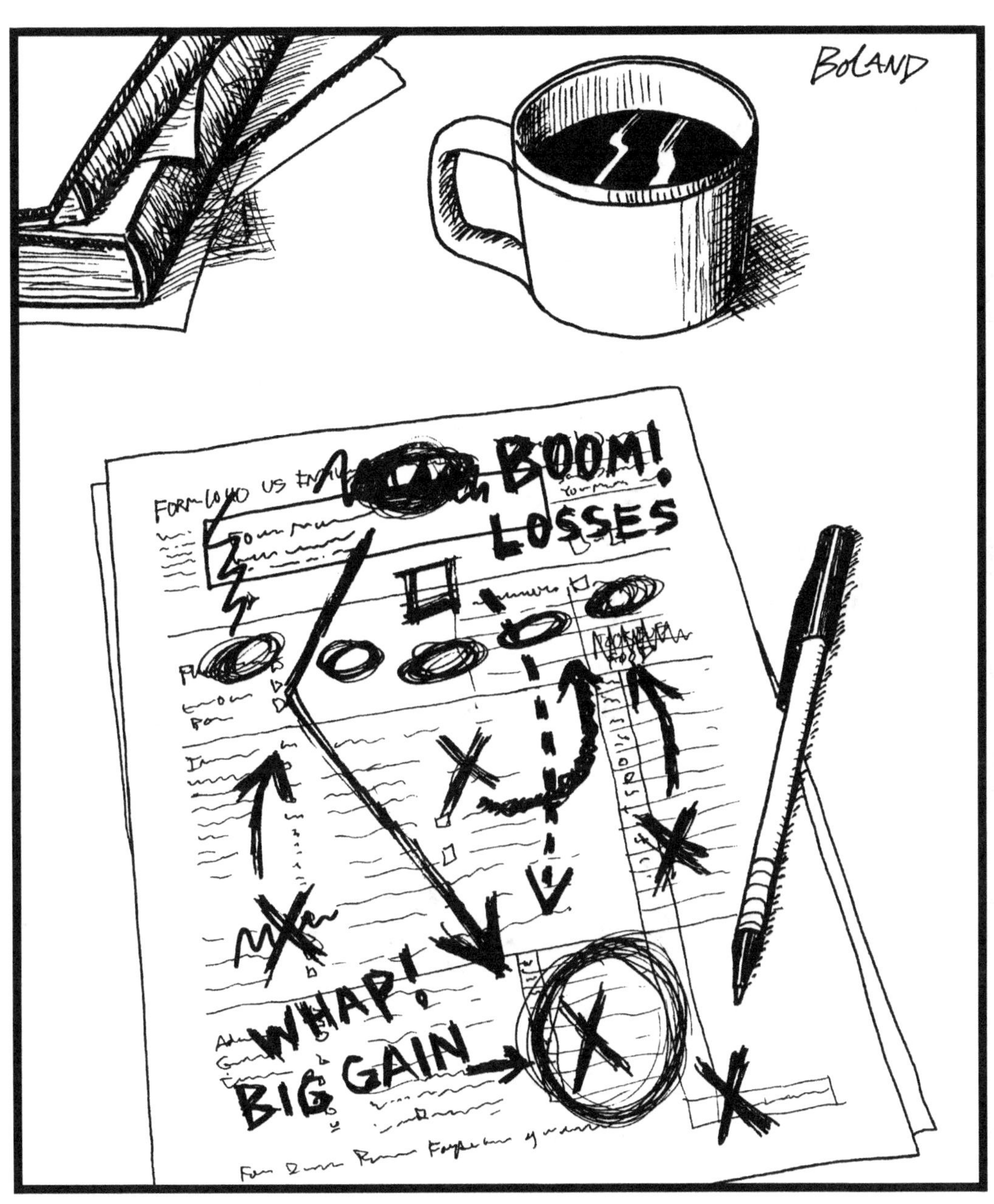

John Madden's tax forms

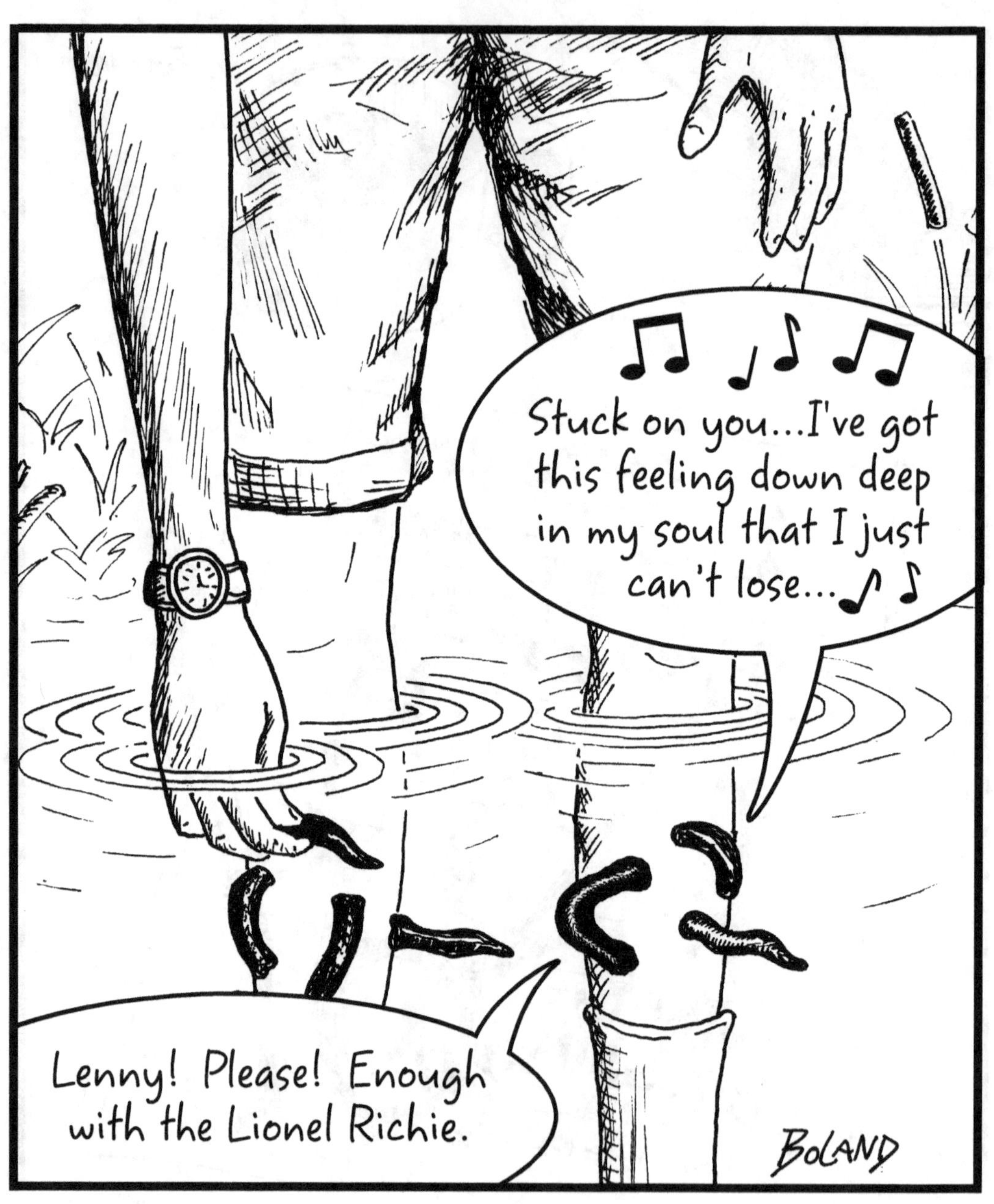
Stuck on you...I've got this feeling down deep in my soul that I just can't lose...
Lenny! Please! Enough with the Lionel Richie.
BOLAND

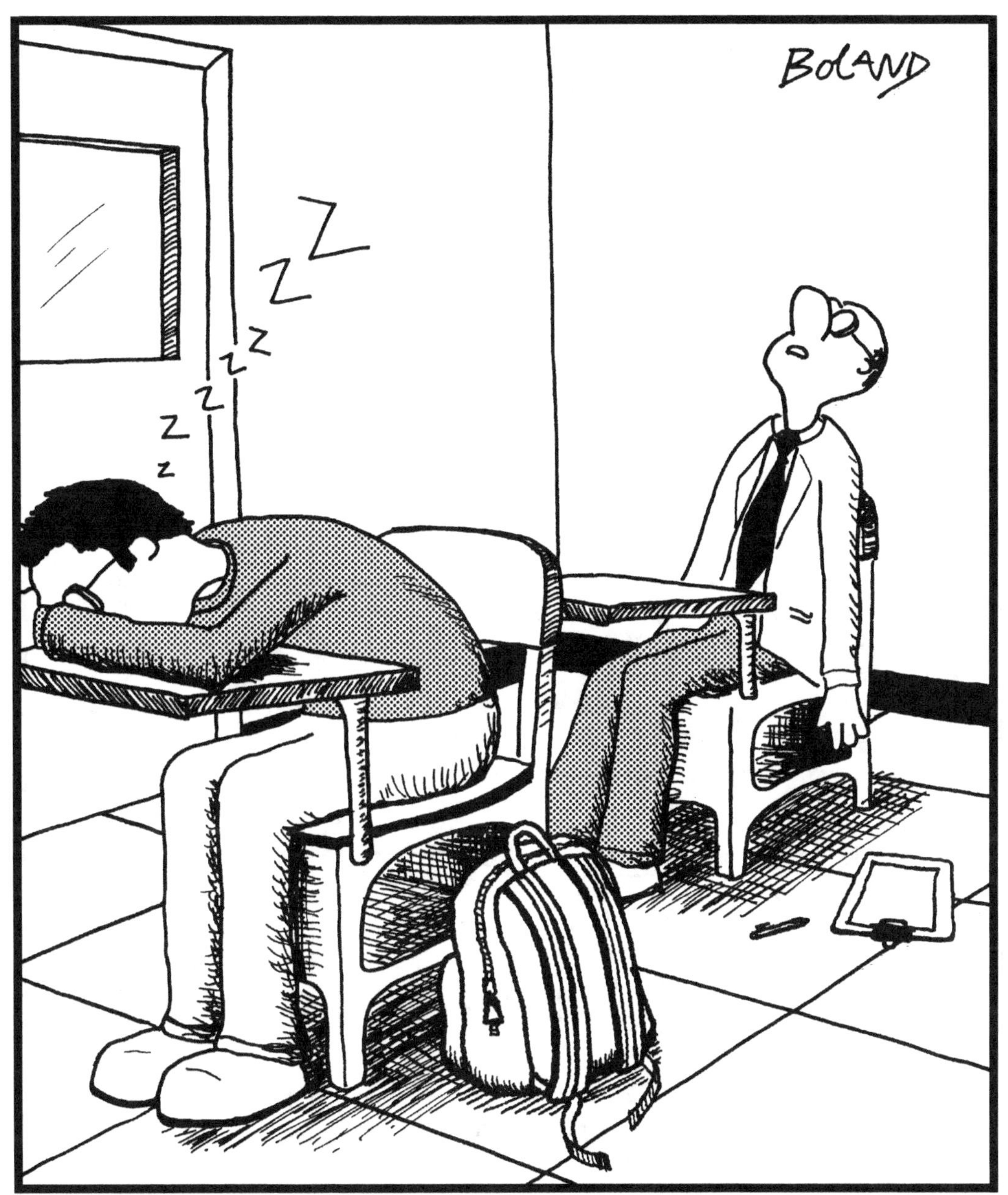

Another failed attempt to scientifically link college lectures and drowsiness

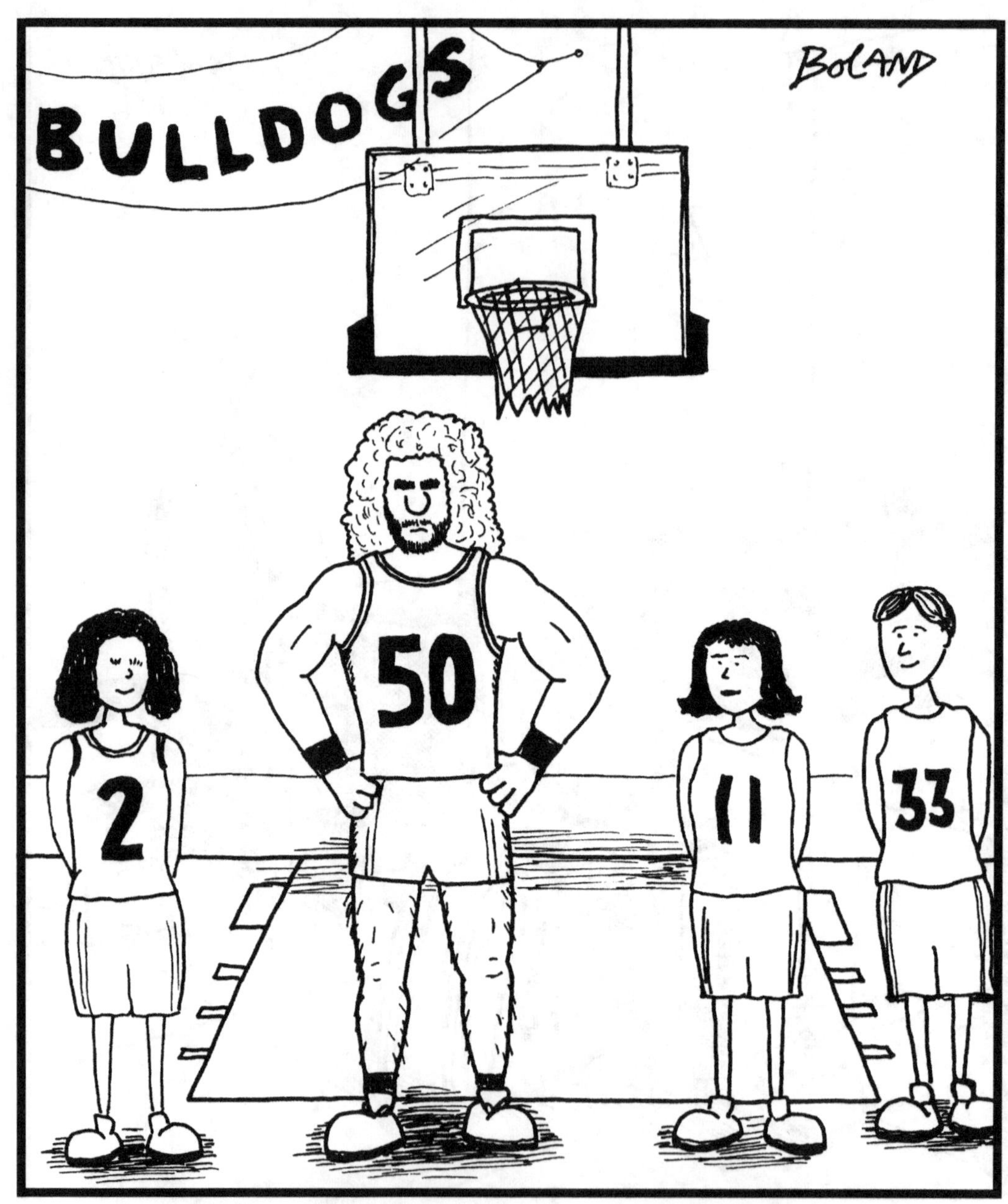

The Lady Bulldogs were undefeated until someone uncovered a scandal involving Helga, the team's center.

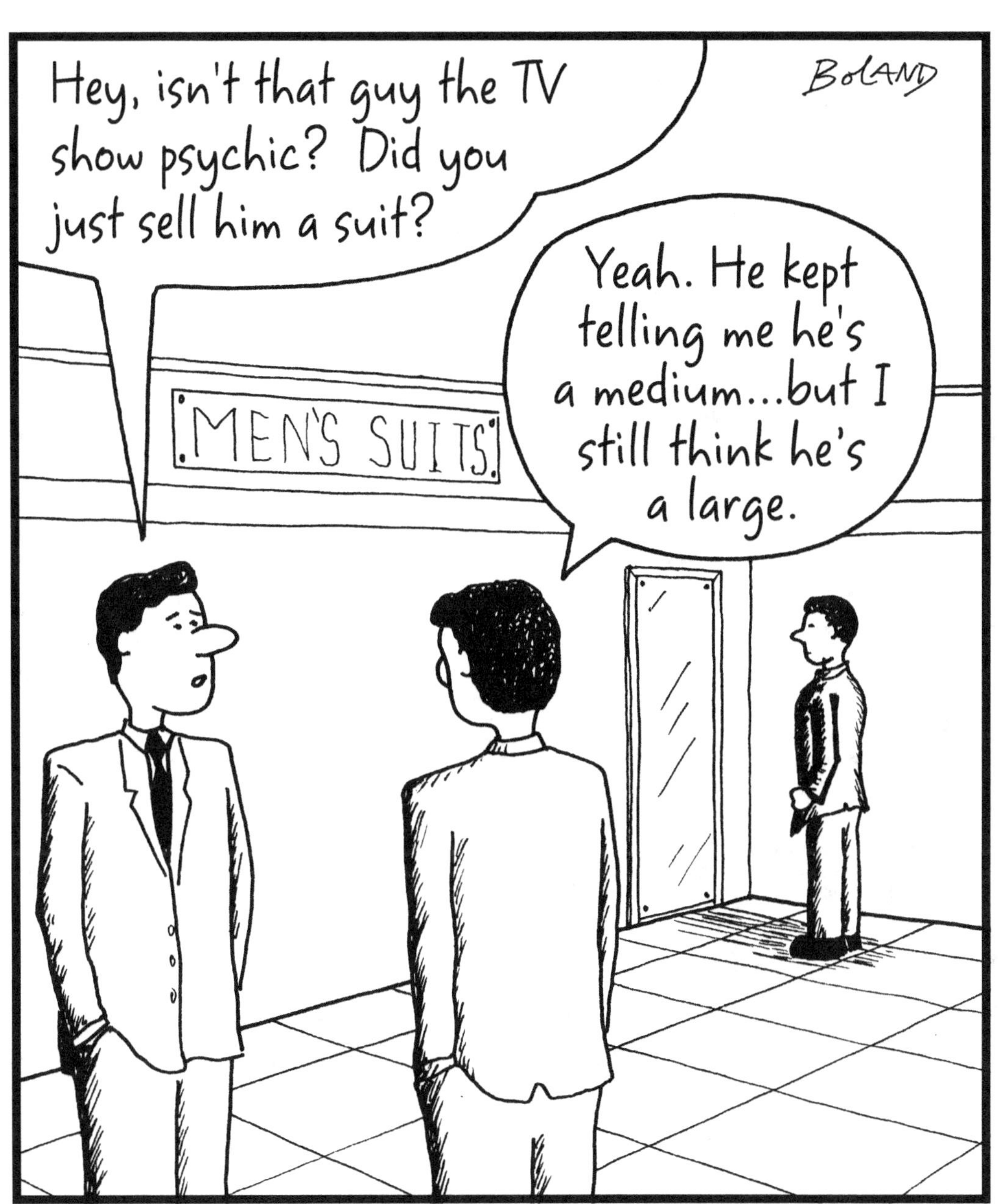
BOLAND
Hey, isn't that guy the TV show psychic? Did you just sell him a suit?
Yeah. He kept telling me he's a medium...but I still think he's a large.
MEN'S SUITS

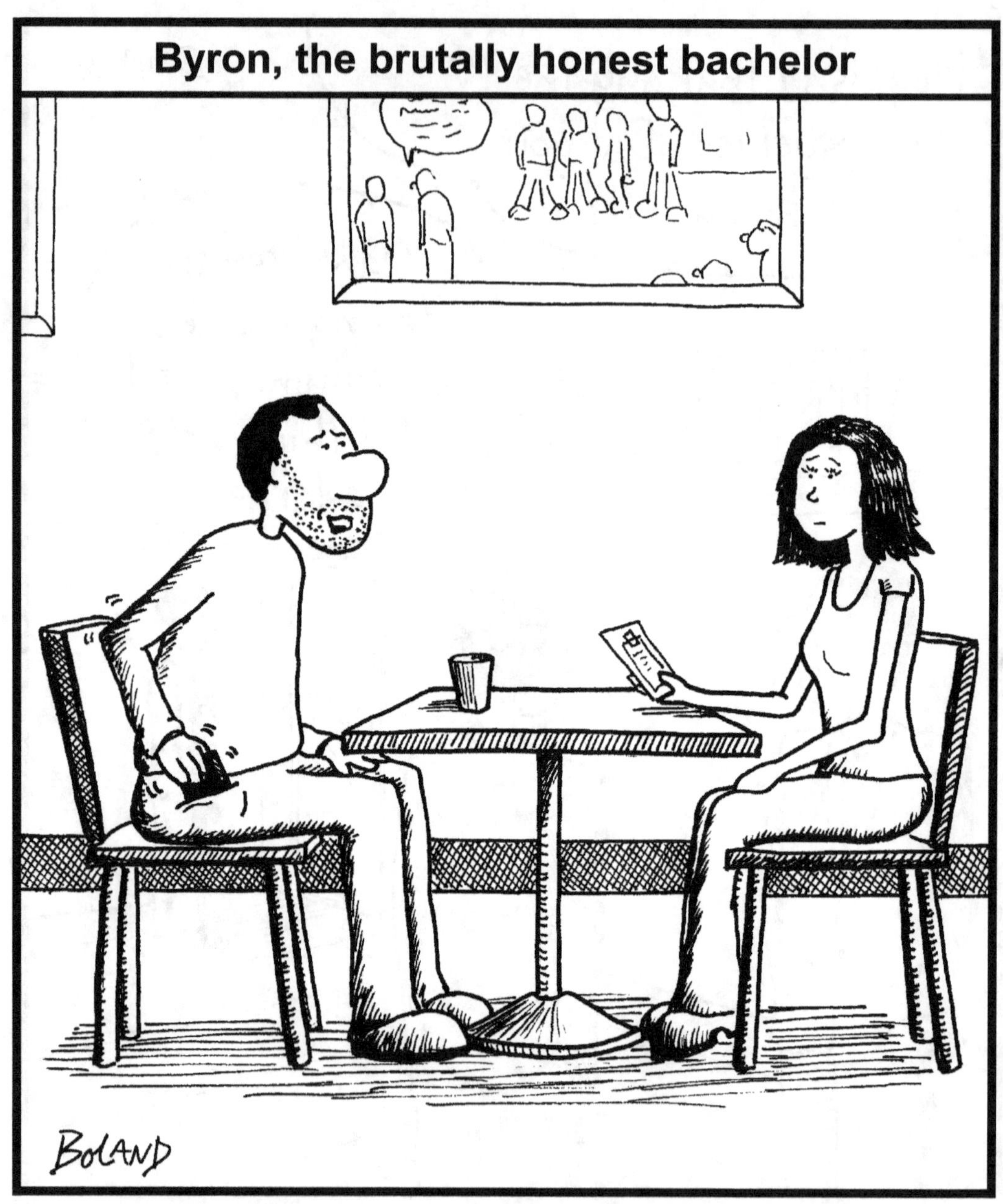

"Oh, don't worry about It. I'll pay for dinner. My parents still give me an allowance."

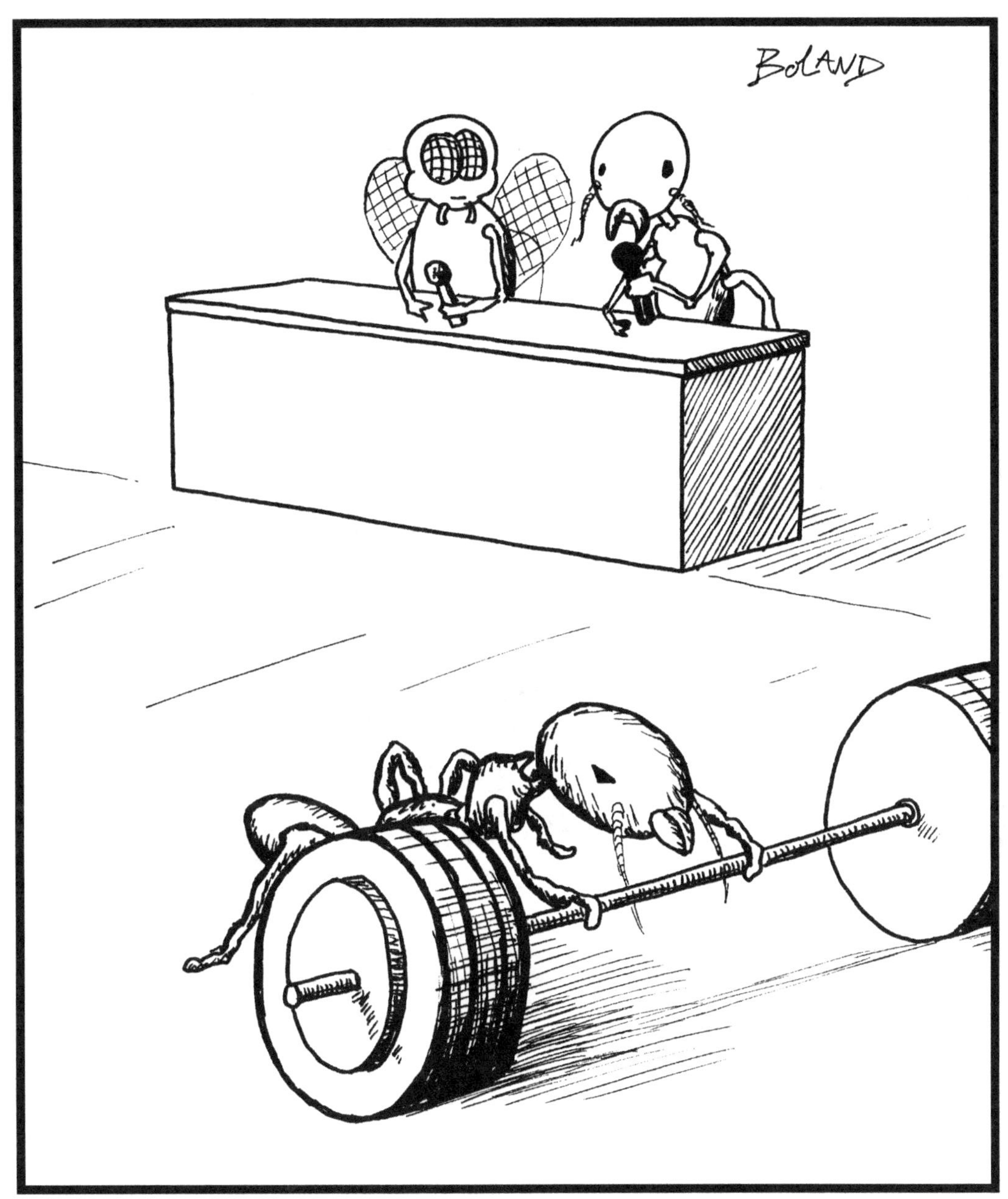

"To the astonishment of myrmecologists around the world, this young ant has already lifted over 70 times his own body weight. Tonight, as he attempts another record, you can't help but wonder, Bob, whether the recent accusations are true... Did he, in fact, consume performance enhancing bugs?"

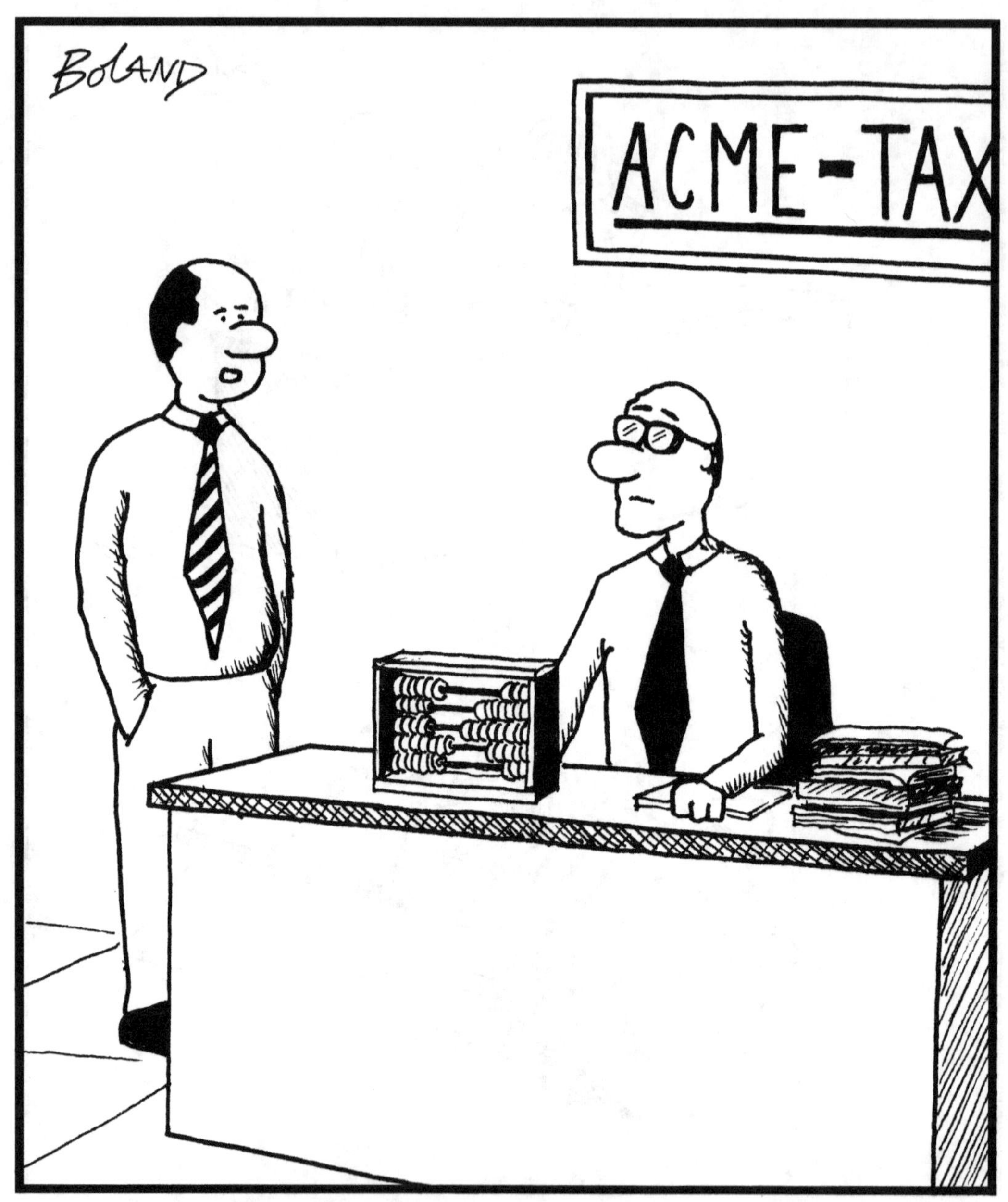

"Tom, when I said that we needed to get back to the basics, I didn't mean it literally."

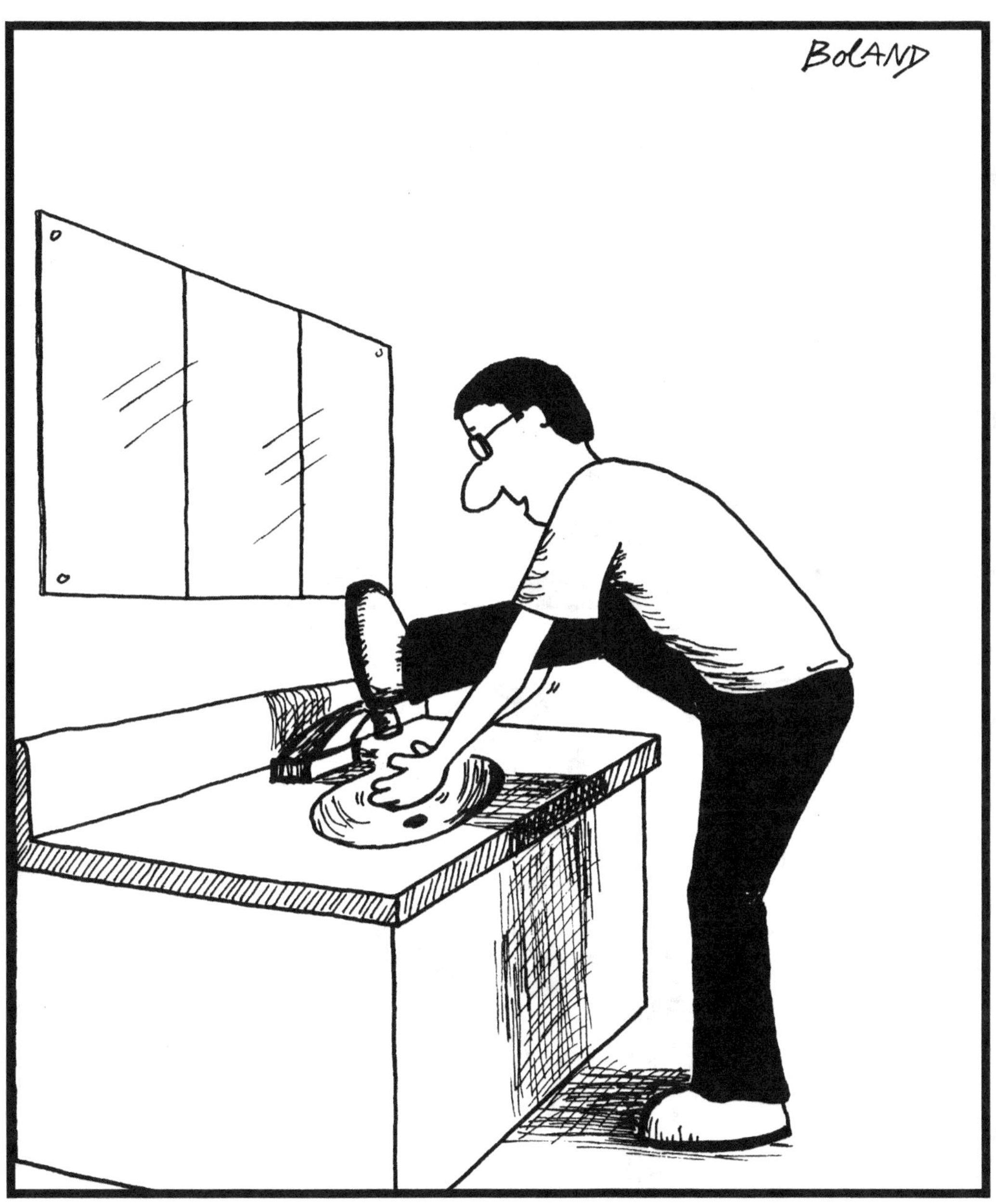

Annoyed by push-down faucets in restrooms, Ron devised his own method for washing up with both hands.

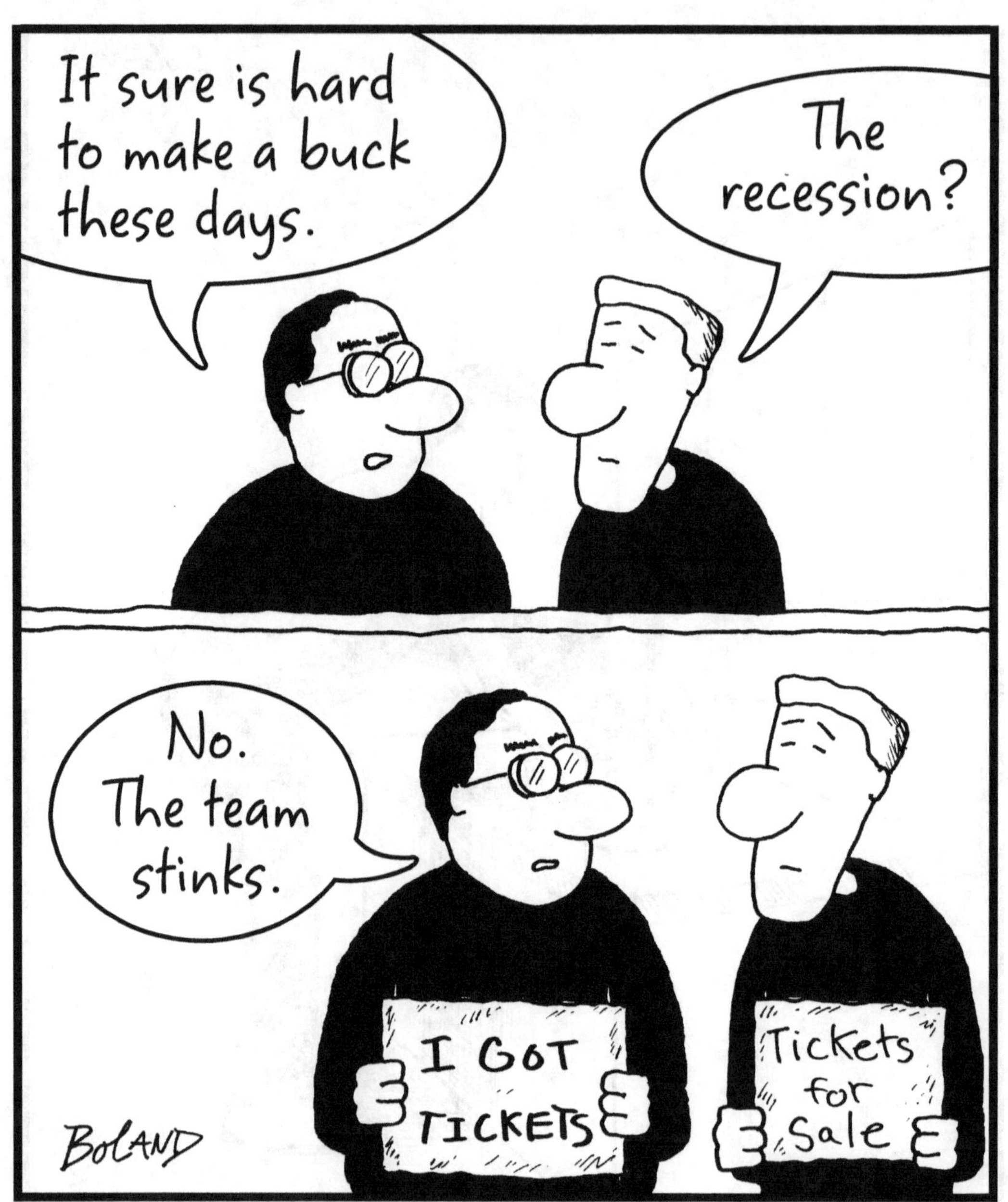
It sure is hard to make a buck these days.
The recession?
No. The team stinks.
I GOT TICKETS
Tickets for Sale
BOLAND

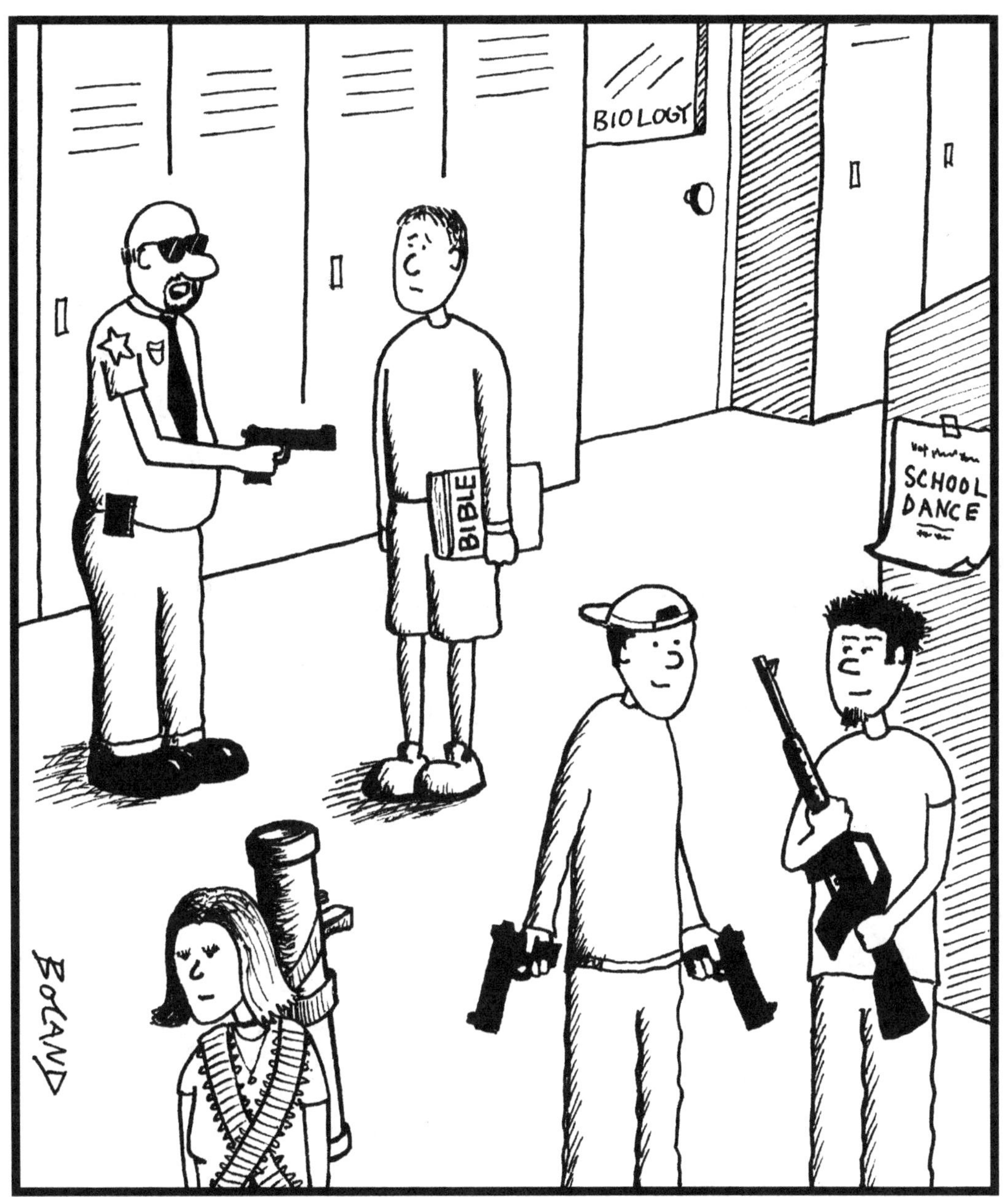

"Son, I'm going to have to ask you to step away from the Bible and put your hands behind your head."

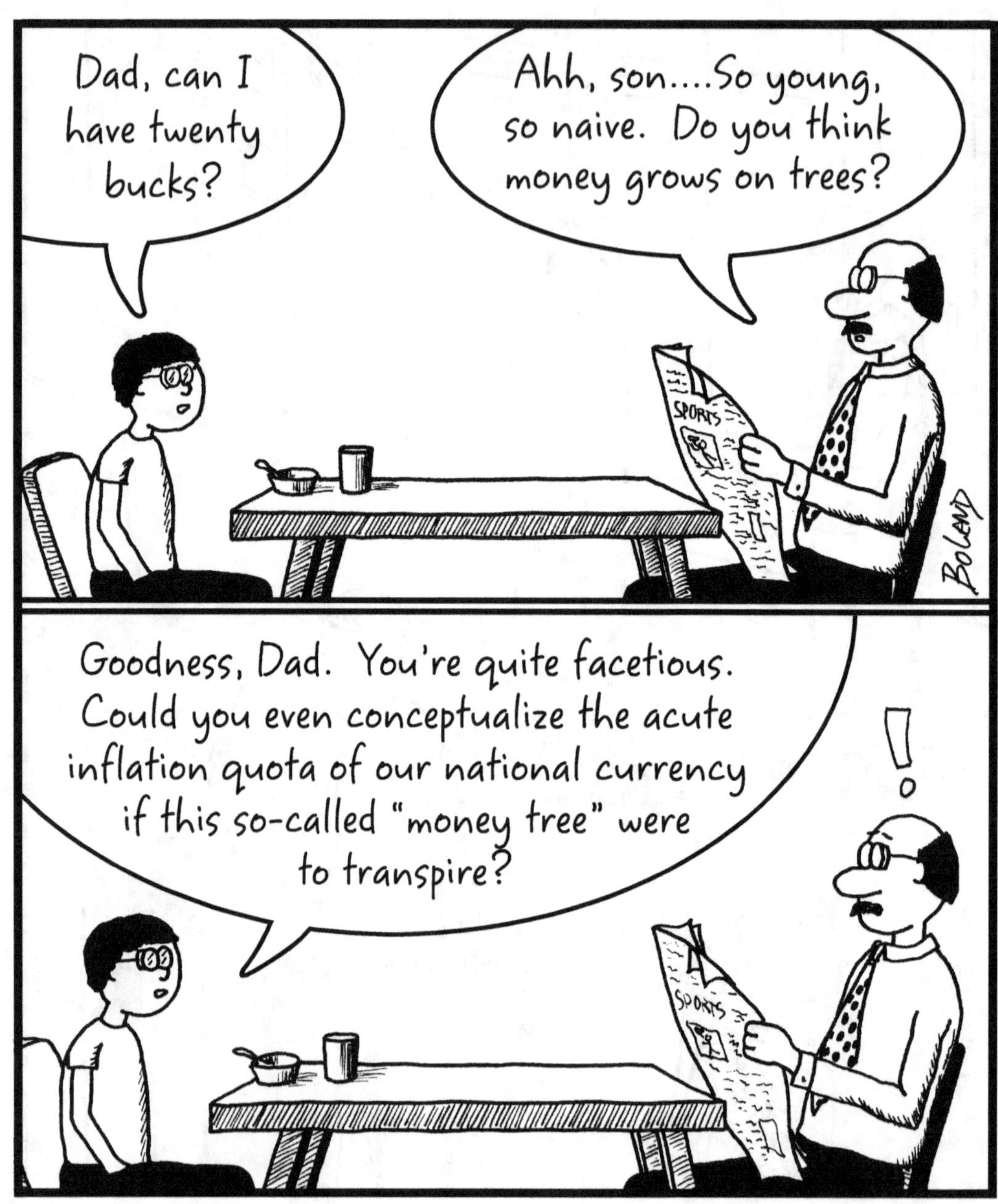
Dad, can I have twenty bucks?
Ahh, son....So young, so naive. Do you think money grows on trees?
SPORTS
BOLAND
Goodness, Dad. You're quite facetious. Could you even conceptualize the acute inflation quota of our national currency if this so-called "money tree" were to transpire?
!
SPORTS

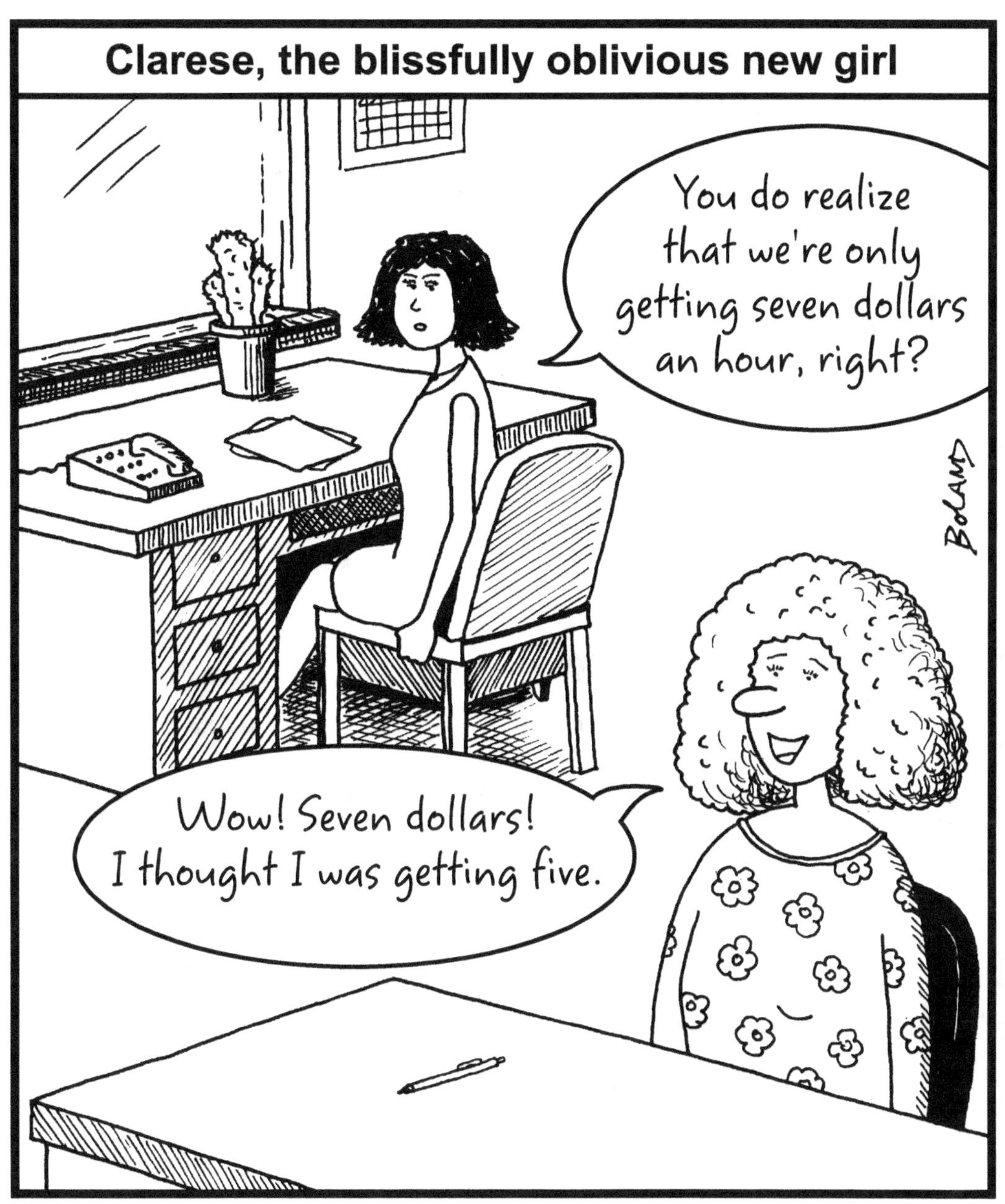

Clarese, the blissfully oblivious new girl

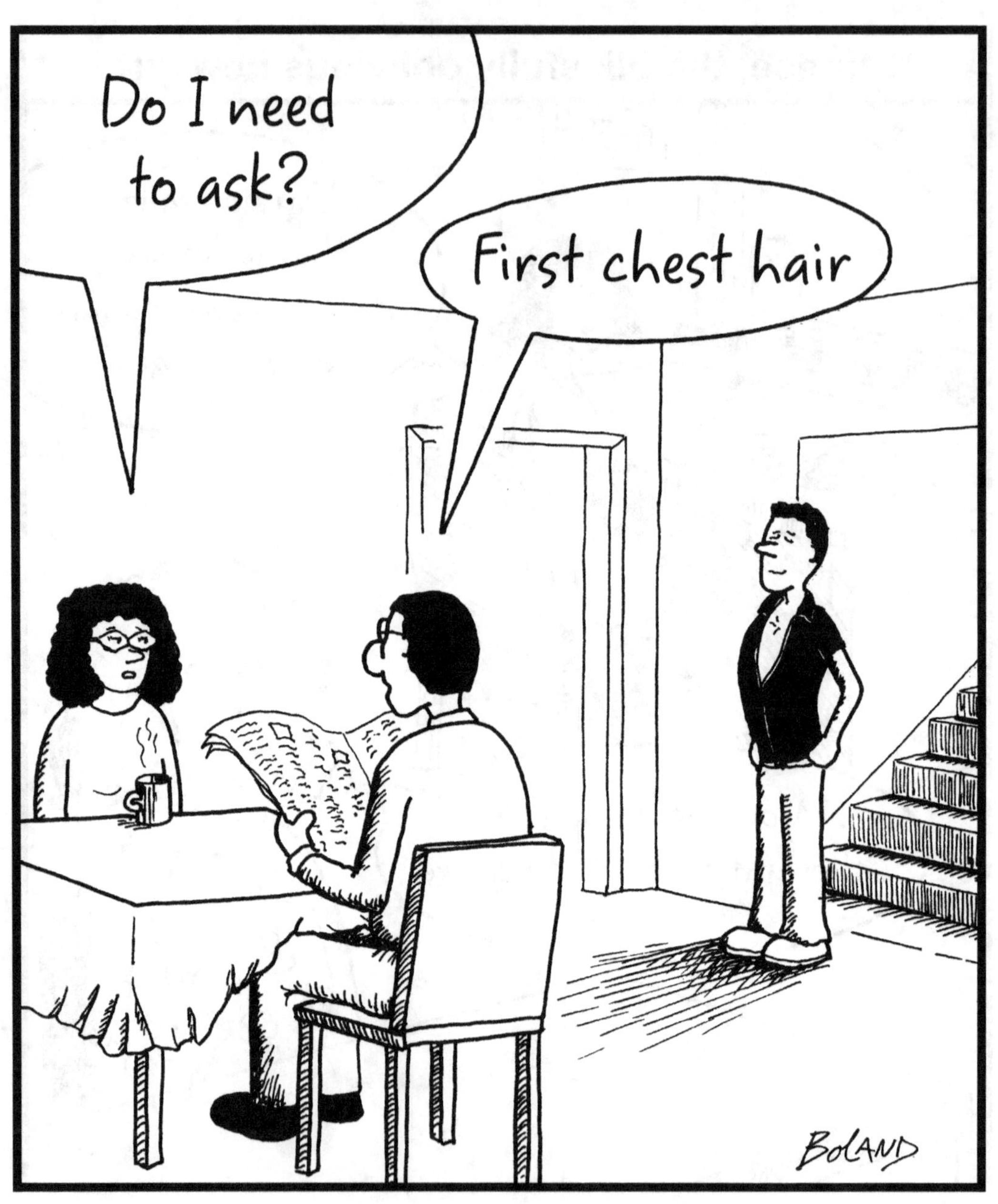
Do I need to ask?
First chest hair
BOLAND

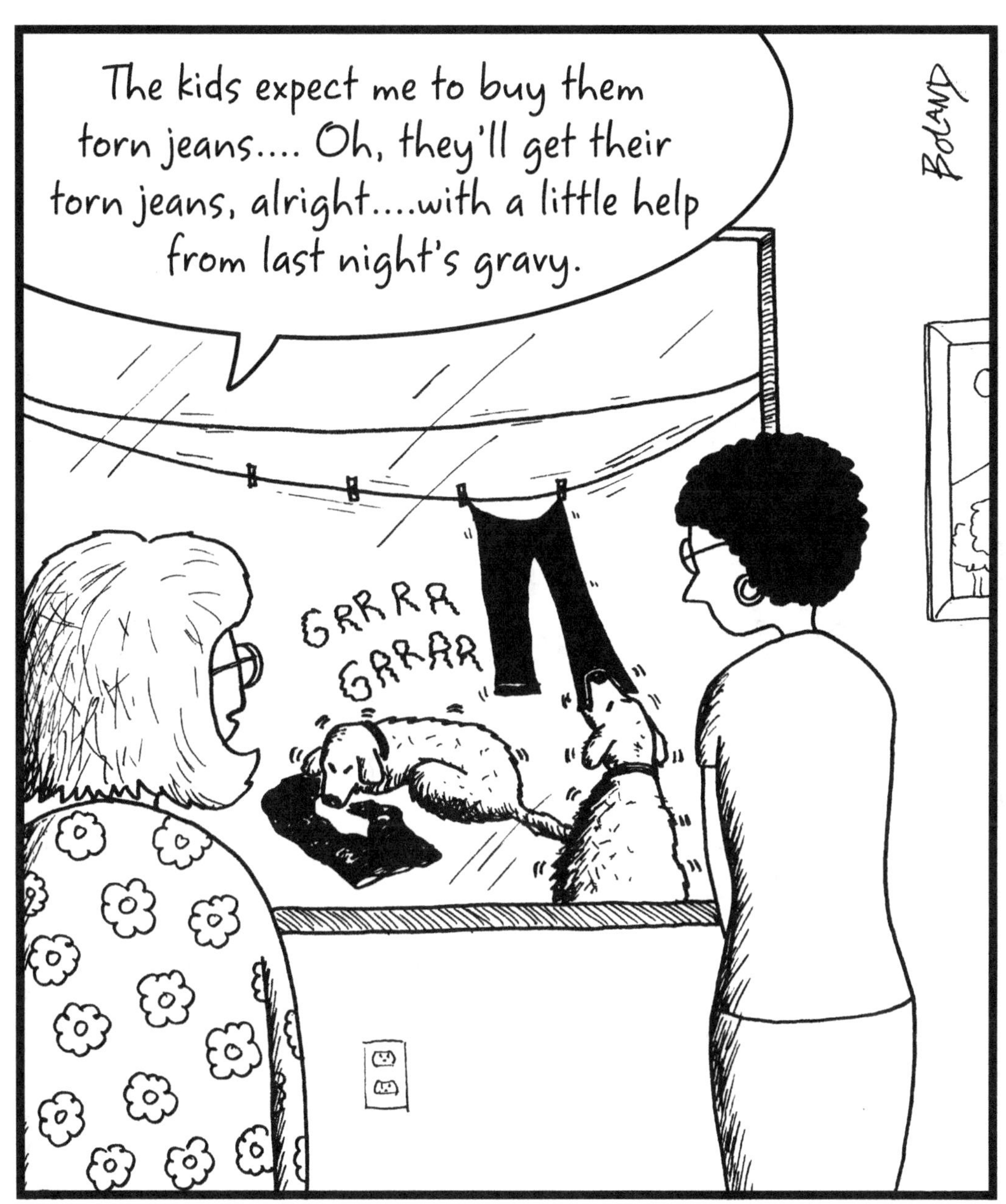
The kids expect me to buy them torn jeans.... Oh, they'll get their torn jeans, alright....with a little help from last night's gravy.
GRRRR
GRRRR
BOLAND

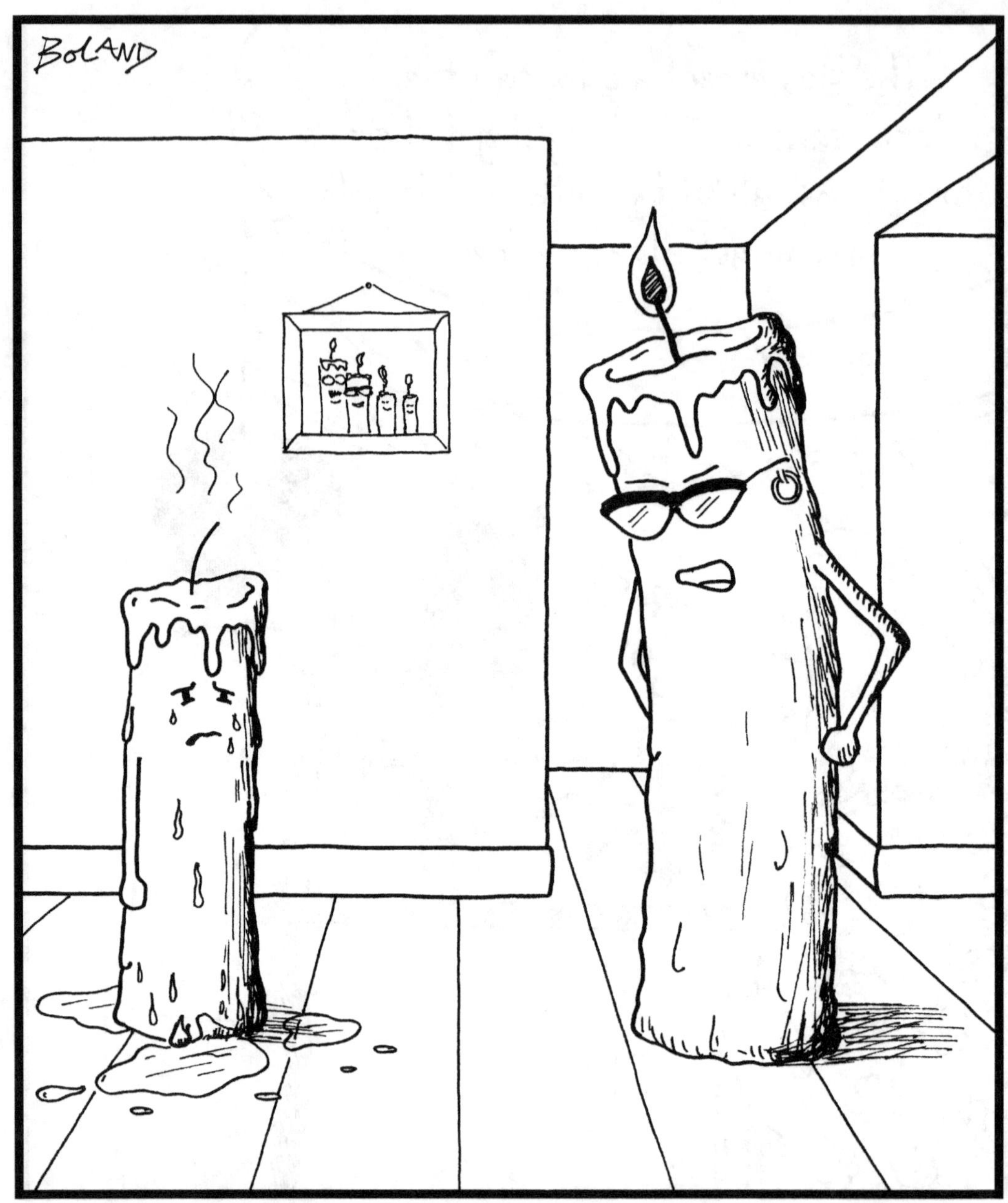

"Don't you come crying to me. How many times have I told you?...If you play with water, you're going to get snuffed."

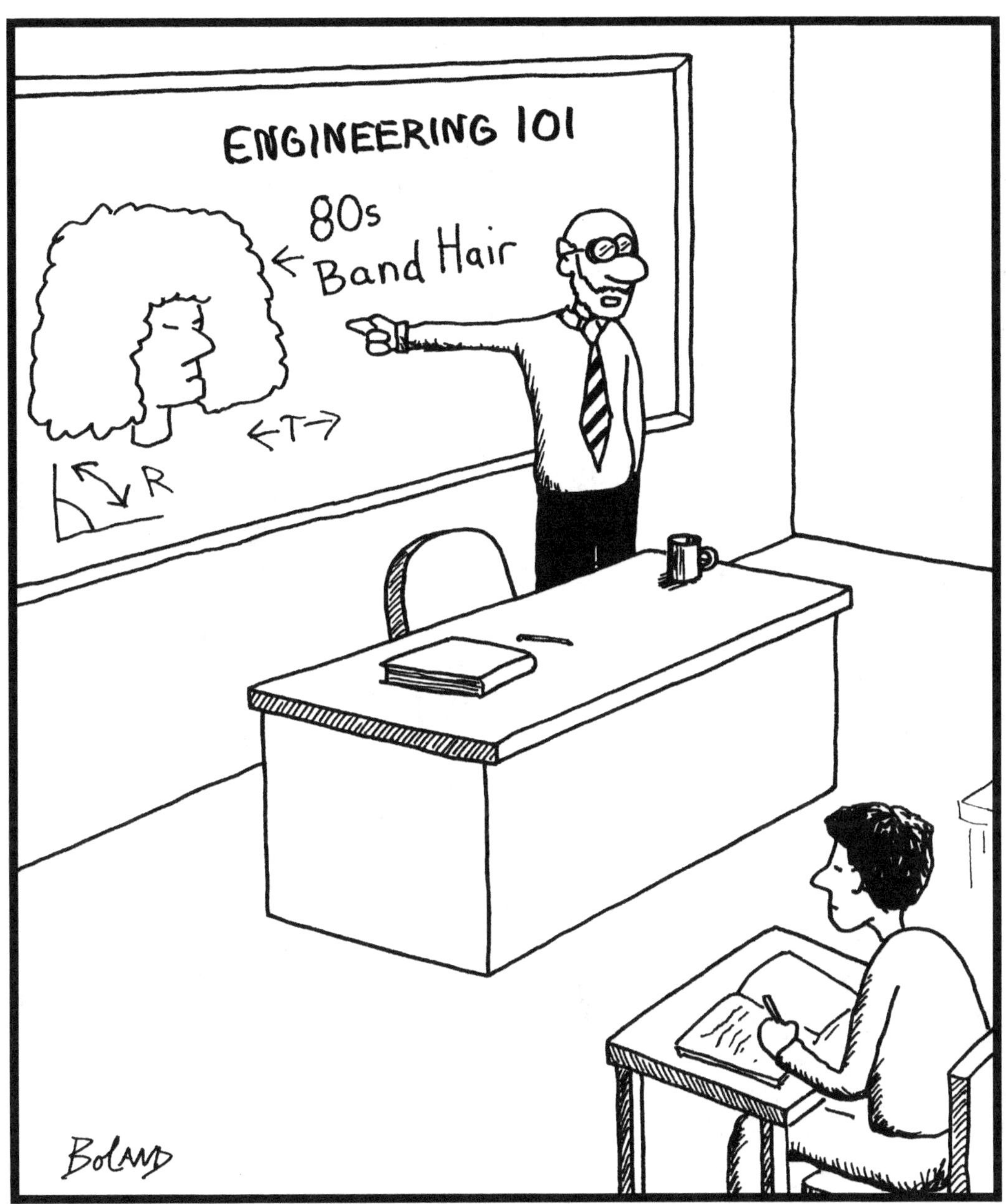

"...and to this day, engineers still marvel at how it was possible for this structure to get so extremely massive without collapsing under its own weight."

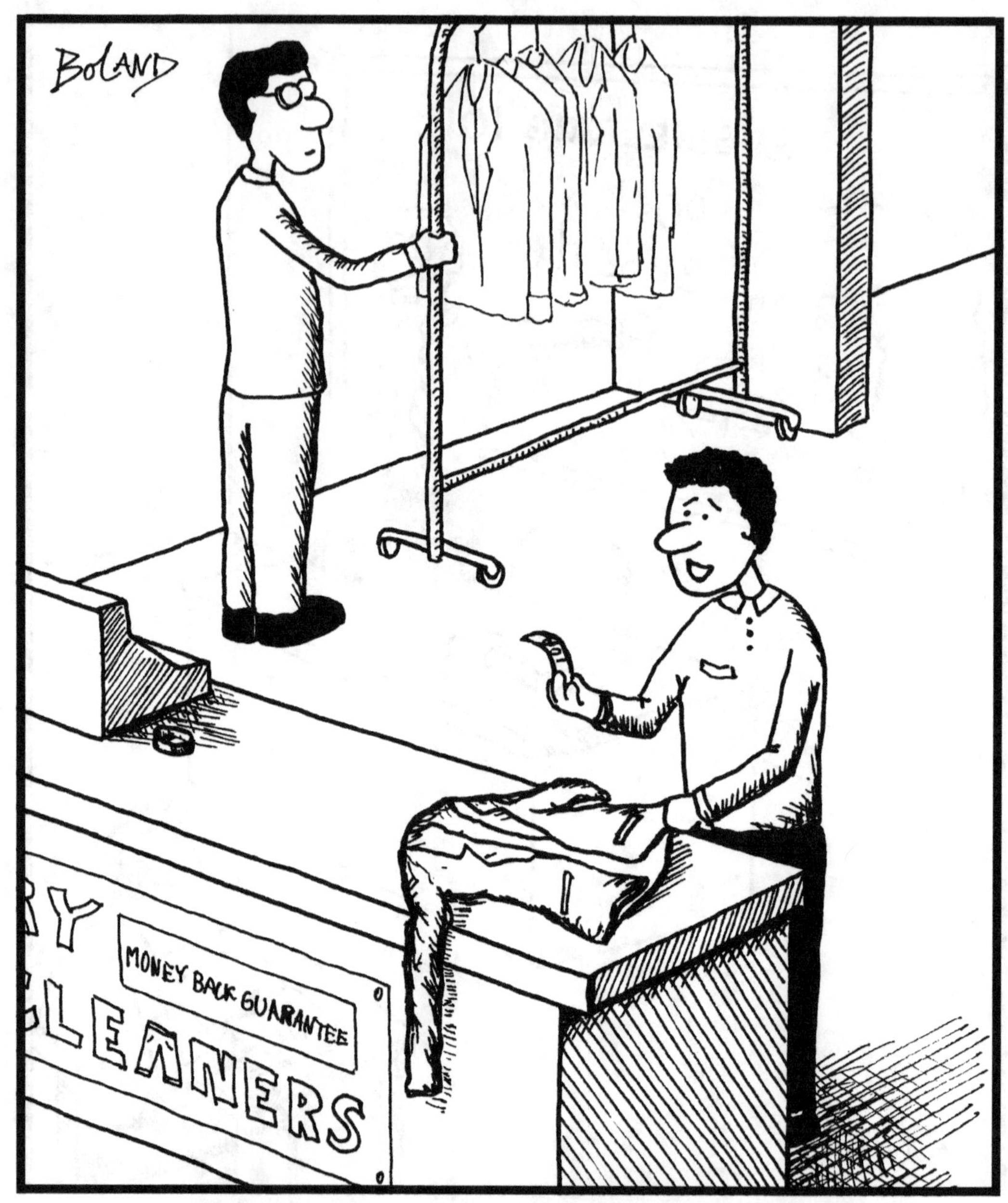

"Check this out! Bob Barker left a hundred bucks in his pocket from the show! I sure hope he keeps 'coming on down'."

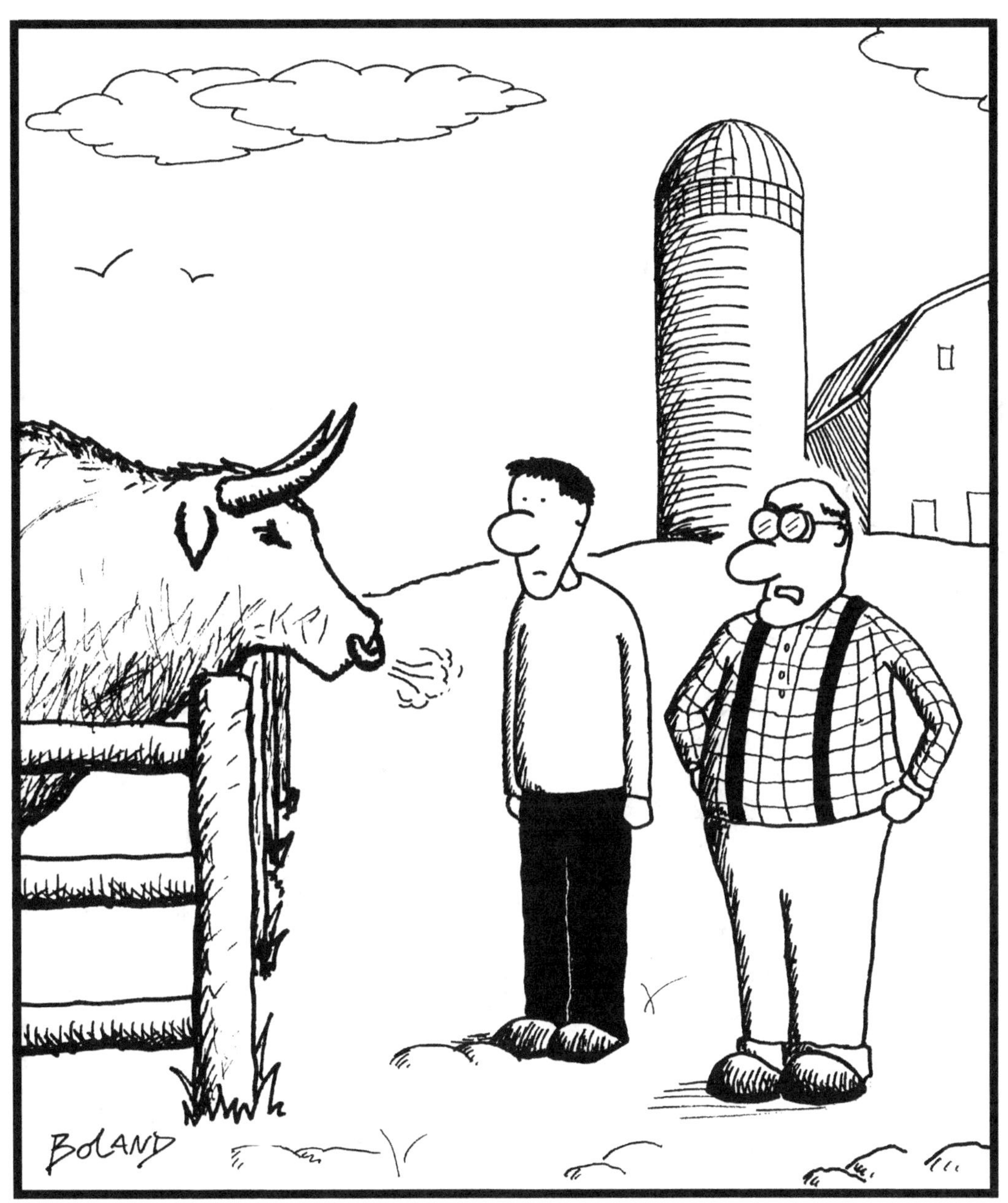

"Take it from personal experience, son. Don't turn your back on that bull...unless you know a good proctologist."

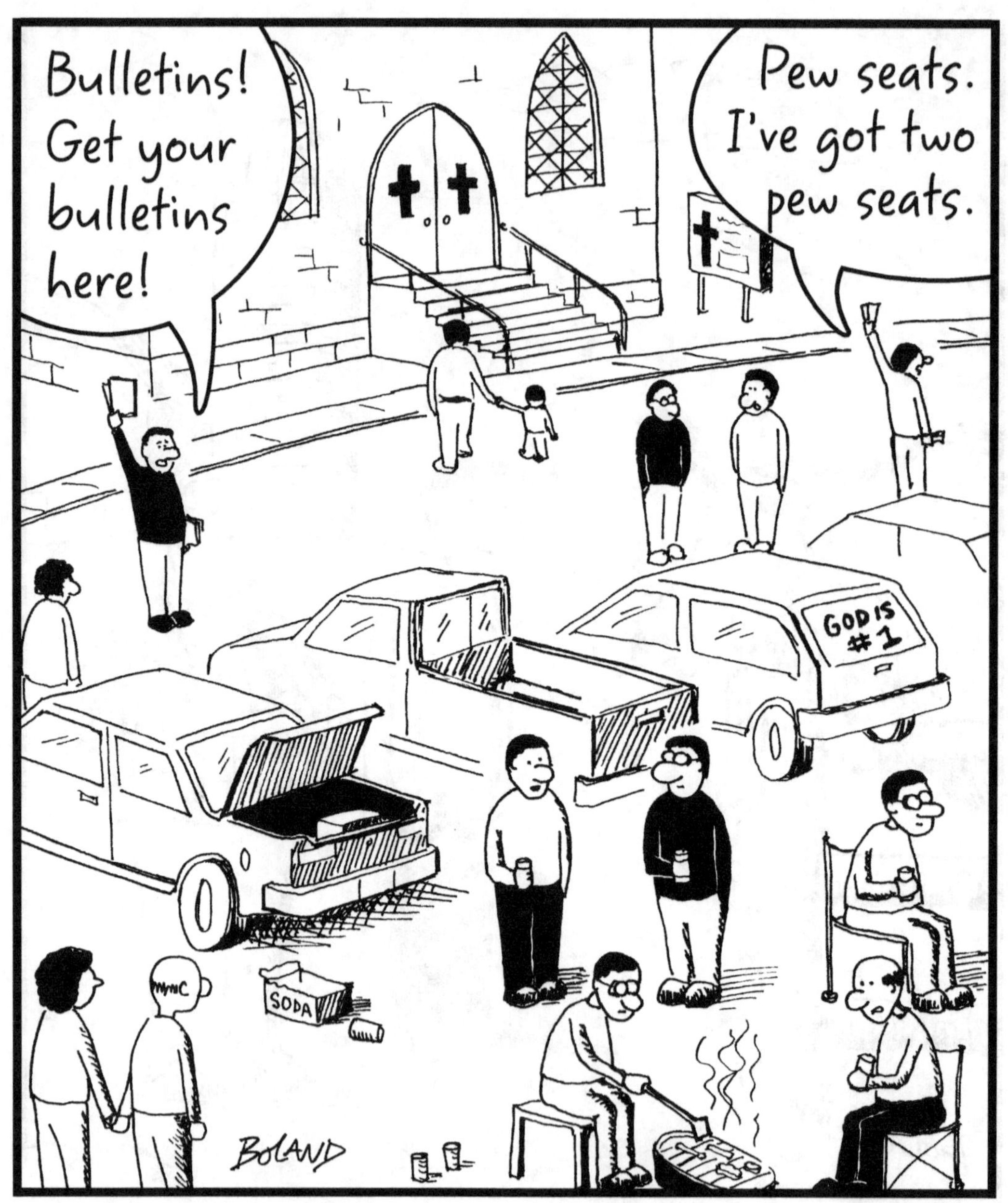

Tailgating Withdrawal: A common occurrence after football season.

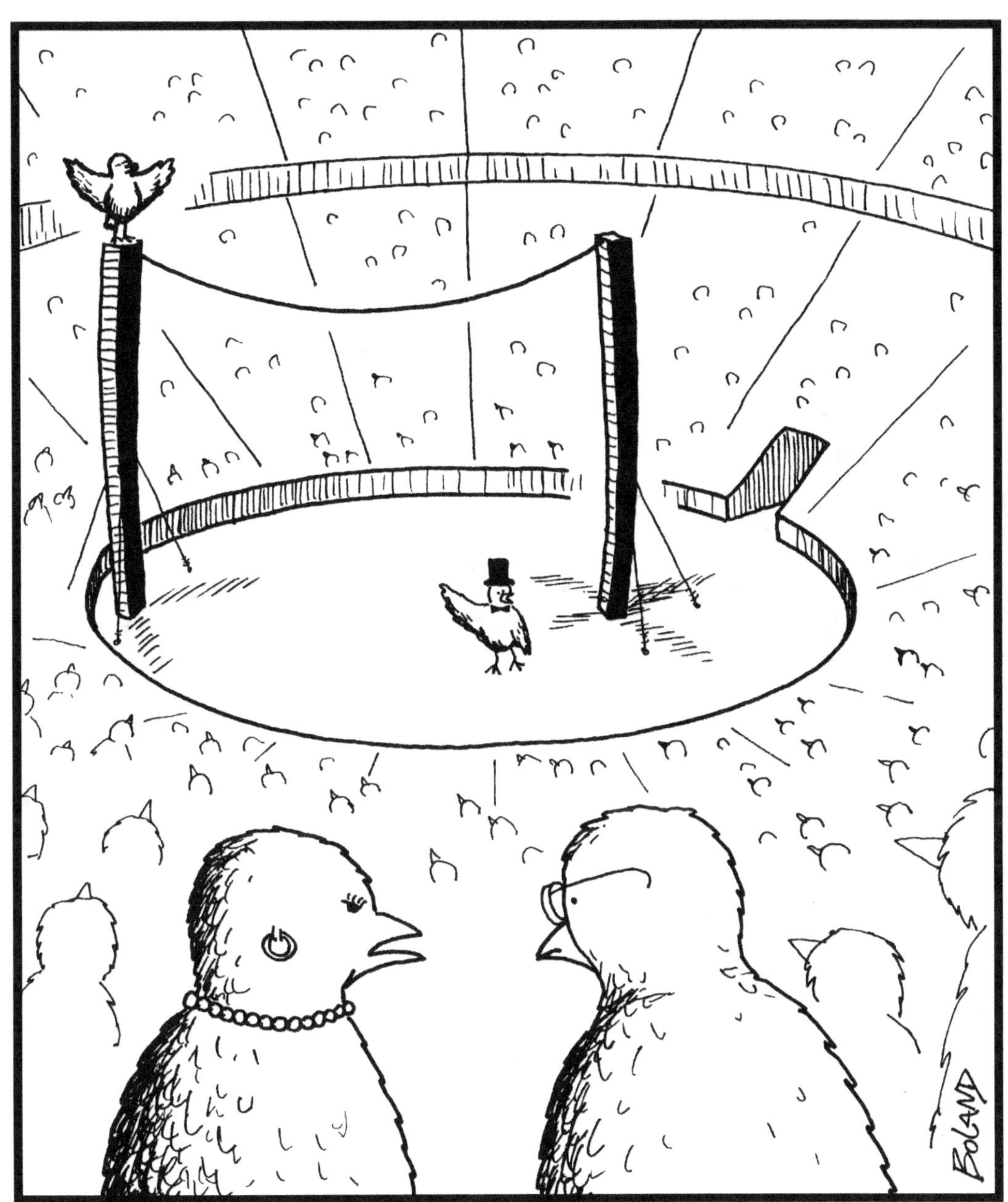

"We paid to see THIS? Come on, Henry... We're going home."

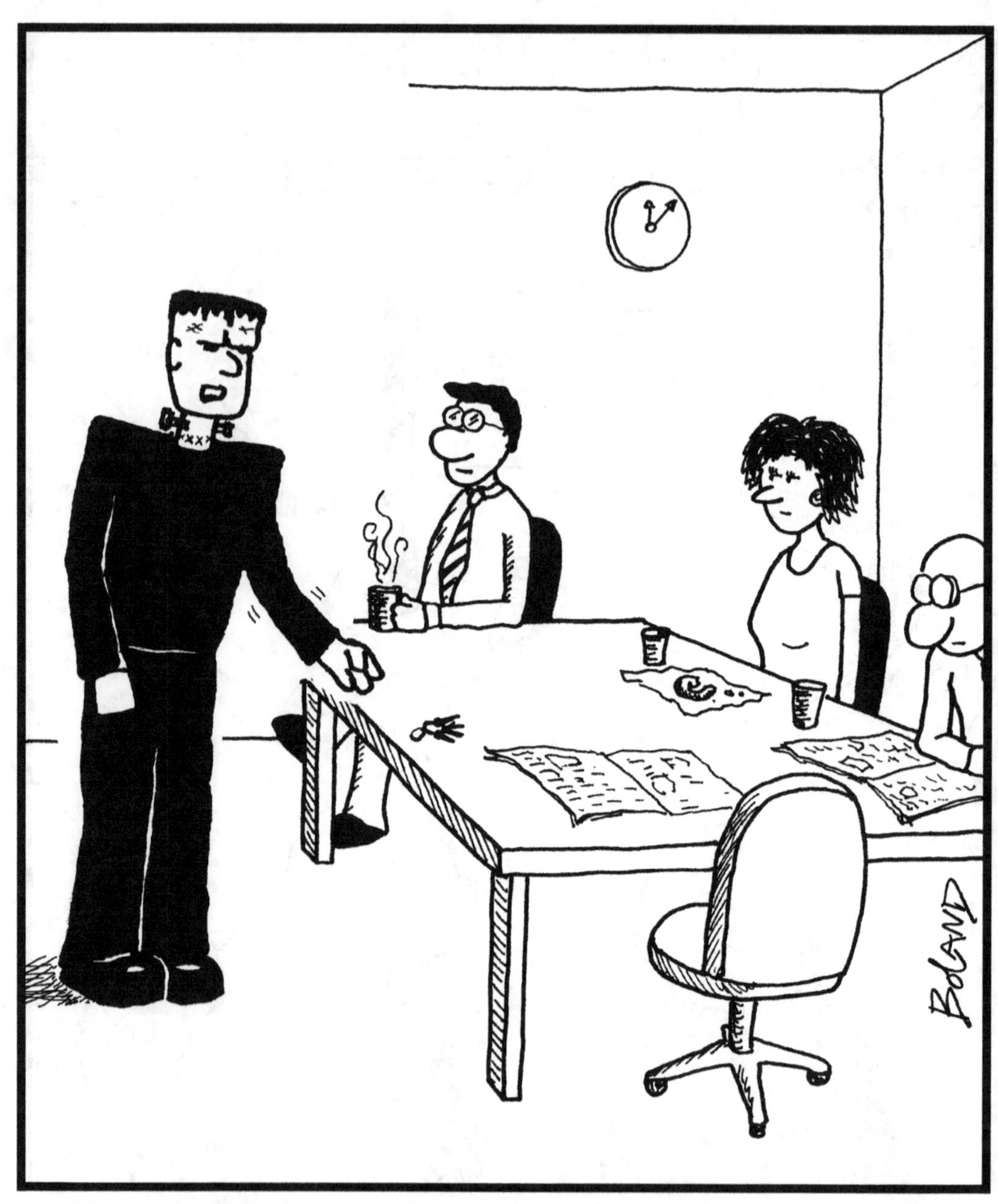

"There they are. I've been looking all over for these keys. I swear I'd lose my head if it wasn't attached."

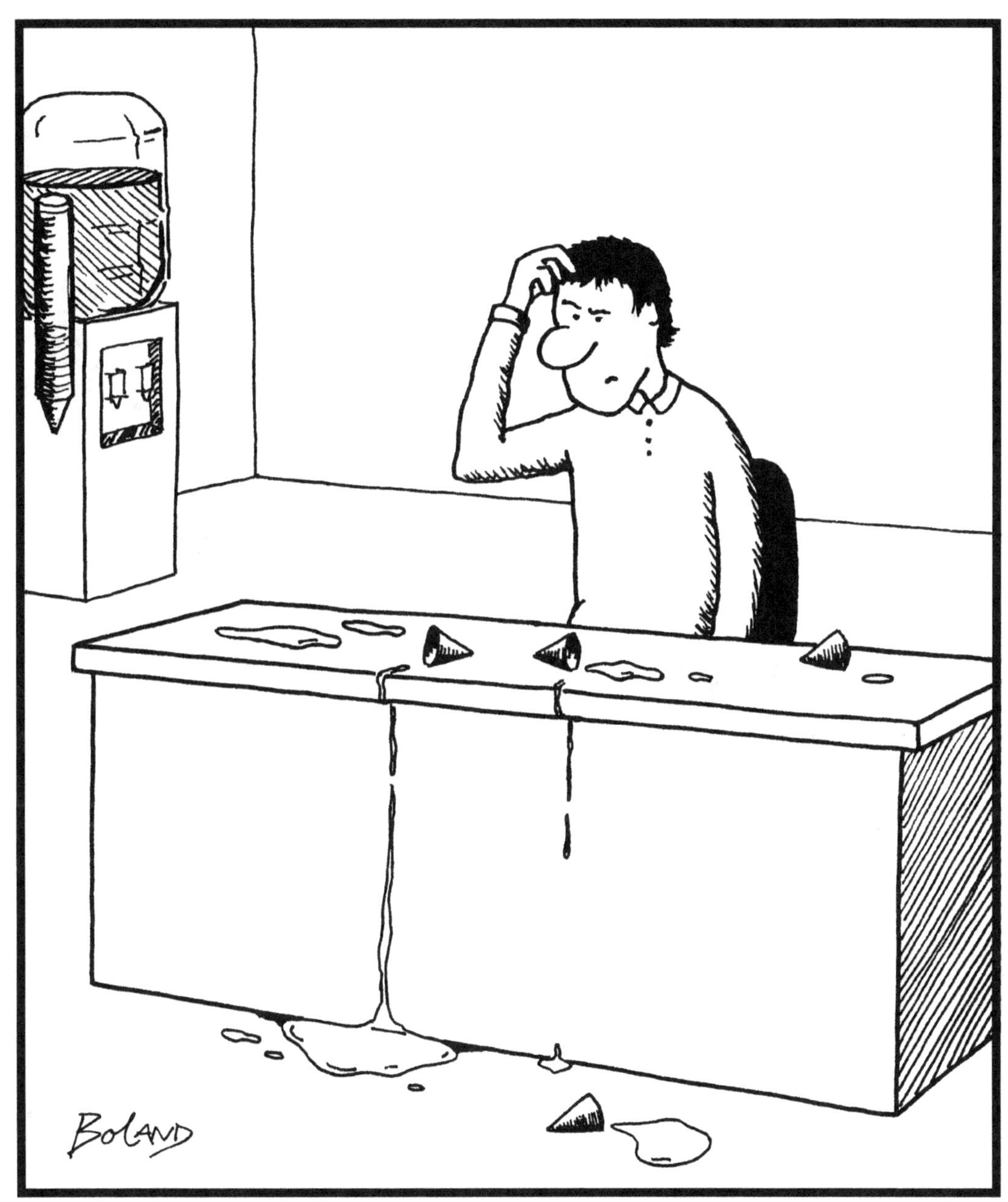

Jimmy, the office idiot

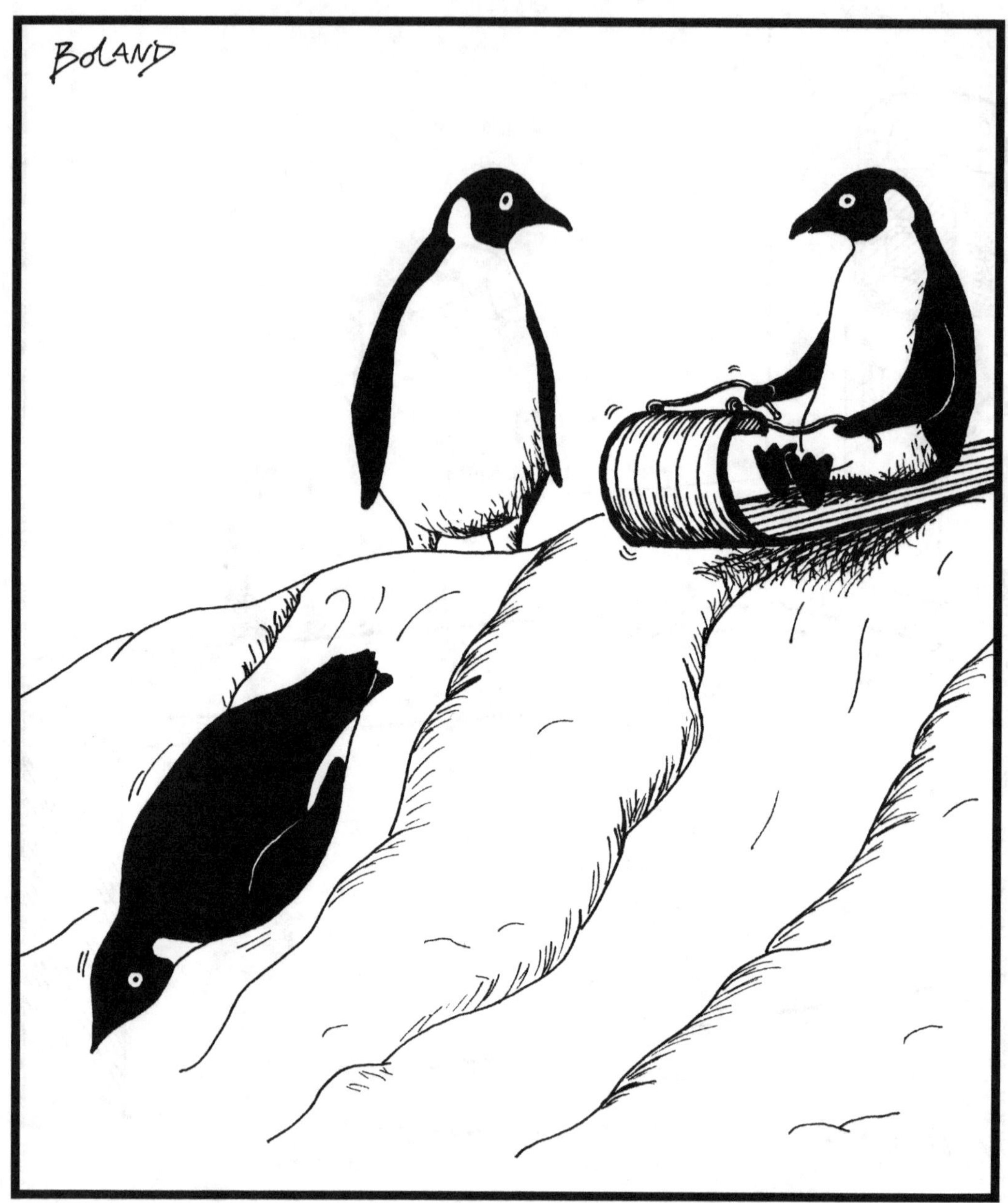
BOLAND

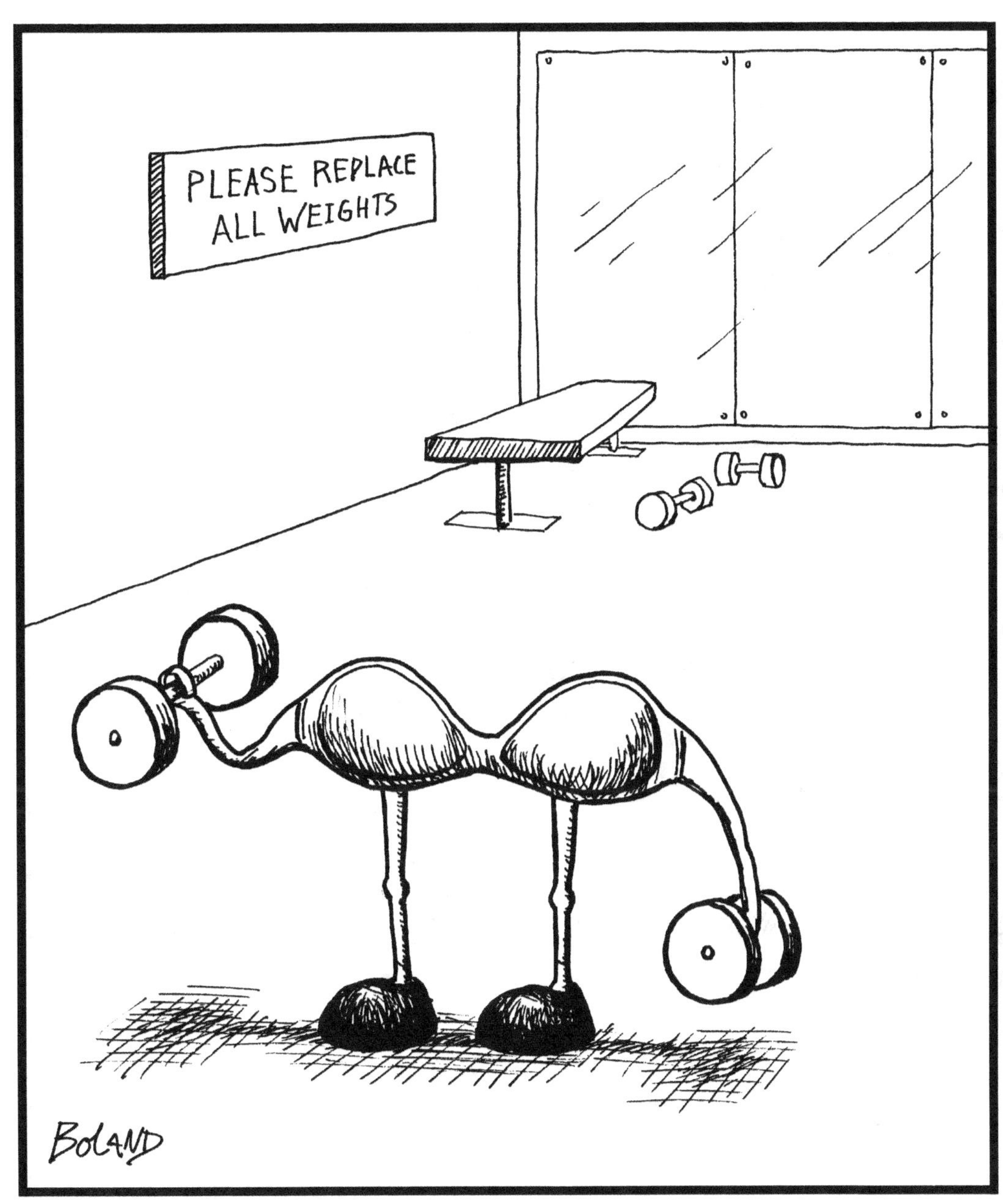

Training Bra

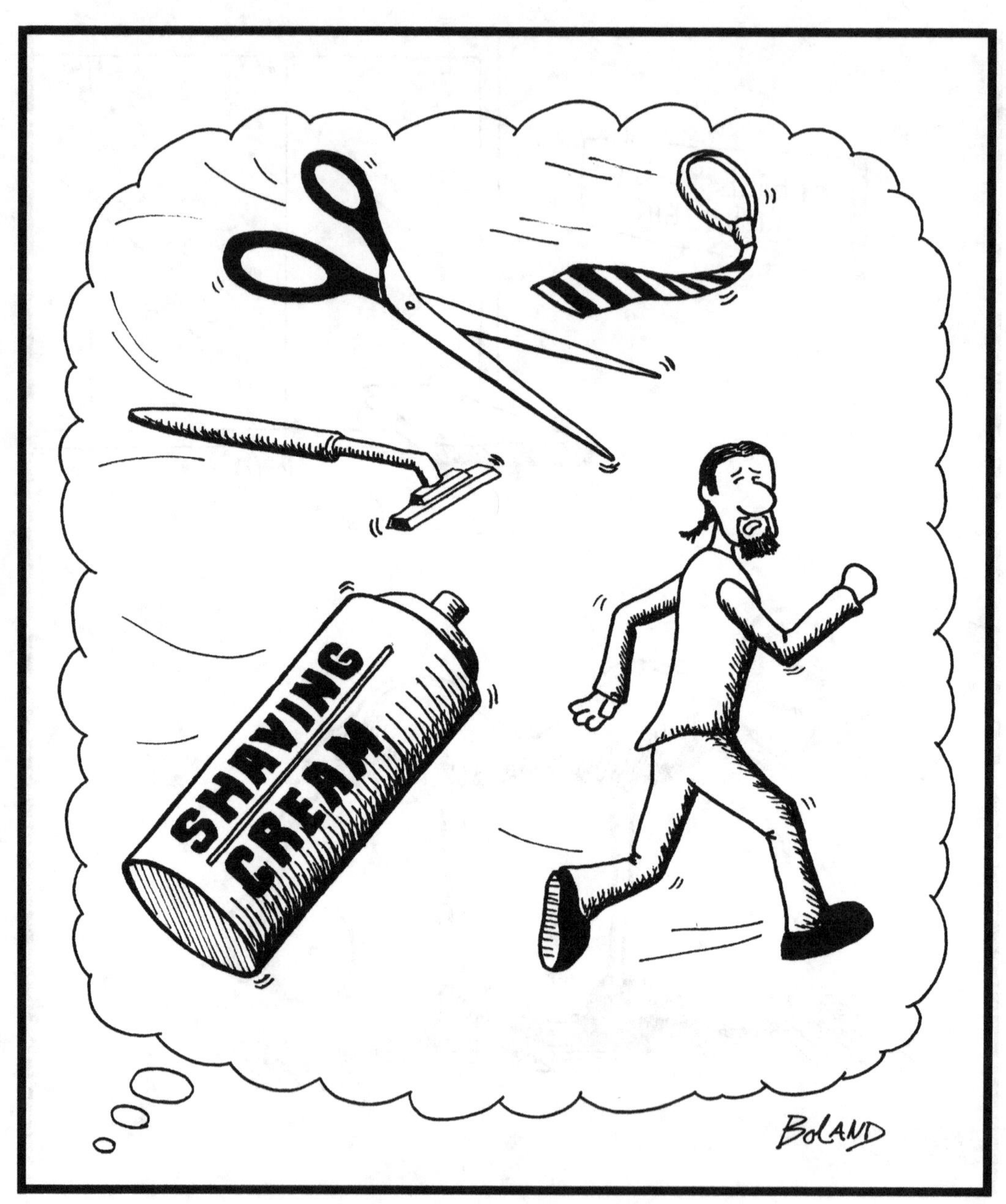

Artist Nightmares

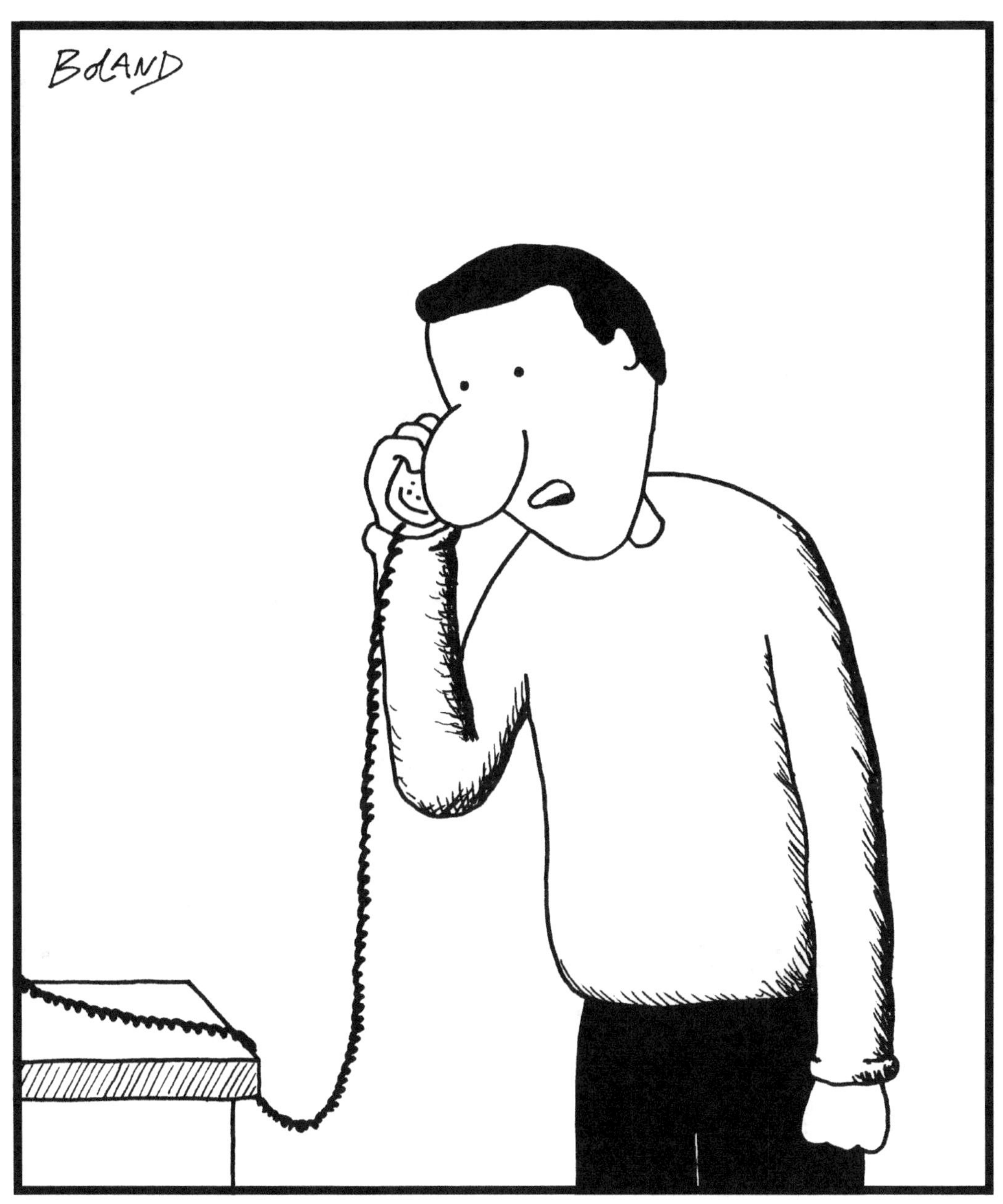

"Hi Doc. I know it's kind of late, but I just saw this commercial and I have no idea what it's for... So, I was just wondering... ....Is Zuritan right for me?"

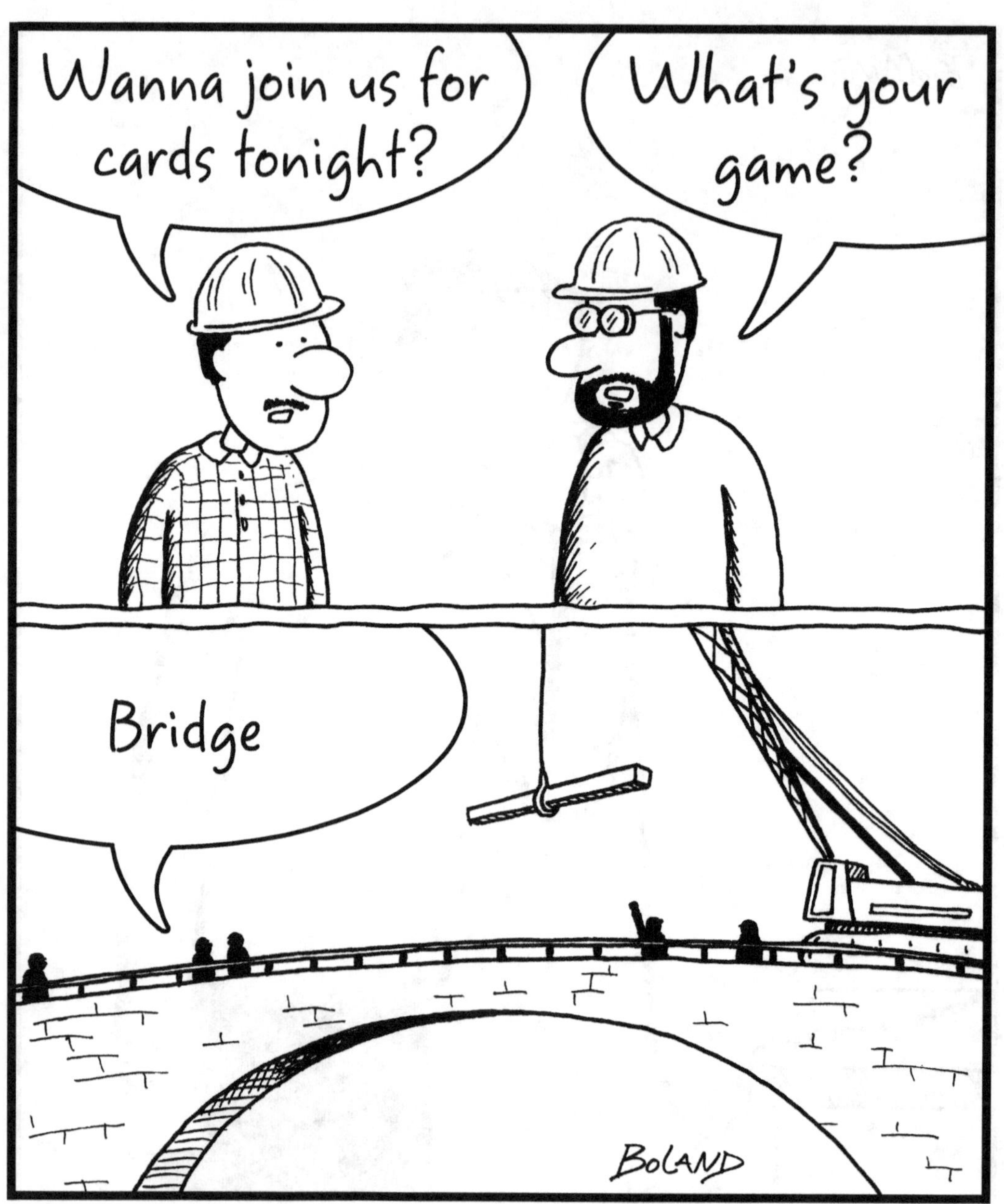
Wanna join us for cards tonight?
What's your game?
Bridge
BOLAND

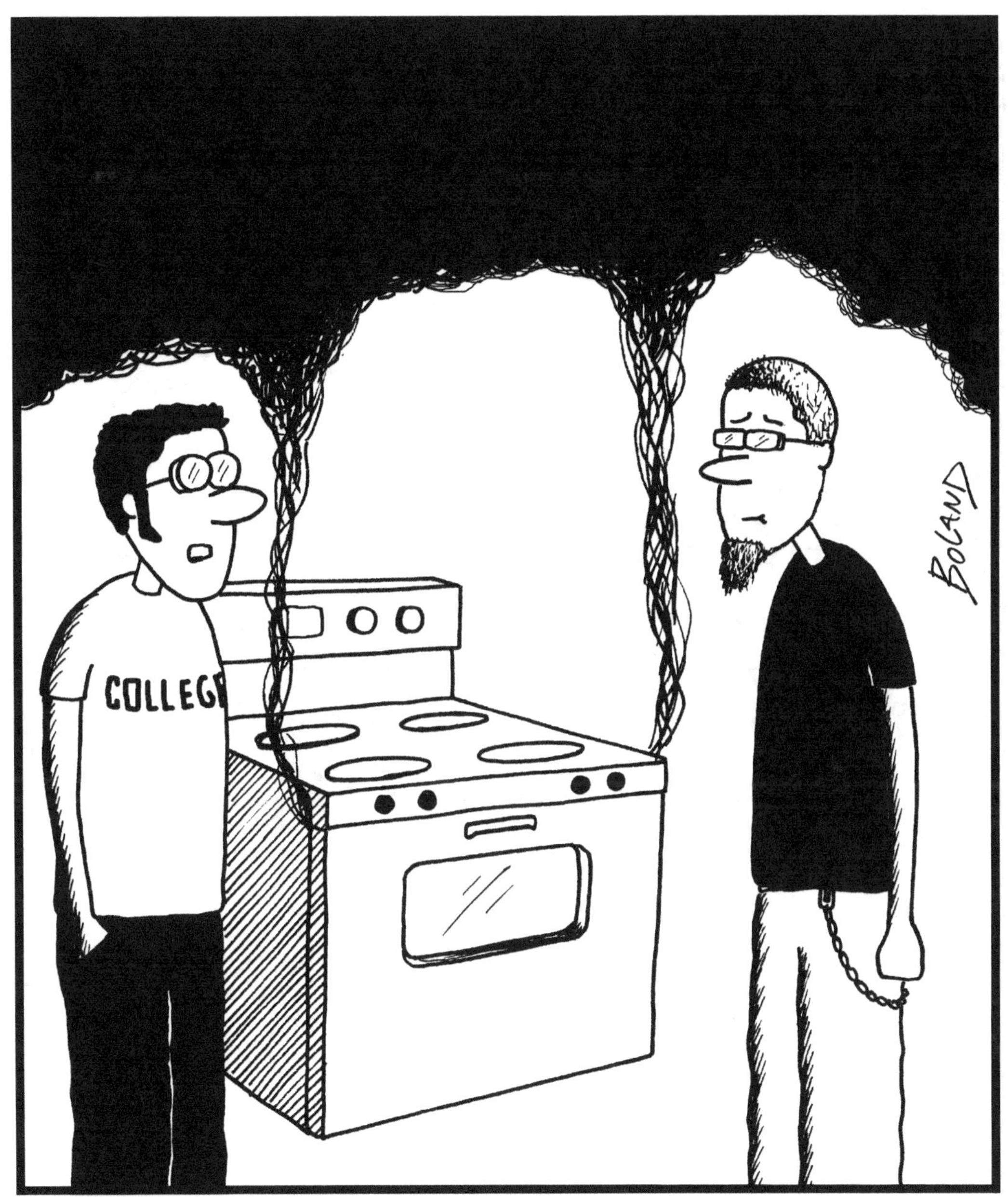

"Trust me, man. Two pizzas...just double the temp. It's simple math."

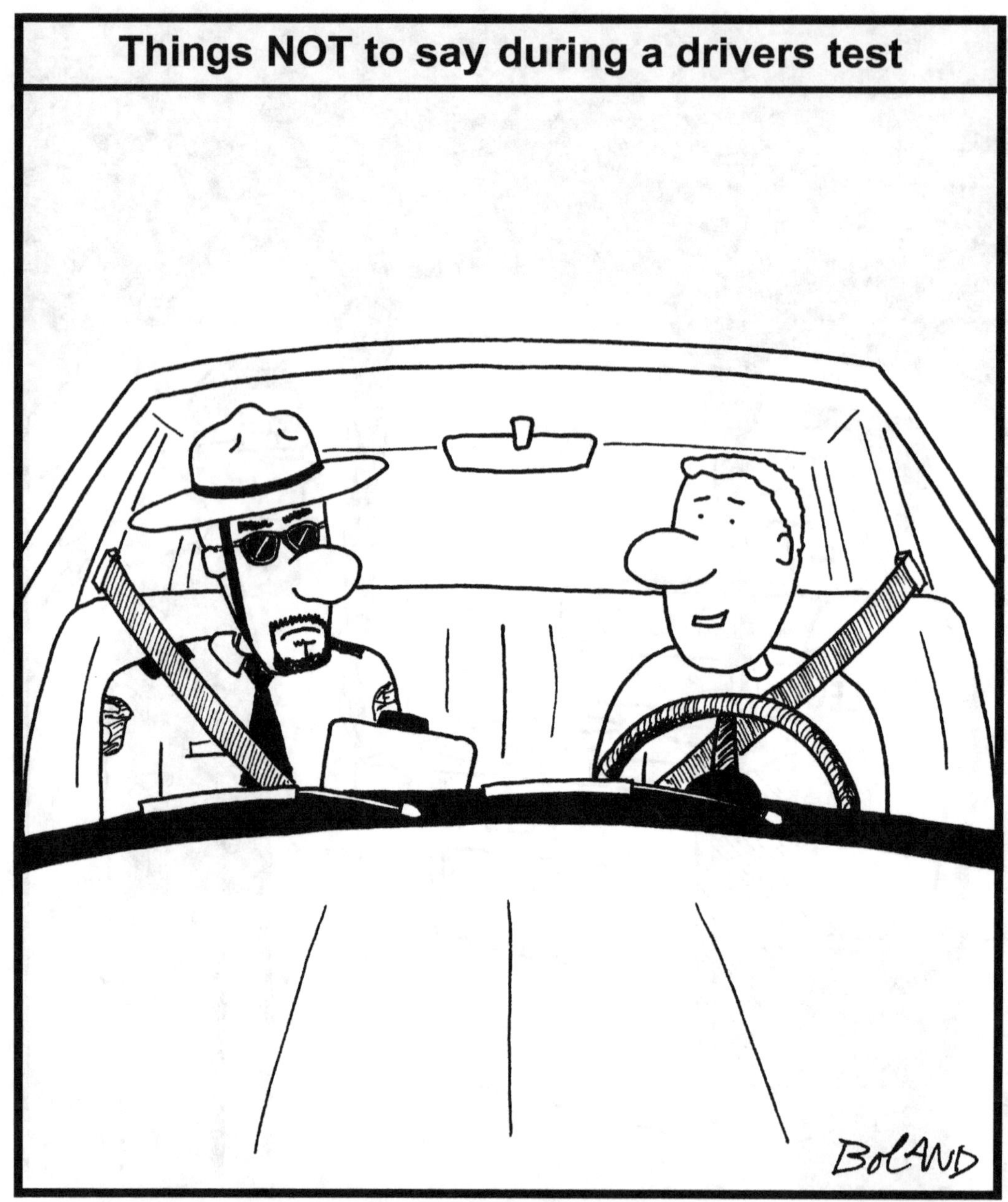

"Sorry about the seat. Taking a turn at 60 with tortillas and nacho cheese in your lap... not as doable as you'd think."

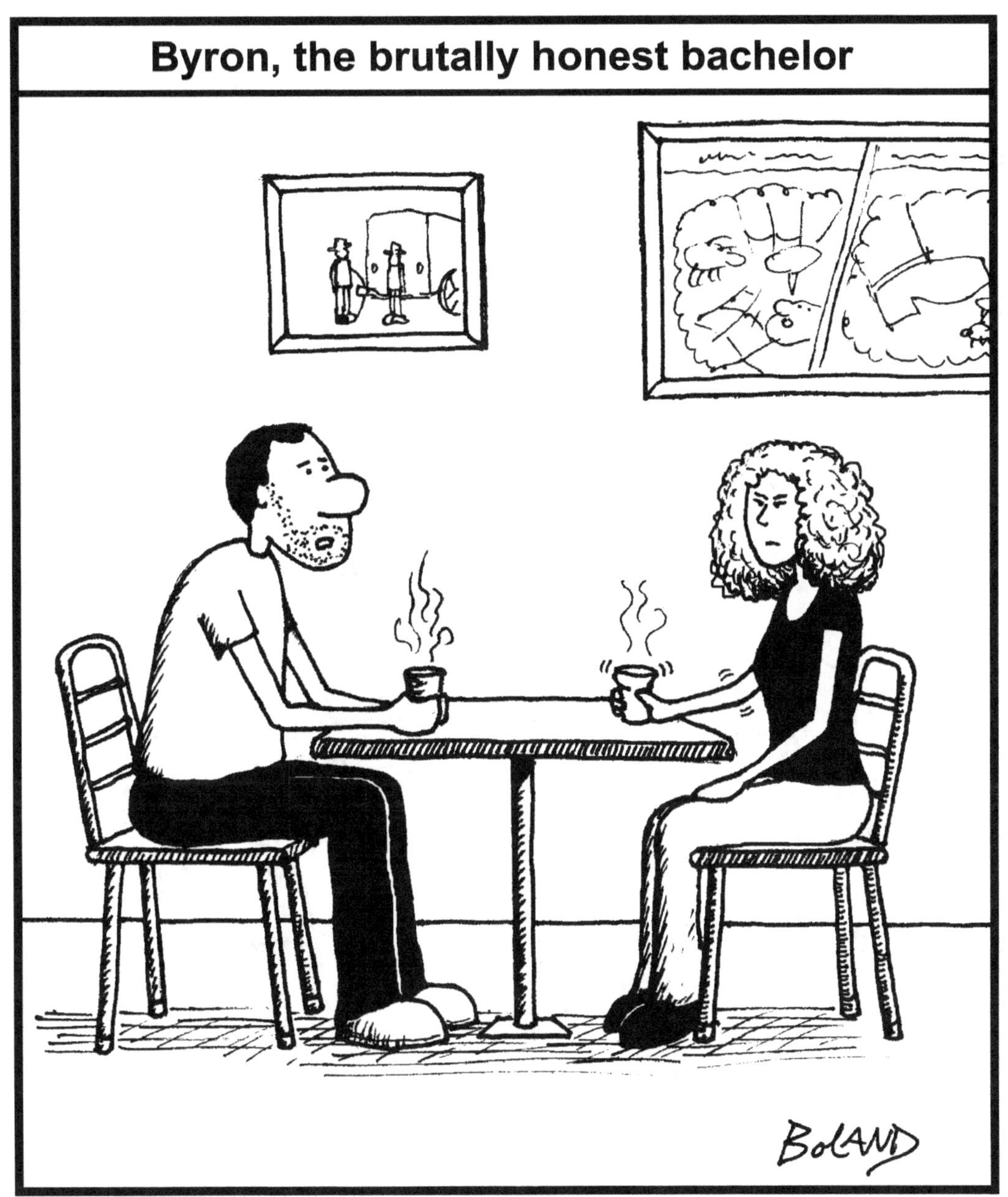

"I love what you're trying to do with your hair."

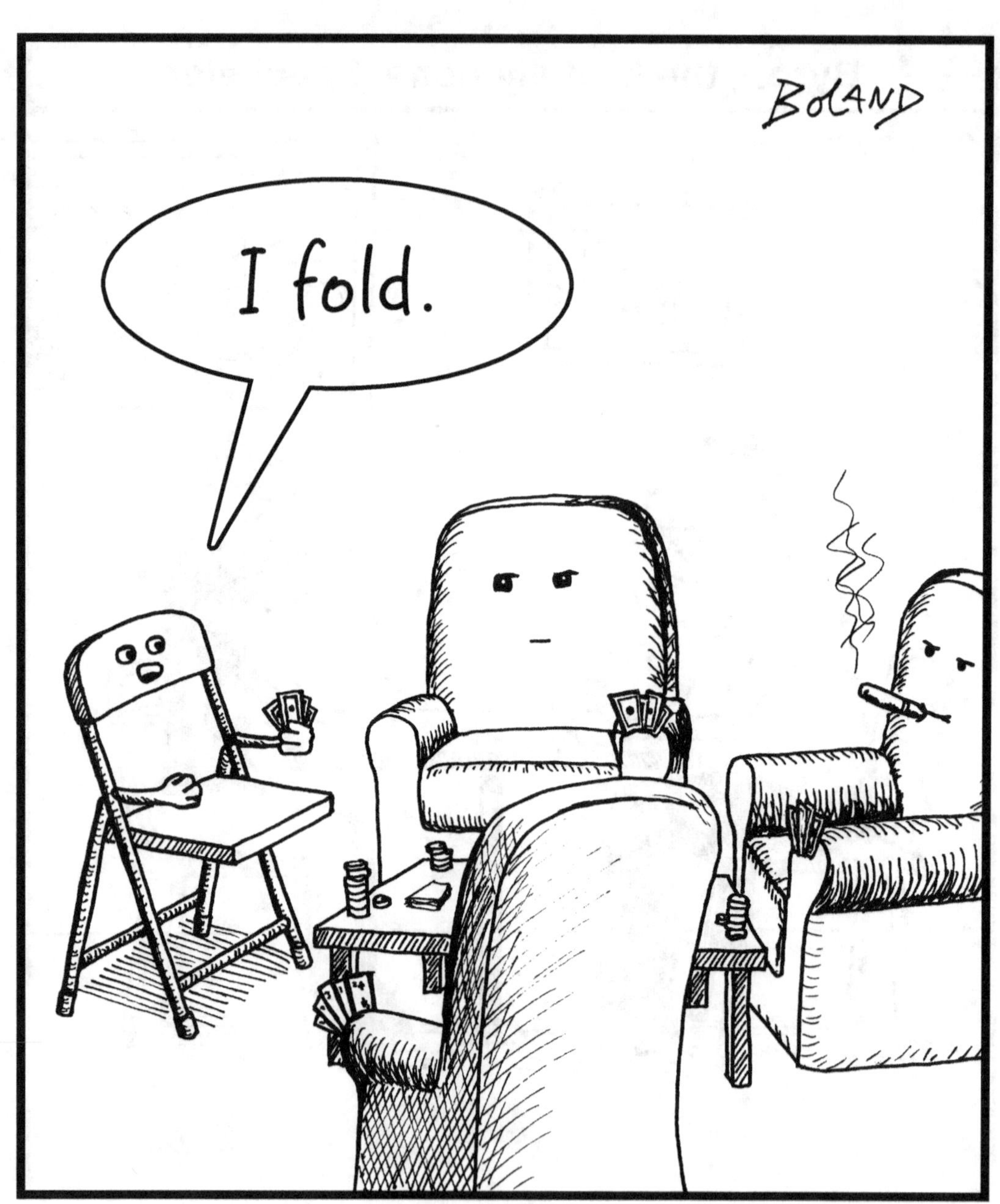
BOLAND
I fold.

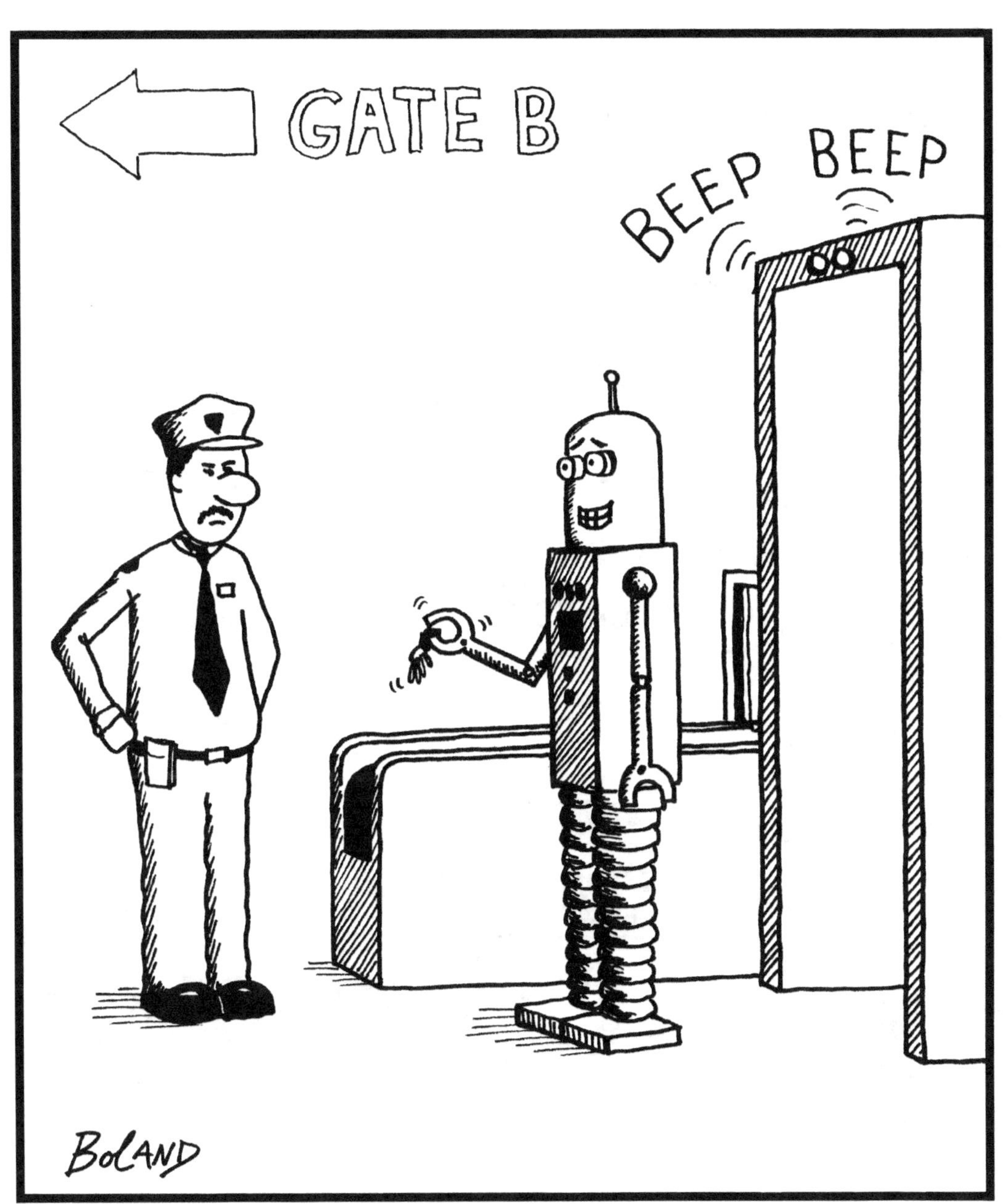

"Sorry. Must be the keys."

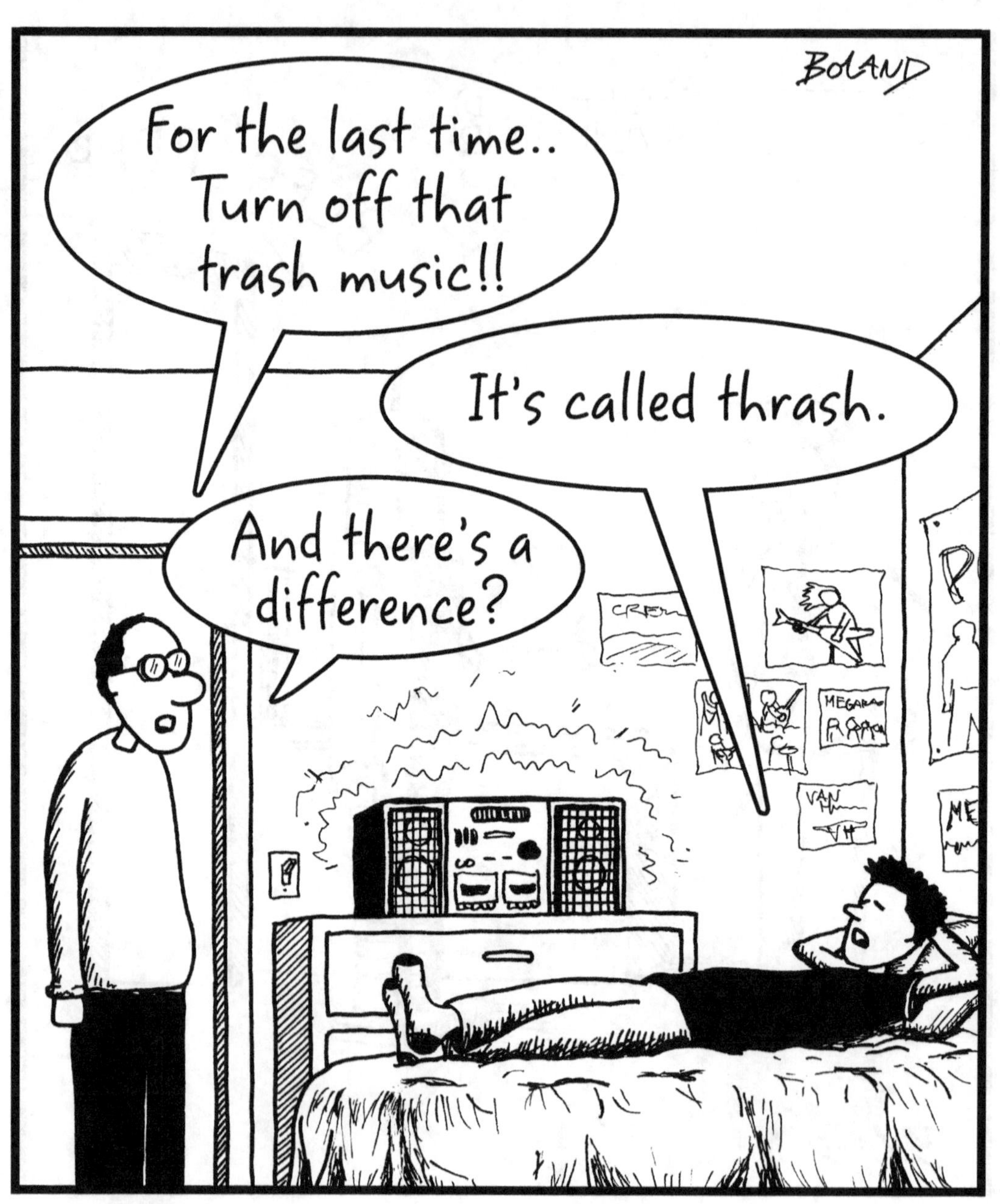
BOLAND
For the last time.. Turn off that trash music!!
It's called thrash.
And there's a difference?

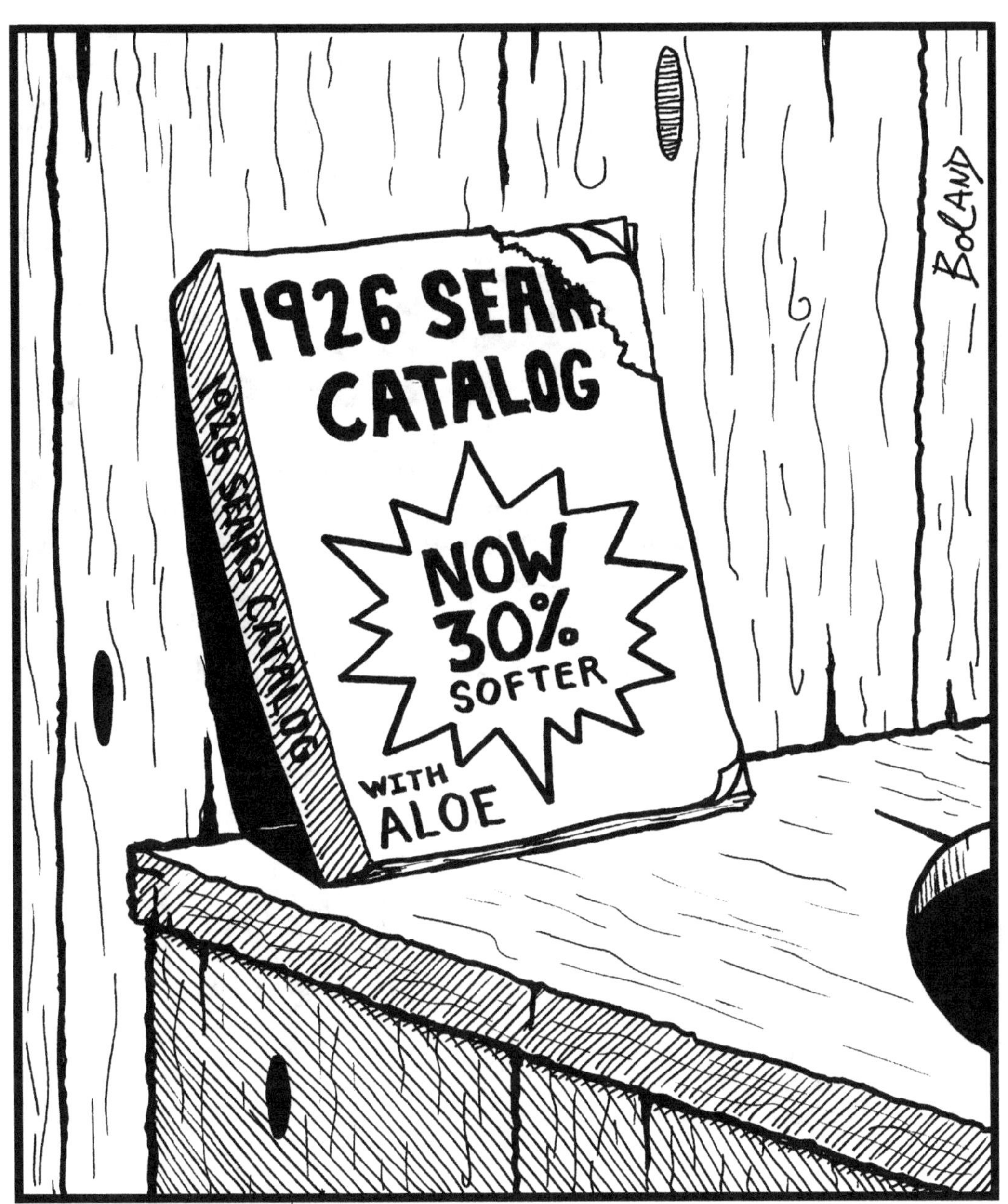
1926 SEAR
CATALOG
1926 SEARS CATALOG
NOW 30% SOFTER
WITH ALOE
BOLAND

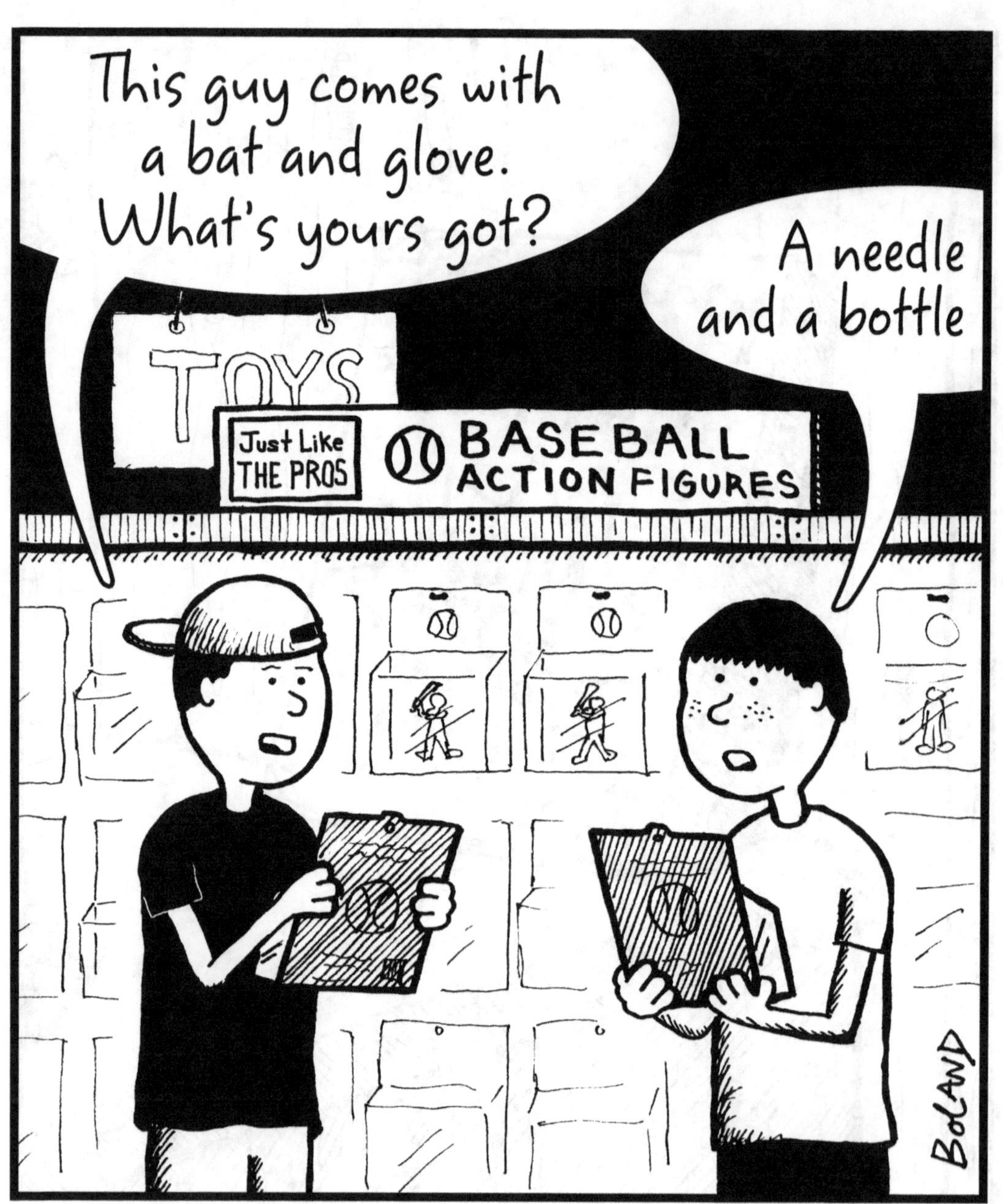
This guy comes with a bat and glove. What's yours got?
A needle and a bottle
TOYS
Just Like THE PROS
BASEBALL ACTION FIGURES
BOLAND

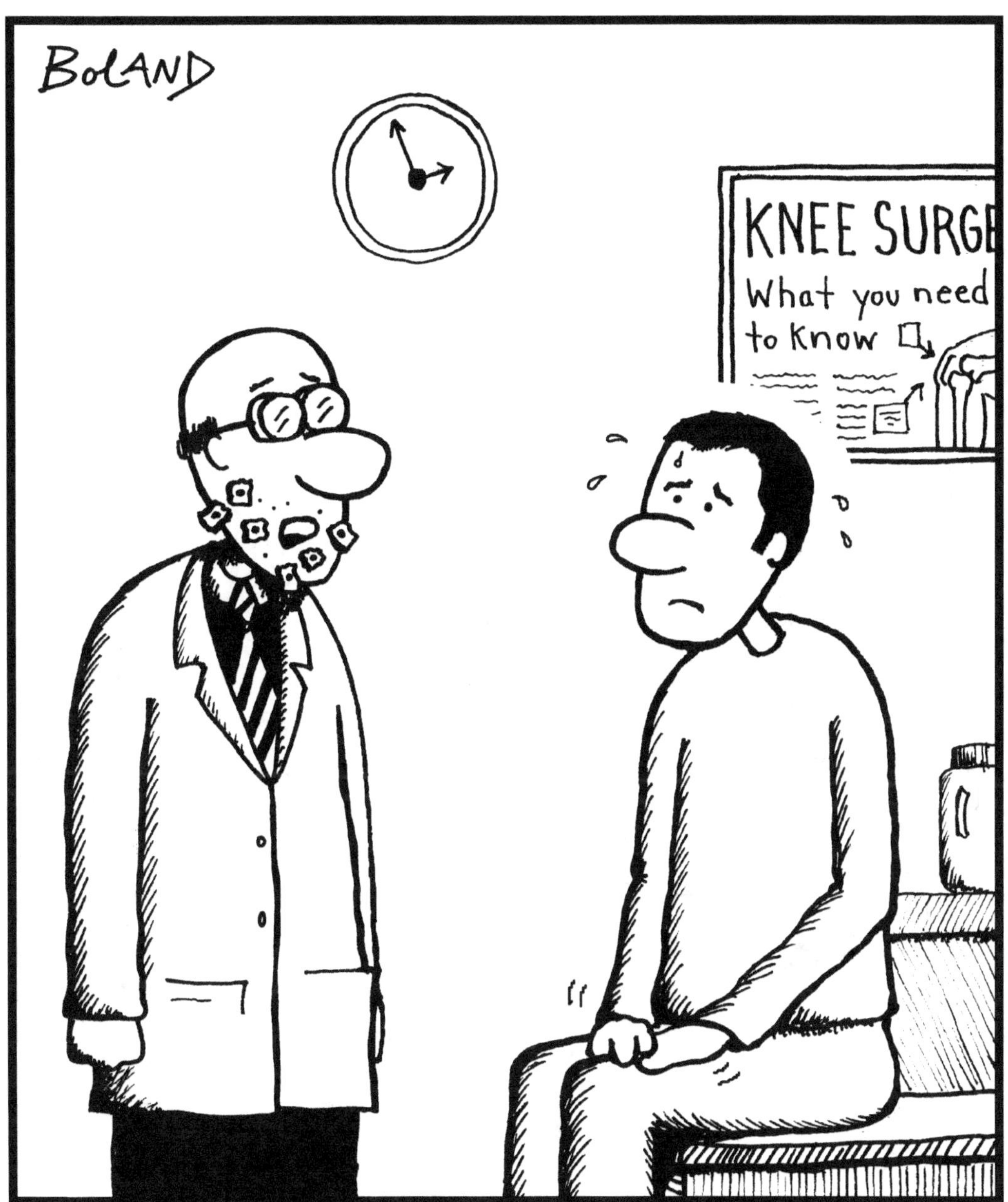

"Mr. Farbs, I completely understand your fears about surgery, but I can assure you that I have the steadiest hands in the profession."

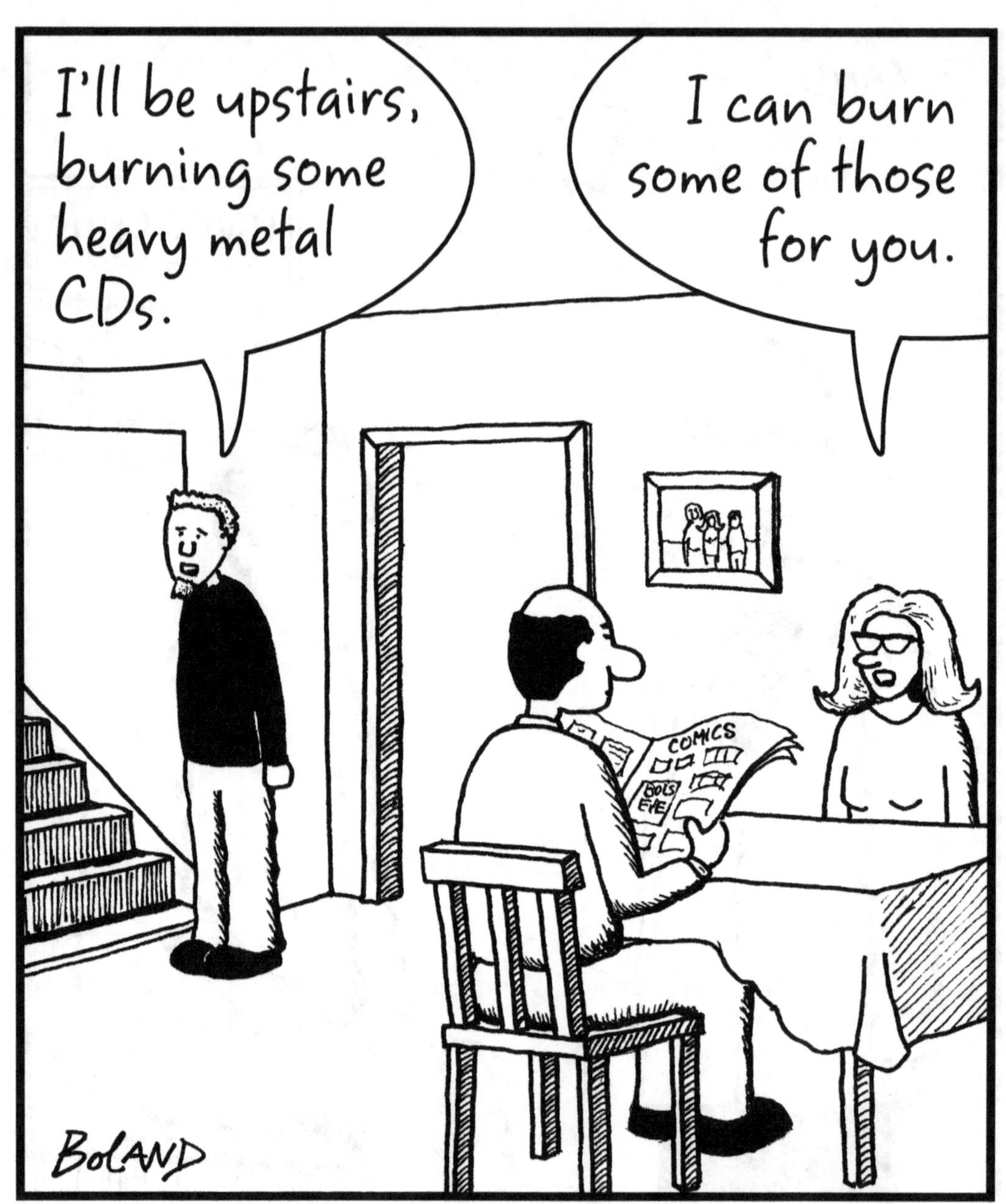
I'll be upstairs, burning some heavy metal CDs.
I can burn some of those for you.
COMICS
BOLAND

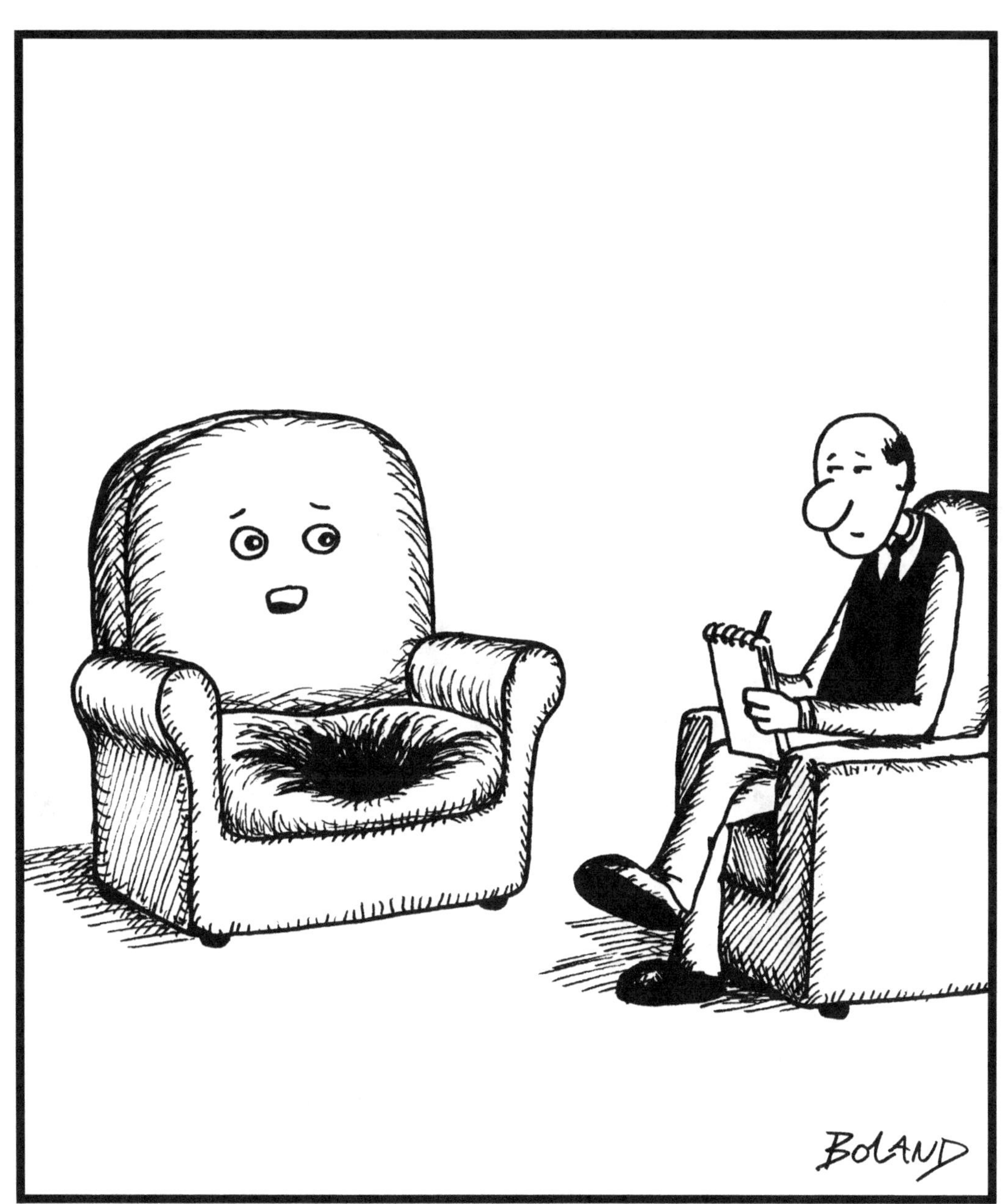

"I'm depressed, Doc."

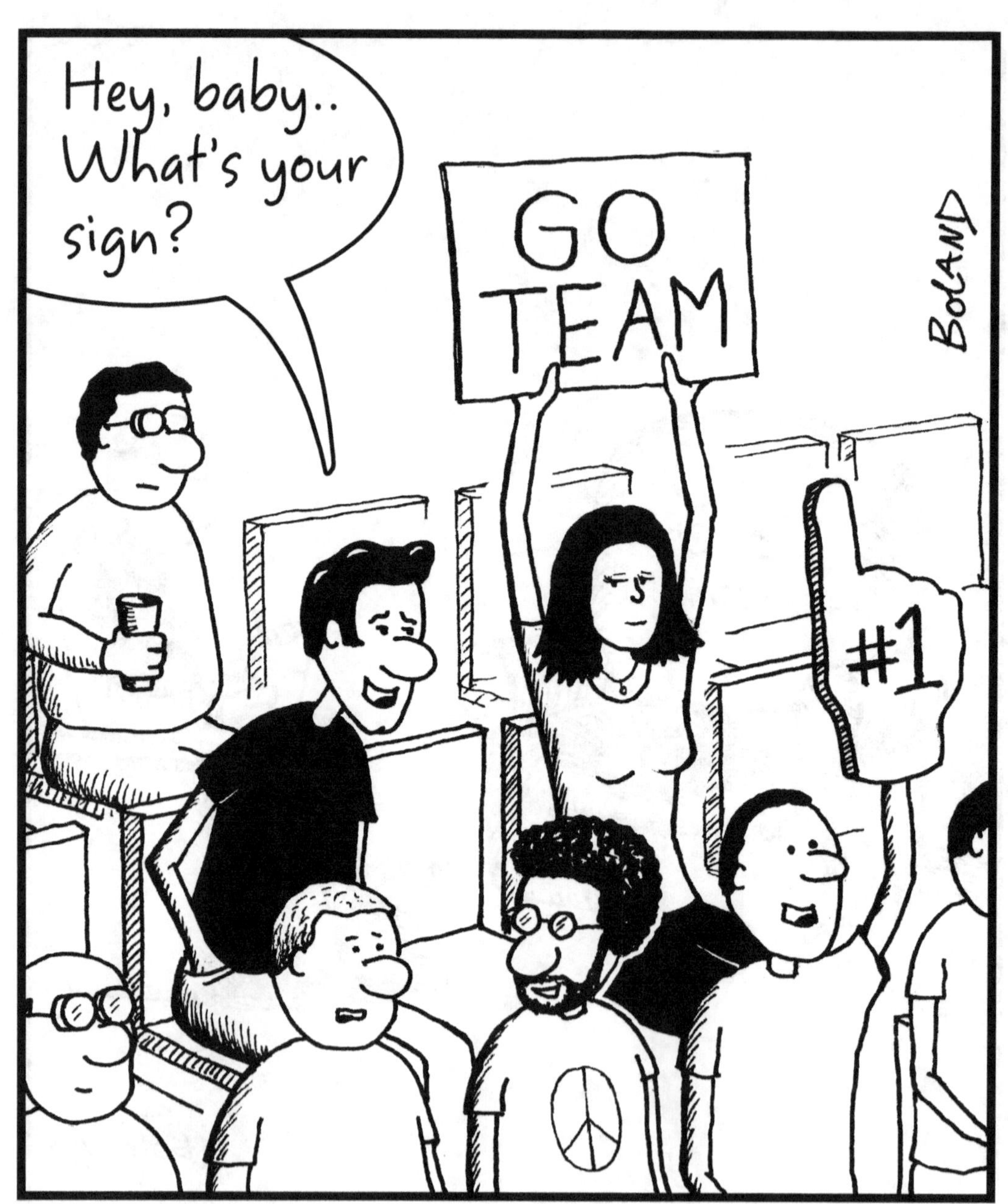
Hey, baby.. What's your sign?
GO TEAM
#1
BOLAND

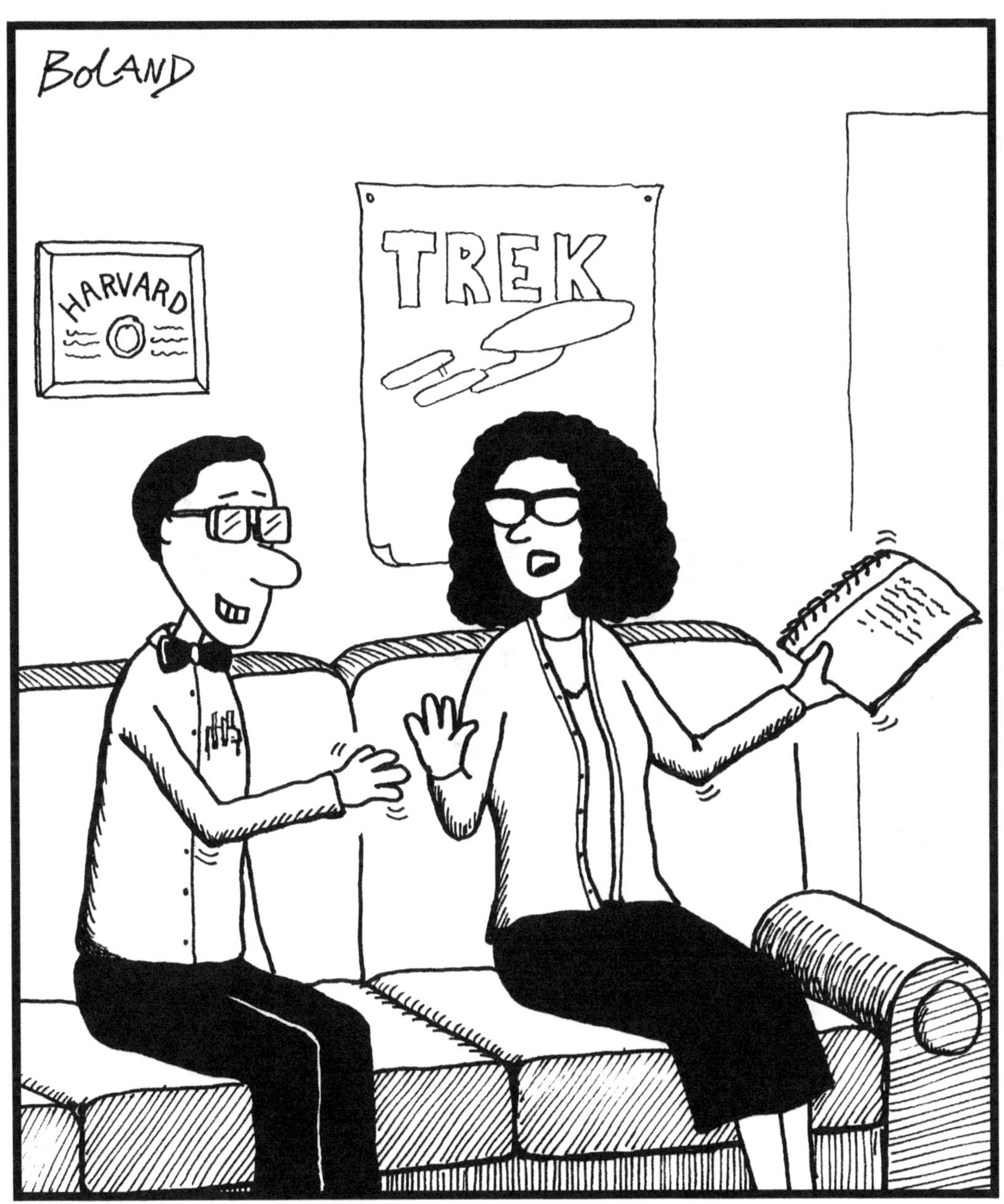

"I'm sorry, Ned...but I'm not that kind of girl. I don't give out my quantum physics theories on the first date."

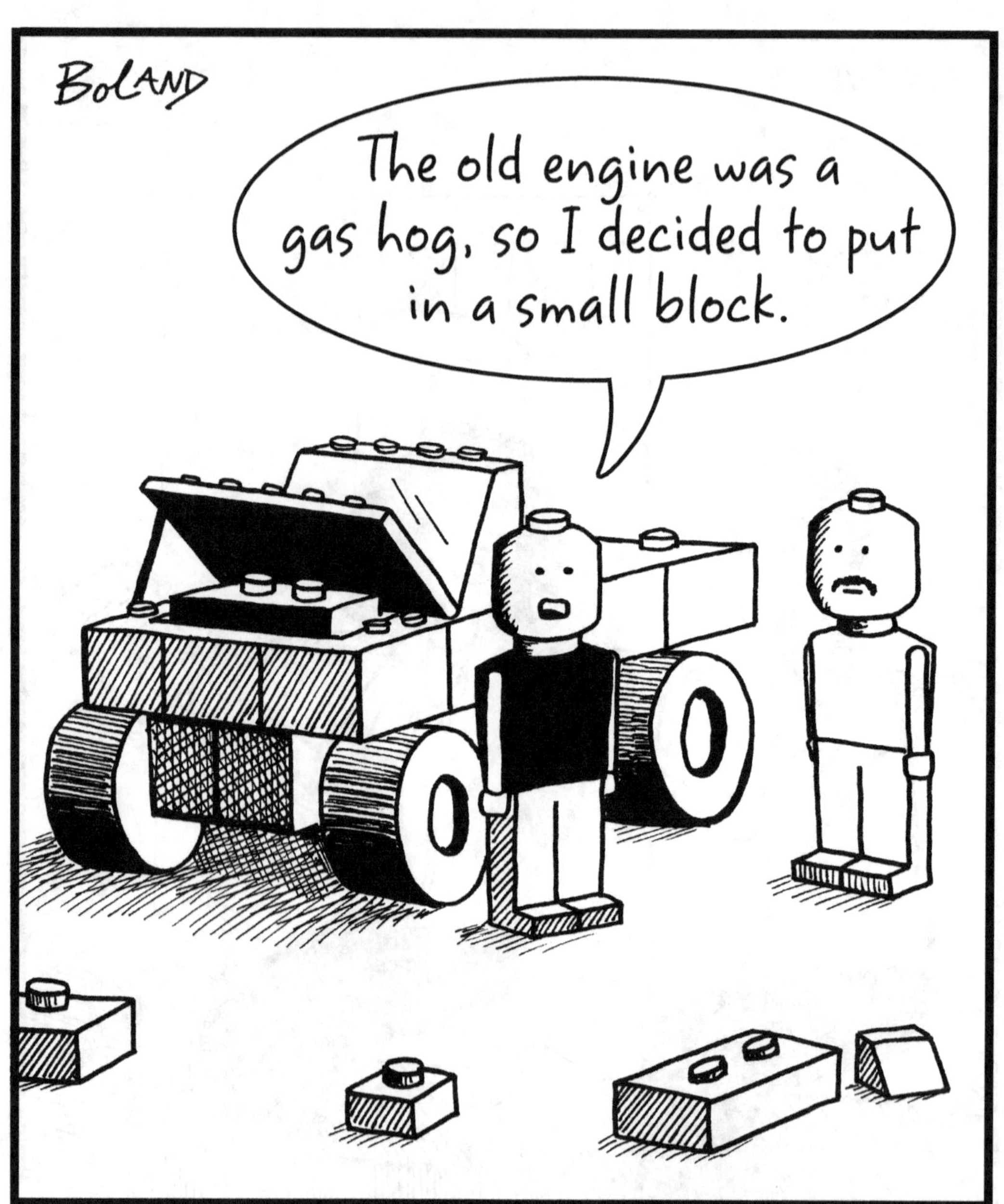
BoLAND
The old engine was a gas hog, so I decided to put in a small block.

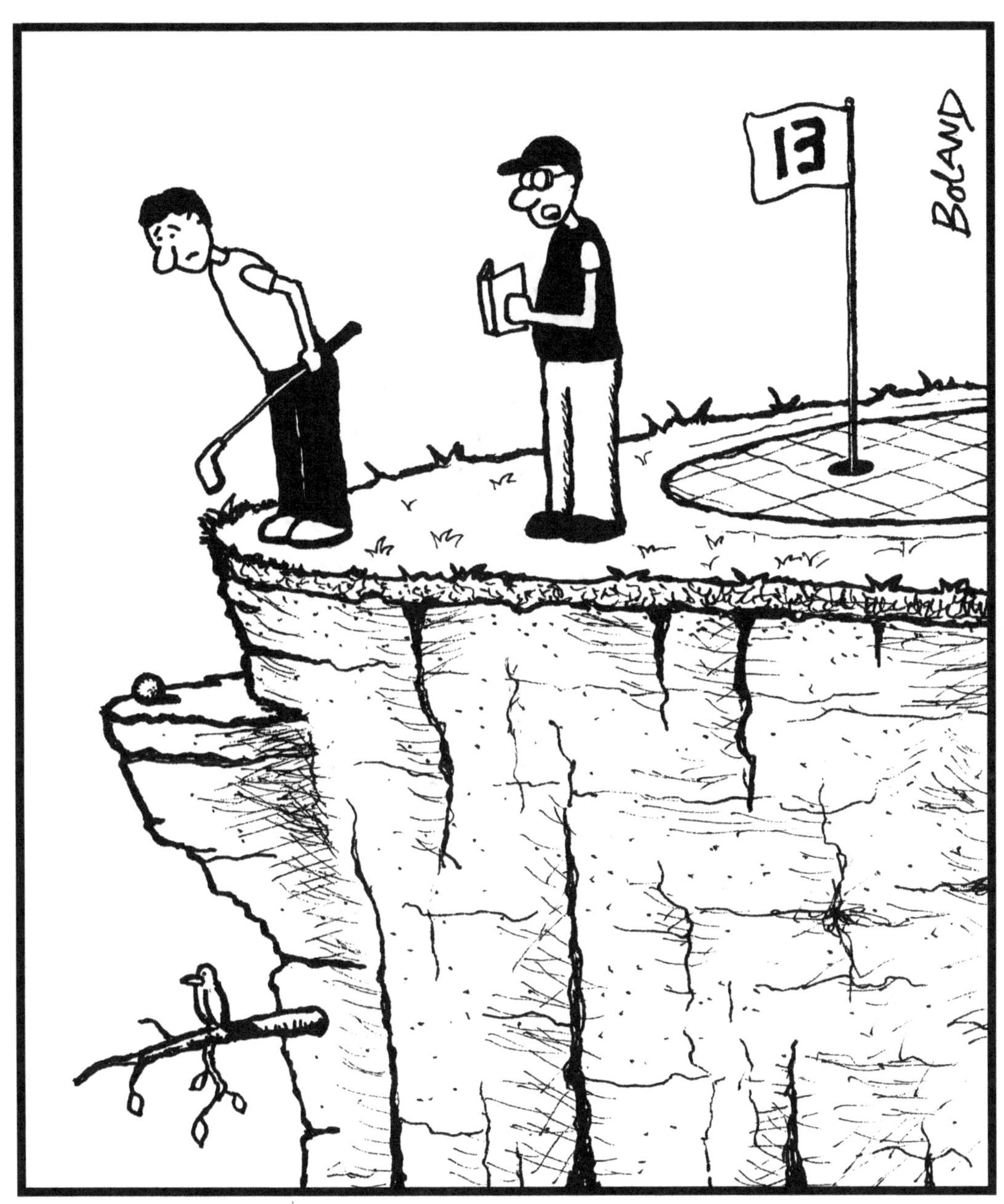

"Well, lookie here. Page 42: 'Ball must be played as it lies.' Well, rules are rules....you know, just like you said earlier when my ball was against that tree. Anyway, good luck with that. Feel free to borrow my bent 9-iron."

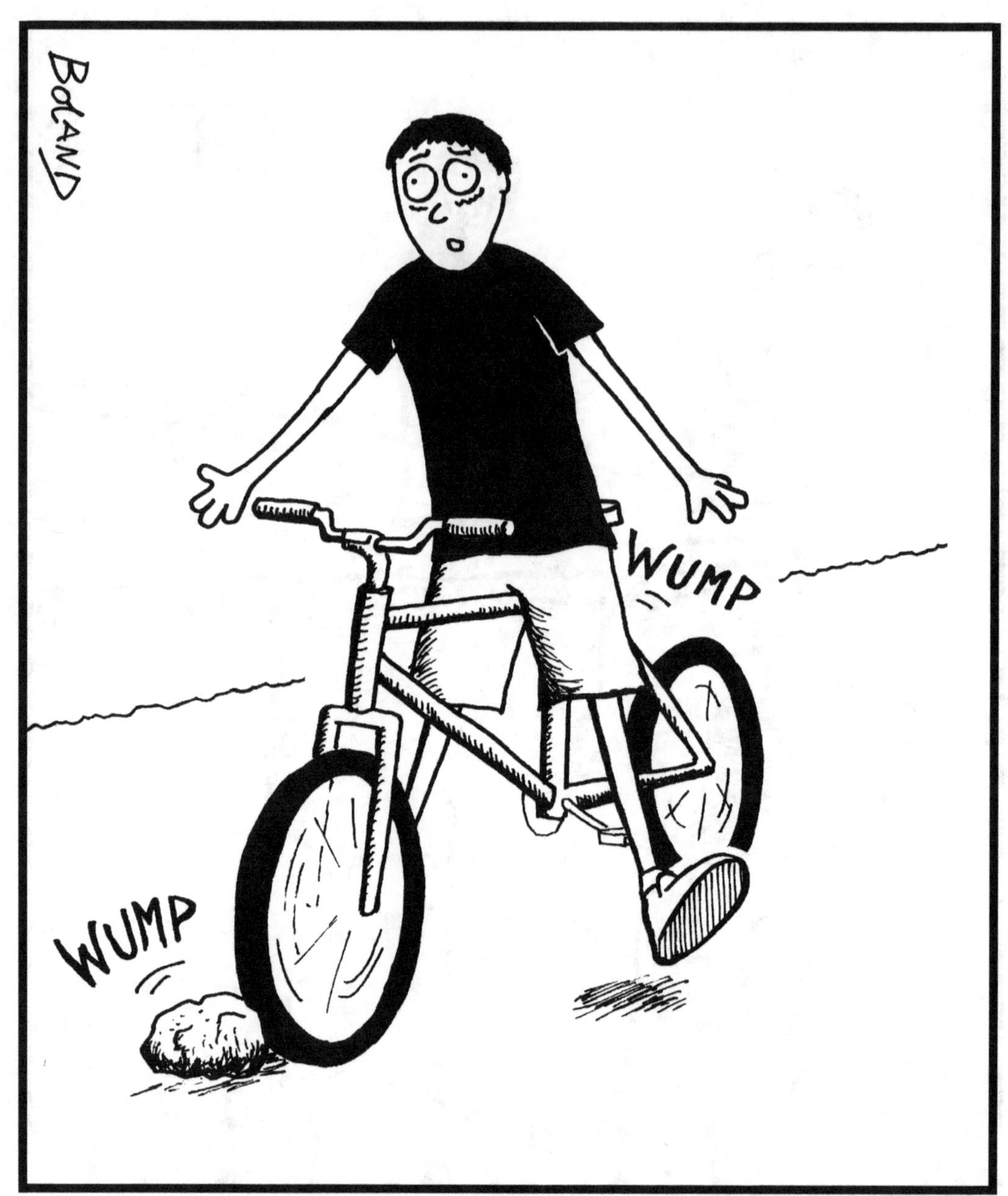

And in that moment, Billy learned the painful irony that a boys bike has a straight crossbar, while a girls bike does not.

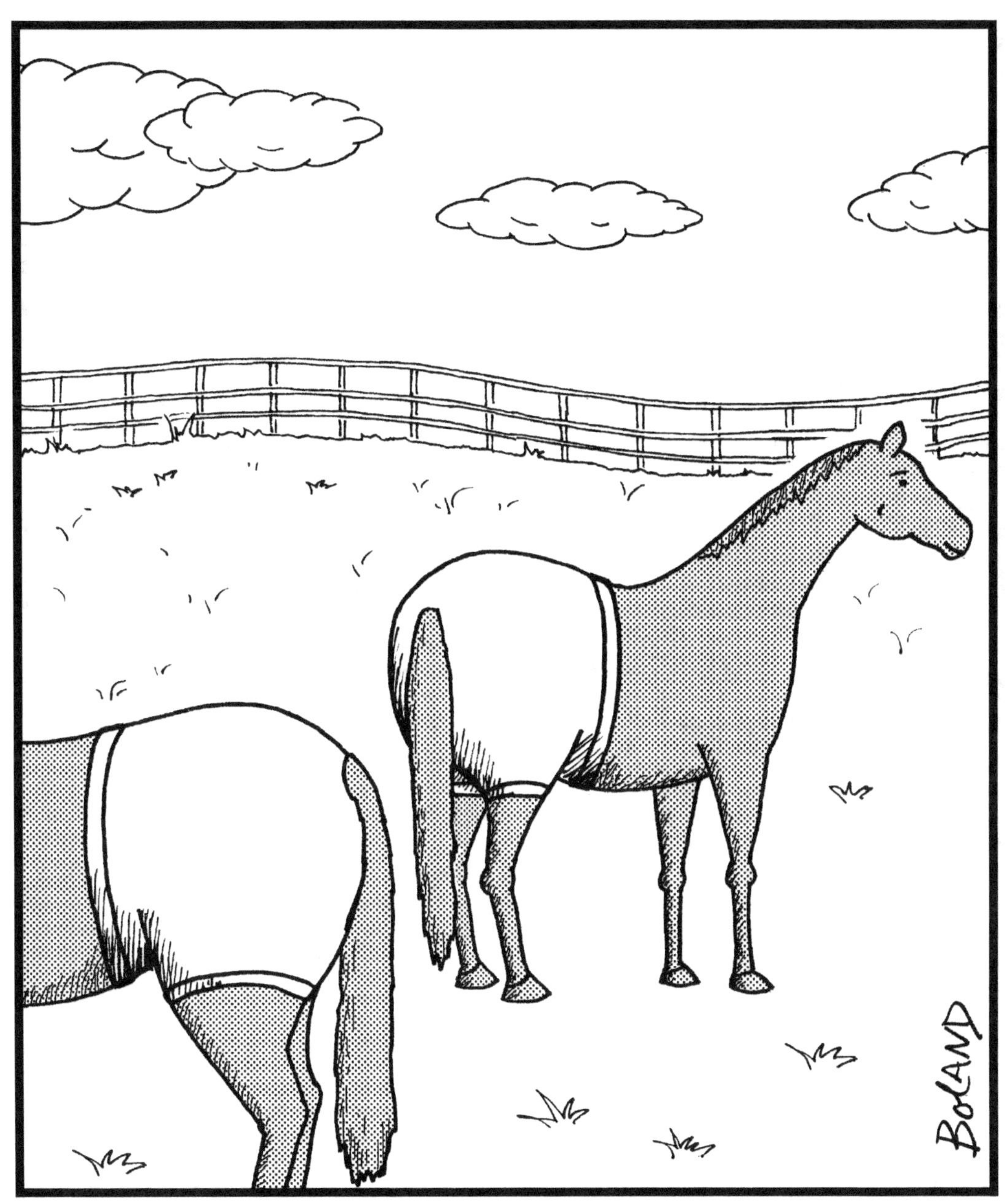

Jockeys on horses

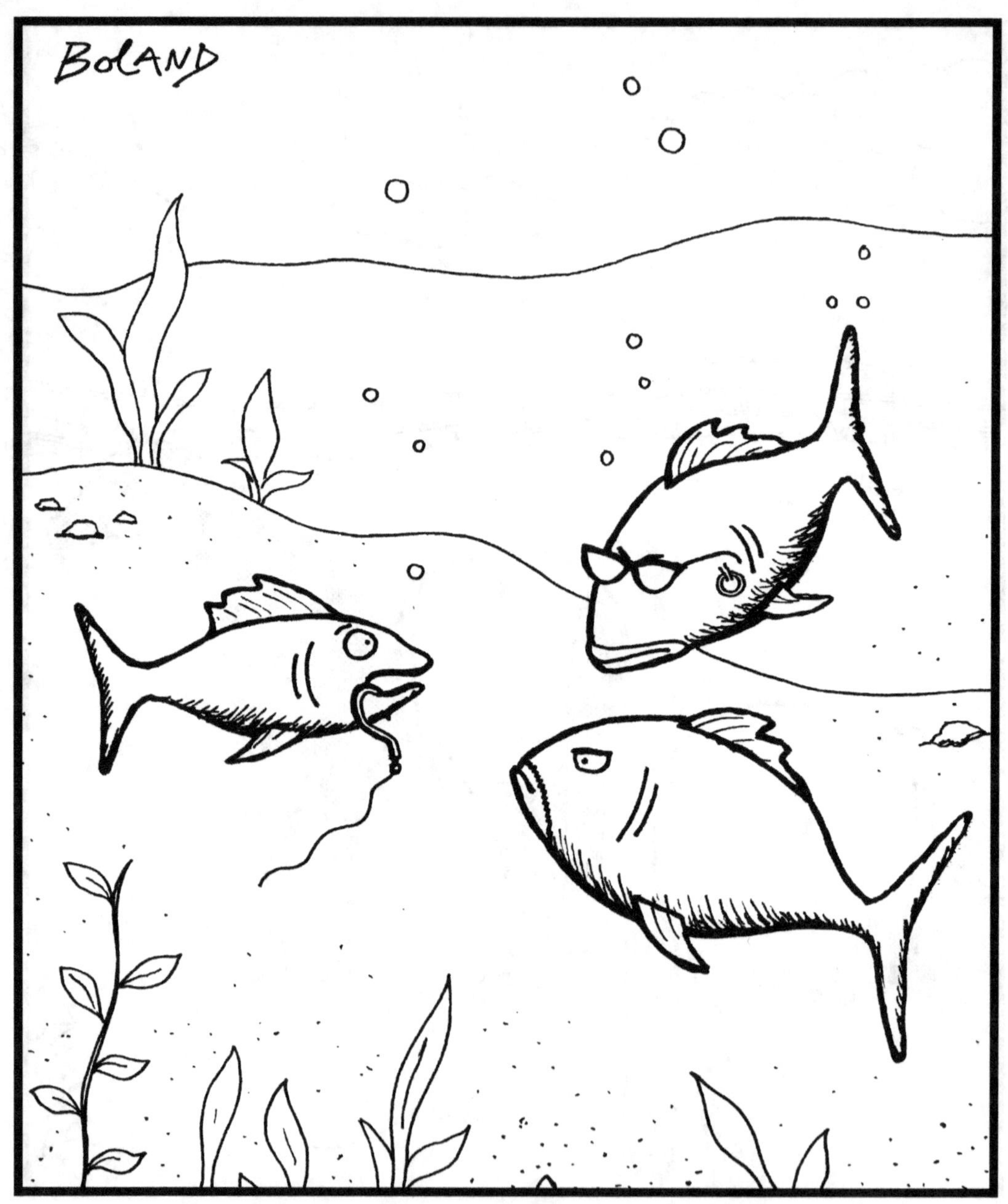

"But, Mom..Dad... Everybody else is getting one."

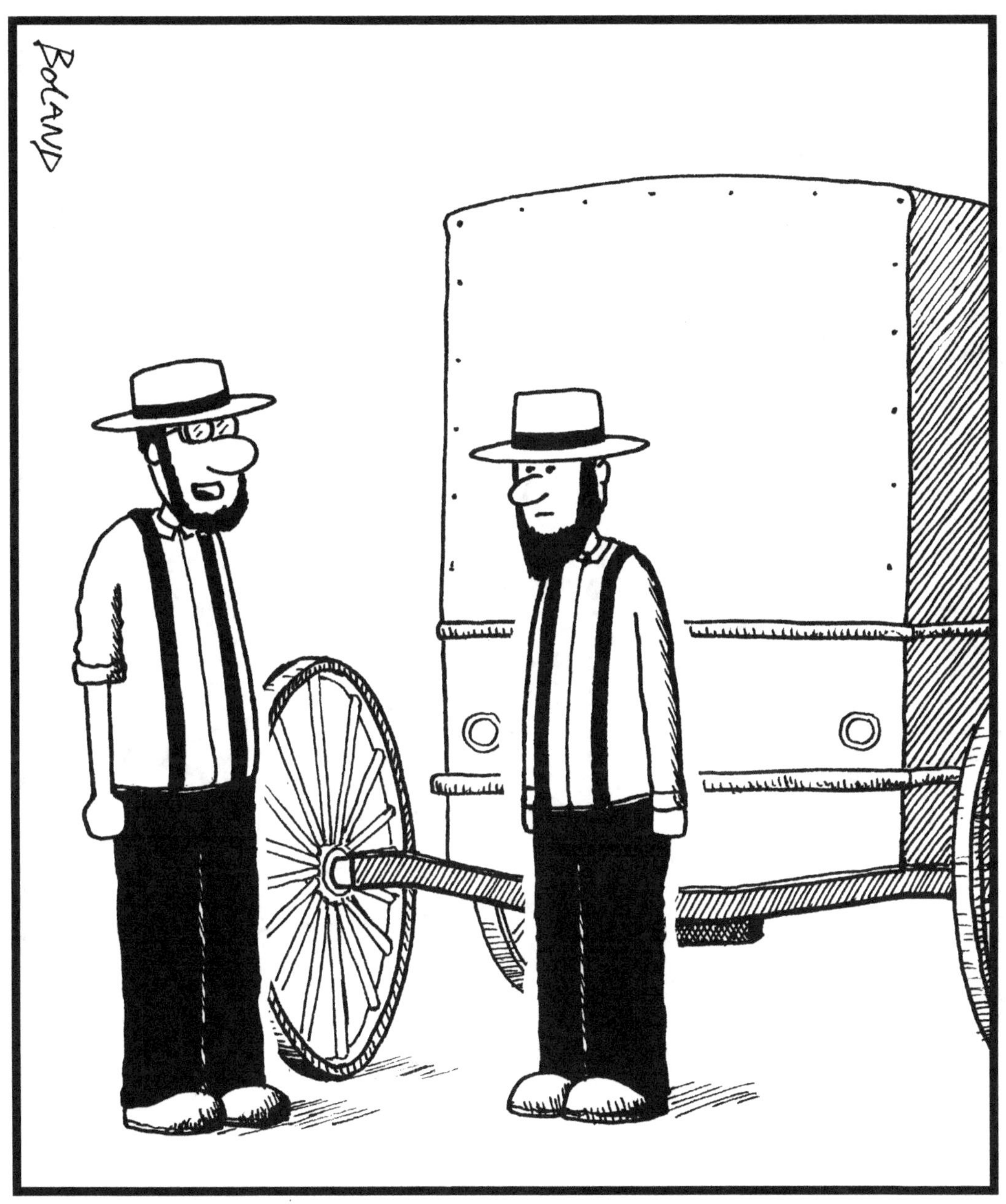

"Sweet ride. How many horses does she have?"

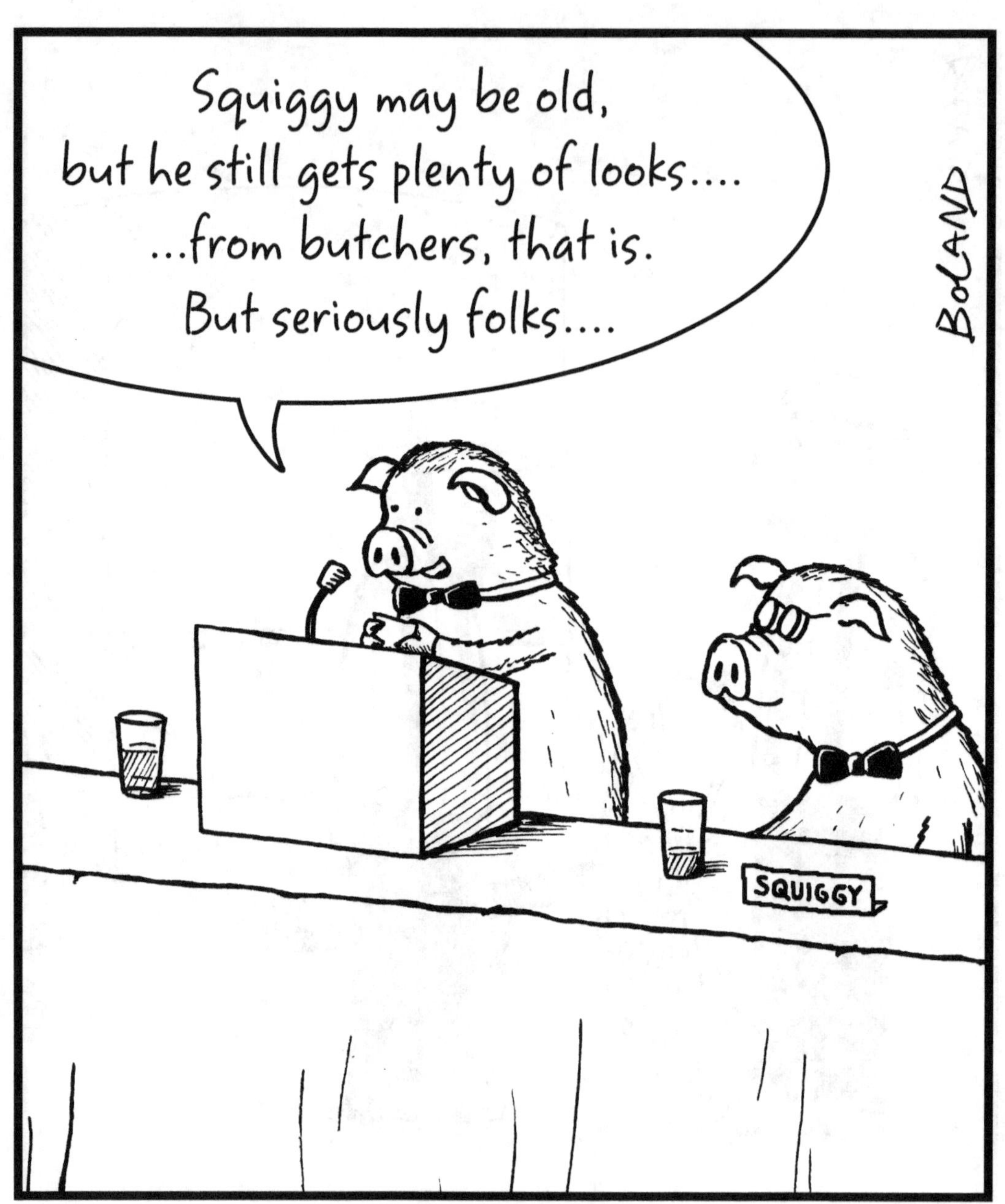
Squiggy may be old,
but he still gets plenty of looks....
...from butchers, that is.
But seriously folks....
BOLAND
SQUIGGY

Pig Roast

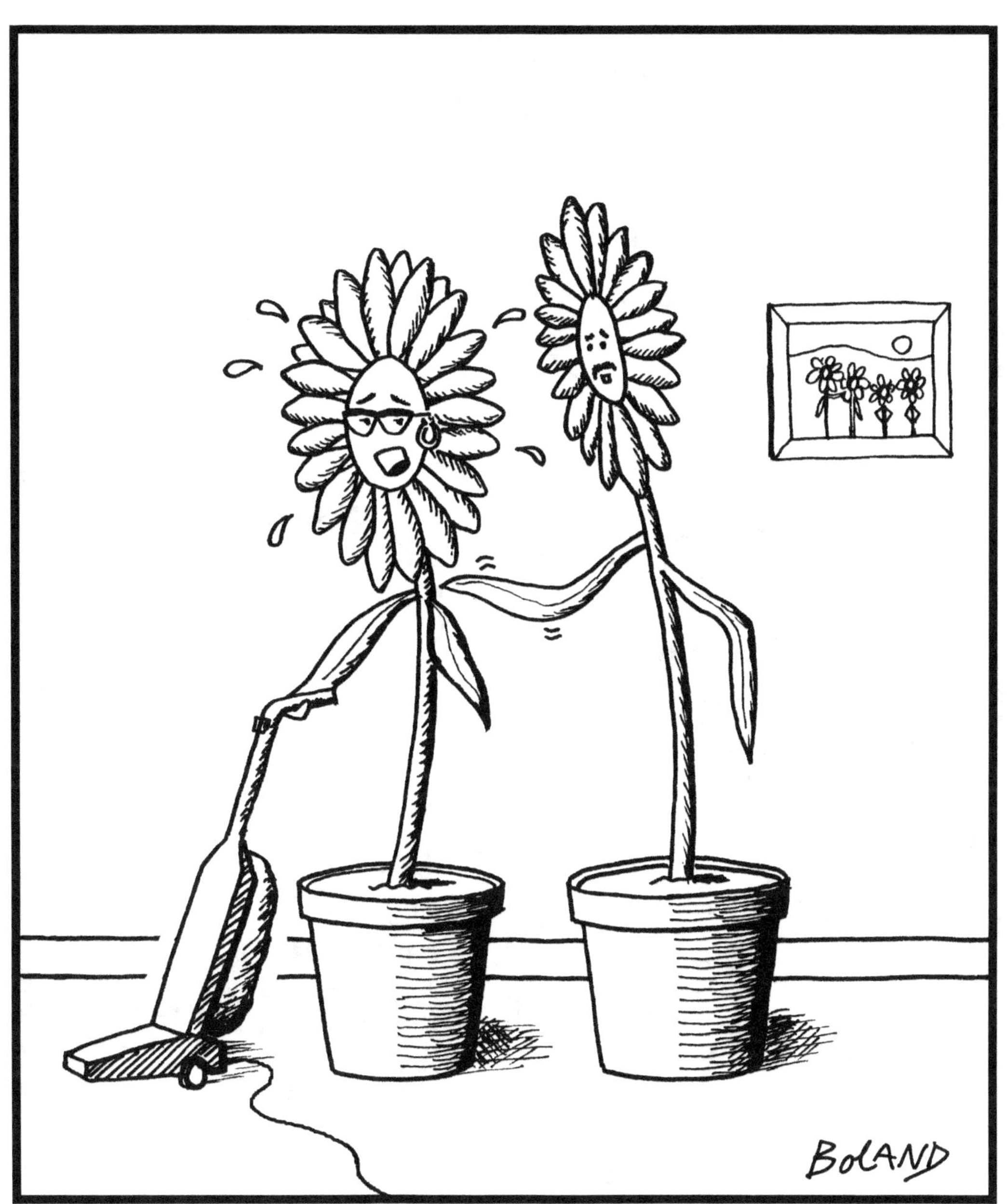

"For heaven's sake, George!! Don't sneak up on me like that! I just about soiled myself."

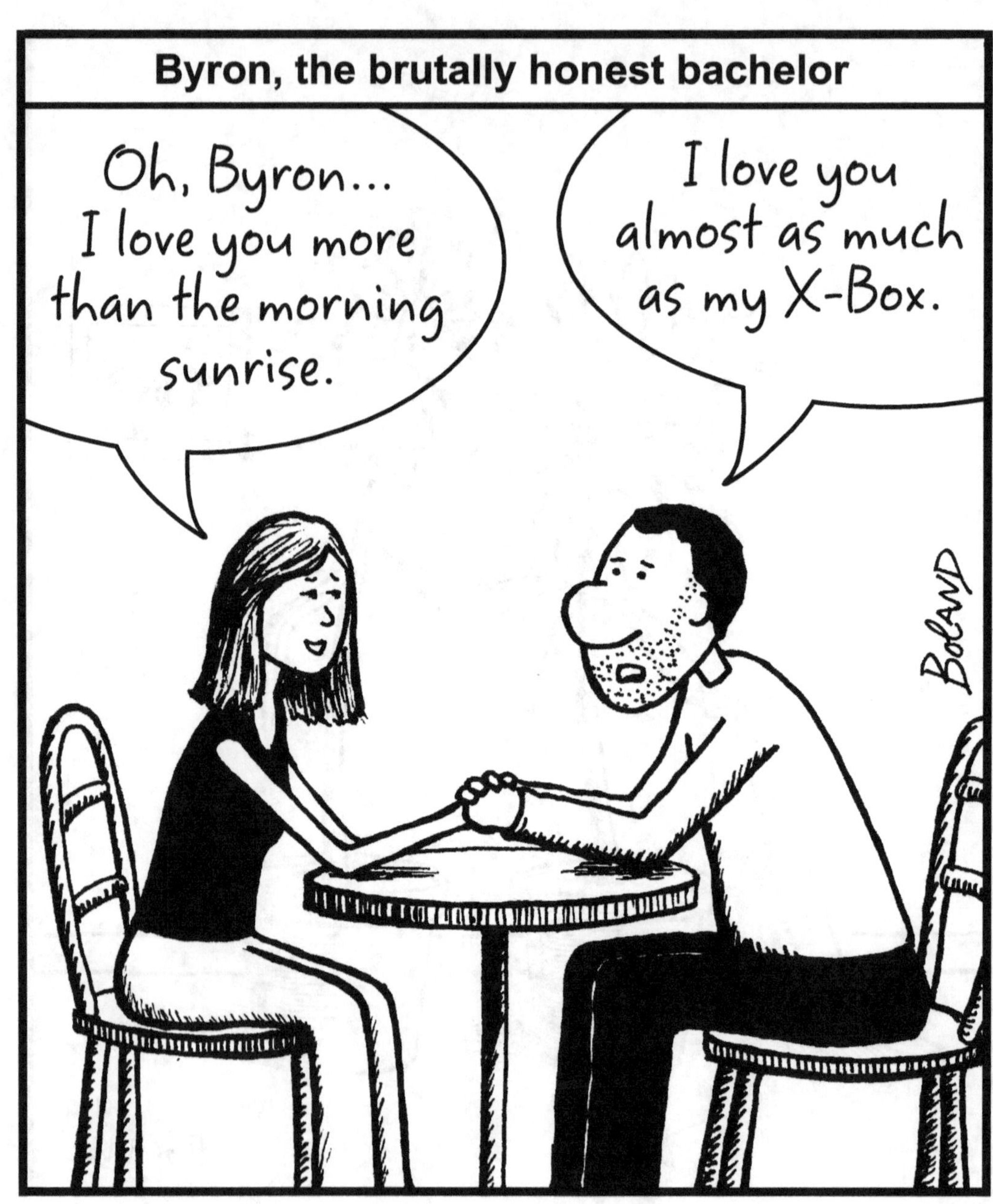
Byron, the brutally honest bachelor
Oh, Byron... I love you more than the morning sunrise.
I love you almost as much as my X-Box.
BOLAND

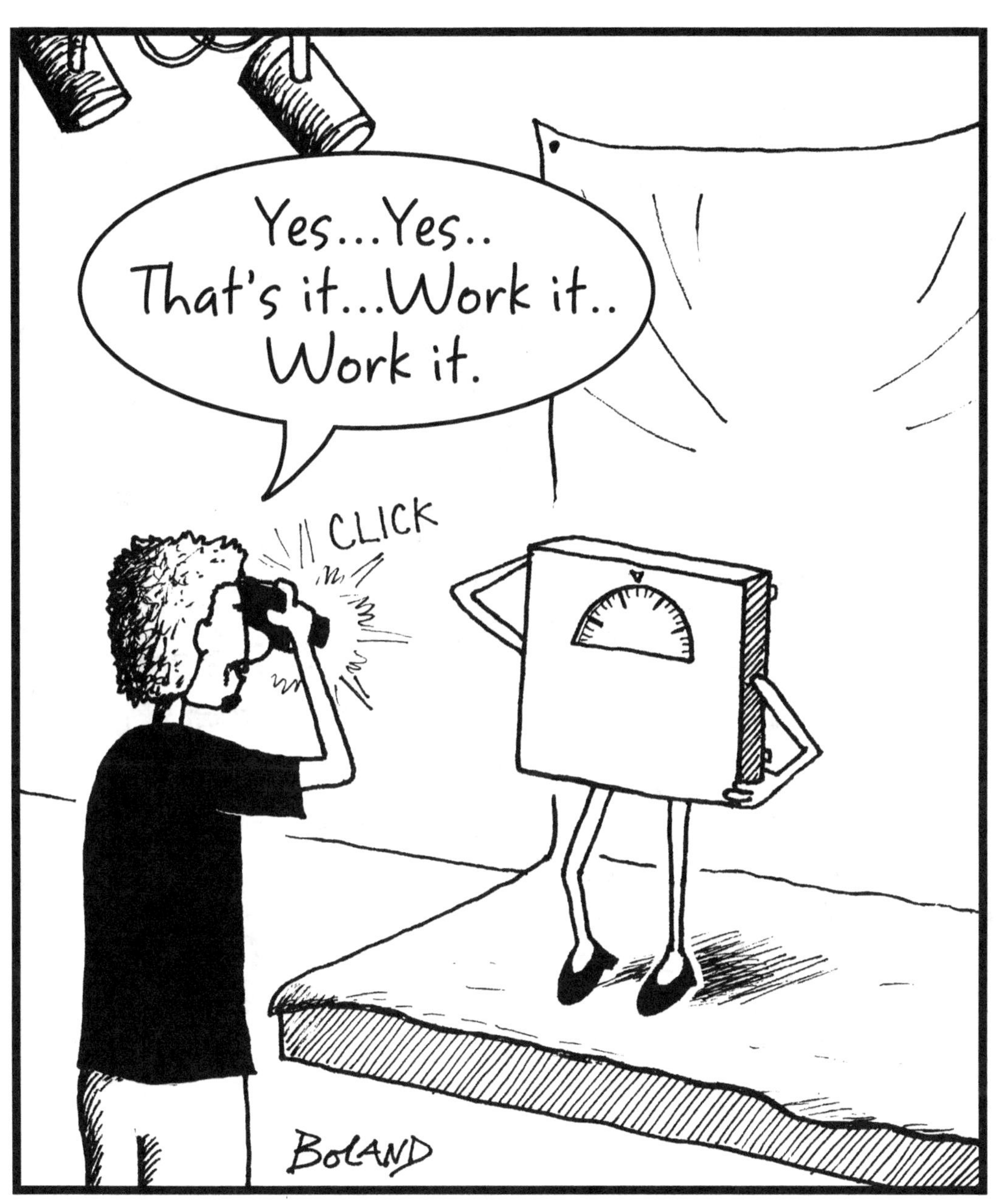

Scale Model

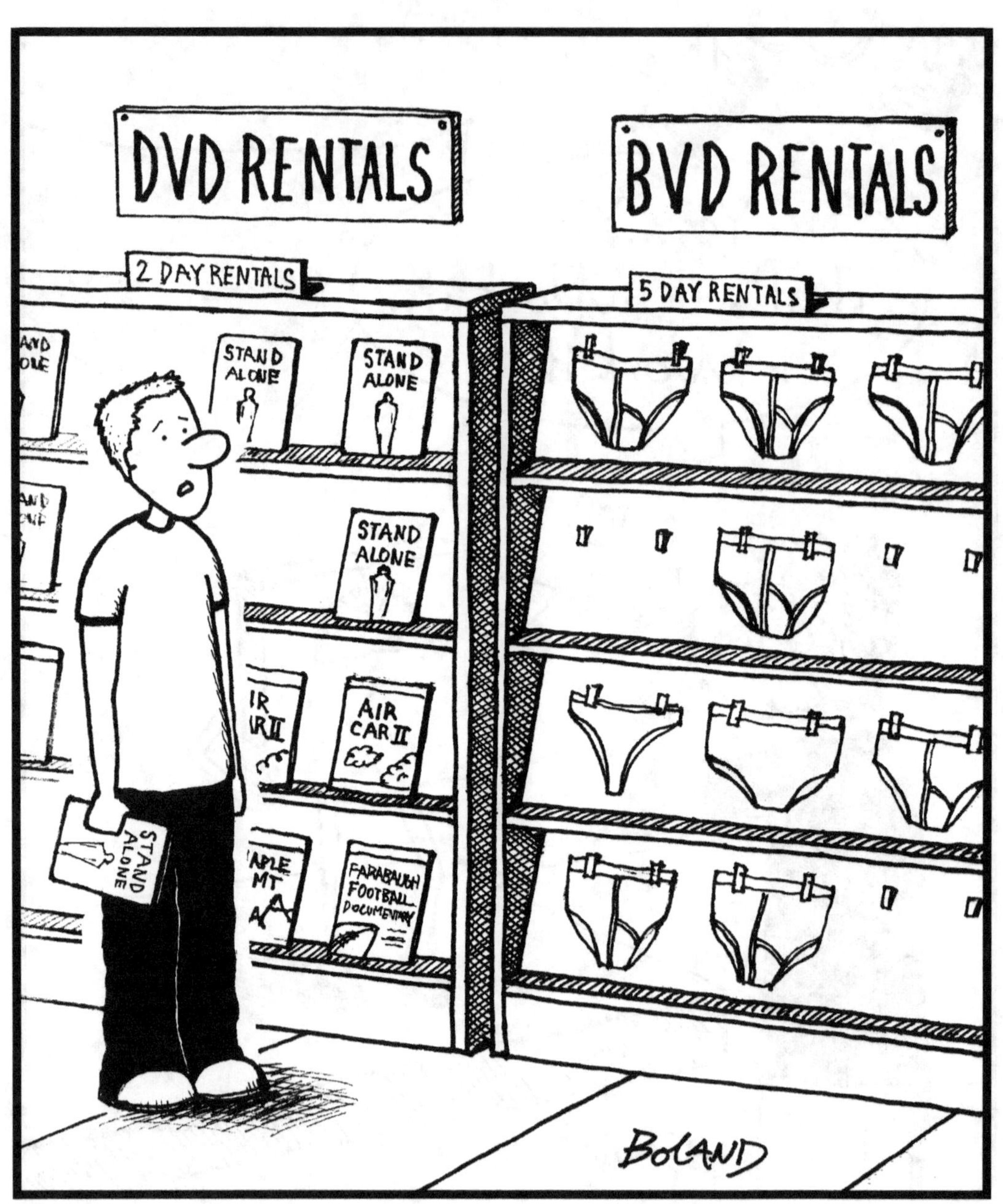
DVD RENTALS
BVD RENTALS
2 DAY RENTALS
5 DAY RENTALS
STAND ALONE
STAND ALONE
STAND ALONE
AIR CAR II
FARABAUGH FOOTBALL DOCUMENTARY
STAND ALONE
BOLAND

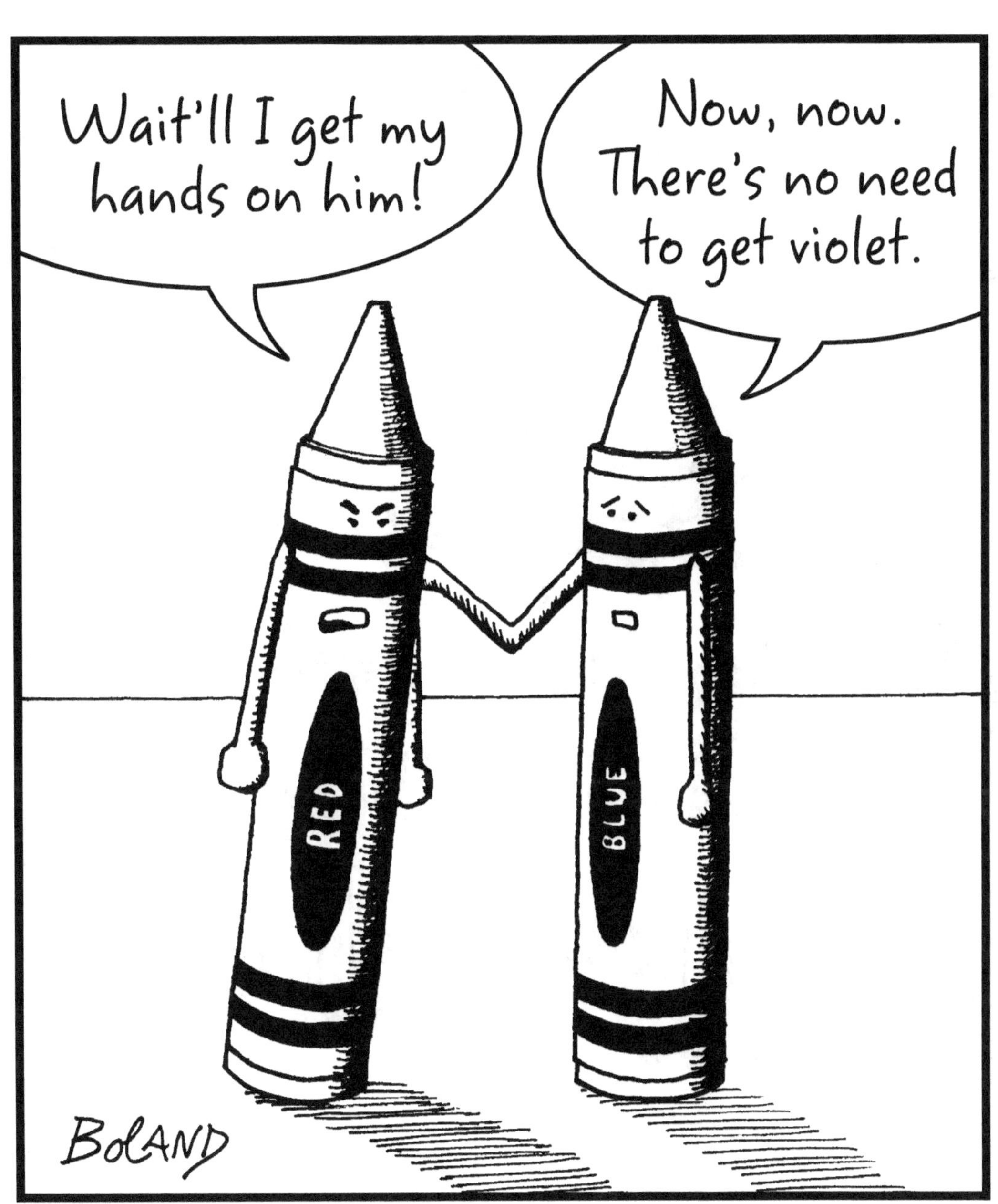
Wait'll I get my hands on him!
Now, now. There's no need to get violet.
RED
BLUE
BOLAND

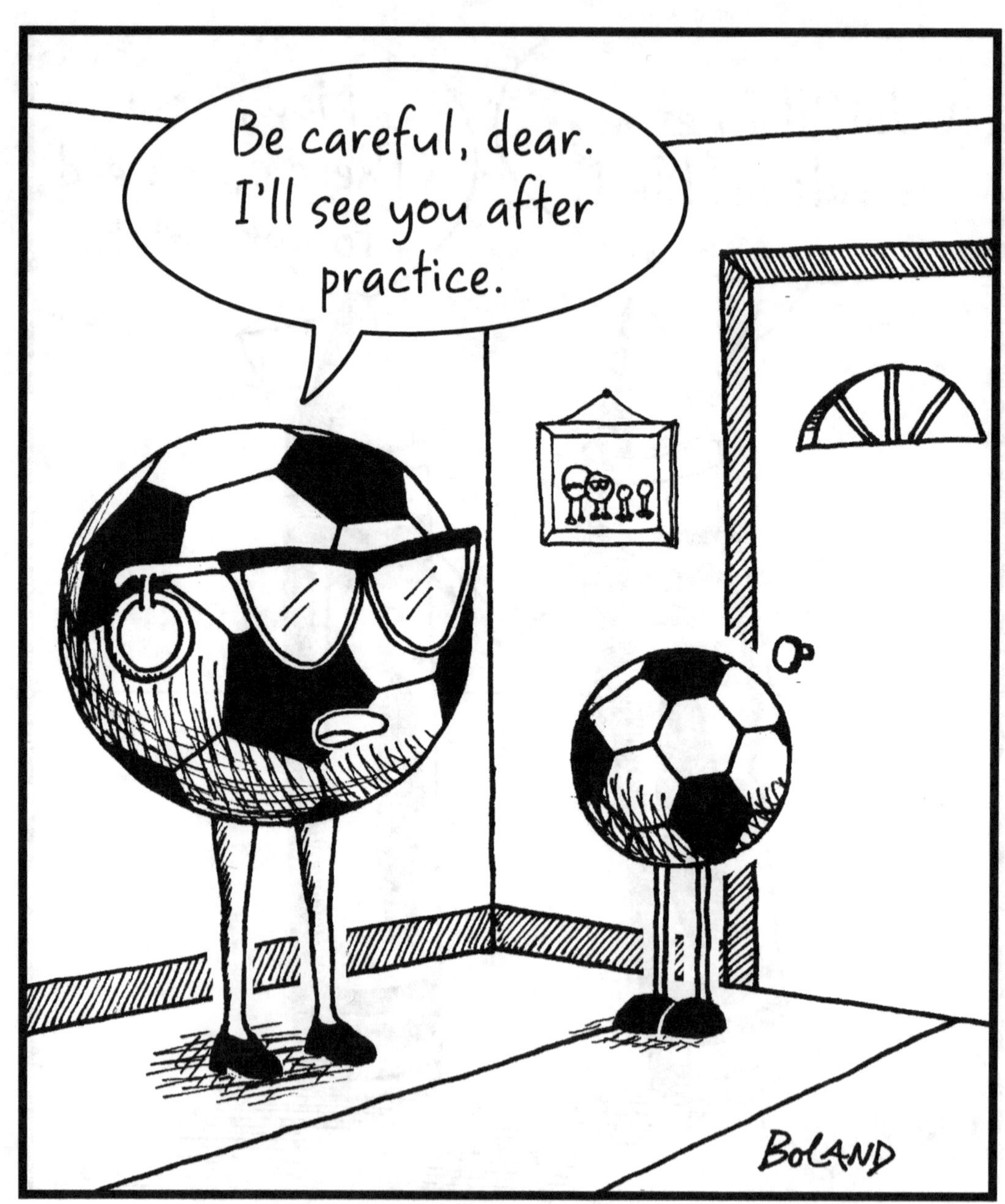

Soccer Mom

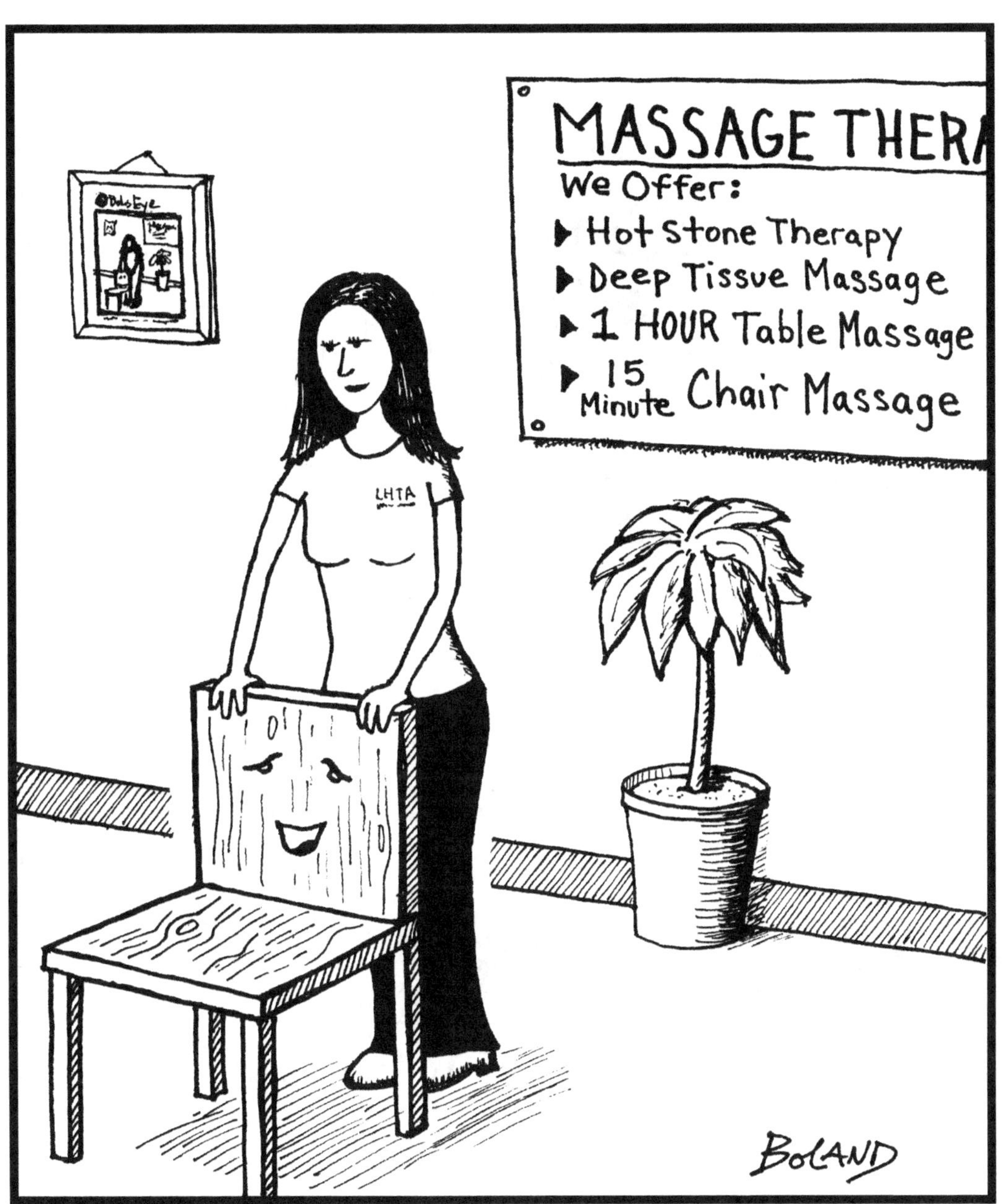

"Ahhh....That feels great. I can feel that knot loosening up already."

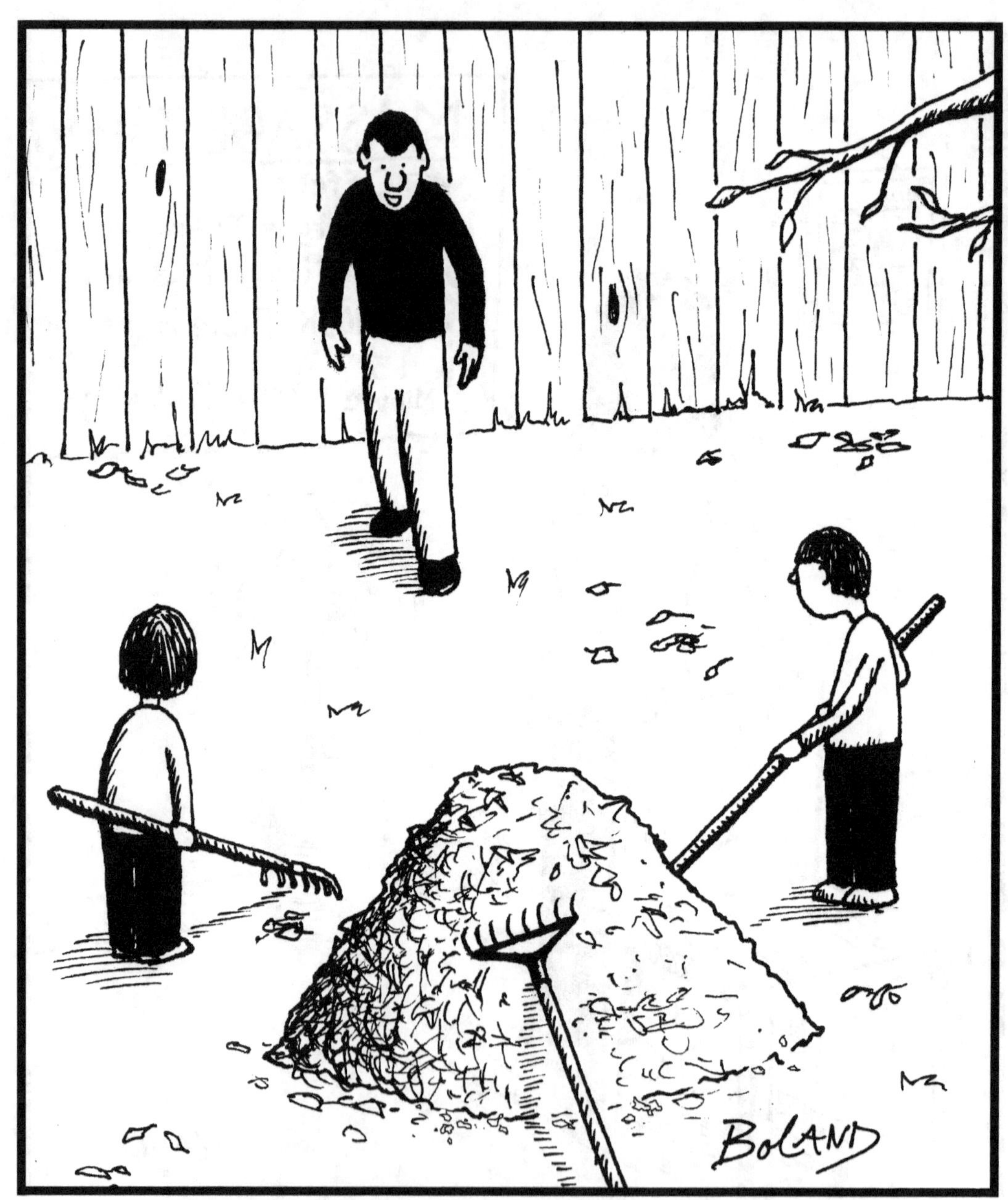

"Step aside kids, and let your old man show you how a real dive is done."

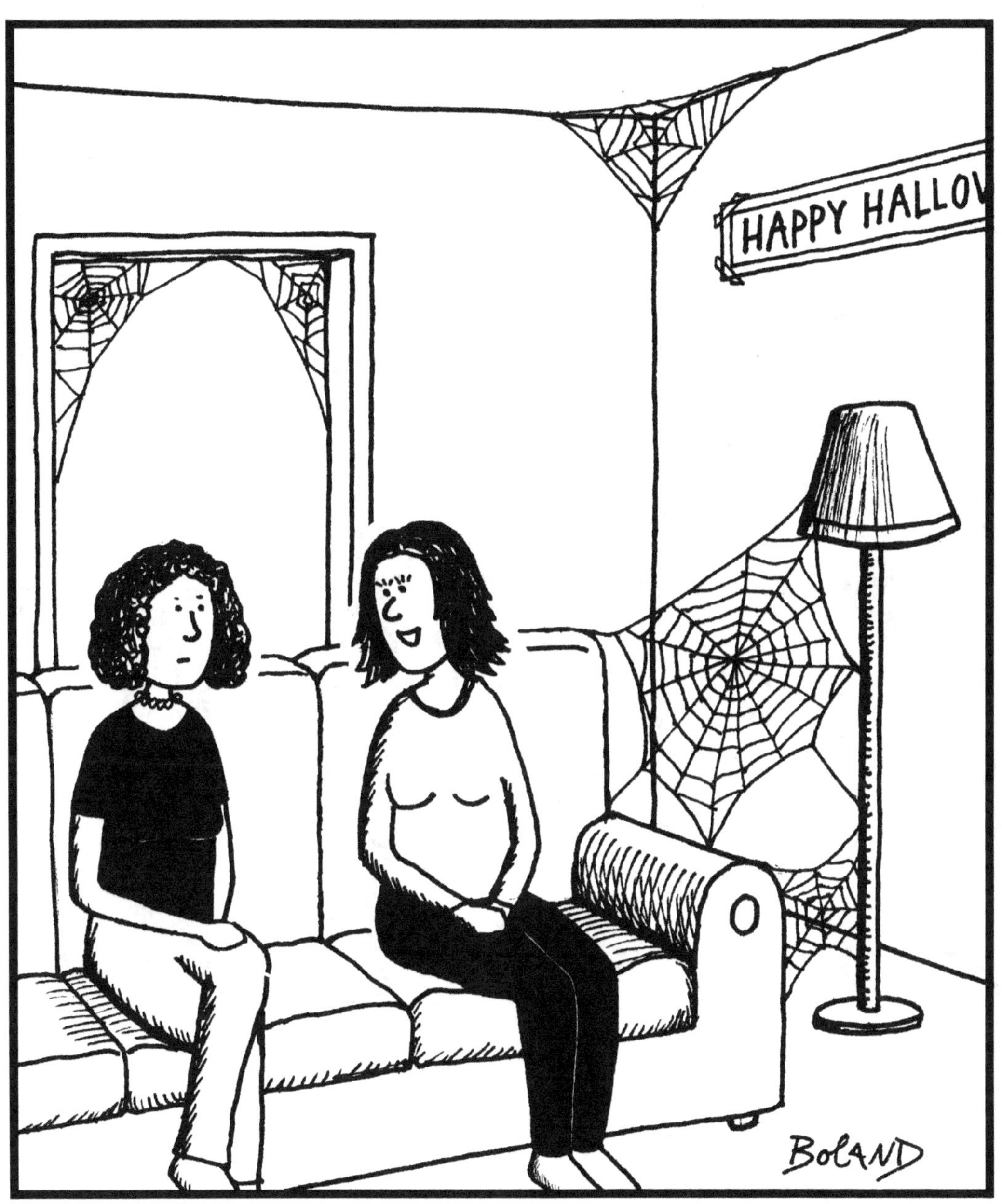

“Thanks. I’ve actually been getting a lot of compliments on the decorating, but between you and me, I haven’t cleaned the house in years.”

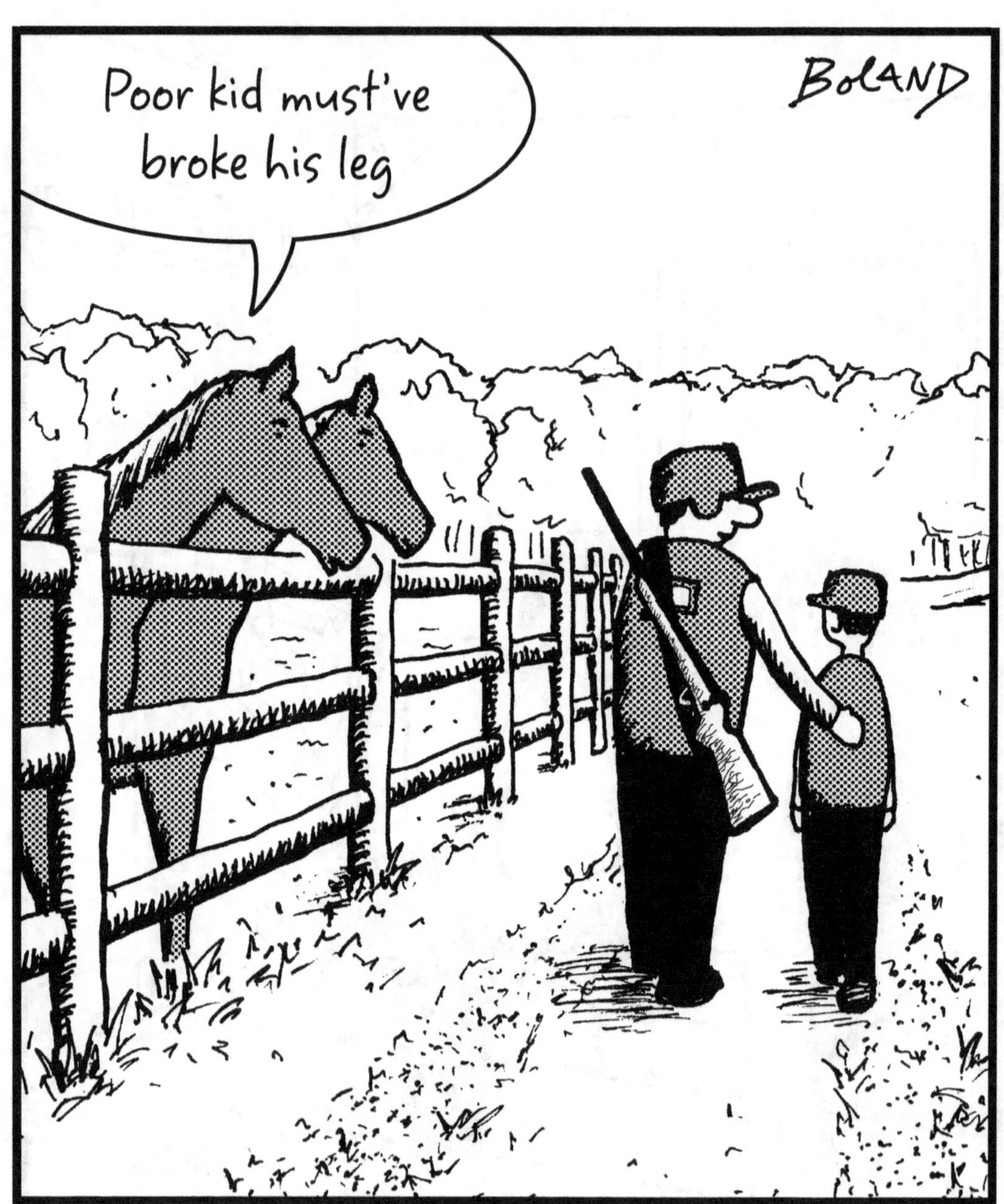
Poor kid must've broke his leg
BOLAND

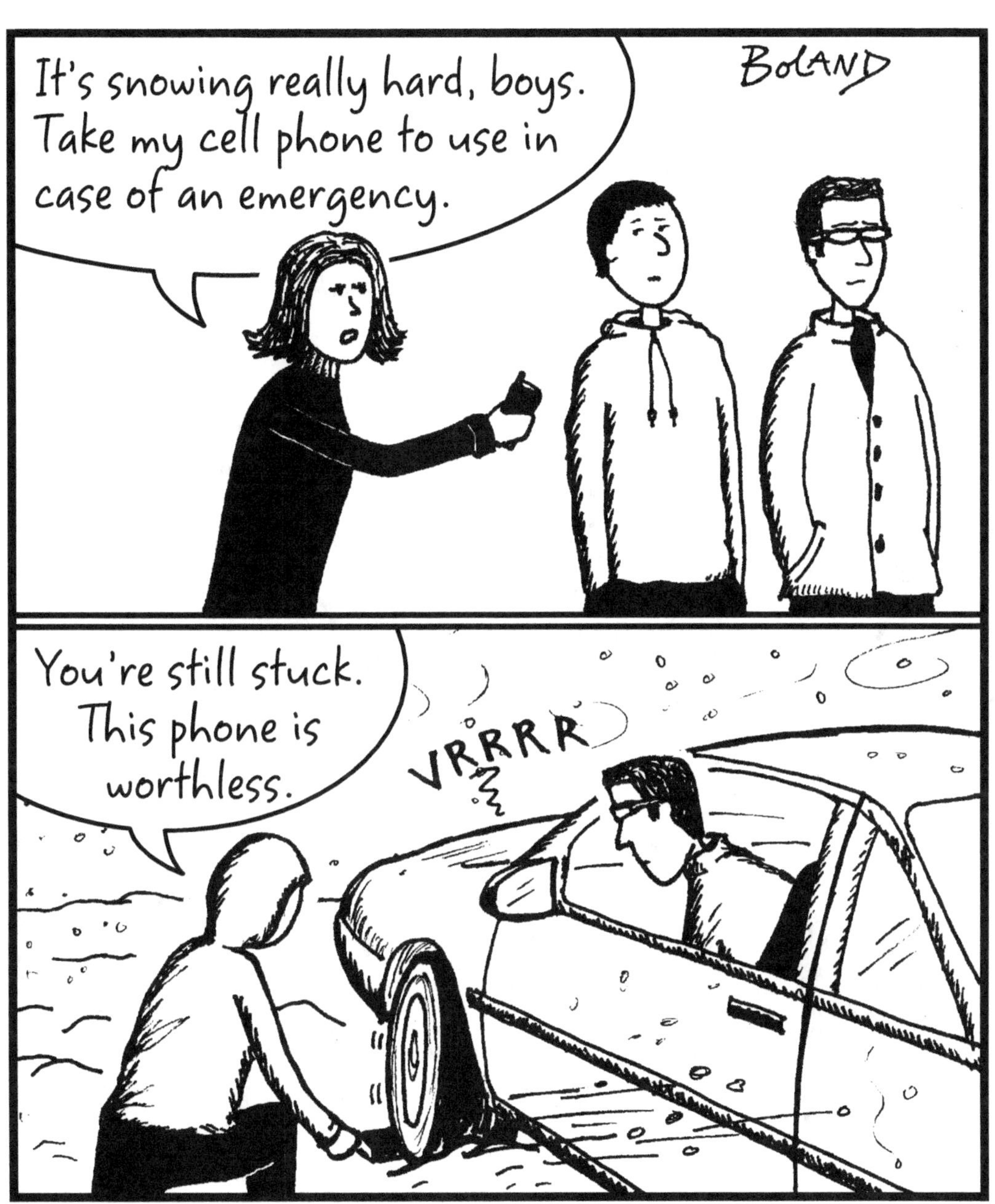
It's snowing really hard, boys. Take my cell phone to use in case of an emergency.
BOLAND
You're still stuck. This phone is worthless.
VRRRR

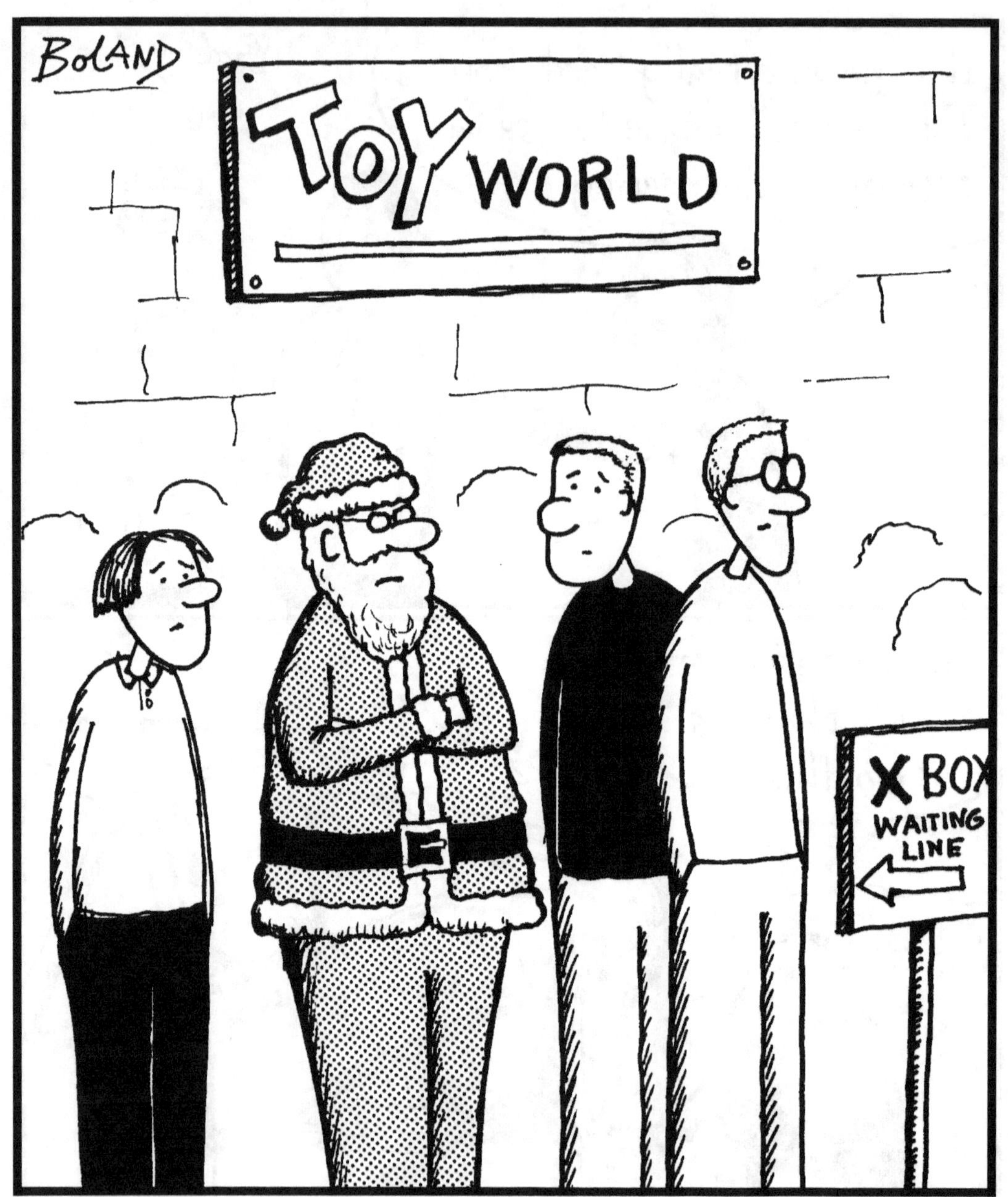
BOLAND
TOY WORLD
X BOX
WAITING LINE

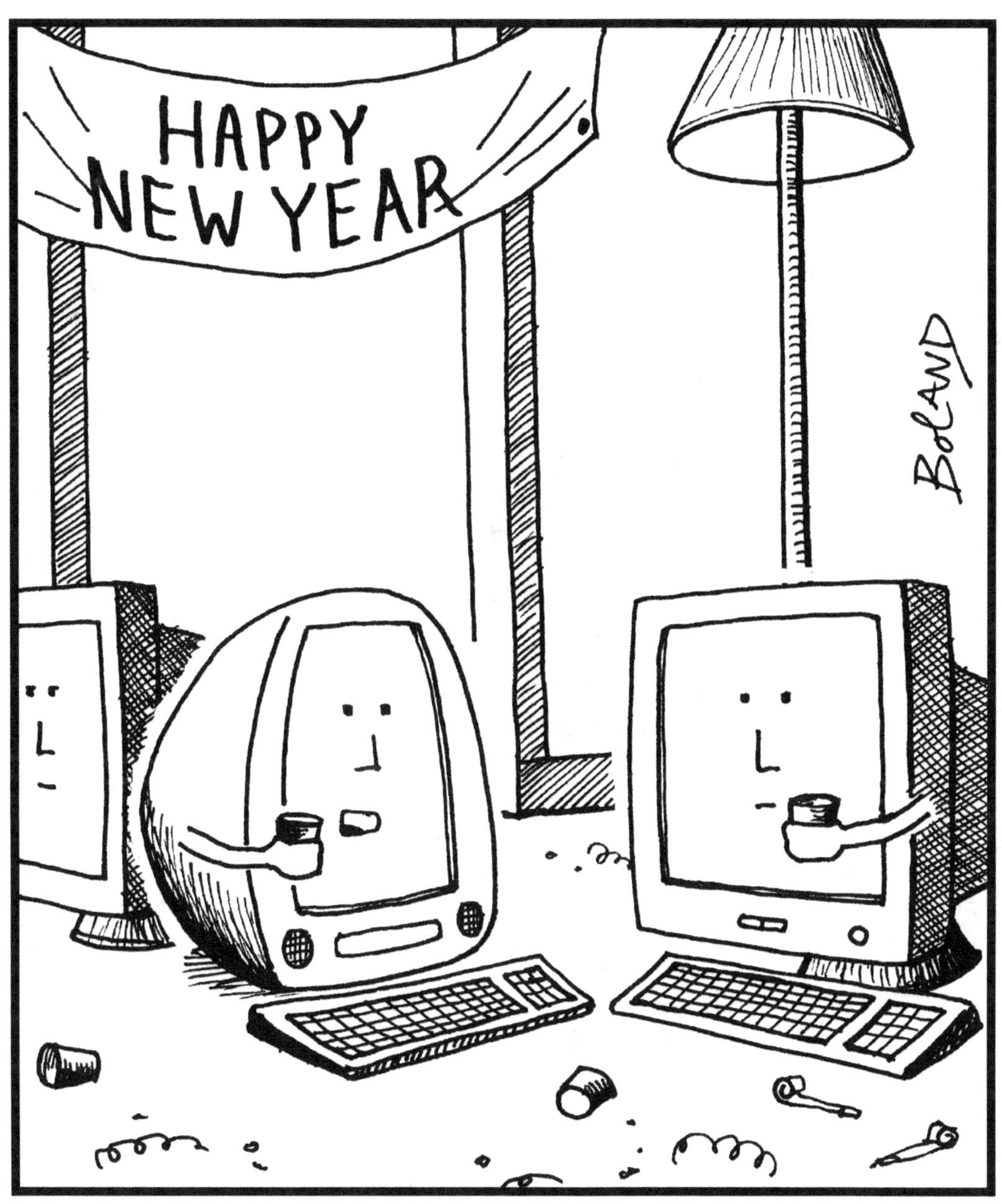

"So, what's your resolution?"

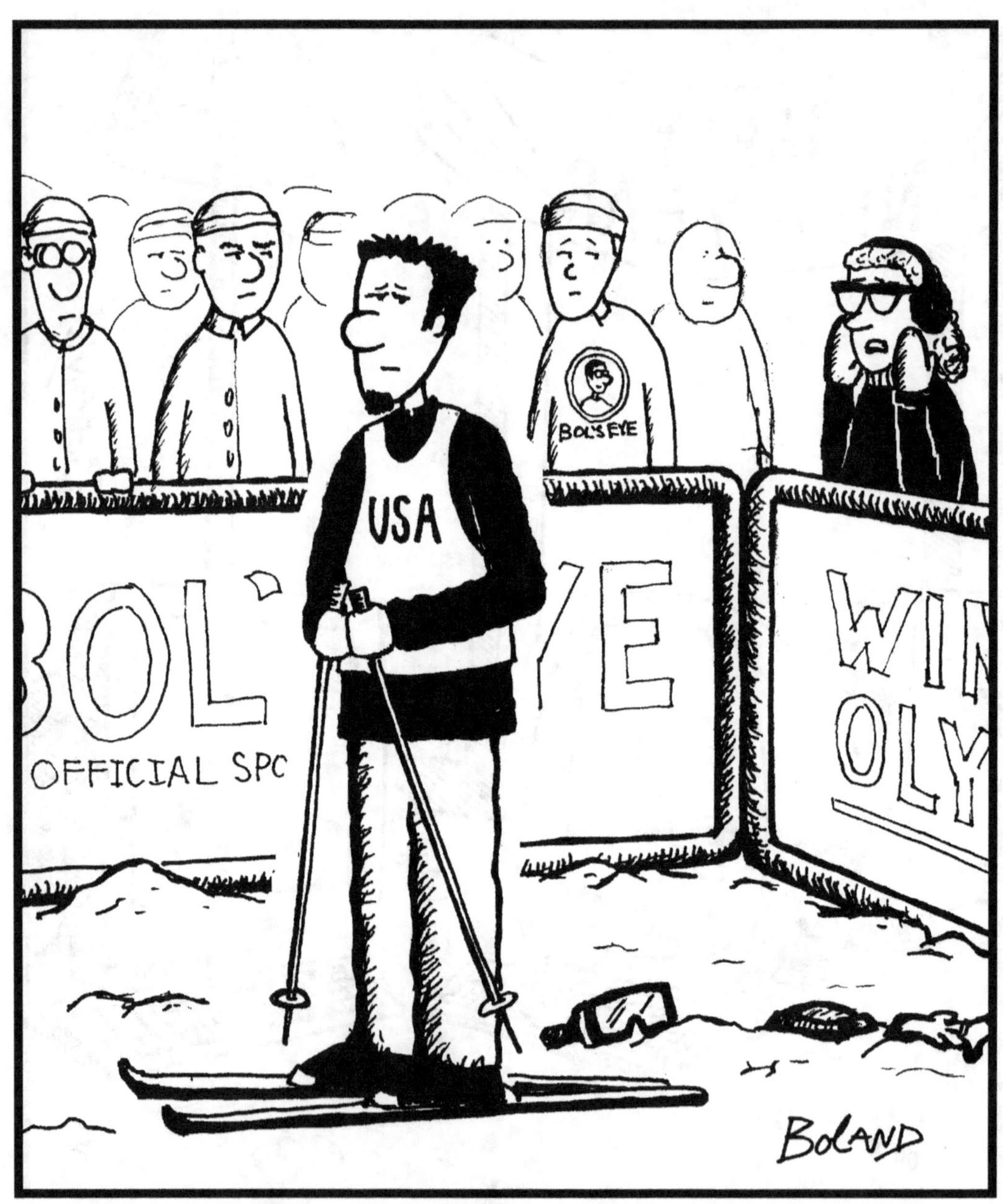

"Jo-ey! Oh, Joey Pooh! Don't forget your hat and glovsies. We wouldn't want you to freeze your cutie pie hands and widdle ears."

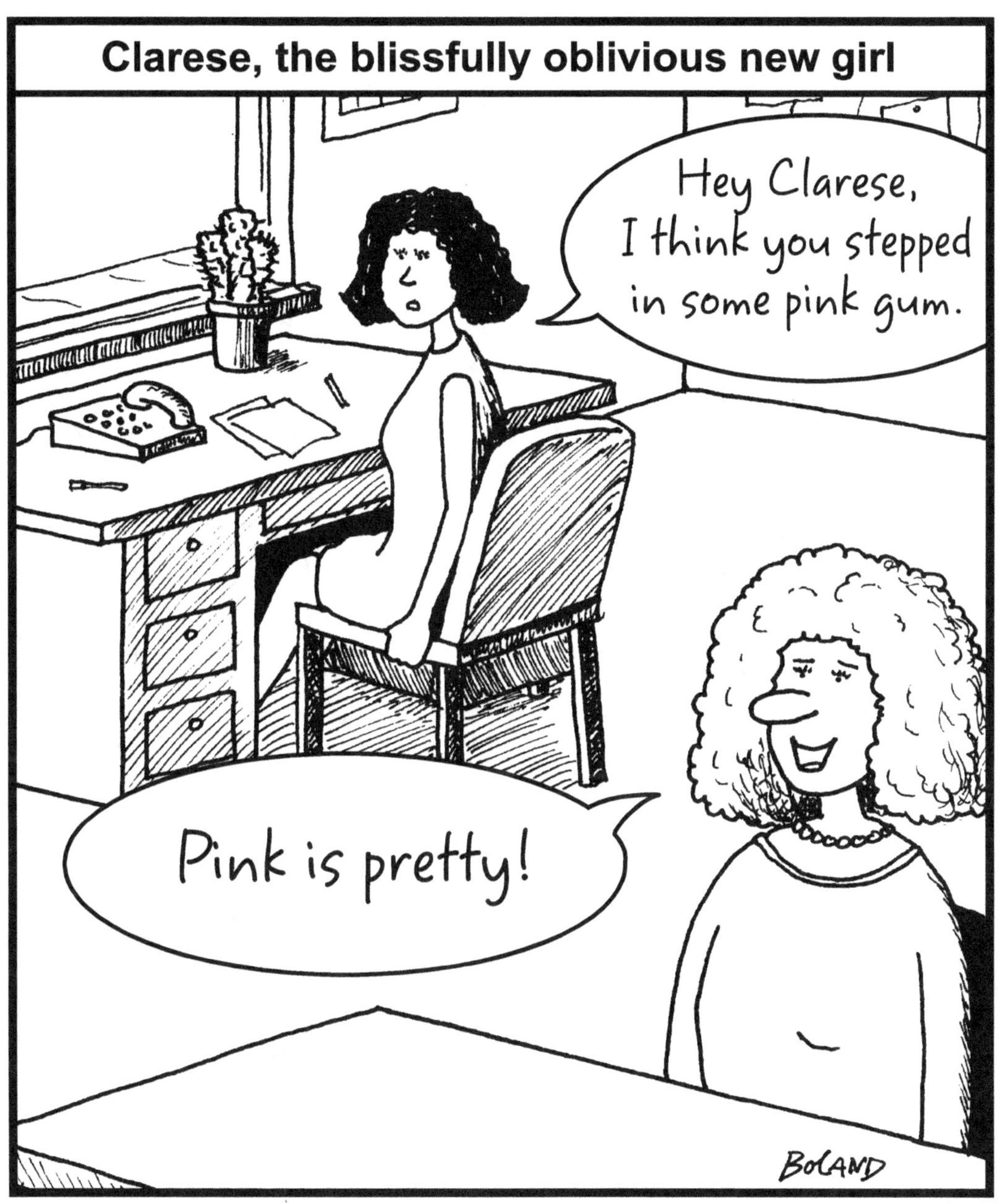
Clarese, the blissfully oblivious new girl
Hey Clarese, I think you stepped in some pink gum.
Pink is pretty!
BOLAND

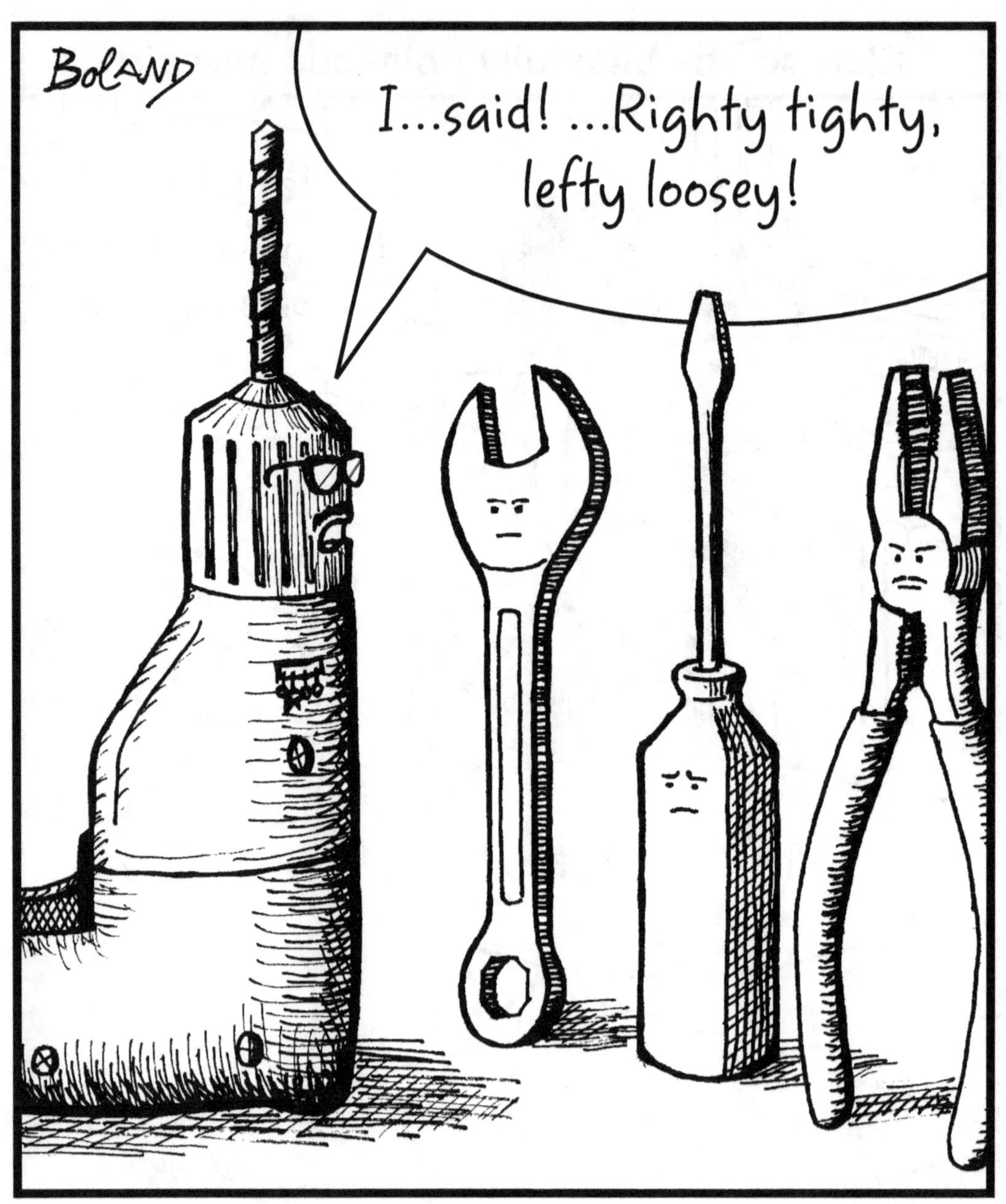

Drill Sergeant

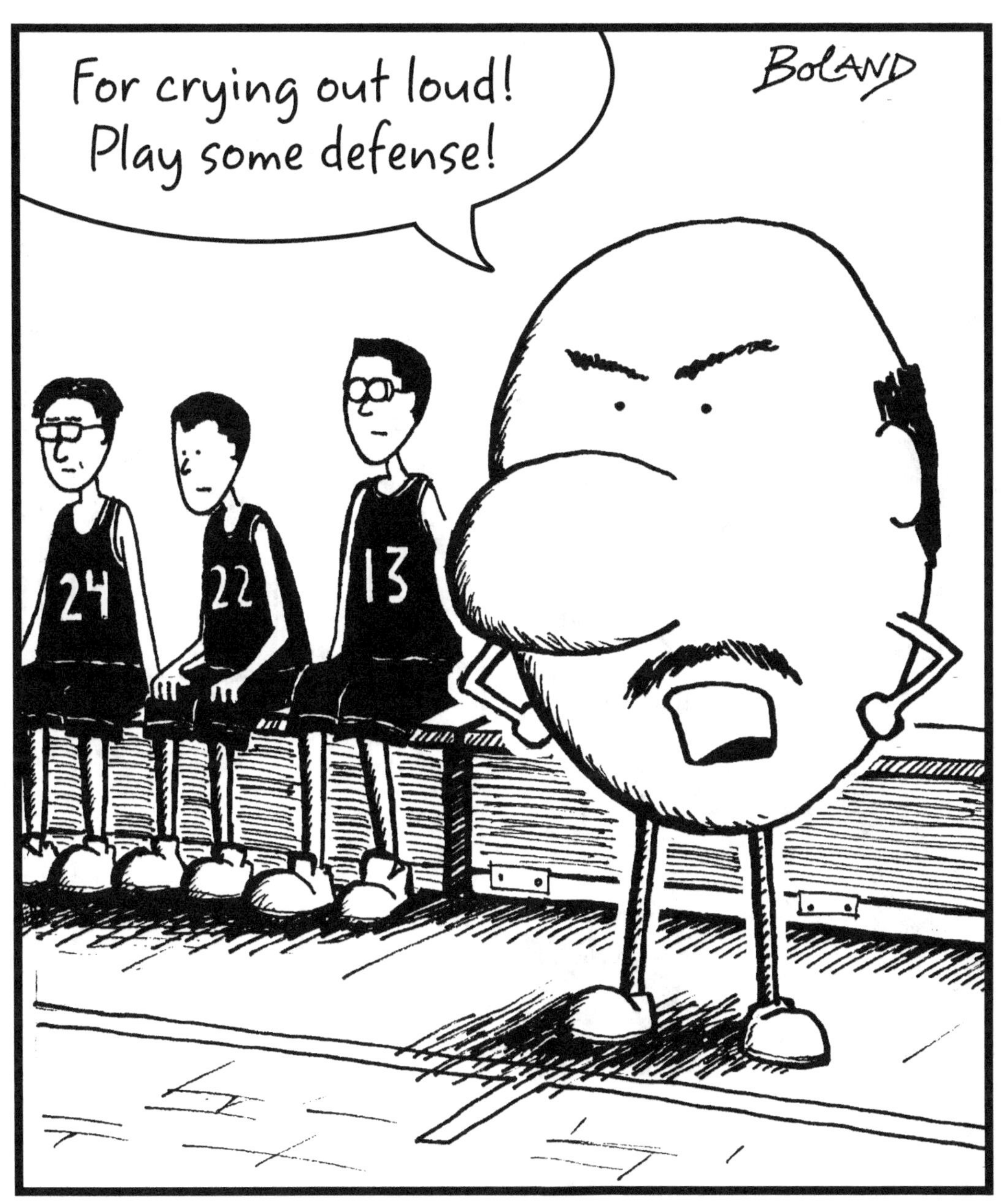

Head Coach

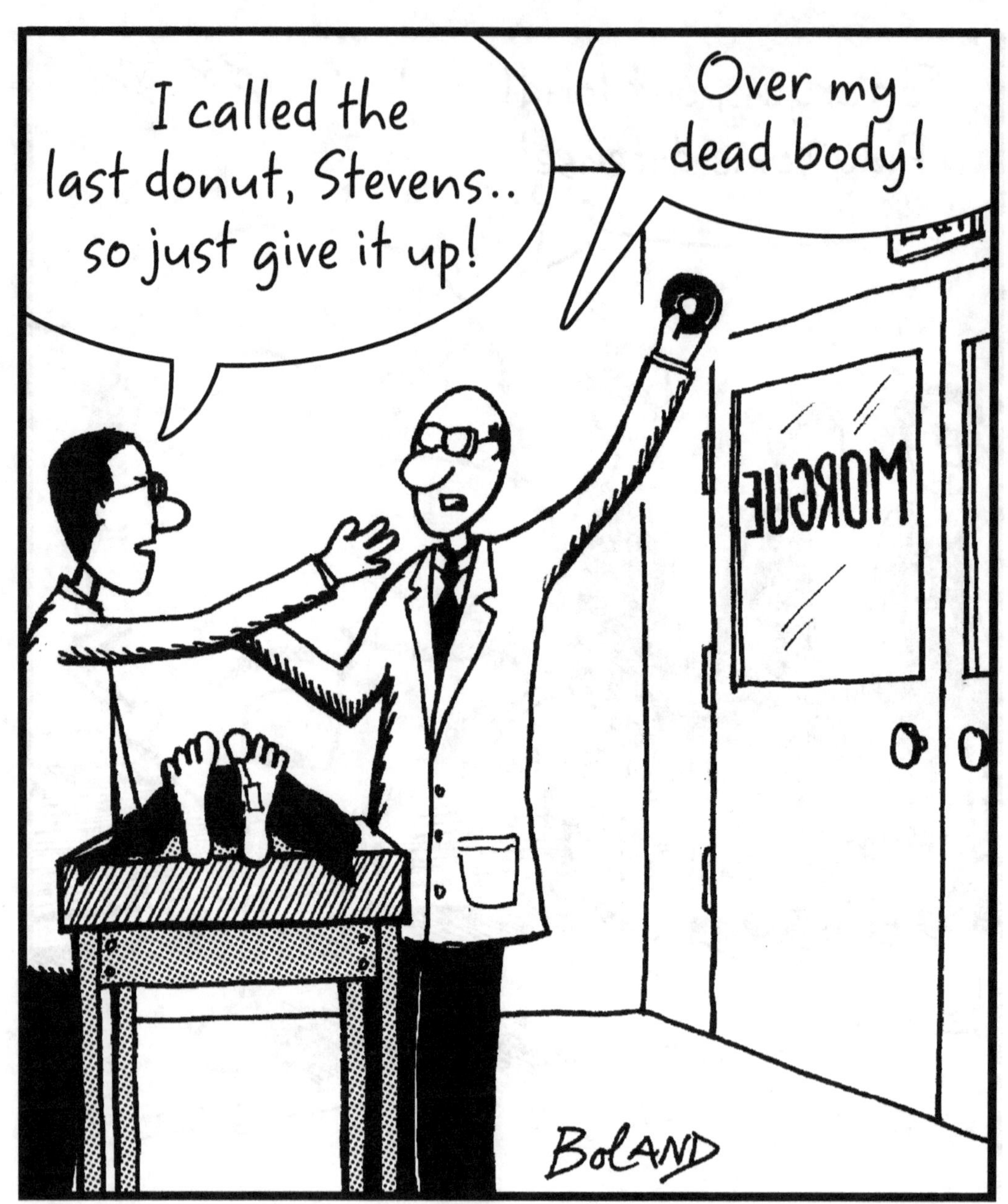
I called the last donut, Stevens.. so just give it up!
Over my dead body!
MORGUE
BoLAND

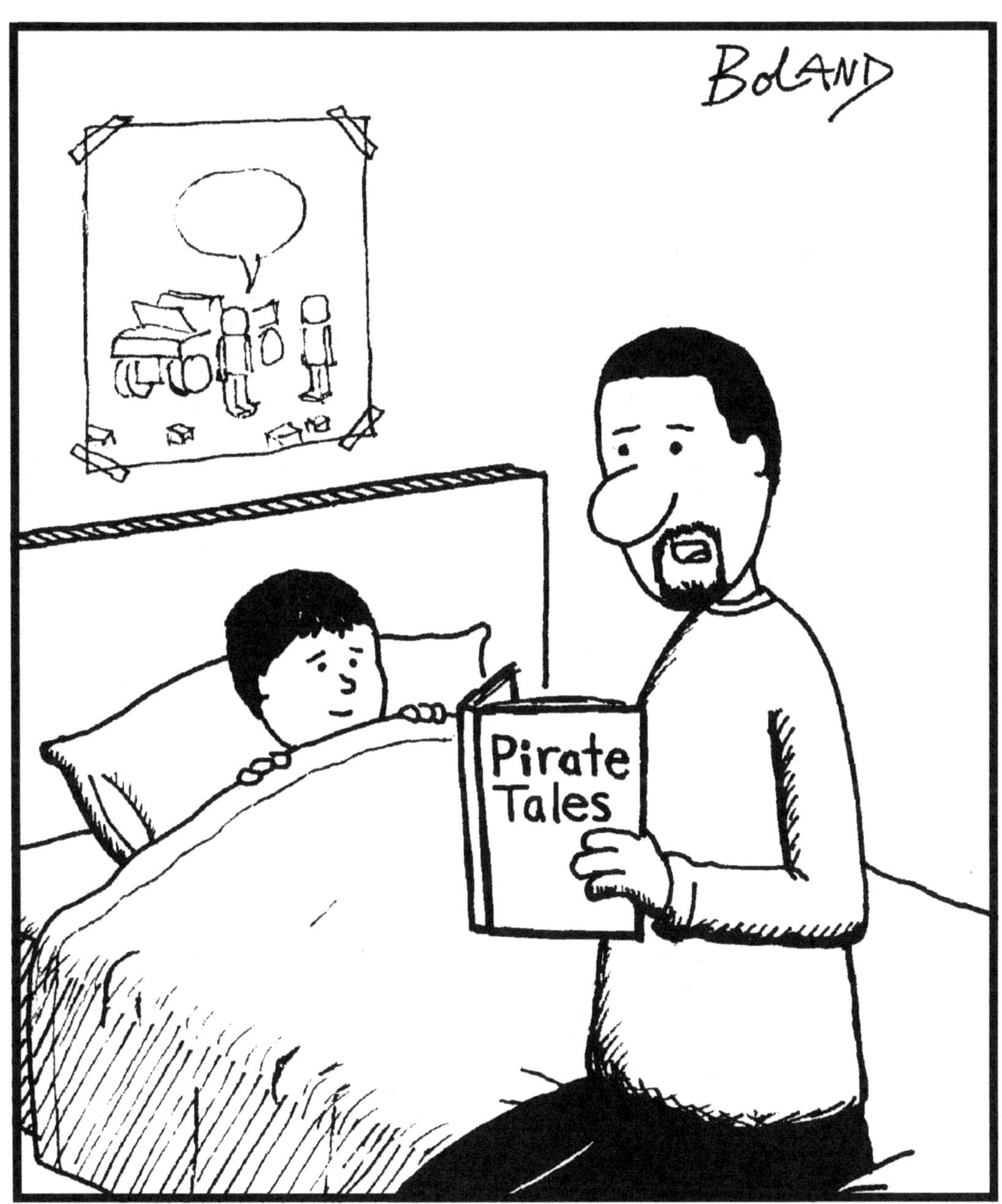

"They pillaged and plundered with no regard for the law. They moved at high speeds, taking whatever they desired. But, alas, their plans were foiled when authorities traced their illegal downloads and took them to court for considerable sums."

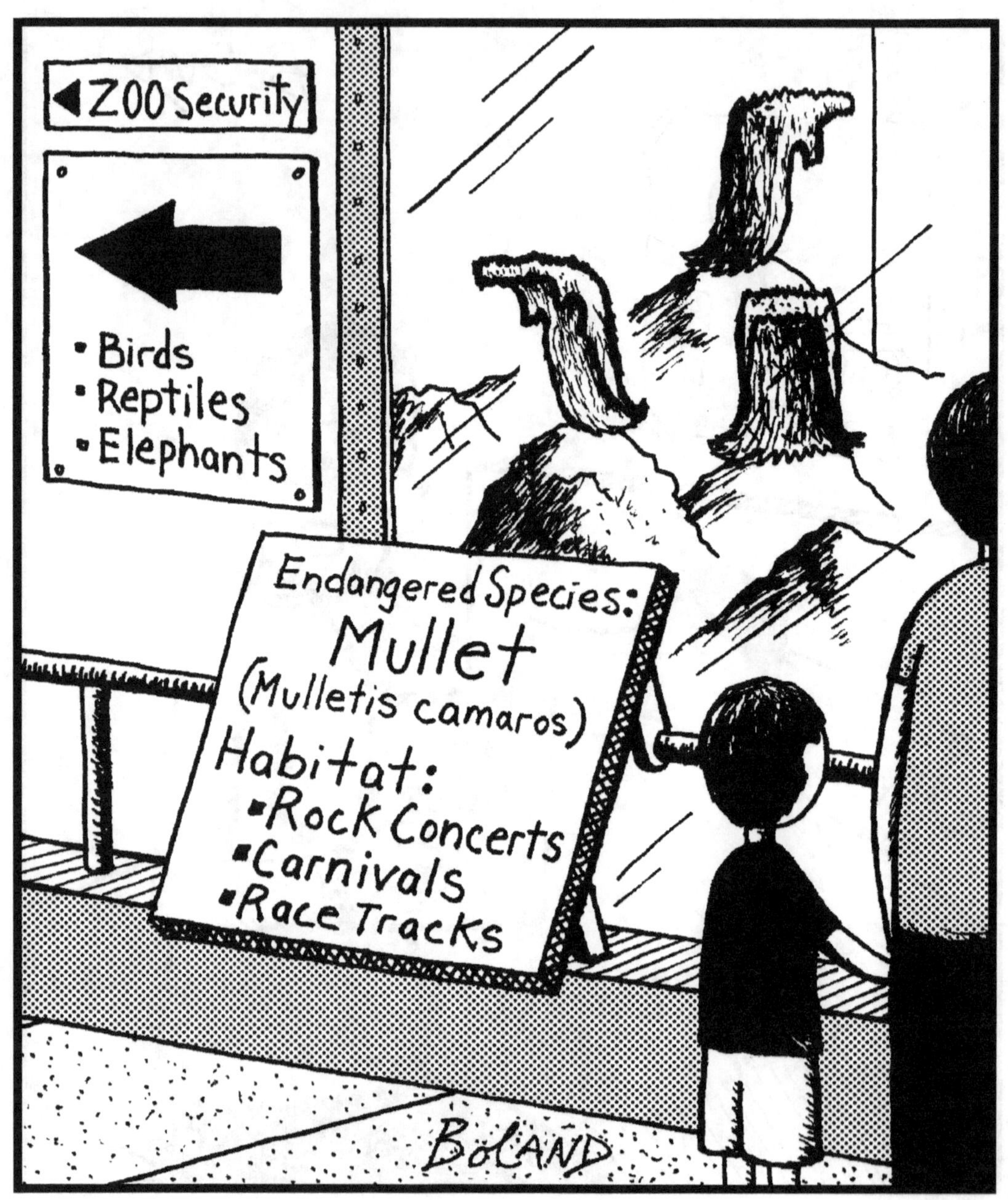
◀ZOO Security
• Birds
• Reptiles
• Elephants
Endangered Species:
Mullet
(Mulletis camaros)
Habitat:
▪Rock Concerts
▪Carnivals
▪Race Tracks
BOLAND

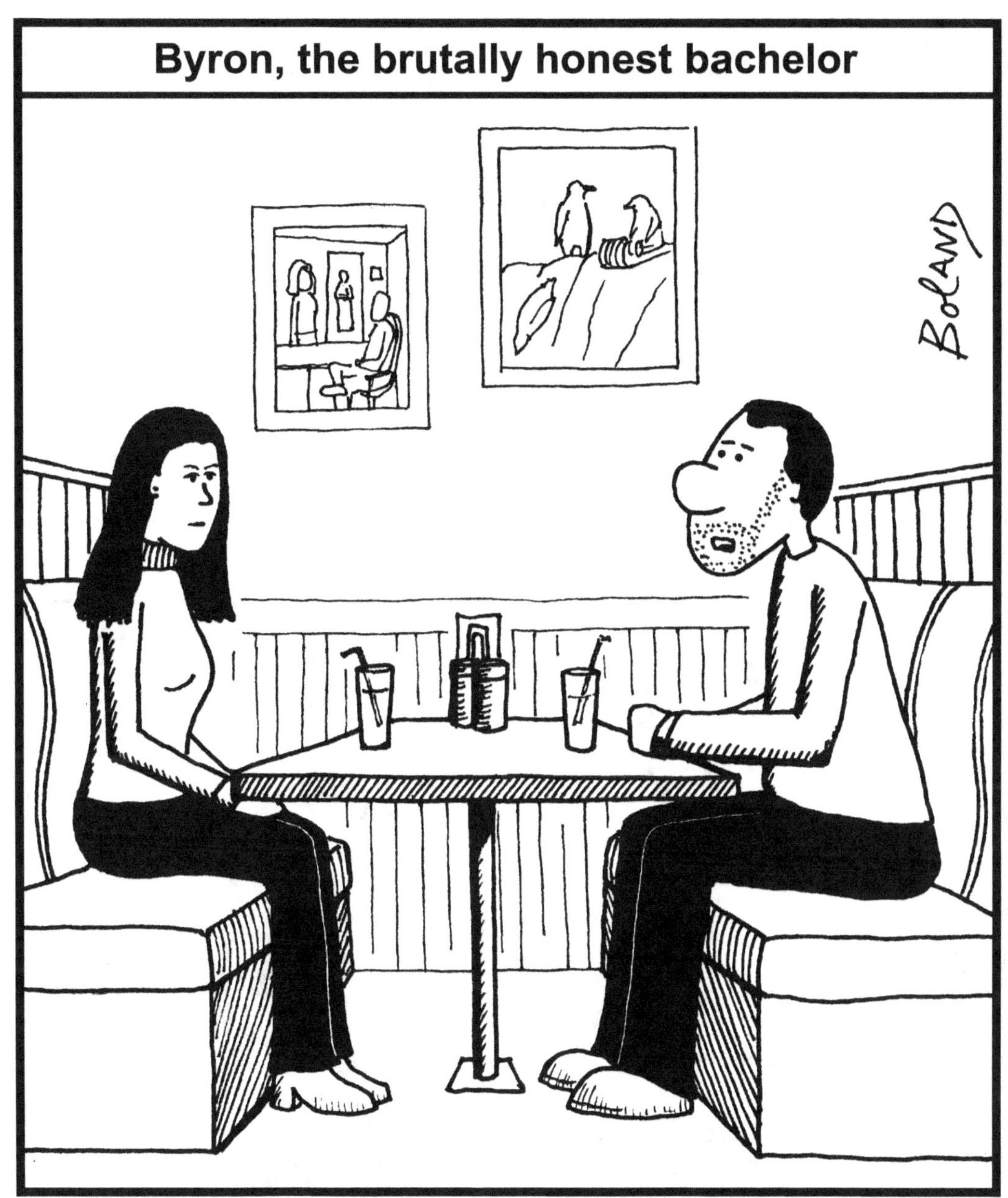

"Could you move your head? I can barely see the game."

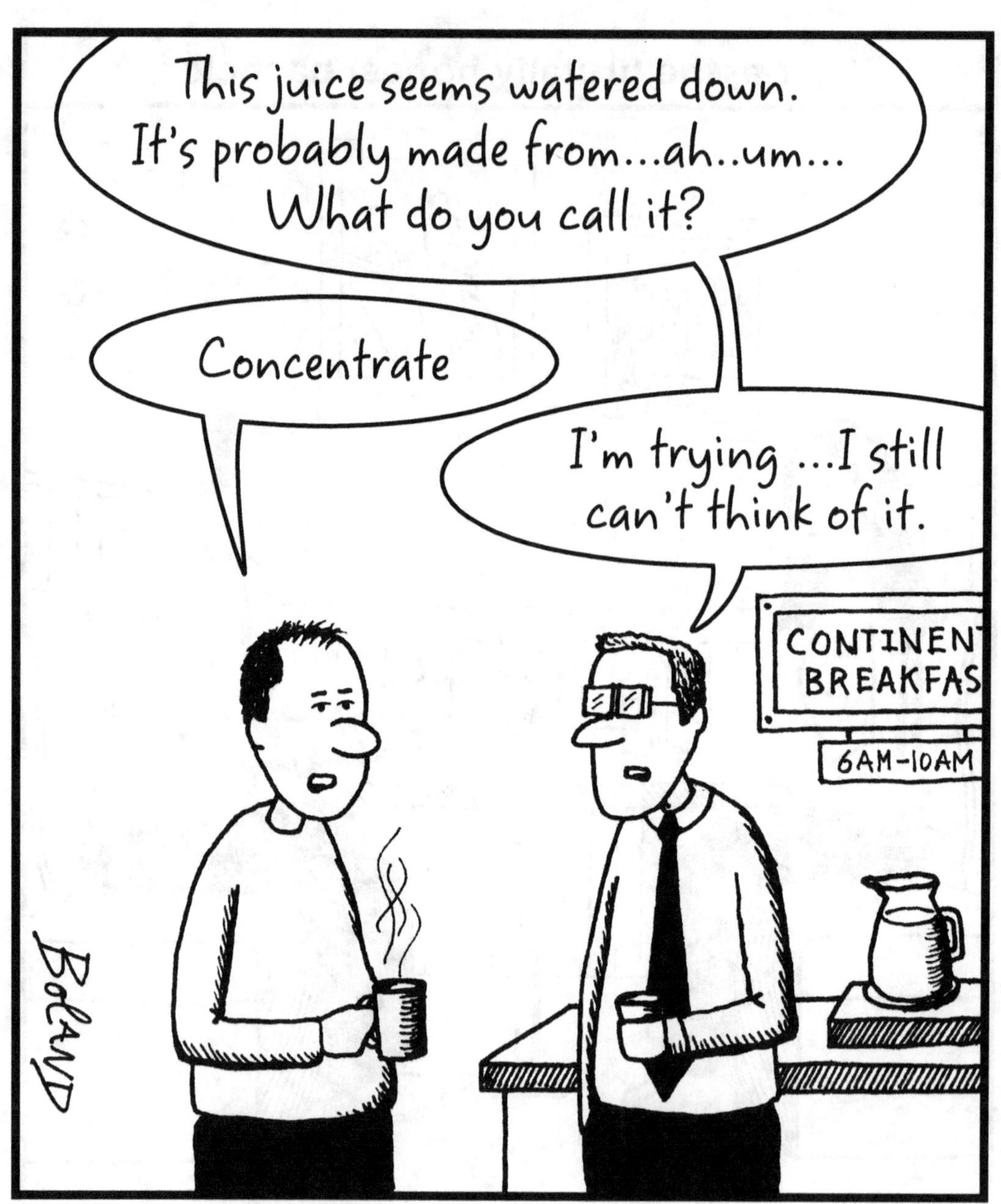
This juice seems watered down. It's probably made from...ah..um... What do you call it?
Concentrate
I'm trying ...I still can't think of it.
CONTINENT
BREAKFAS
6AM–10AM
BOLAND

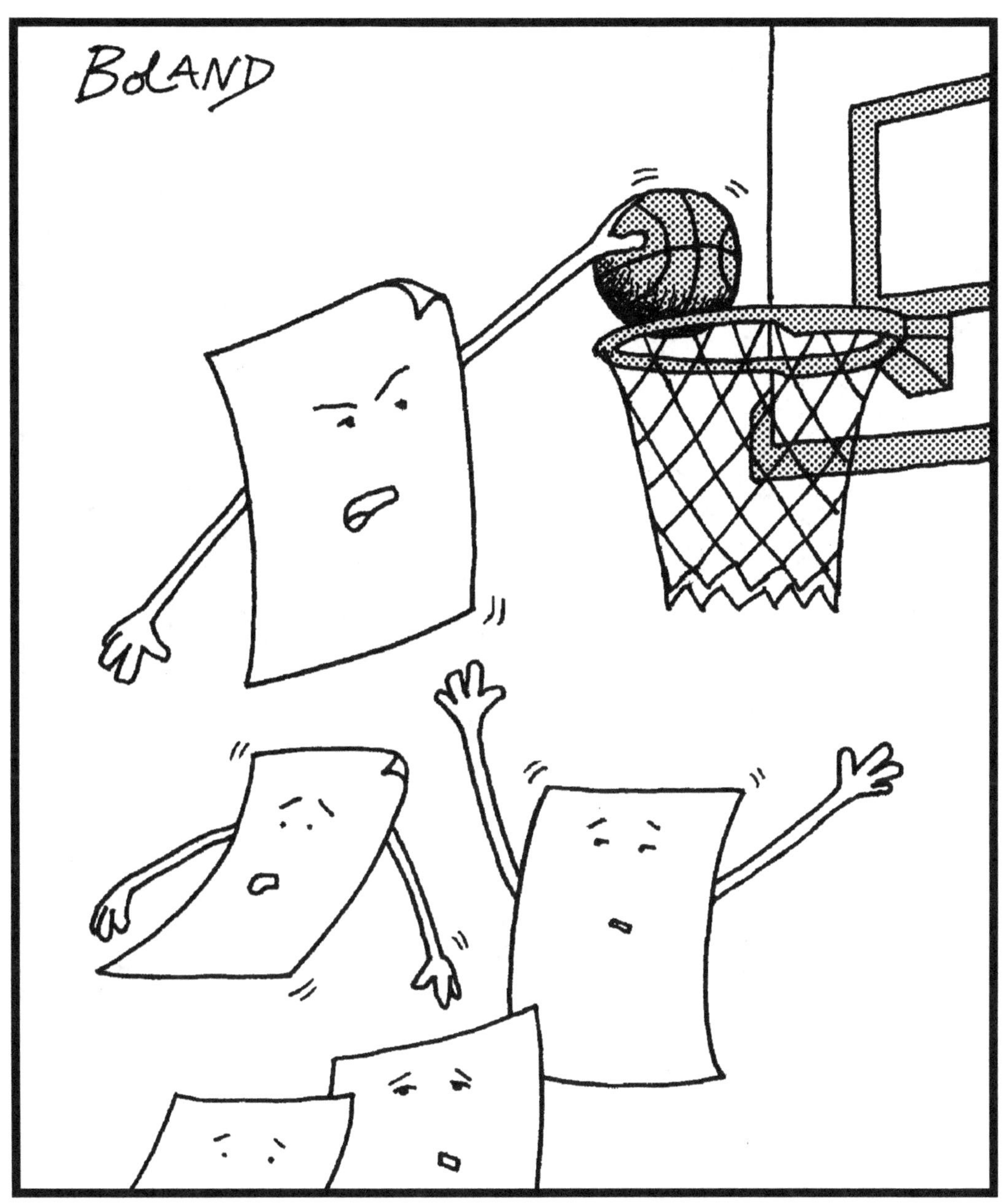

Paper Jam

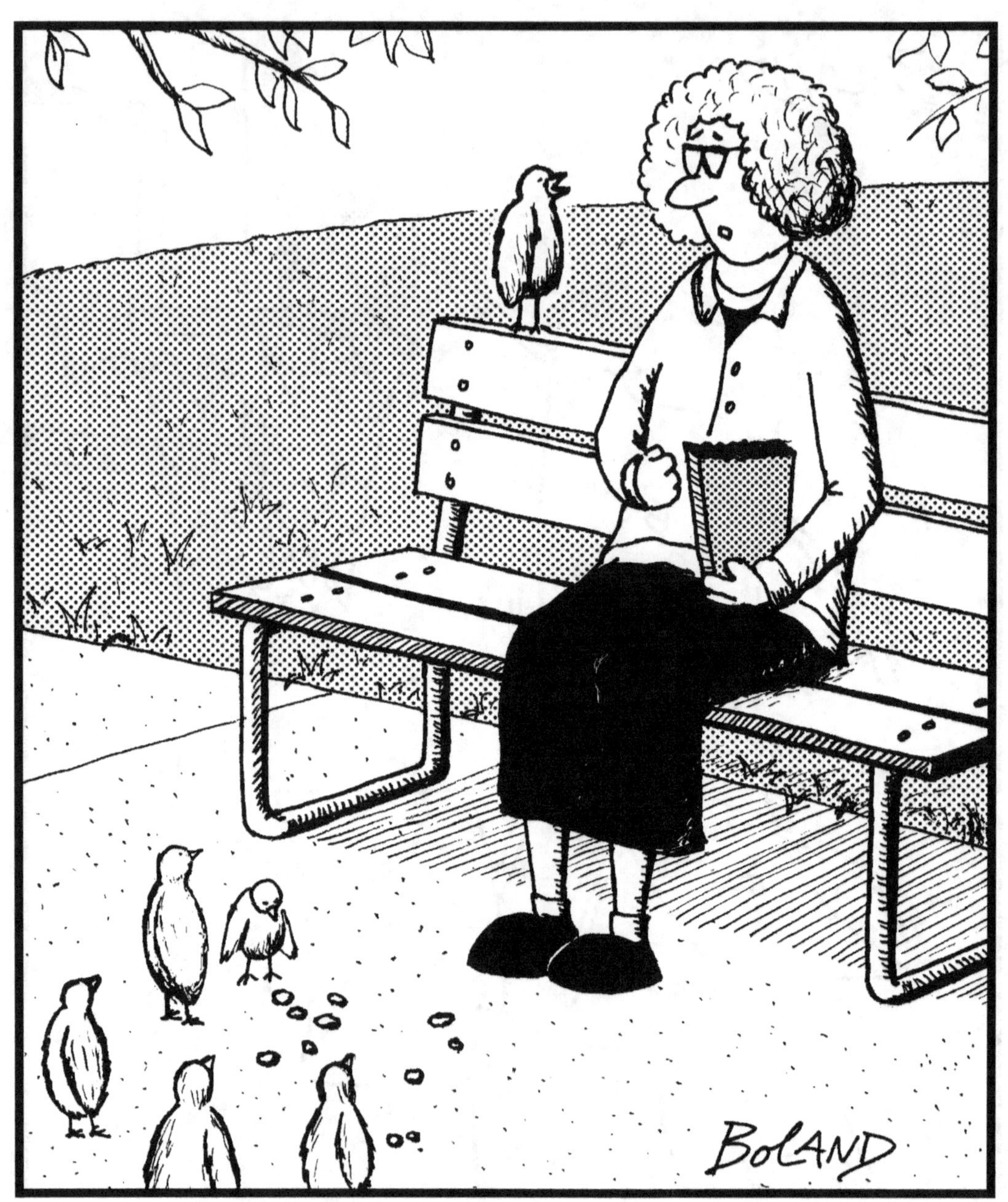

"We only eat low carb now."

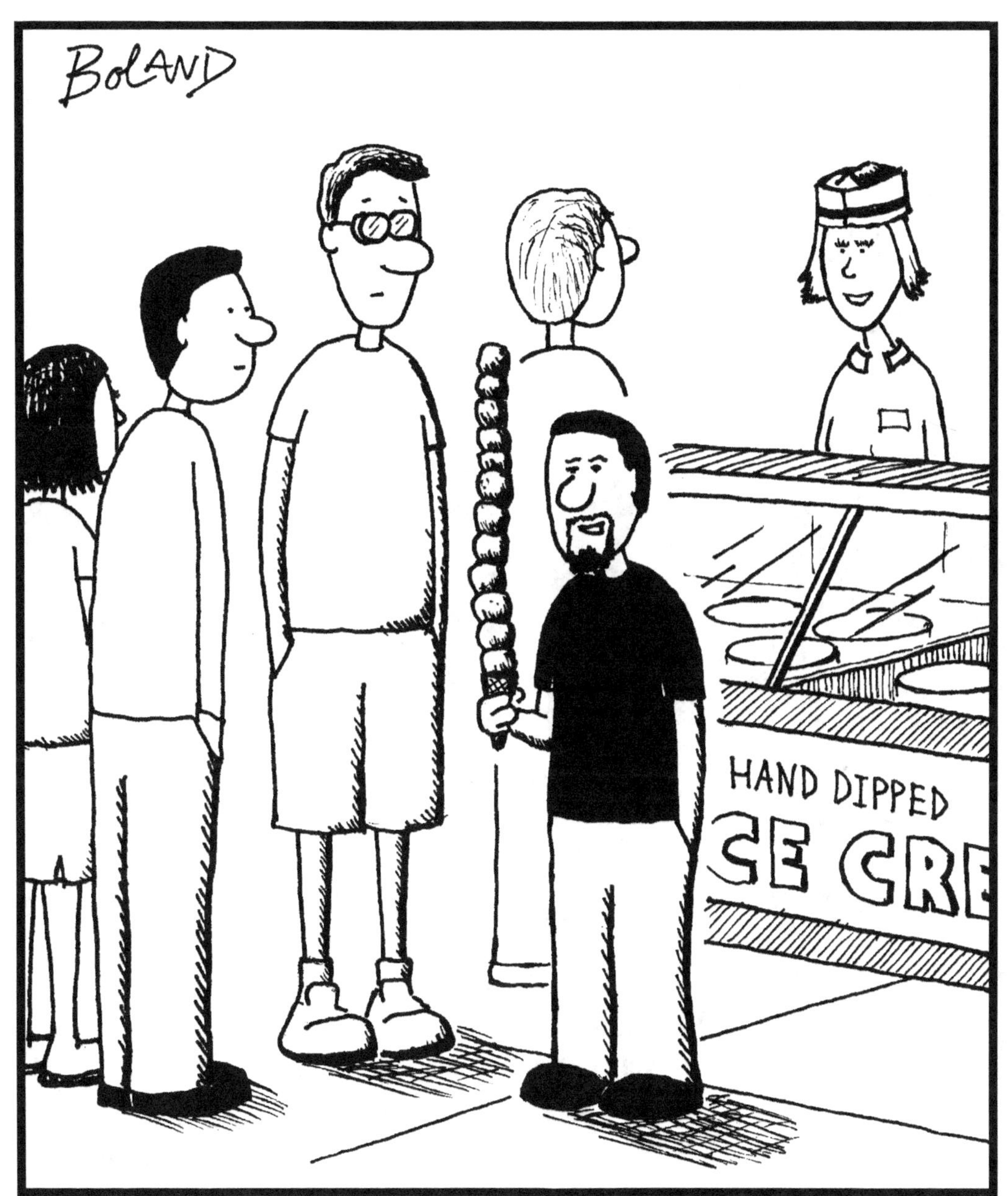

Neapolitan Complex

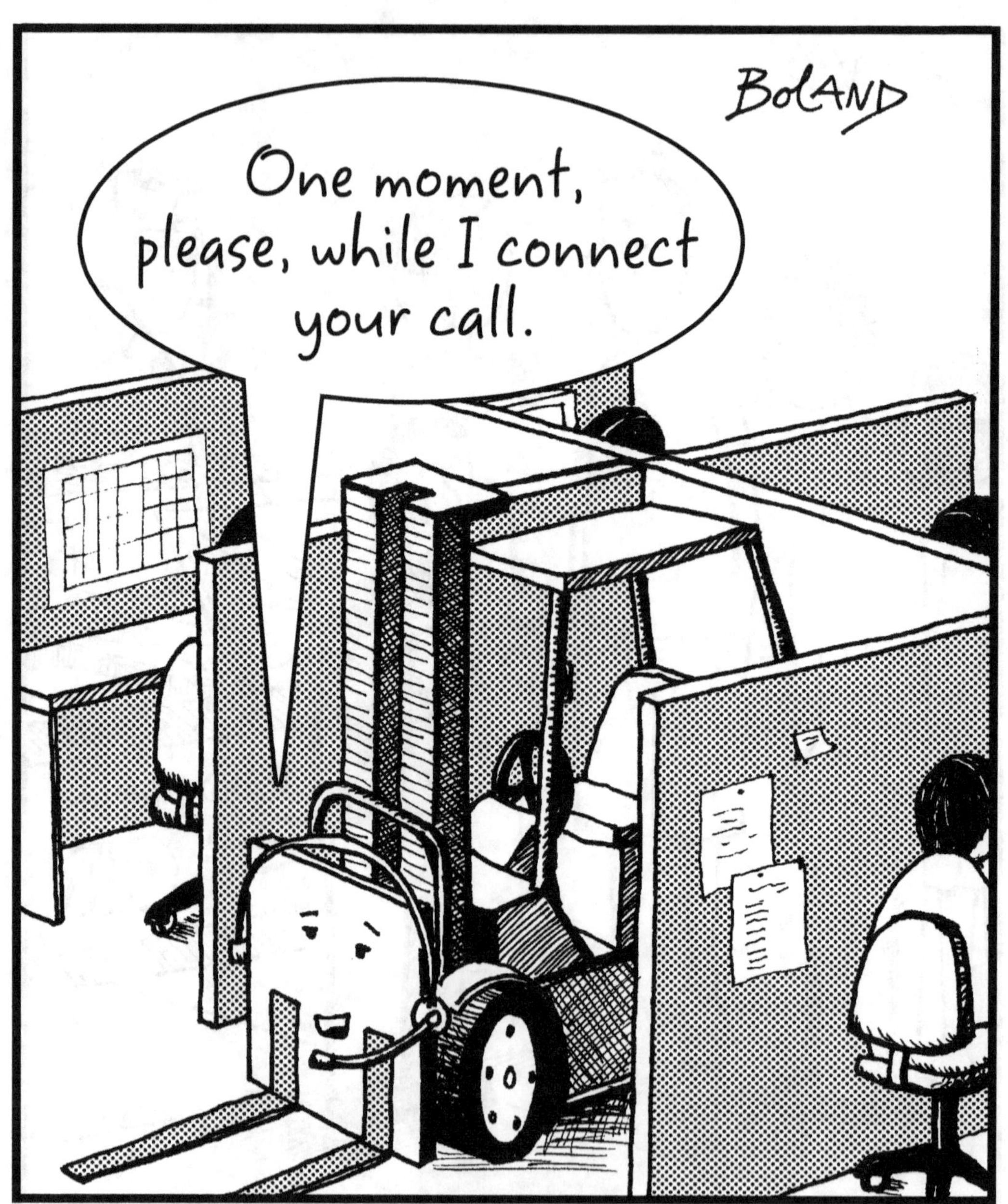

Forklift Operator

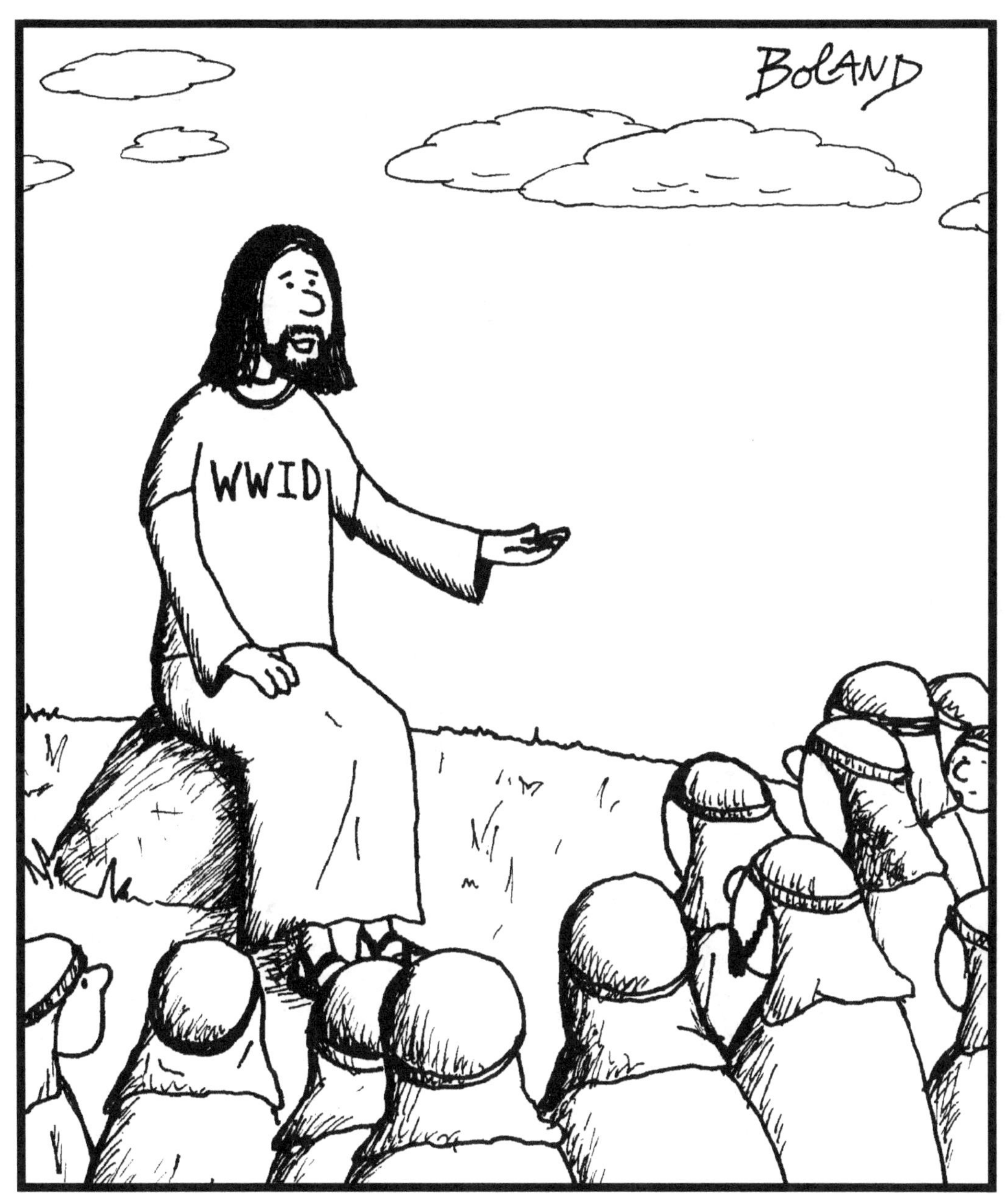
BOLAND
WWID

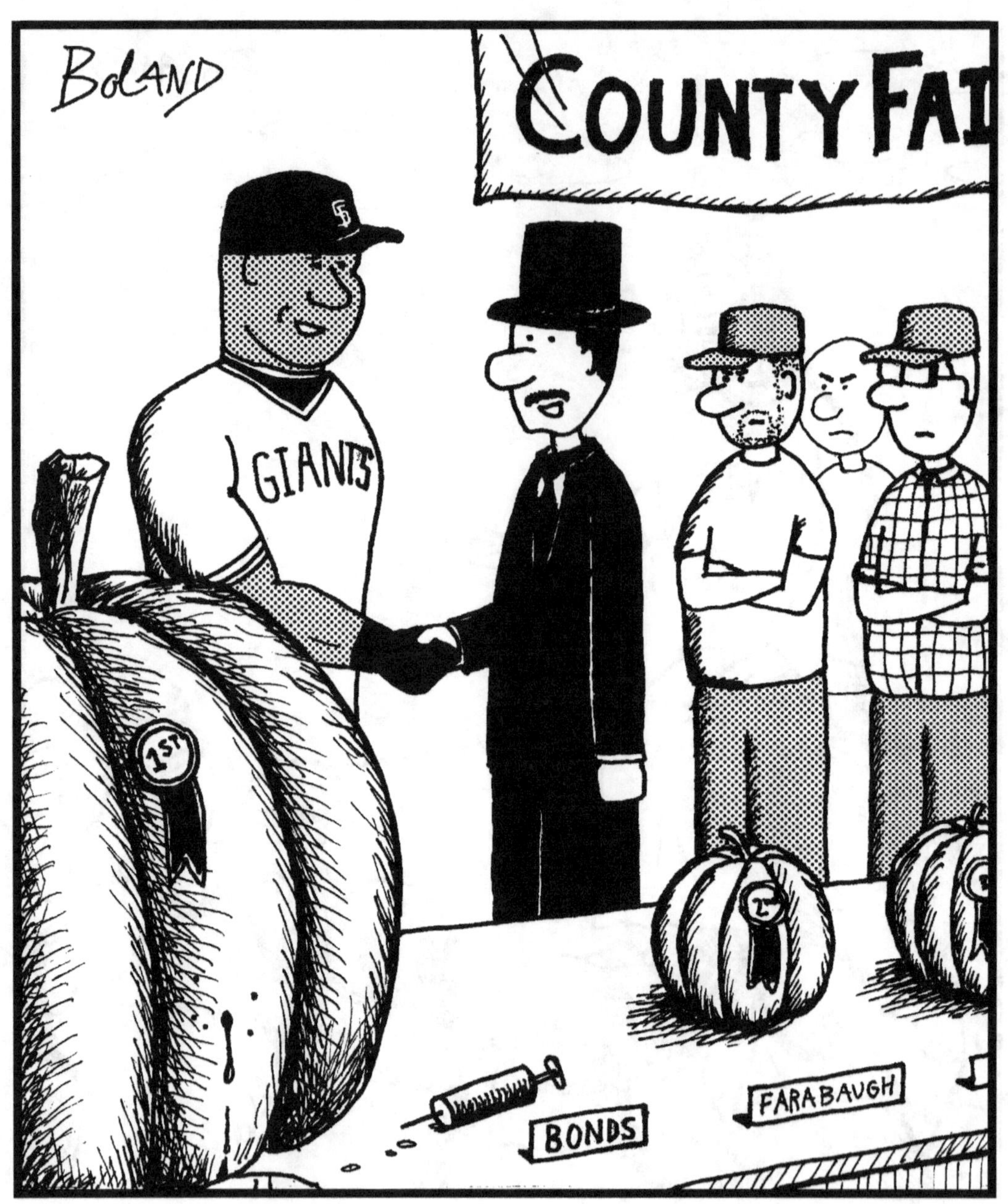
BOLAND
COUNTY FAI
GIANTS
1ST
BONDS
FARABAUGH

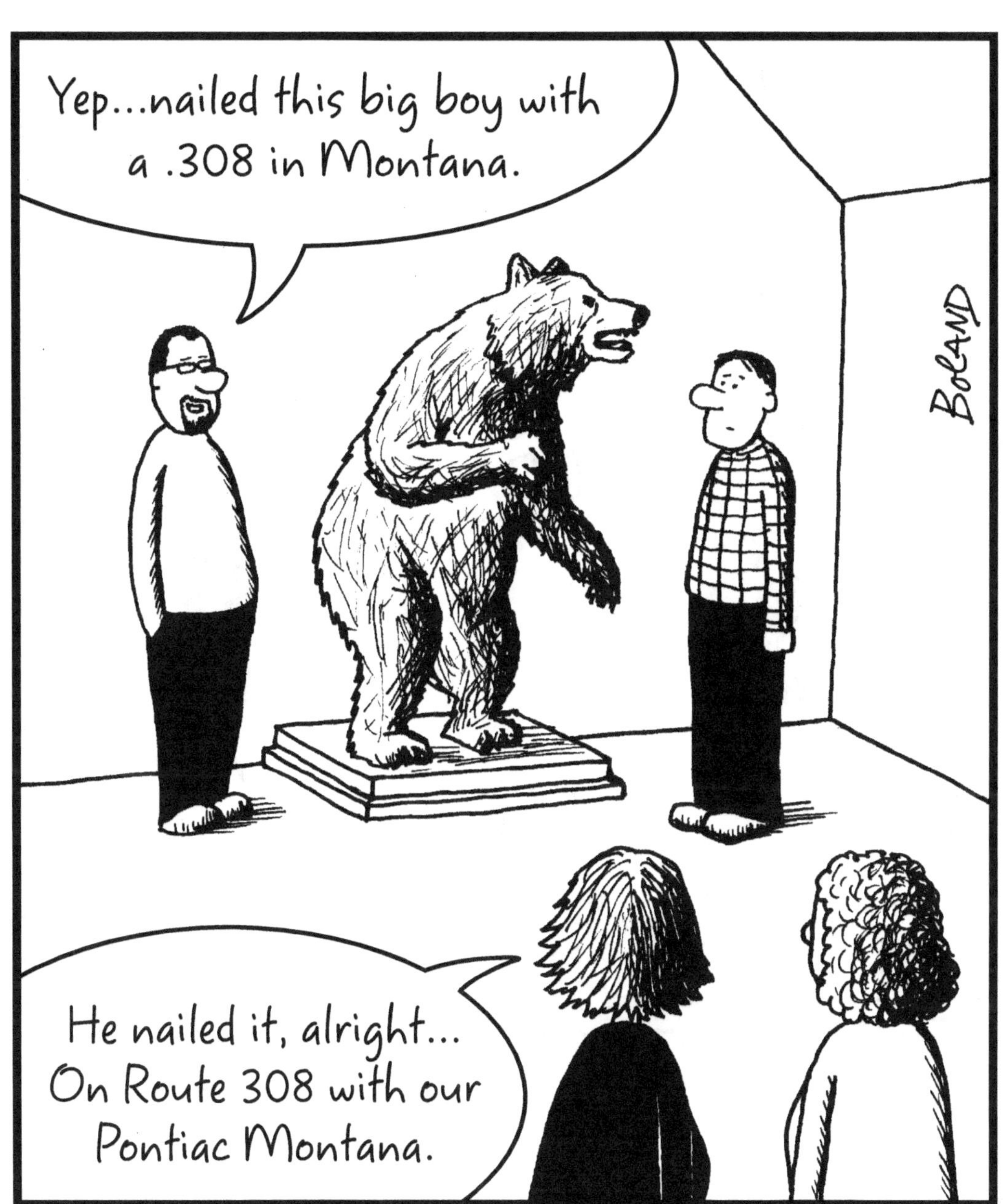
Yep...nailed this big boy with a .308 in Montana.
BOLAND
He nailed it, alright... On Route 308 with our Pontiac Montana.

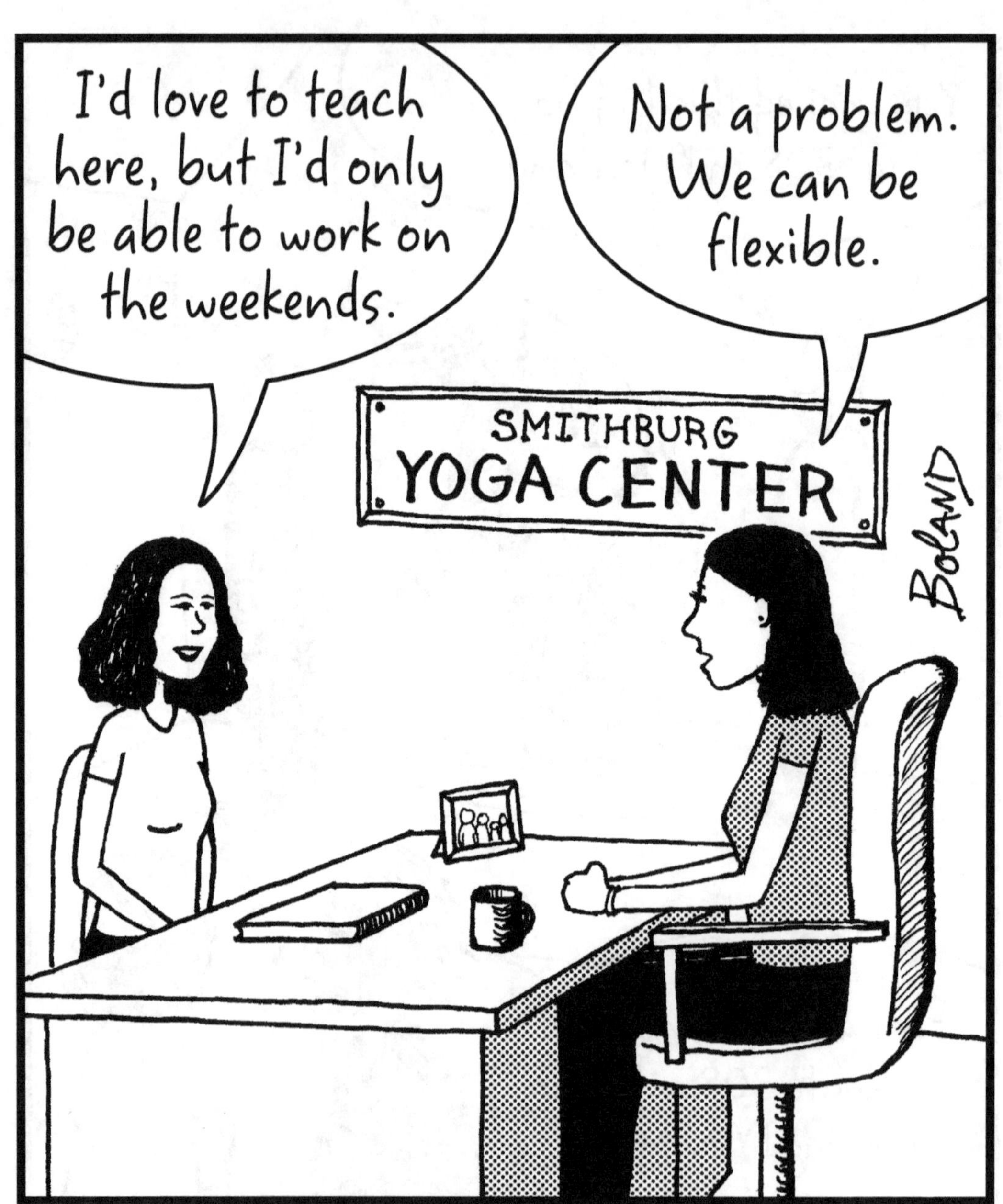
I'd love to teach here, but I'd only be able to work on the weekends.
Not a problem. We can be flexible.
SMITHBURG
YOGA CENTER
BOLAND

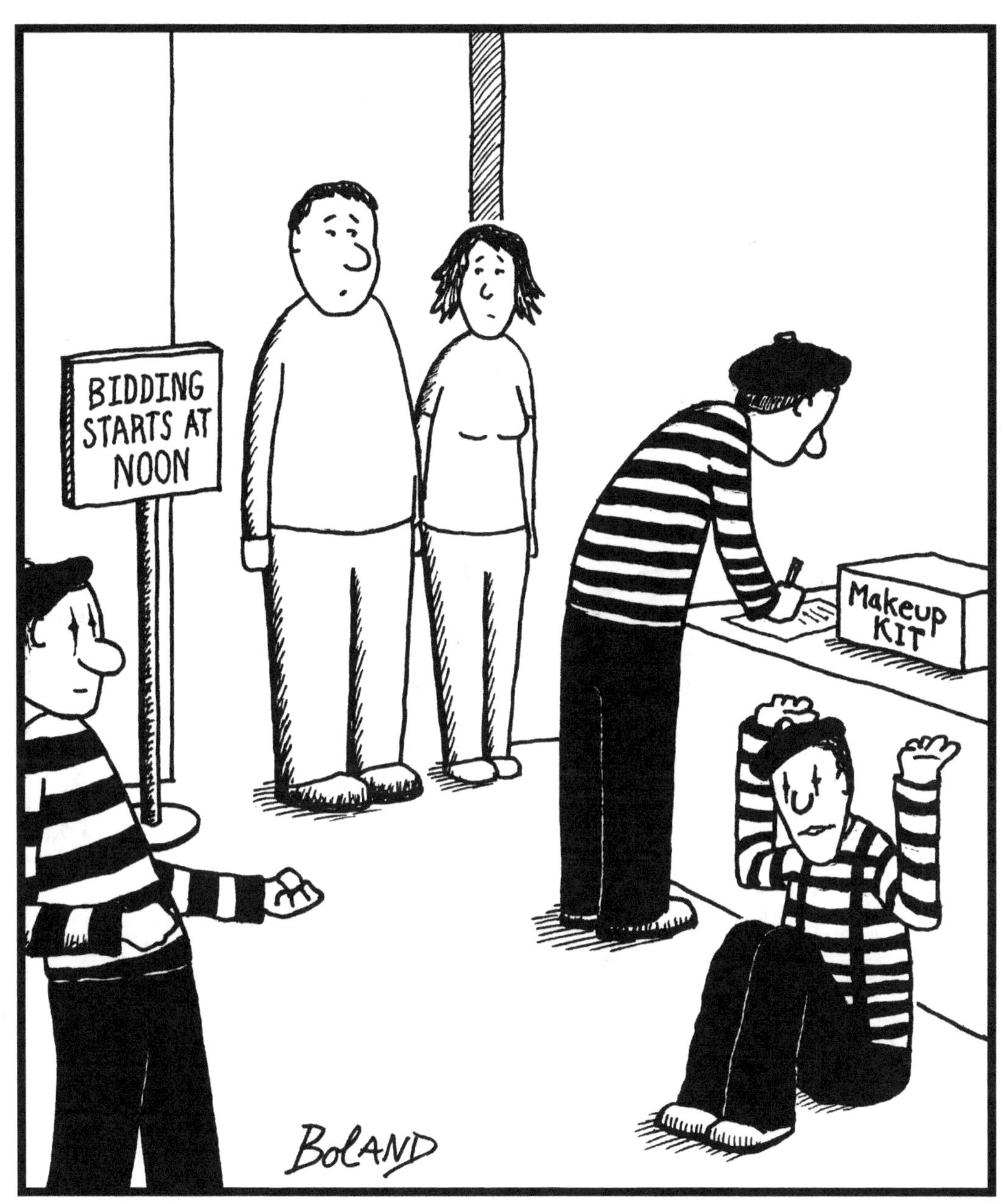

Silent Auction

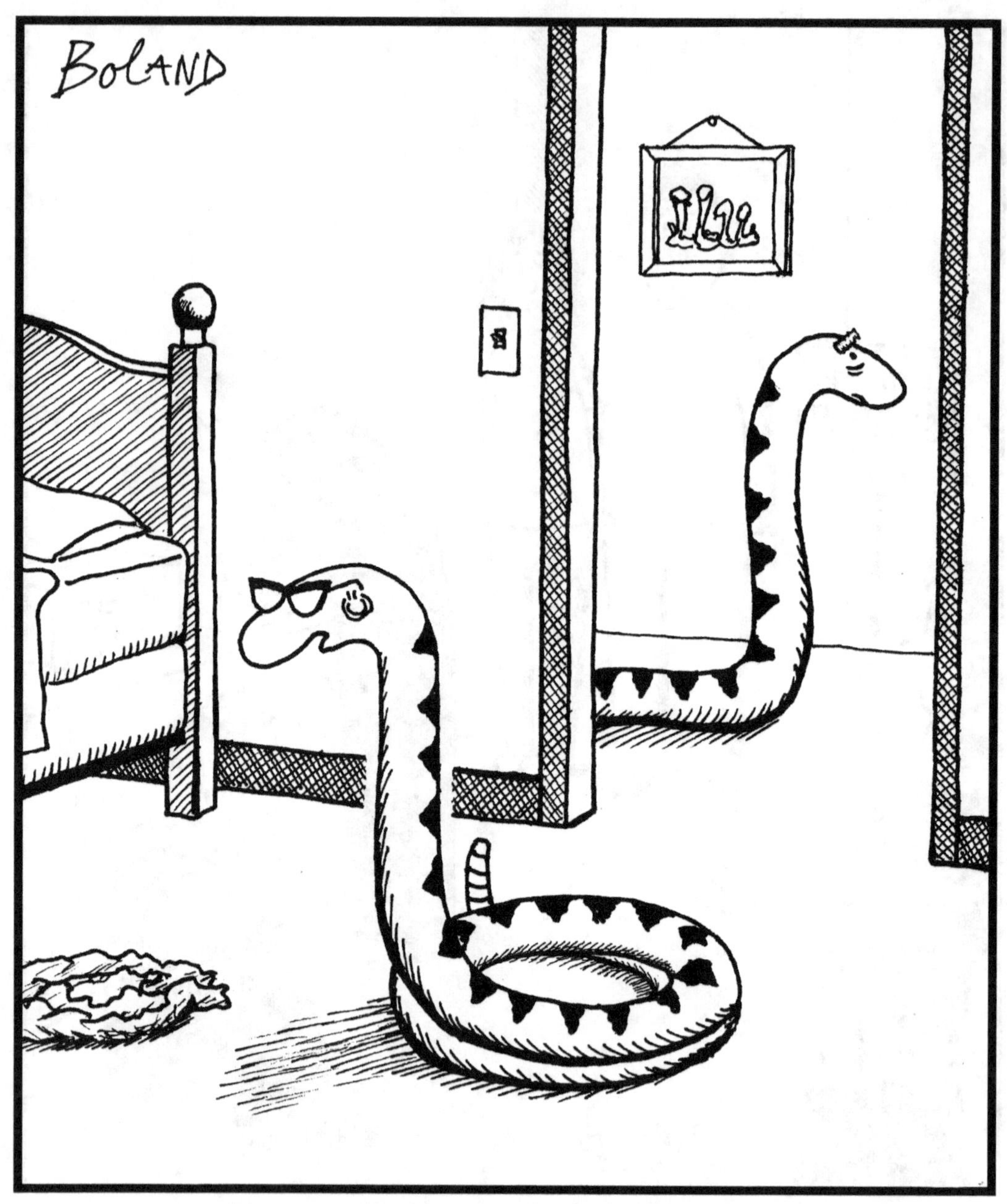

"Arthur!! What did I tell you about leaving your wet skin on the floor?!"

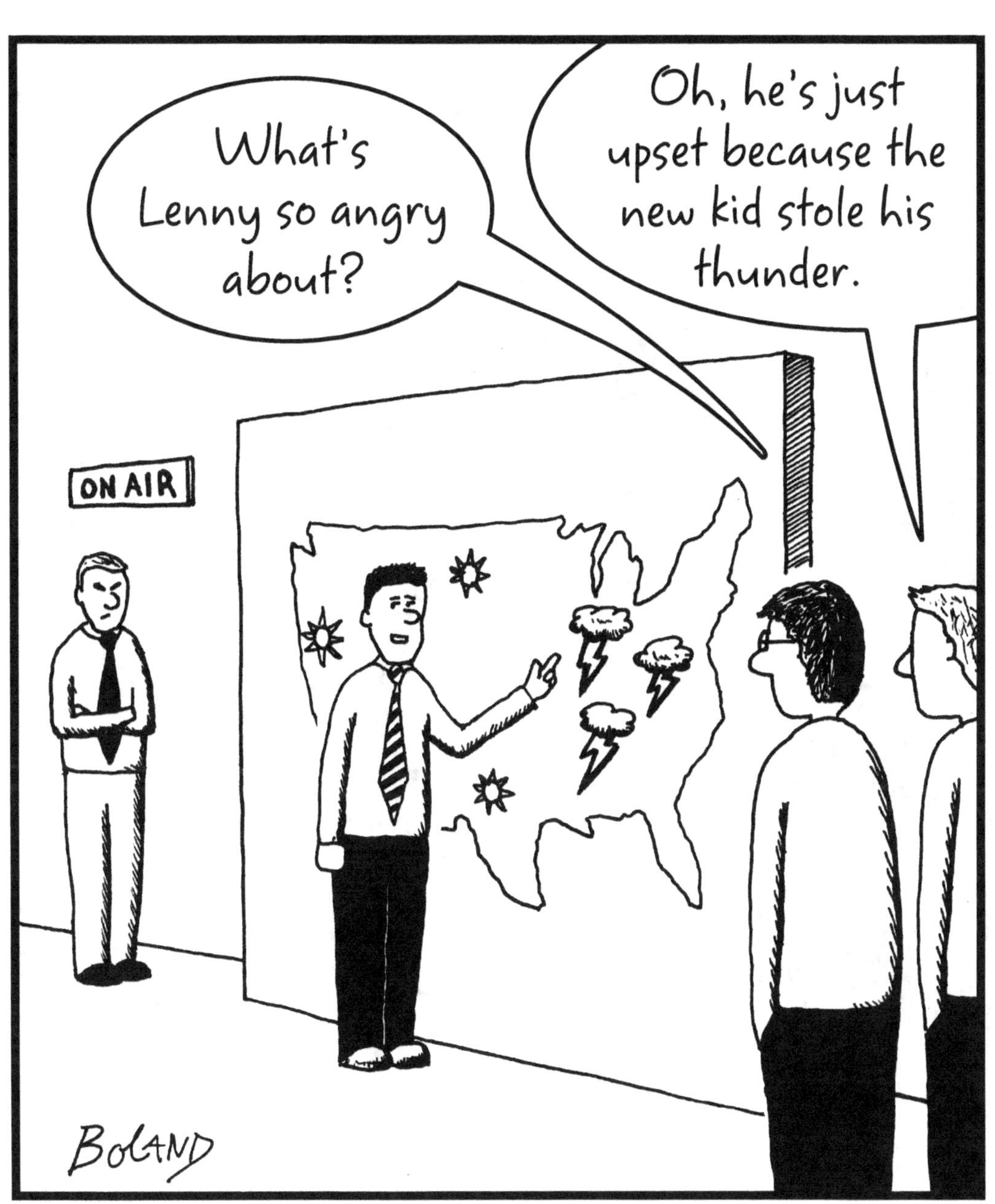
What's Lenny so angry about?
Oh, he's just upset because the new kid stole his thunder.
ON AIR
BOLAND

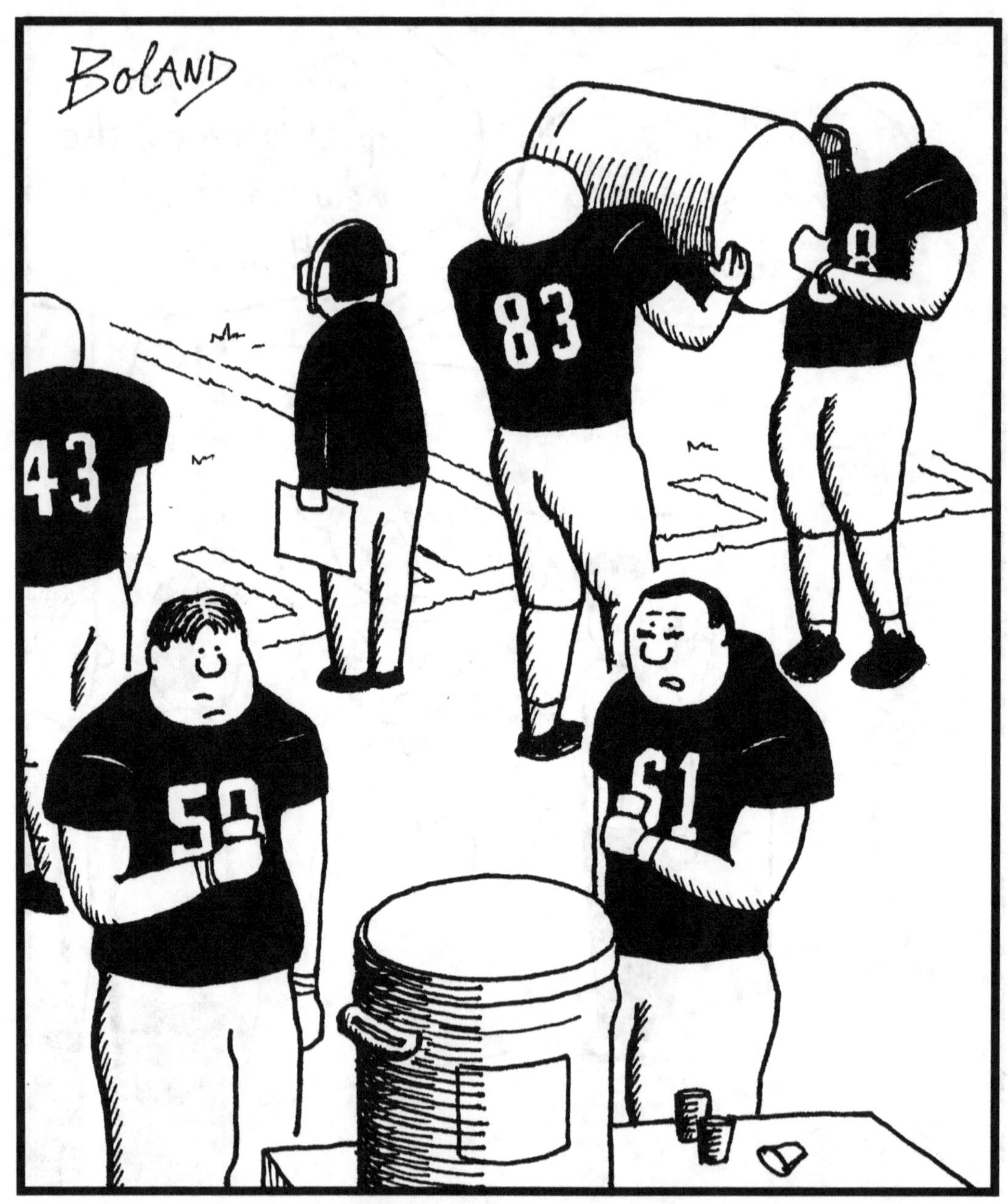

“Water? Where’d the hot chocolate go?”

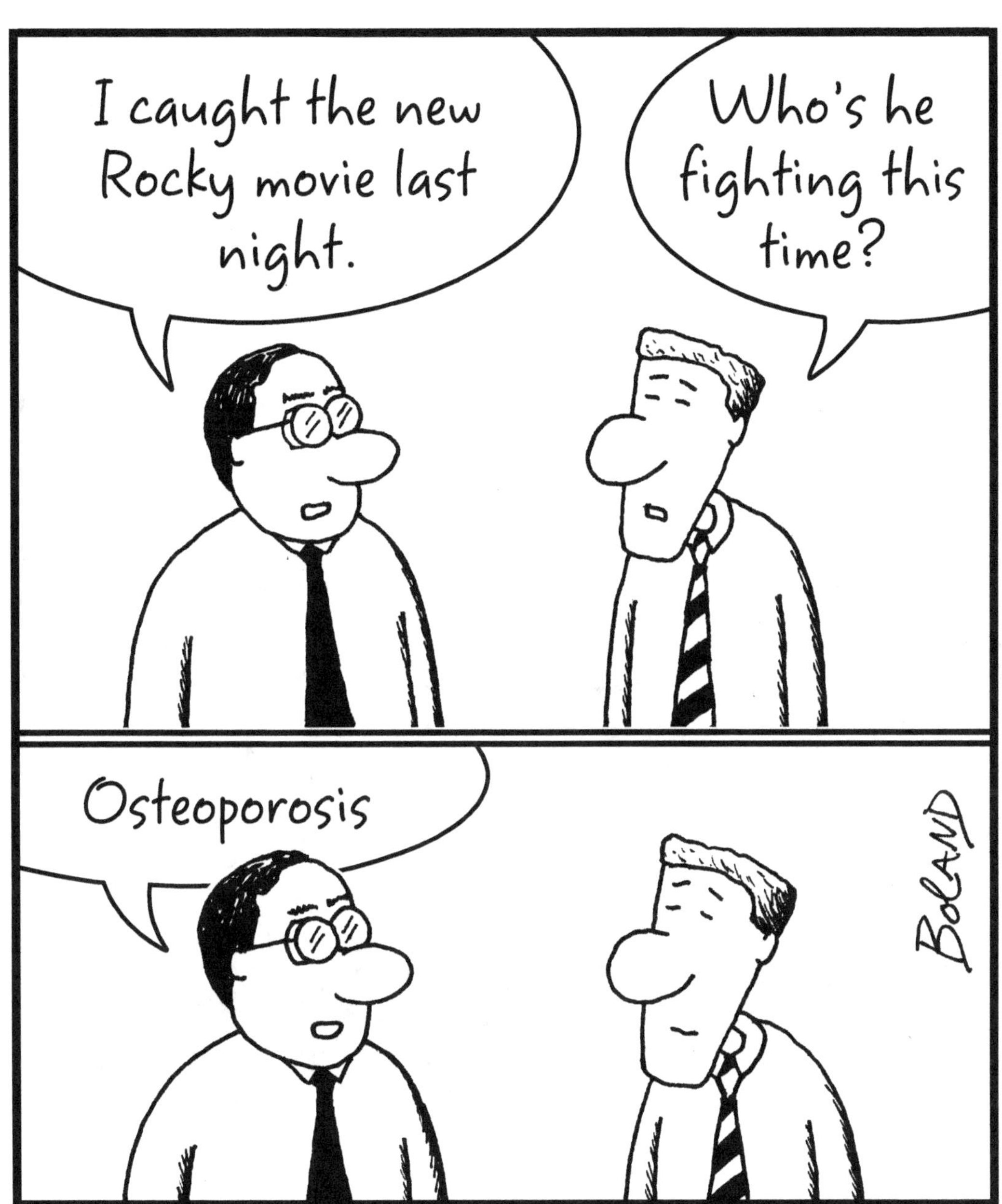
I caught the new Rocky movie last night.
Who's he fighting this time?
Osteoporosis
BOLAND

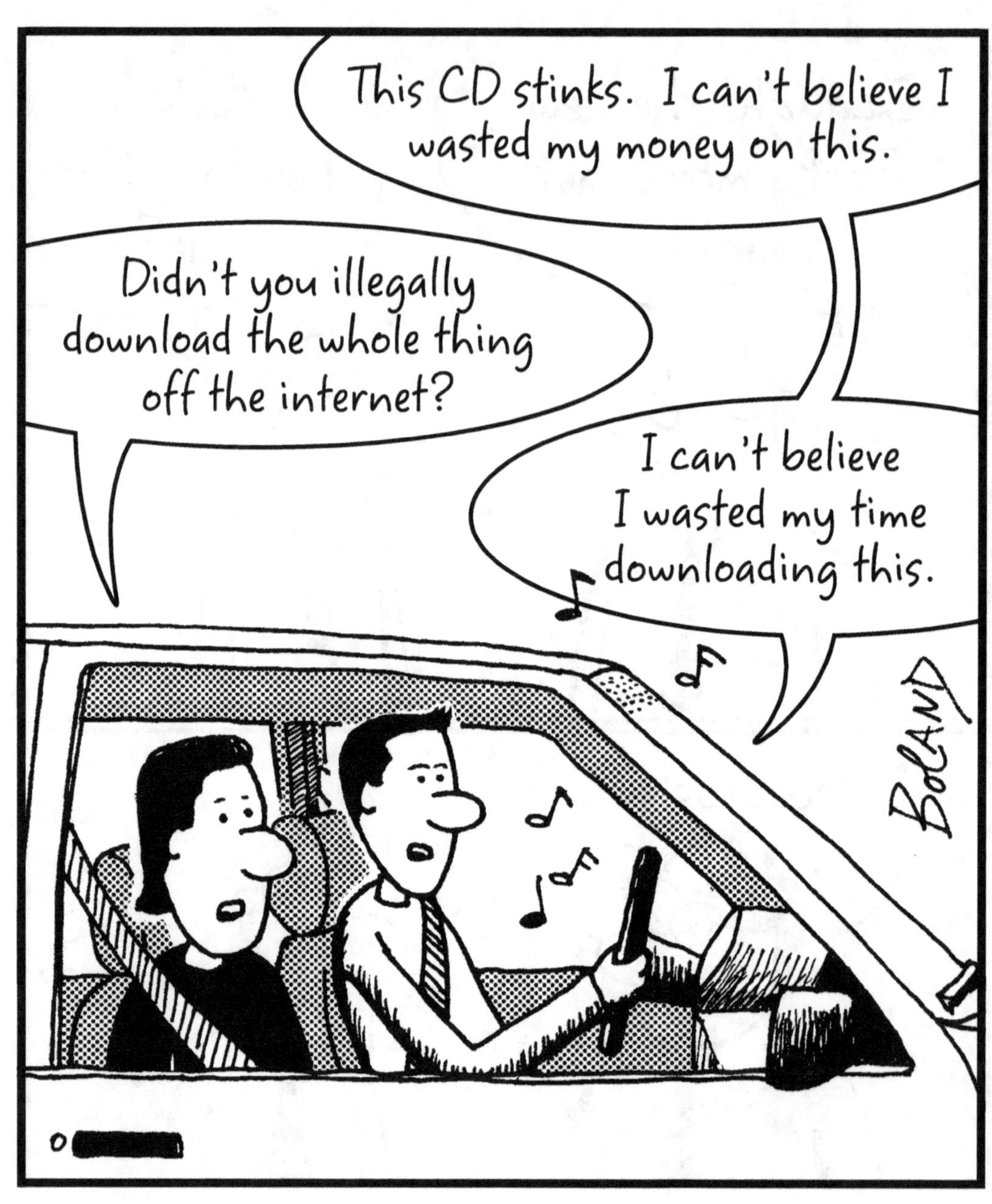
This CD stinks. I can't believe I wasted my money on this.
Didn't you illegally download the whole thing off the internet?
I can't believe I wasted my time downloading this.
BOLAND

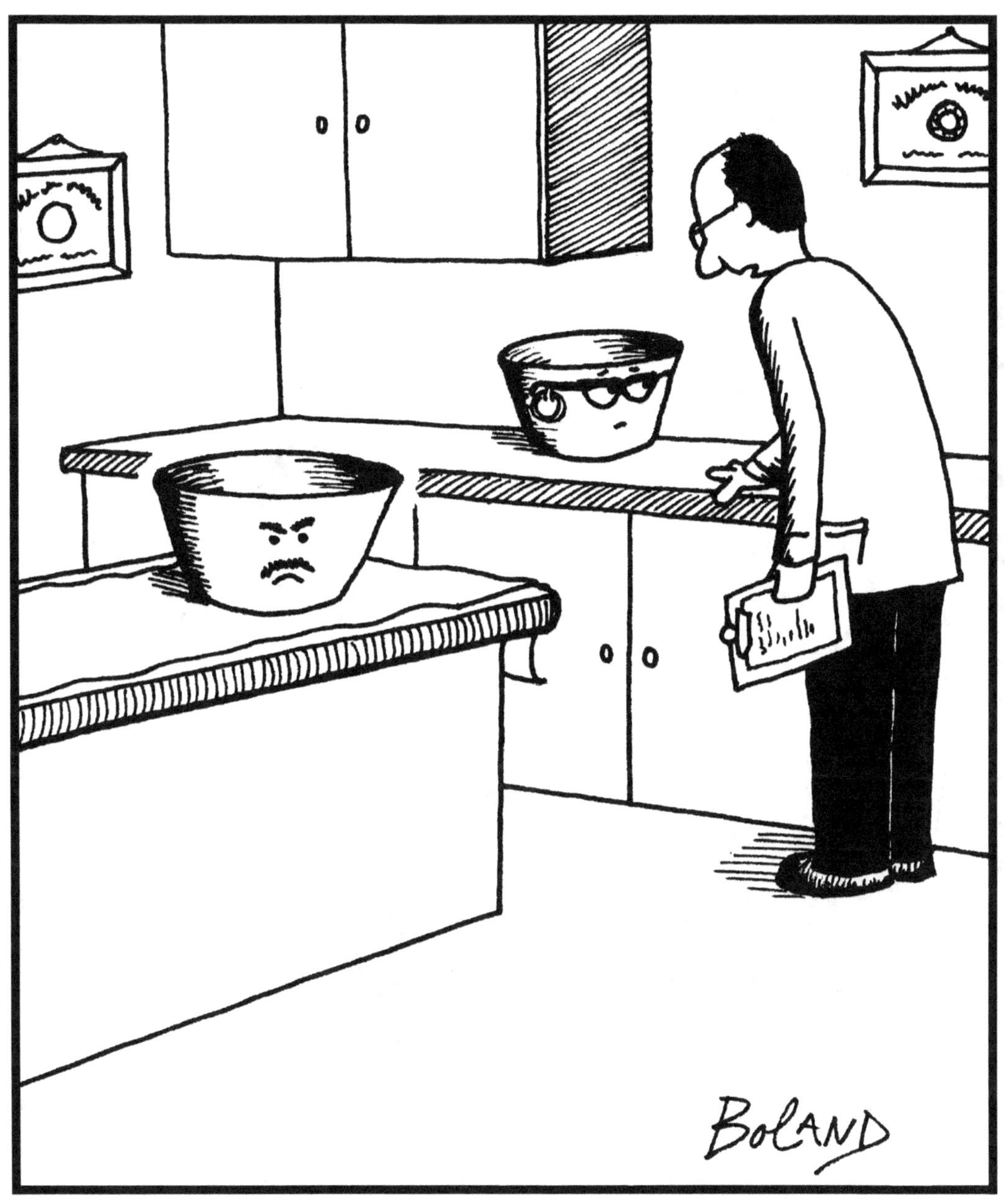

"You can rest easy, ma'am. Your husband simply has a case of irritable bowl syndrome."

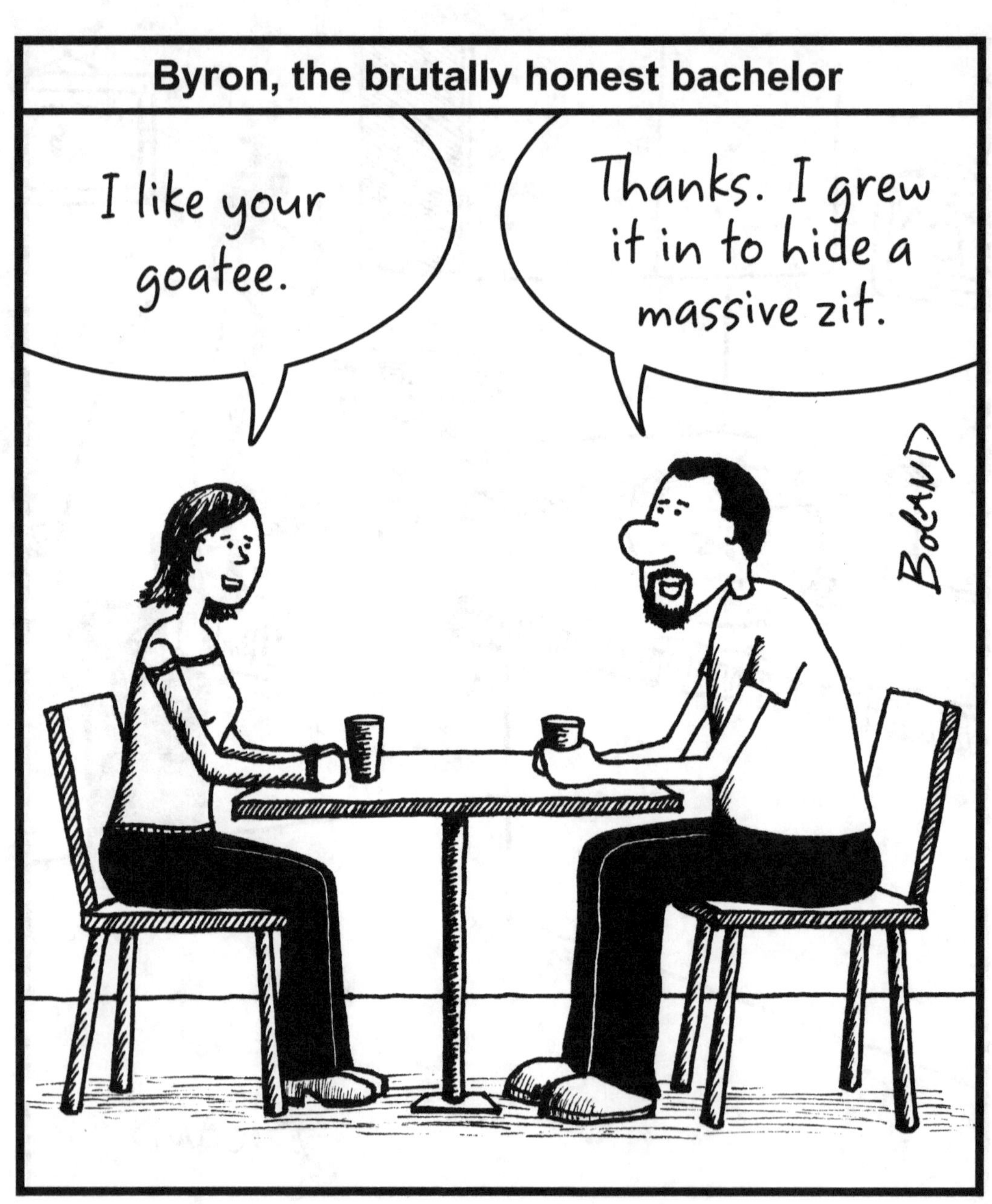
Byron, the brutally honest bachelor
I like your goatee.
Thanks. I grew it in to hide a massive zit.
BOLAND

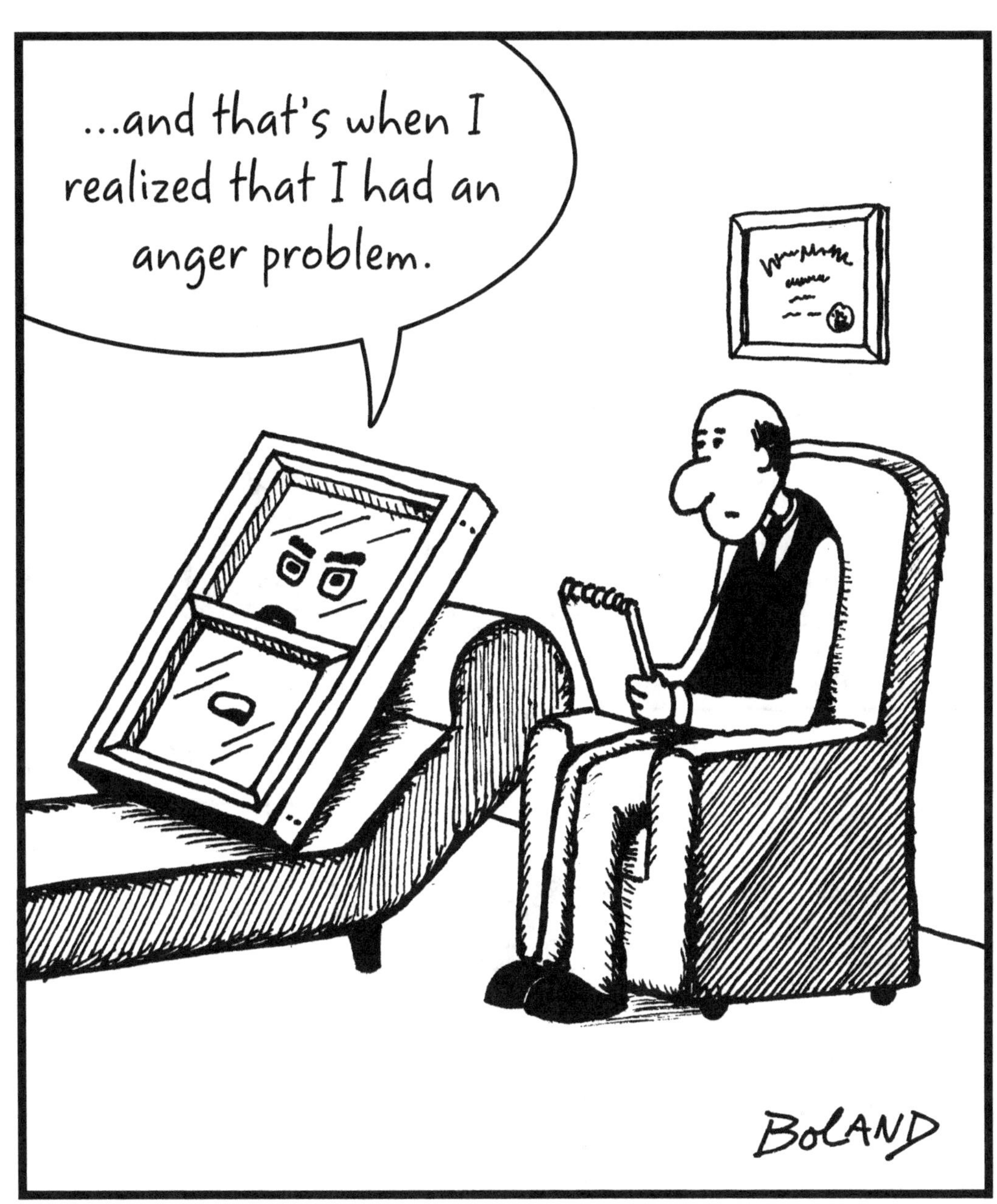

Tempered Glass

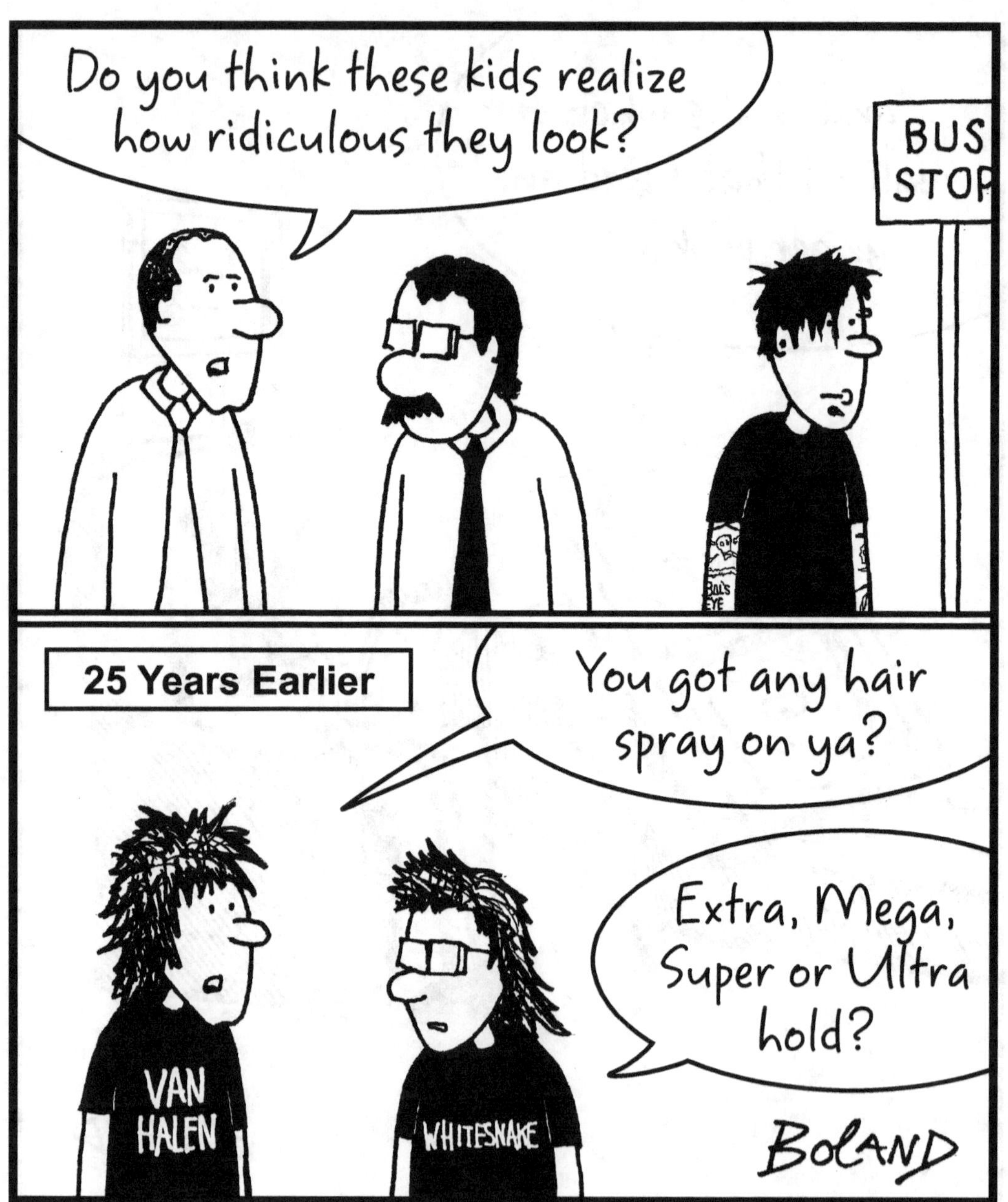
Do you think these kids realize how ridiculous they look?
BUS STOP
25 Years Earlier
You got any hair spray on ya?
Extra, Mega, Super or Ultra hold?
VAN HALEN
WHITESNAKE
BOLAND

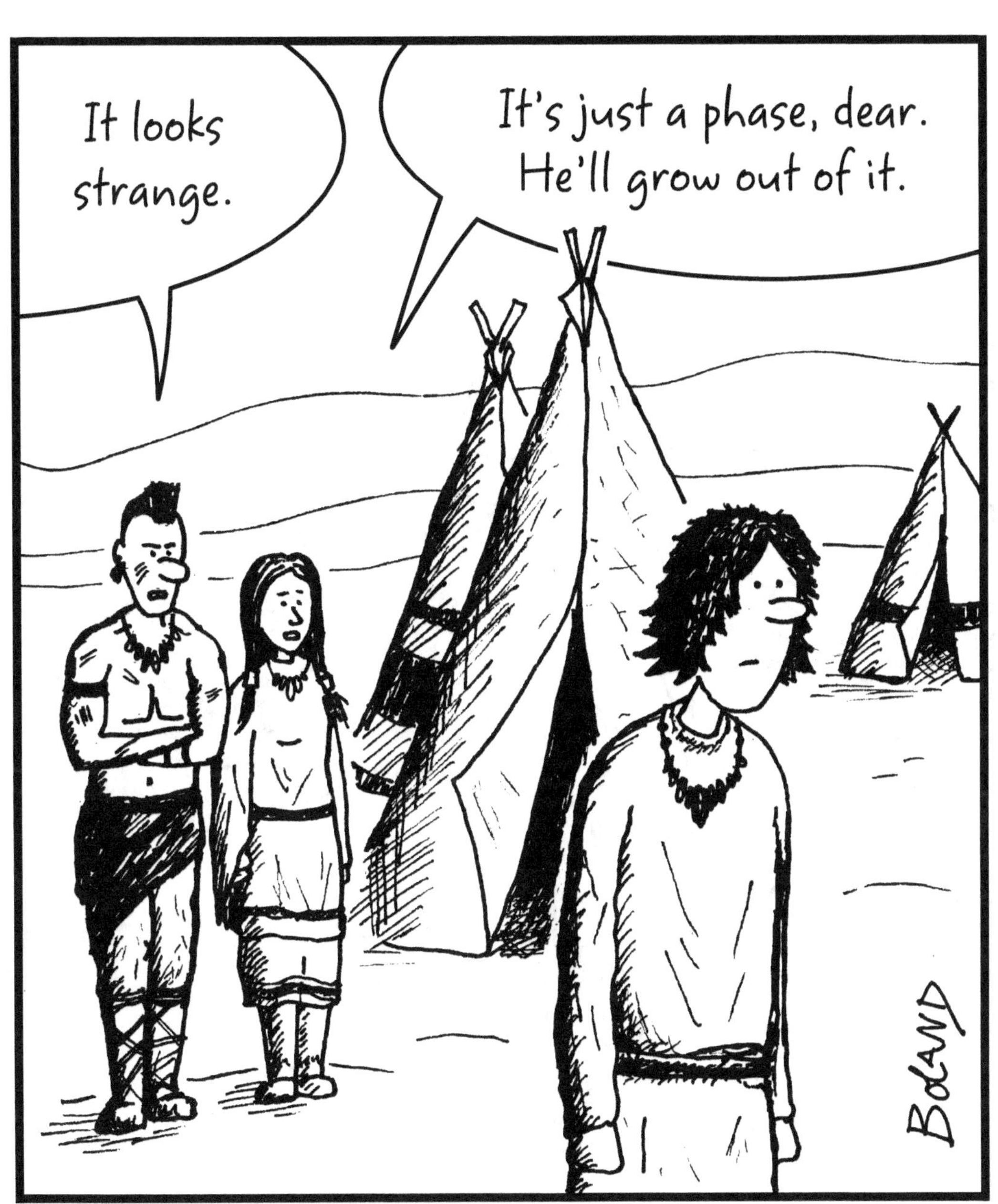
It looks strange.
It's just a phase, dear. He'll grow out of it.
BOLAND

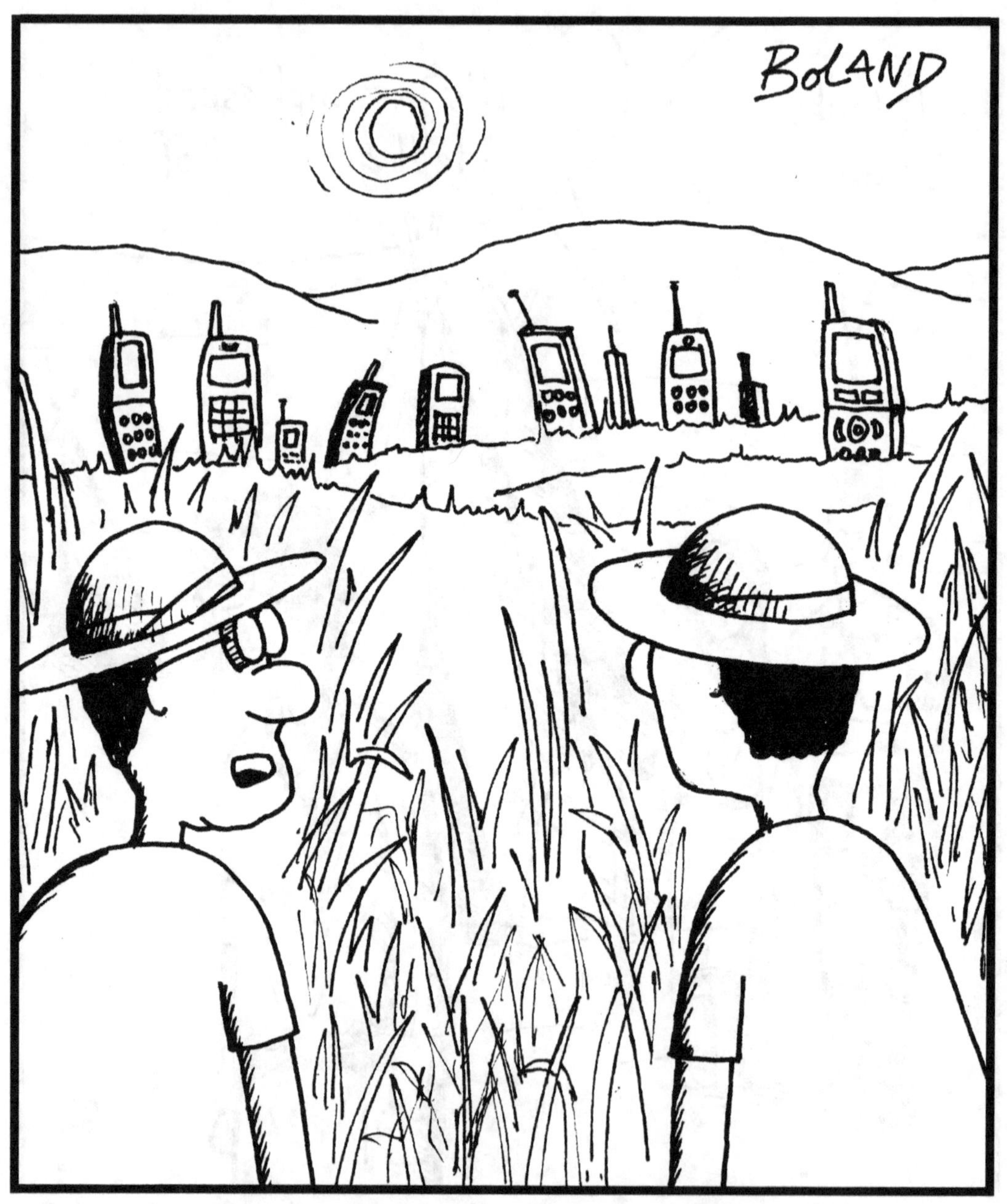

"Look at them, Hayduk. ...So beautiful, so quiet, so distant from civilization. They really are quite majestic when they're roaming."

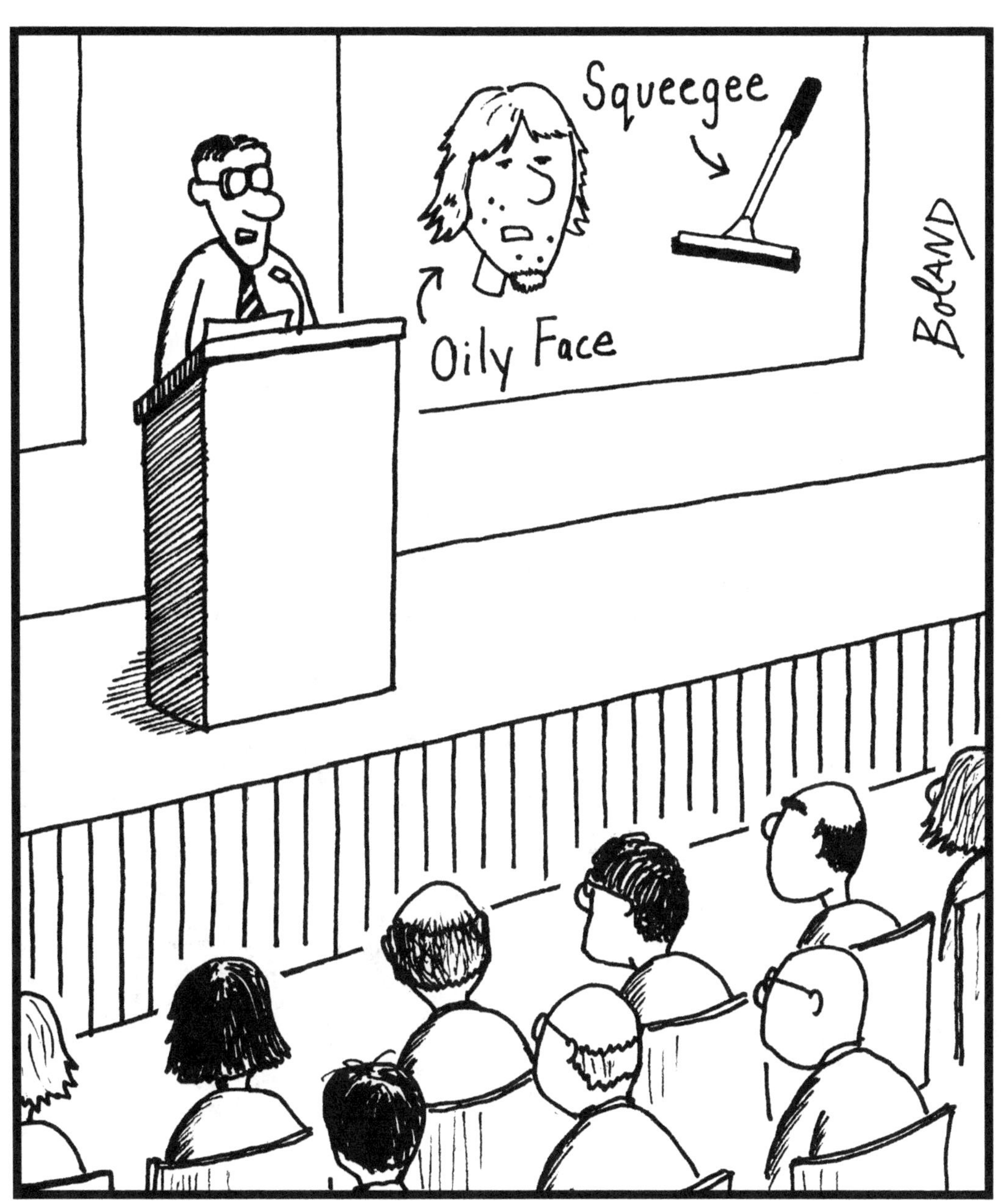

"Ladies and gentlemen, fellow scientists... I present to you the holy grail of renewable energy."

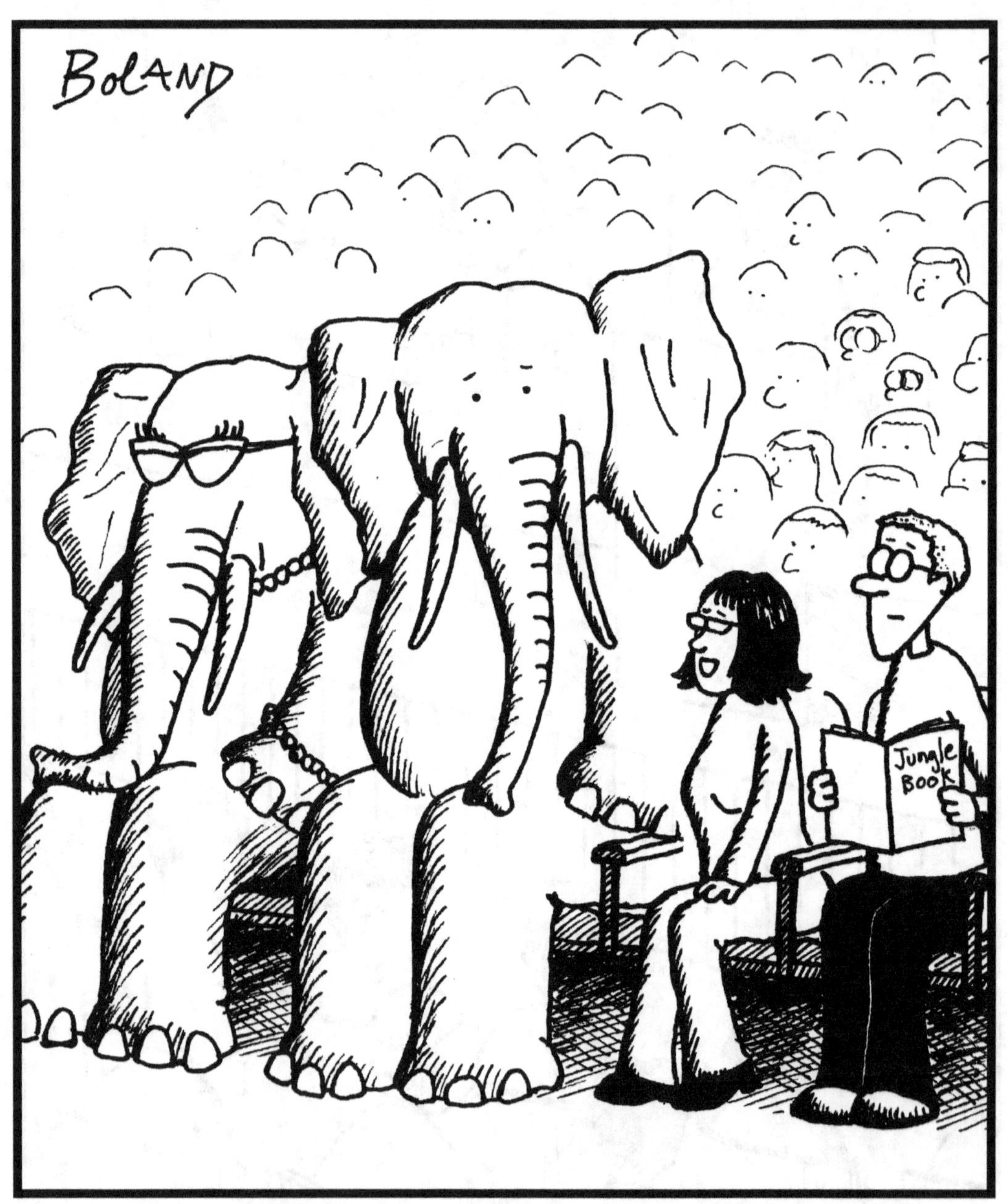

"Our daughter is playing the monkey. Which one did you say was yours, again?"

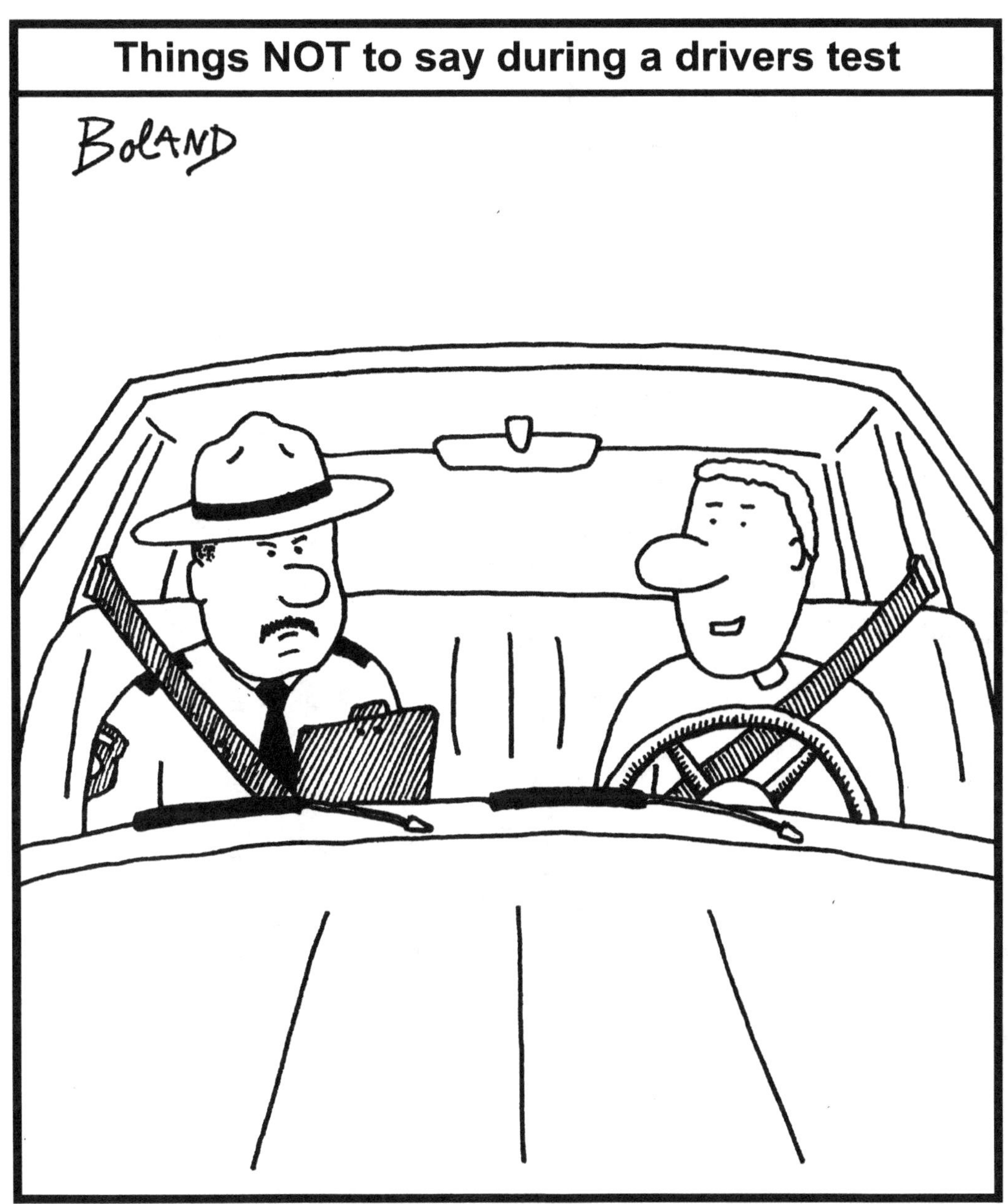

“Can I get bonus points if I drive with my knees?”

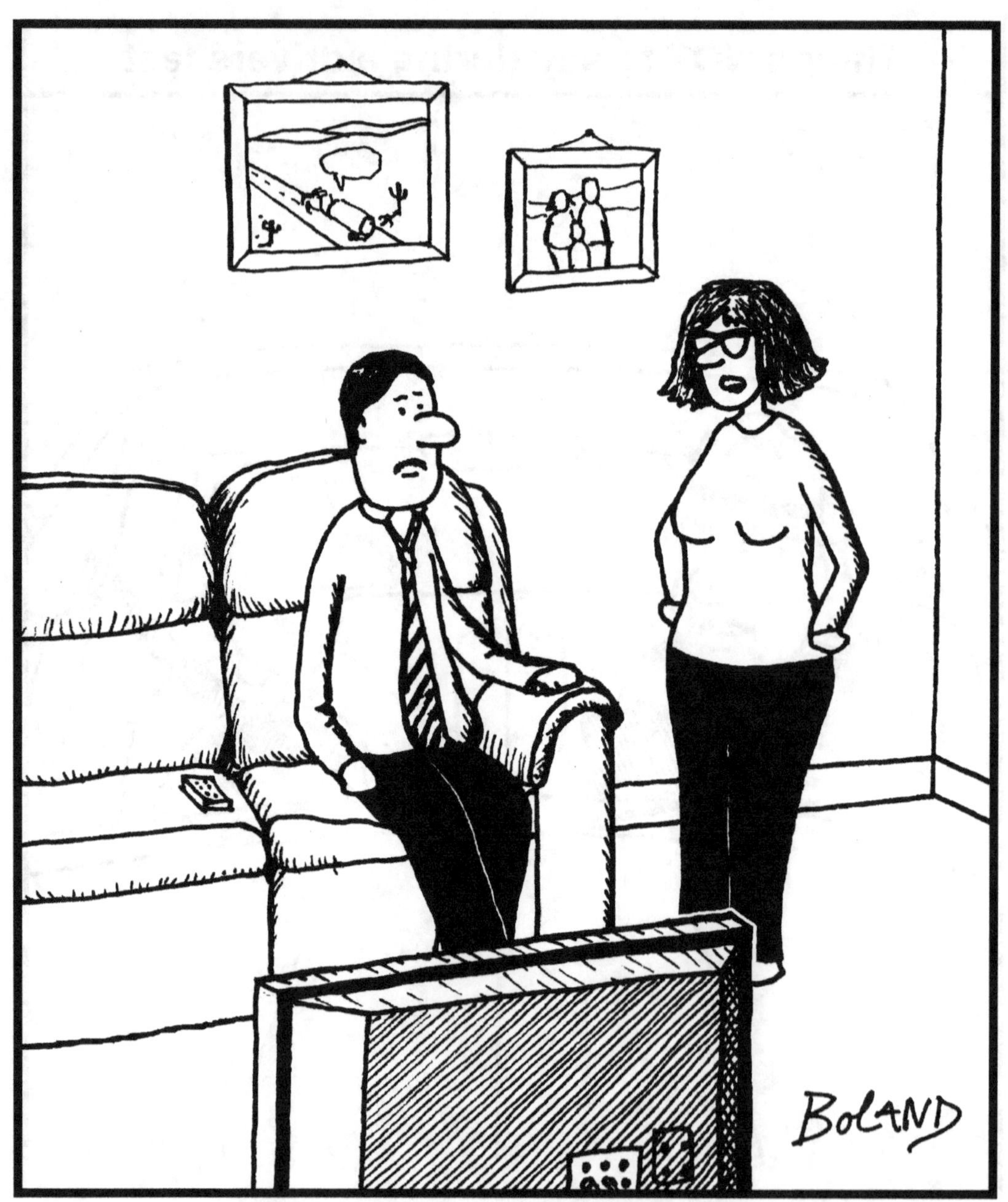

"I don't want Junior watching the news anymore. Today he said he couldn't finish his chores without a bailout."

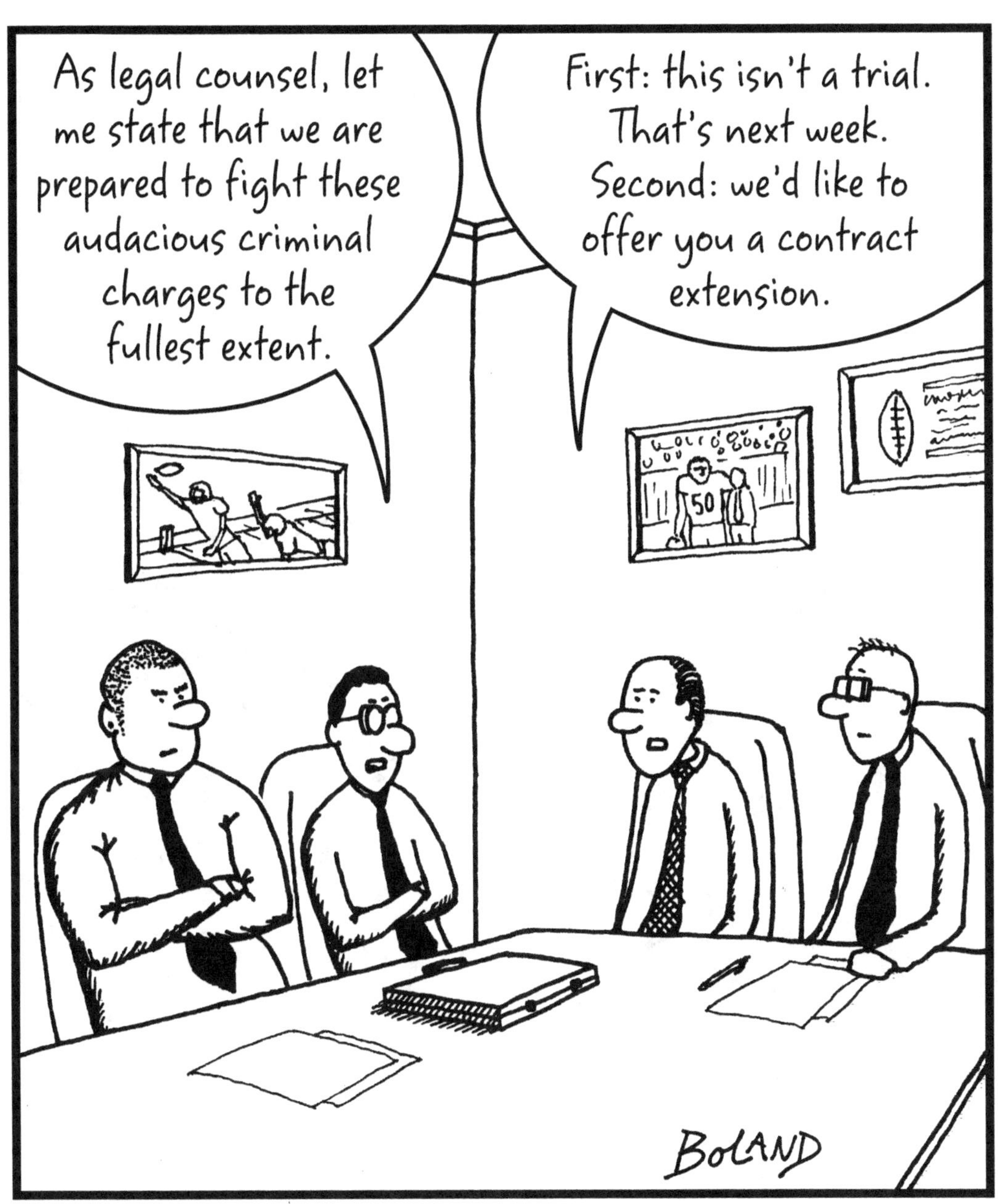
As legal counsel, let me state that we are prepared to fight these audacious criminal charges to the fullest extent.
First: this isn't a trial. That's next week. Second: we'd like to offer you a contract extension.
50
BOLAND

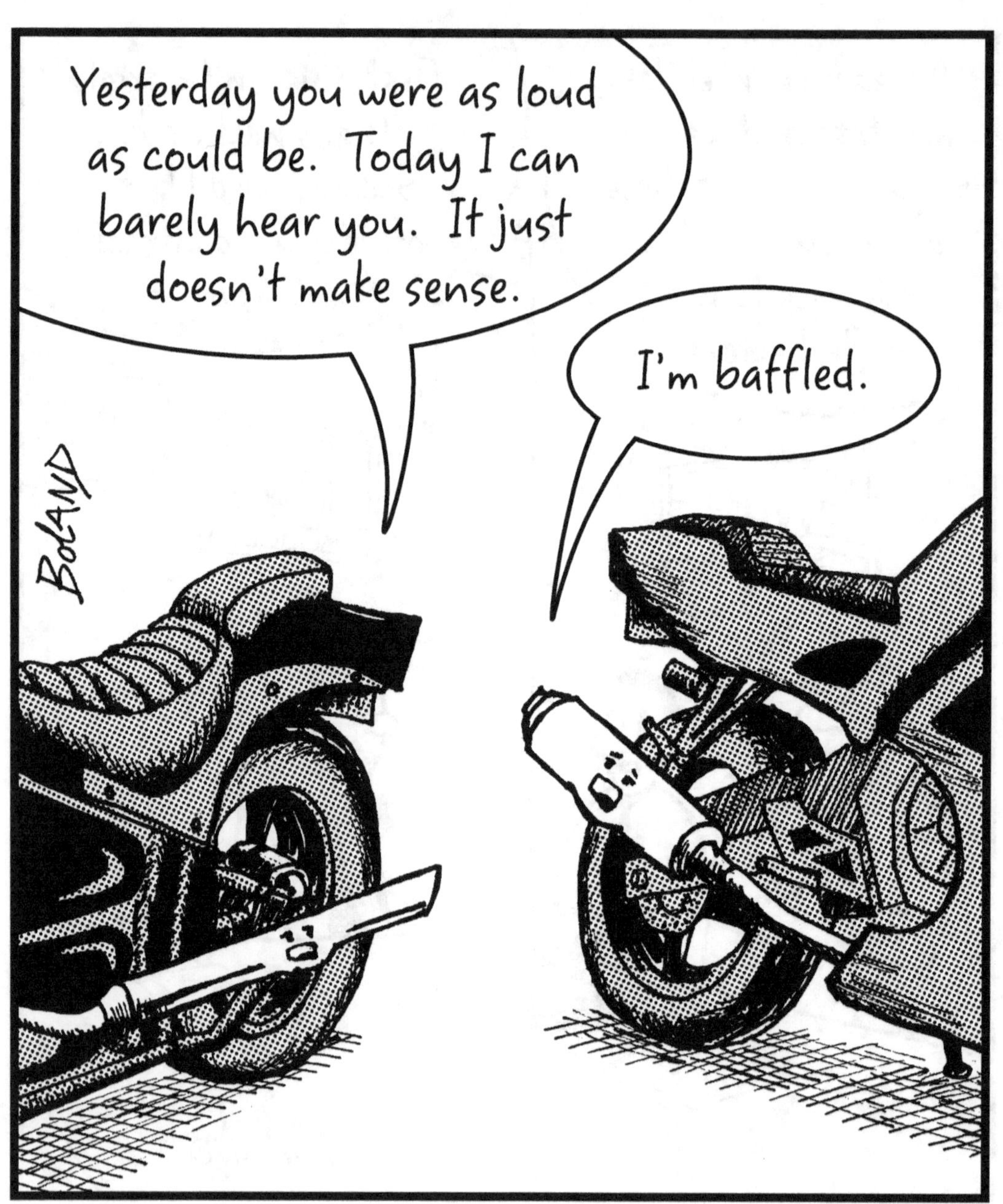
Yesterday you were as loud as could be. Today I can barely hear you. It just doesn't make sense.
I'm baffled.
BoLAND

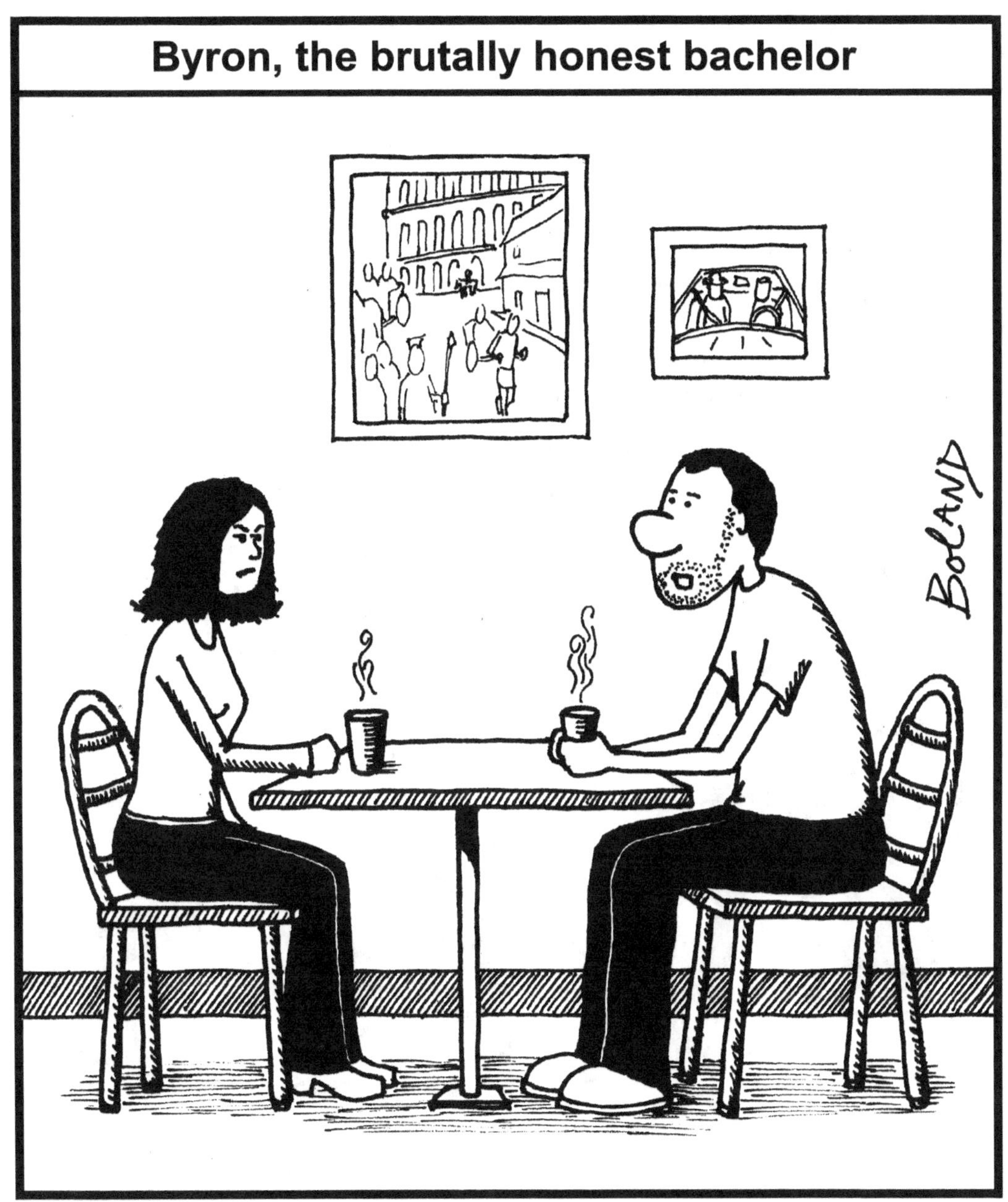

"Whoa..Turn your head. Did I just spot some grays? How old did you say you were?"

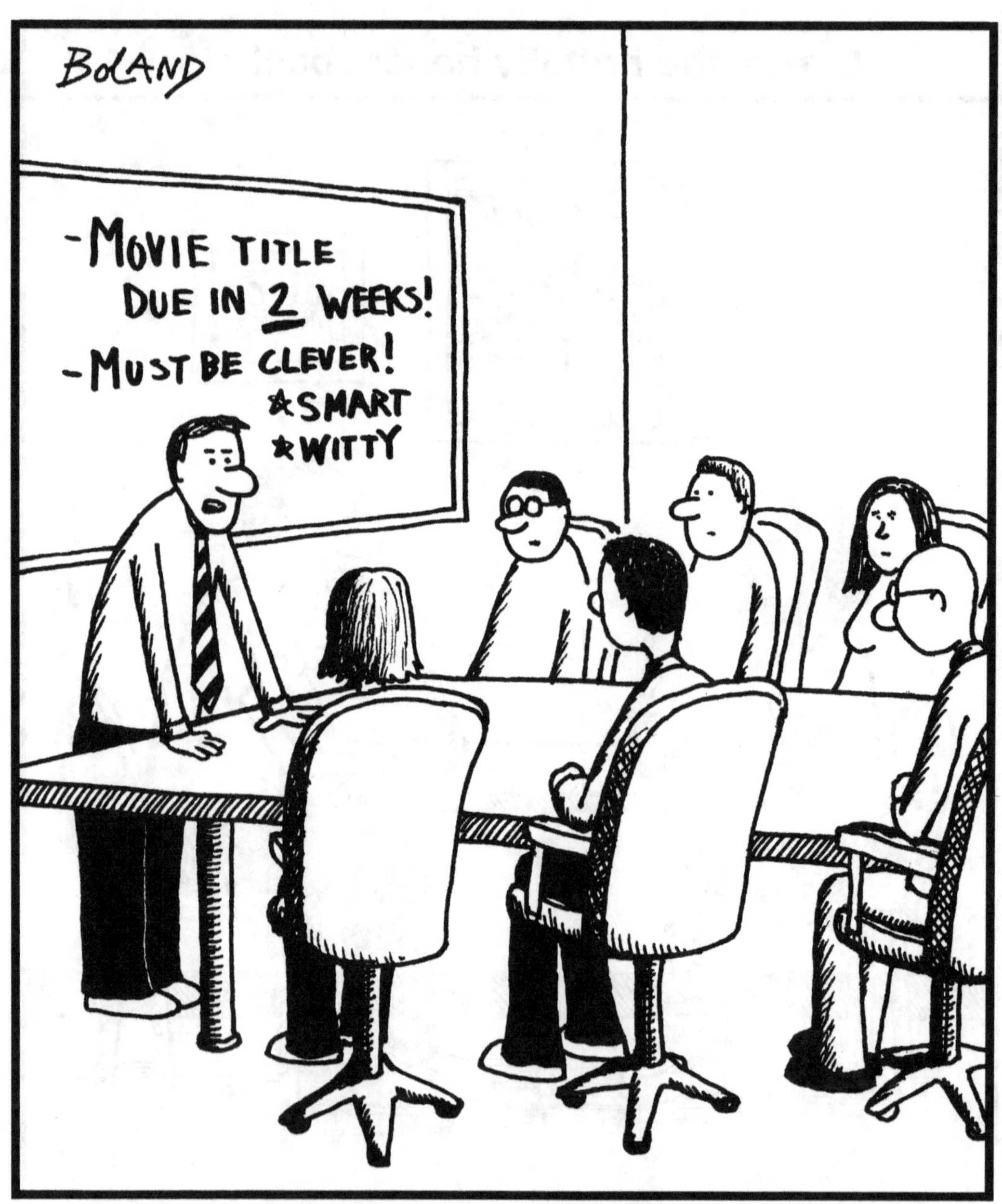

"OK, let's recap, folks. We've got Samuel L. Jackson. We've got snakes. We've got a plane. Now, let's show everybody why we make the big bucks."

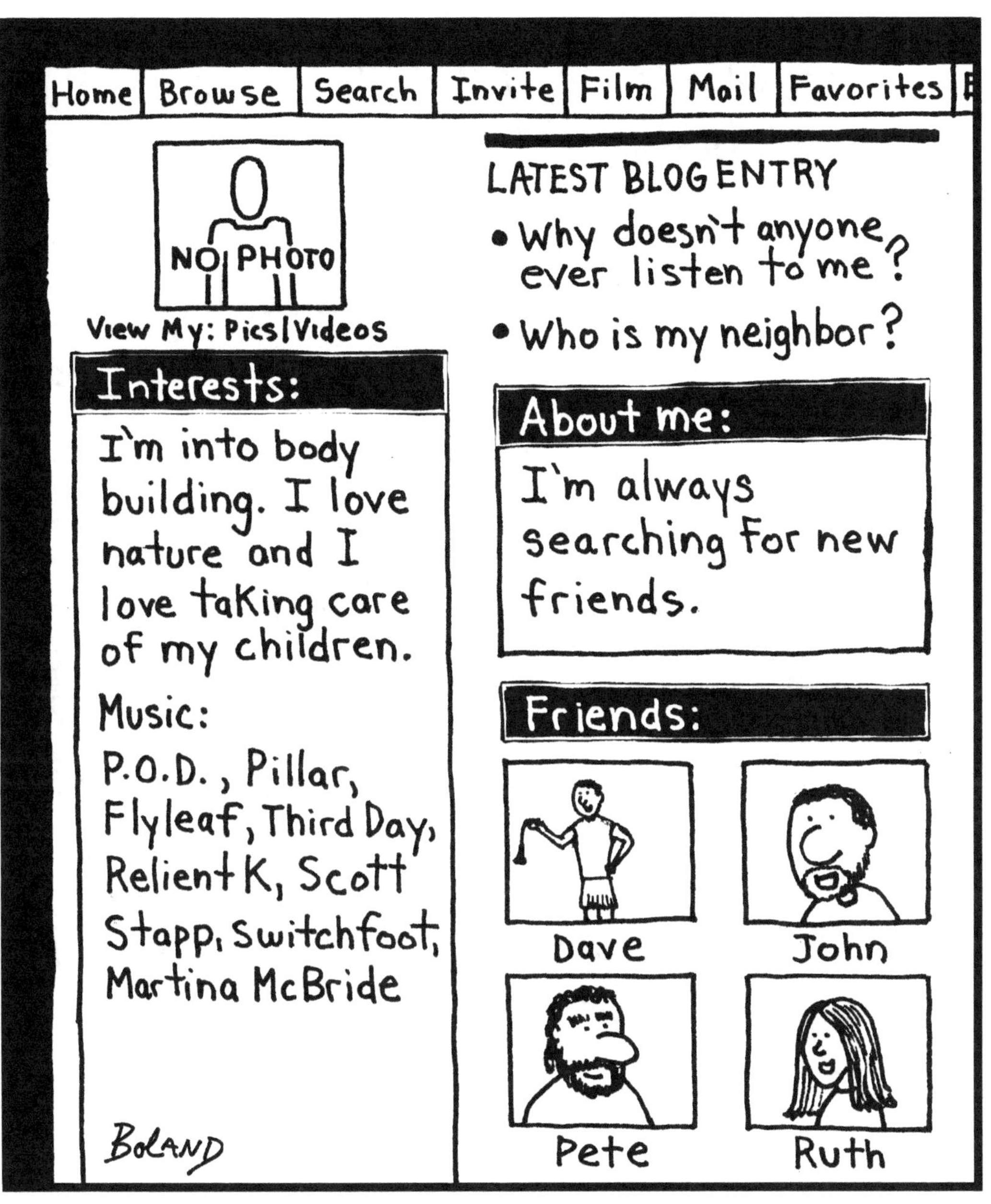

God's social network page

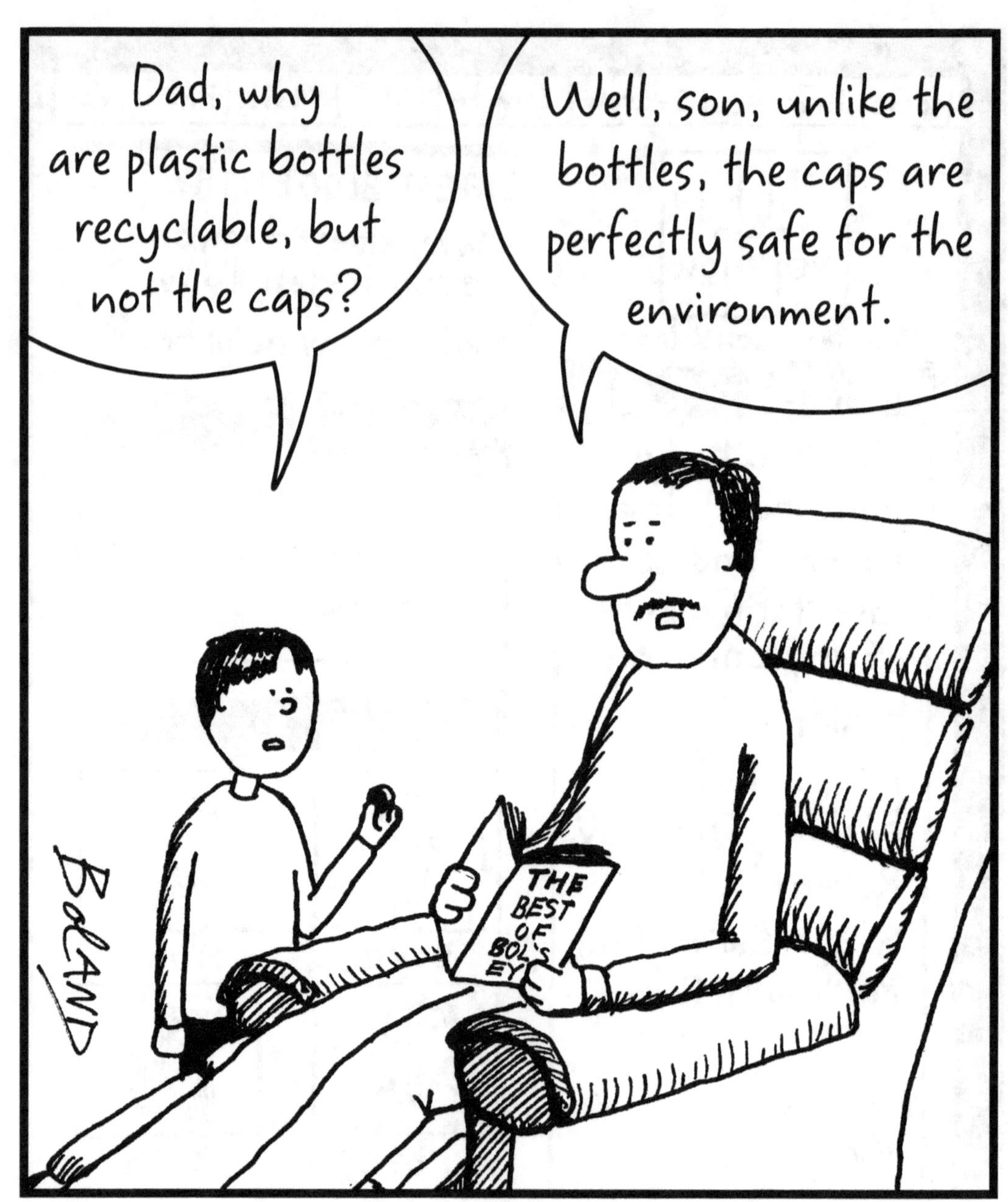
Dad, why are plastic bottles recyclable, but not the caps?
Well, son, unlike the bottles, the caps are perfectly safe for the environment.
THE BEST OF BOL'S EY
BOLAND

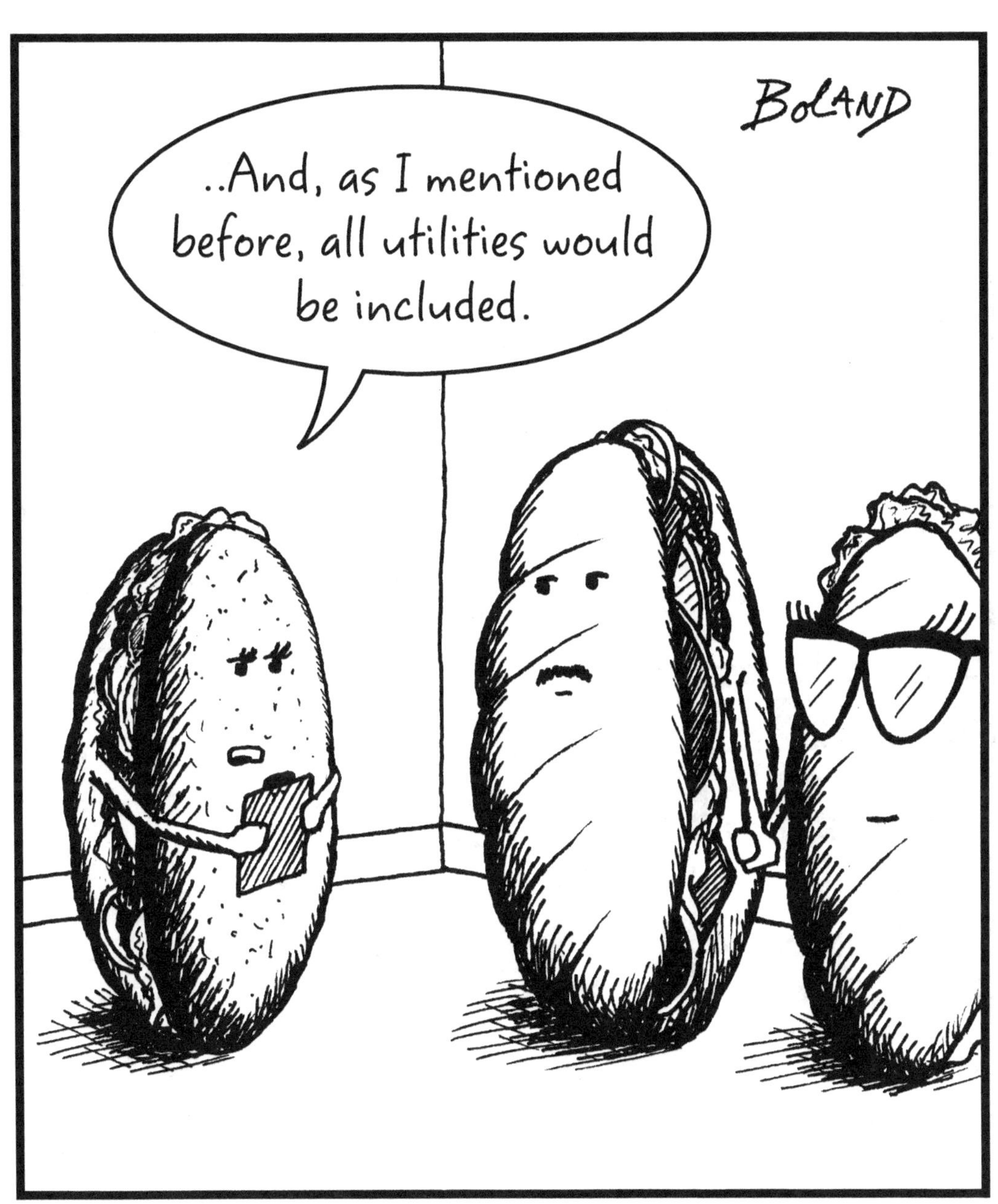
BOLAND
..And, as I mentioned before, all utilities would be included.

Sub Leasing

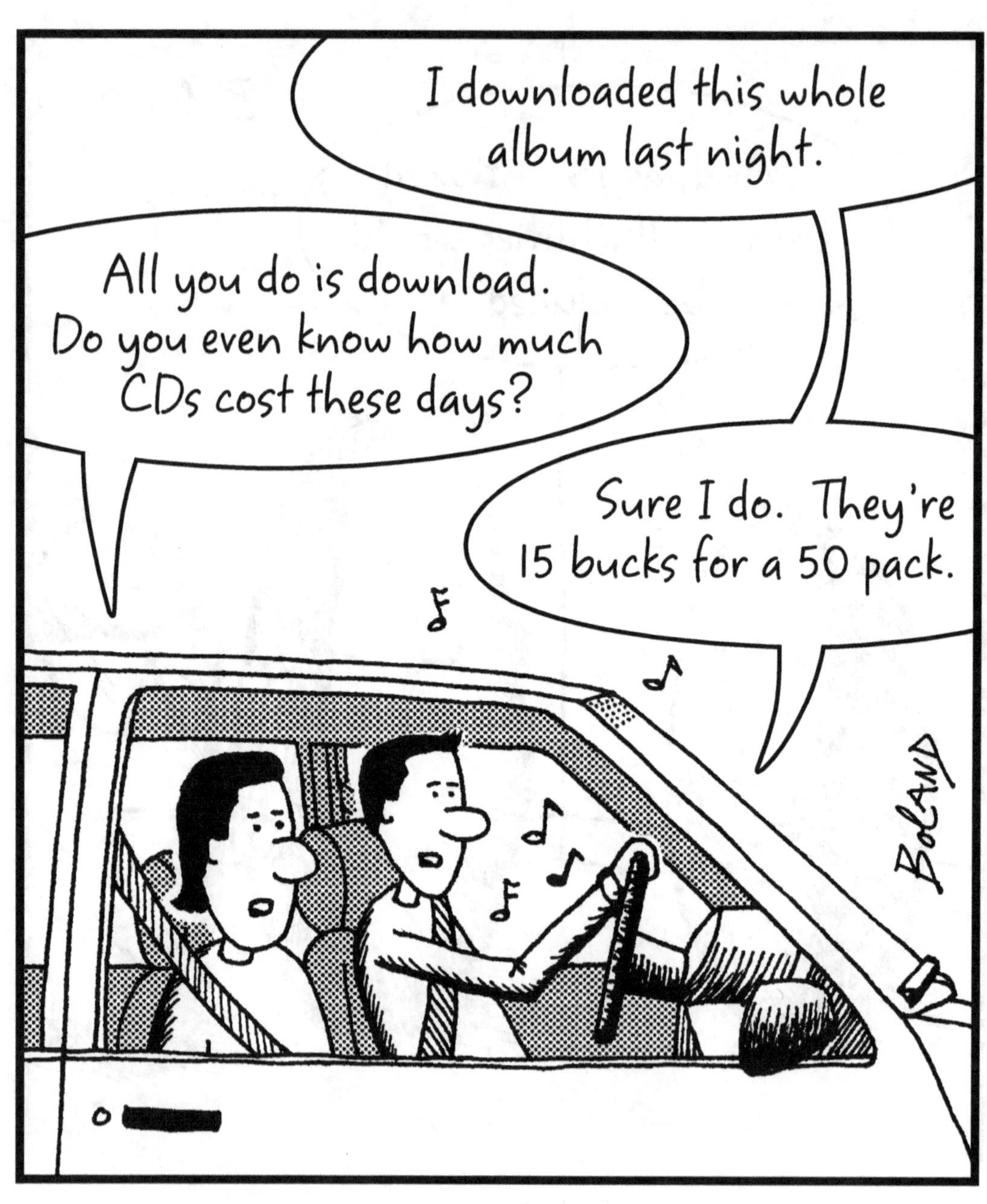
I downloaded this whole album last night.
All you do is download. Do you even know how much CDs cost these days?
Sure I do. They're 15 bucks for a 50 pack.
BOLAND

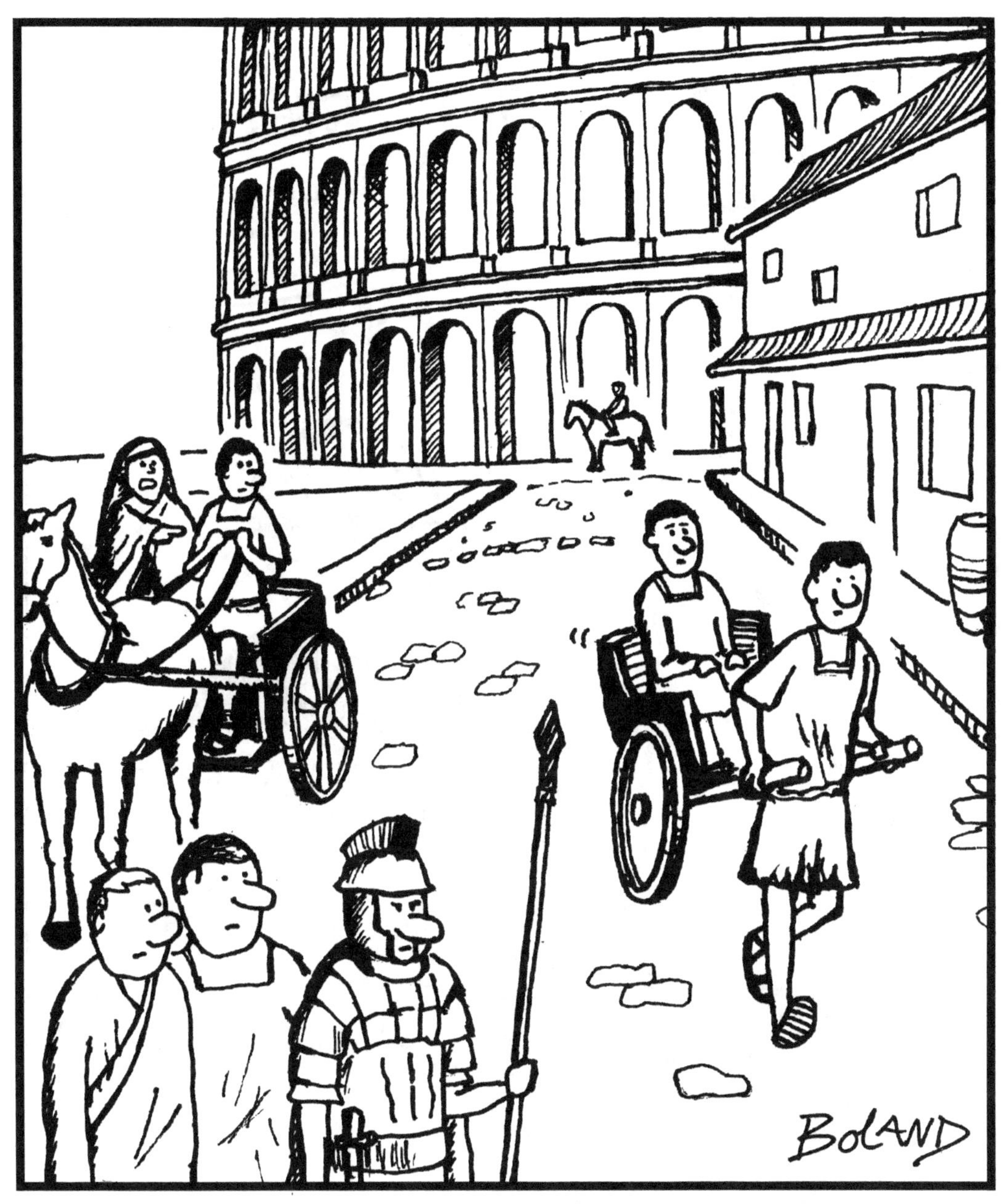

"Look, Dear. It's one of those hybrids."

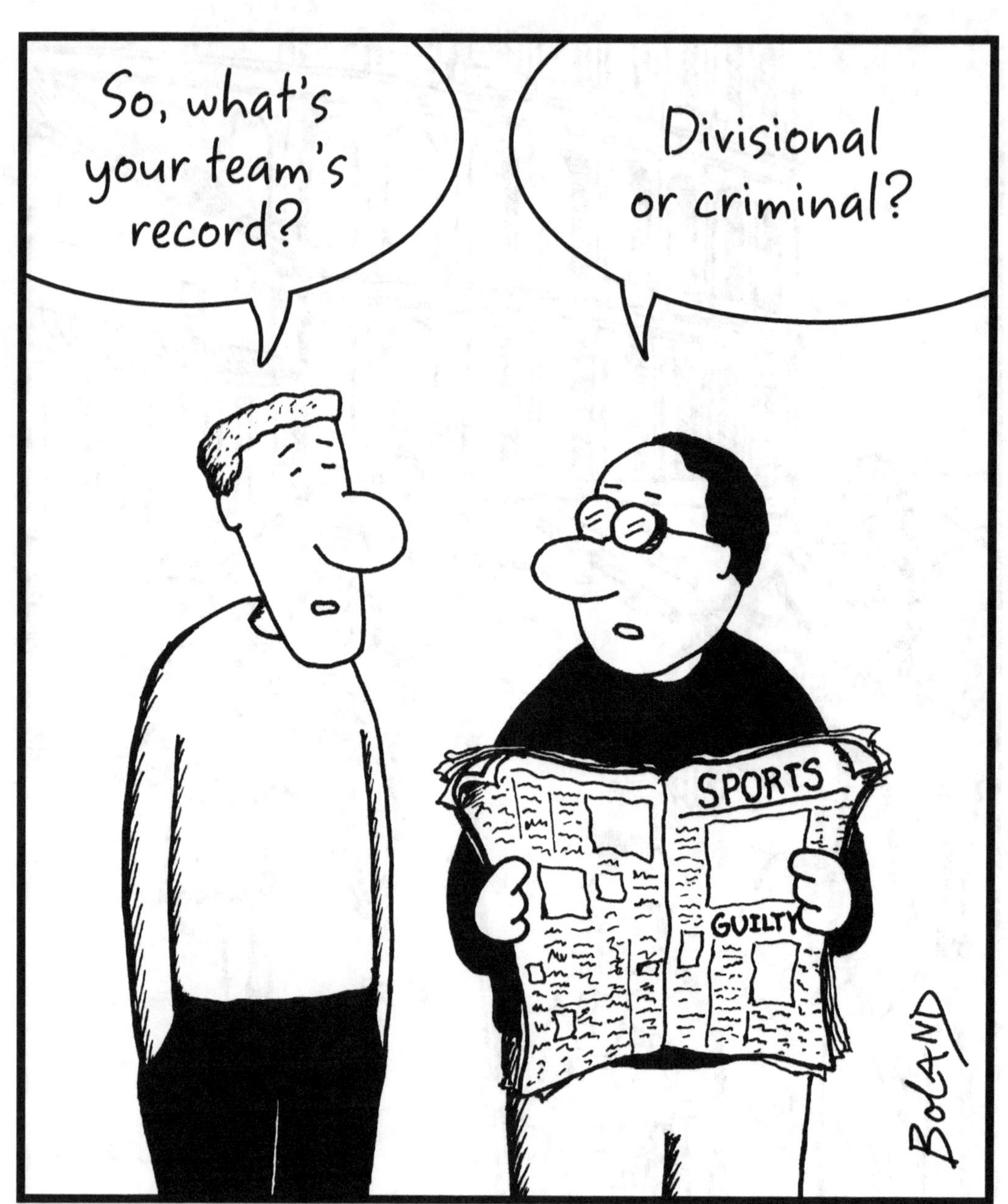
So, what's your team's record?
Divisional or criminal?
SPORTS
GUILTY
BOLAND

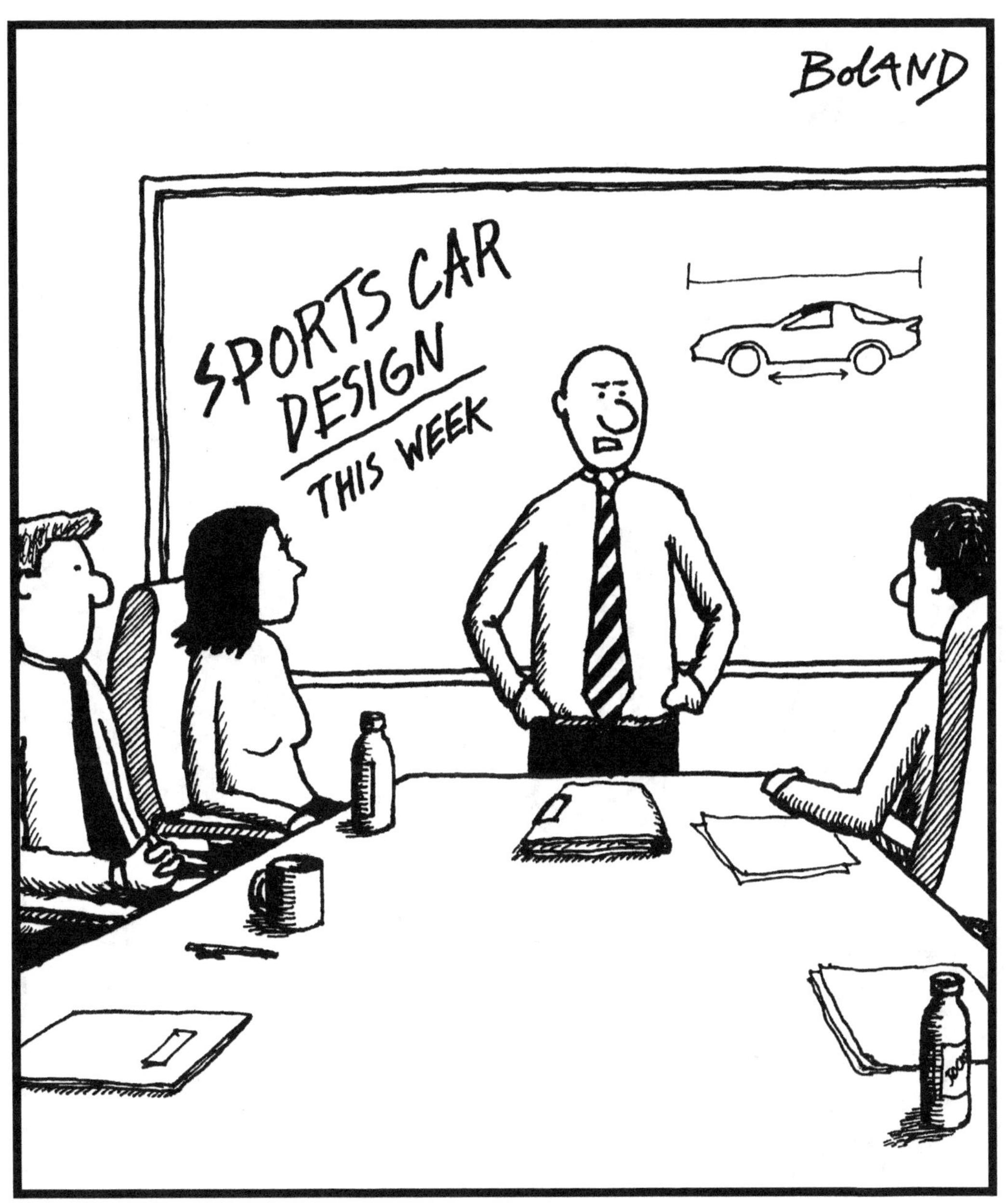

"Here's the plan, folks. We'll put out a design that no one will like. Then, after poor sales we'll discontinue the model. Later, we'll bring it back with a retro look and all get rich. Any questions? Good. Now, let's get out there and make this failure happen."

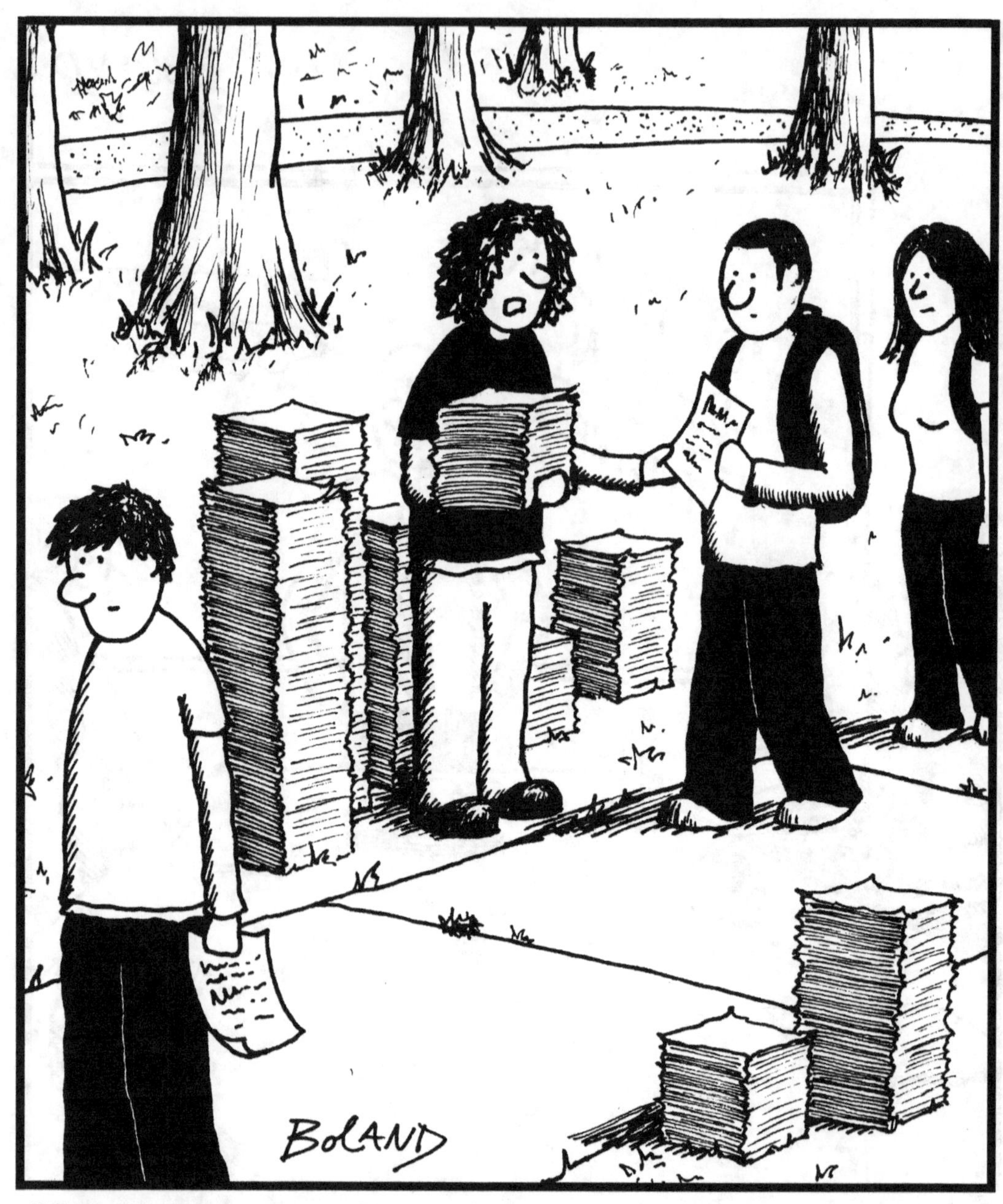

"Save the trees...Save the trees...Save the trees..."

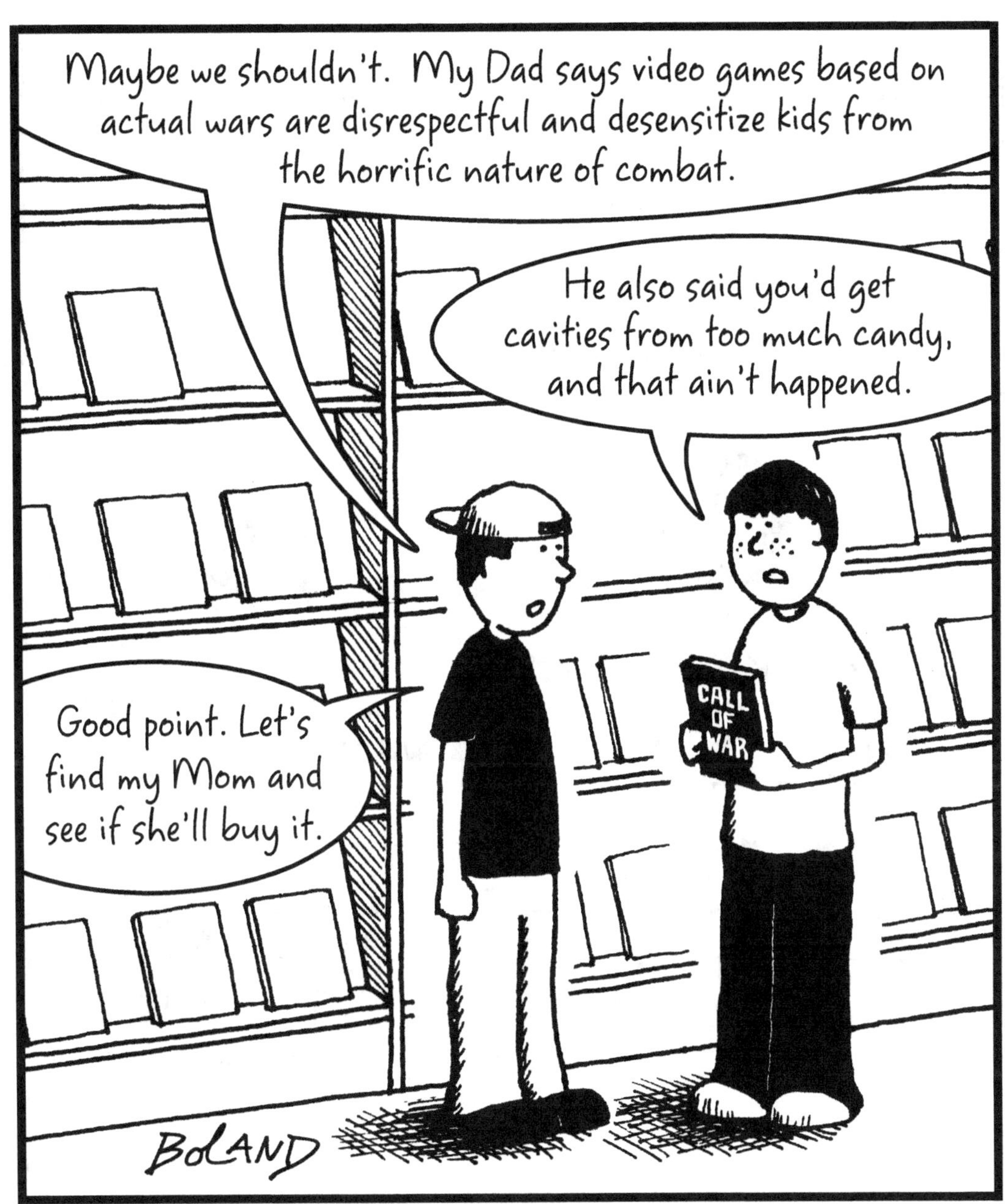
Maybe we shouldn't. My Dad says video games based on actual wars are disrespectful and desensitize kids from the horrific nature of combat.
He also said you'd get cavities from too much candy, and that ain't happened.
Good point. Let's find my Mom and see if she'll buy it.
CALL OF WAR
BOLAND

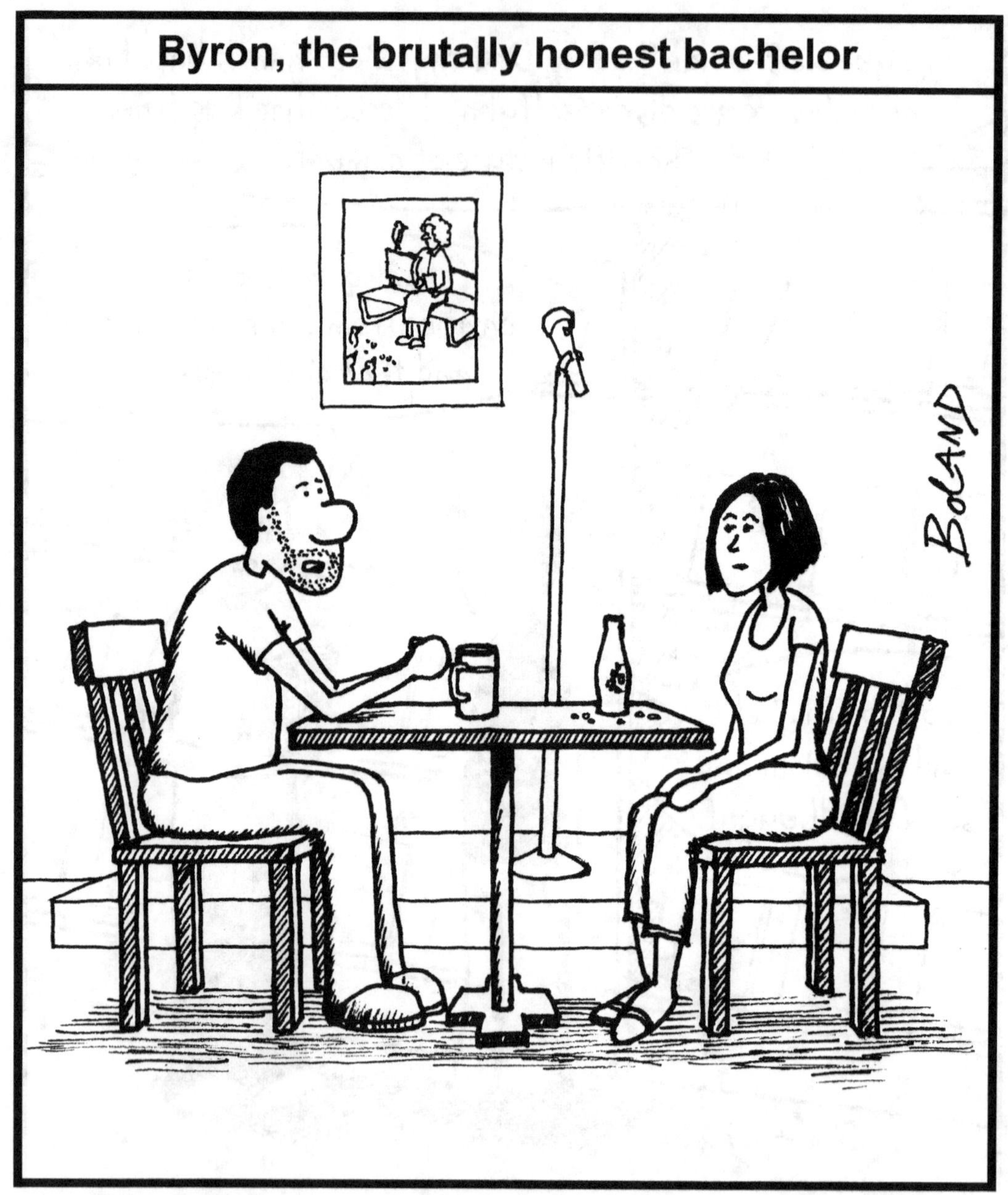

Byron, the brutally honest bachelor

“My friends keep telling me that you’re out of my league, but I told them that you’re the kind of girl that would settle.”

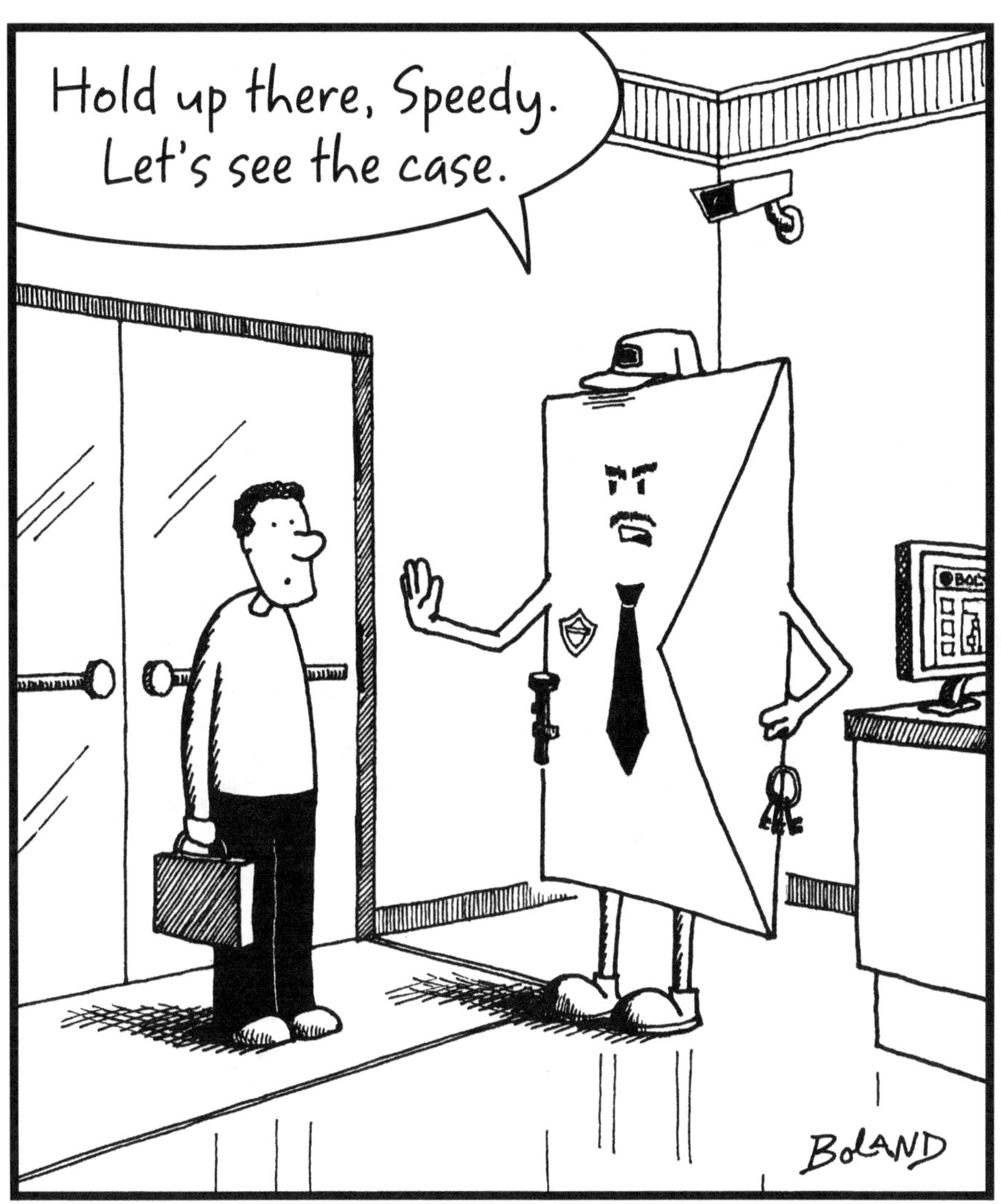

Security Envelope

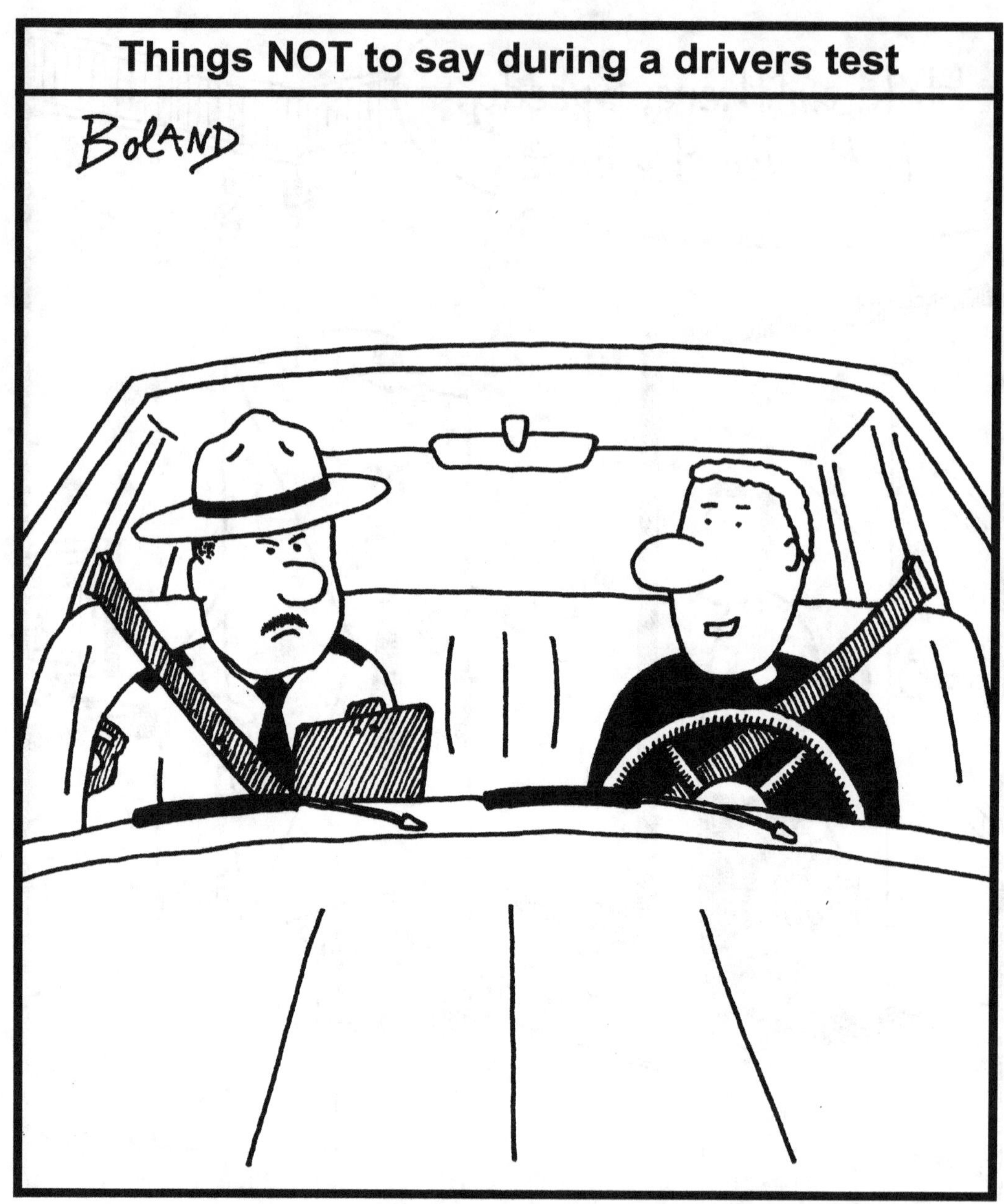

"It's uncanny. You look just like my aunt.... Except she has a fuller mustache"

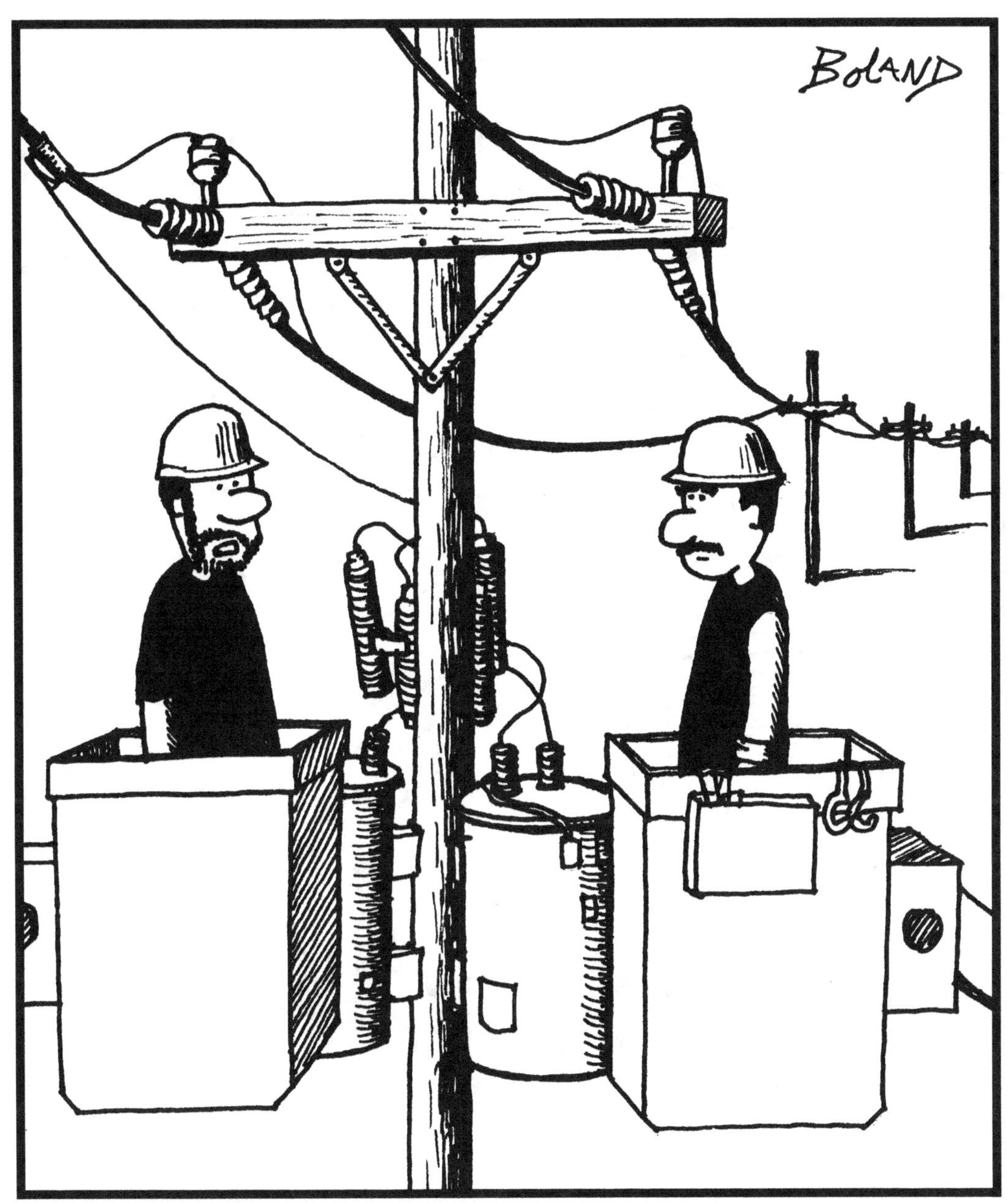

"This isn't what I meant when I asked the boss for a raise."

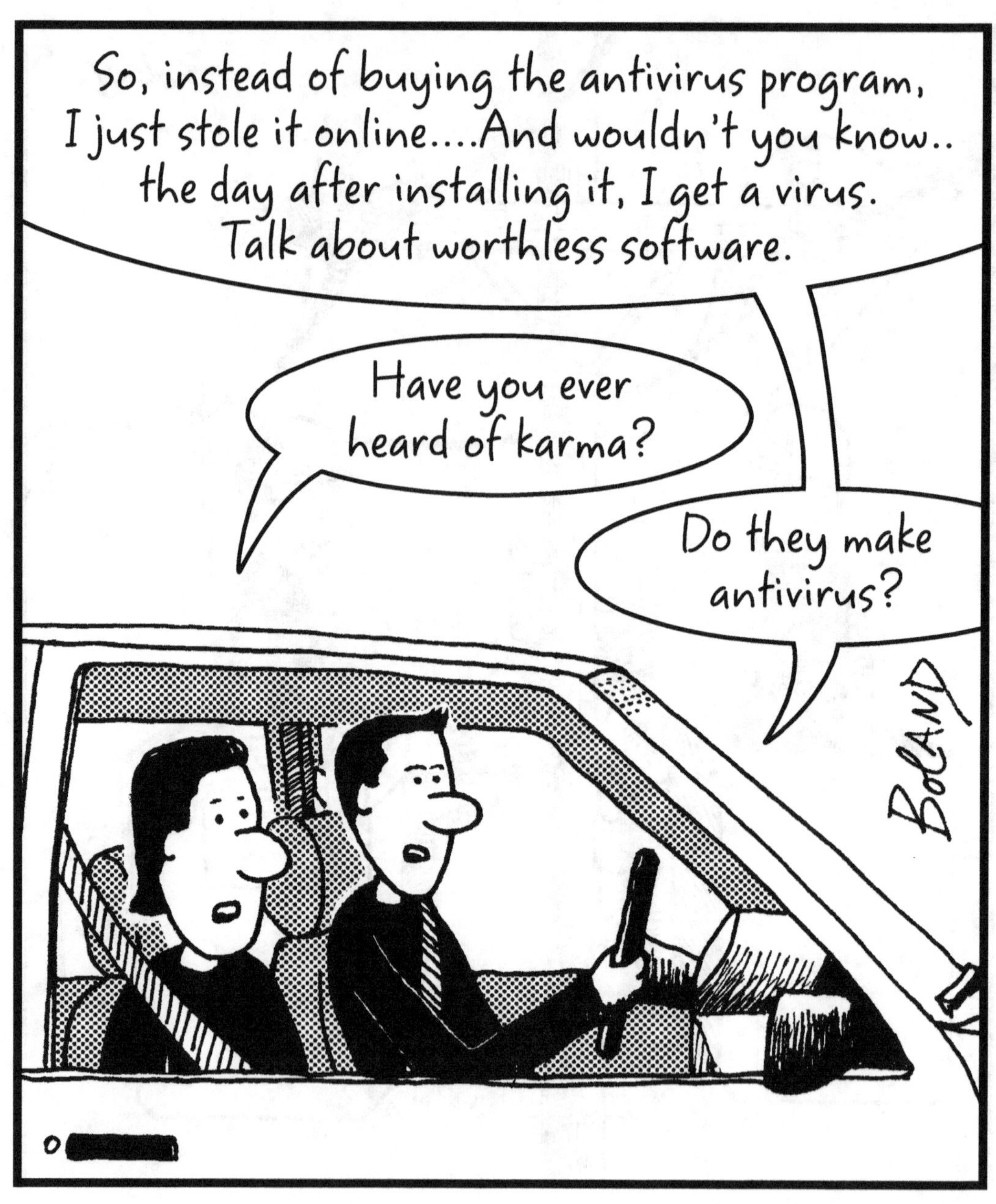
So, instead of buying the antivirus program, I just stole it online....And wouldn't you know.. the day after installing it, I get a virus. Talk about worthless software.
Have you ever heard of karma?
Do they make antivirus?
BOLAND

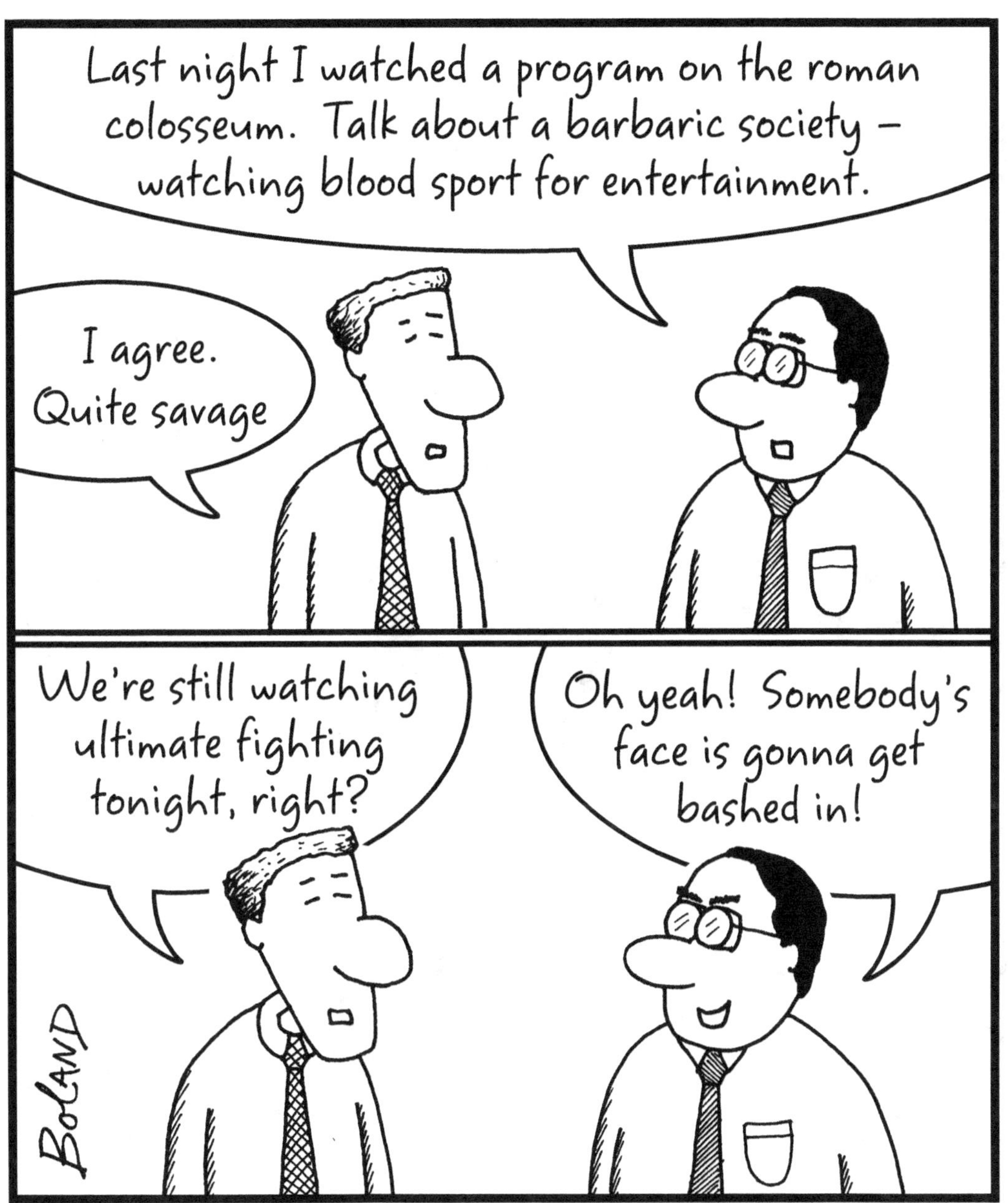
Last night I watched a program on the roman colosseum. Talk about a barbaric society – watching blood sport for entertainment.
I agree. Quite savage
We're still watching ultimate fighting tonight, right?
Oh yeah! Somebody's face is gonna get bashed in!
BOLAND

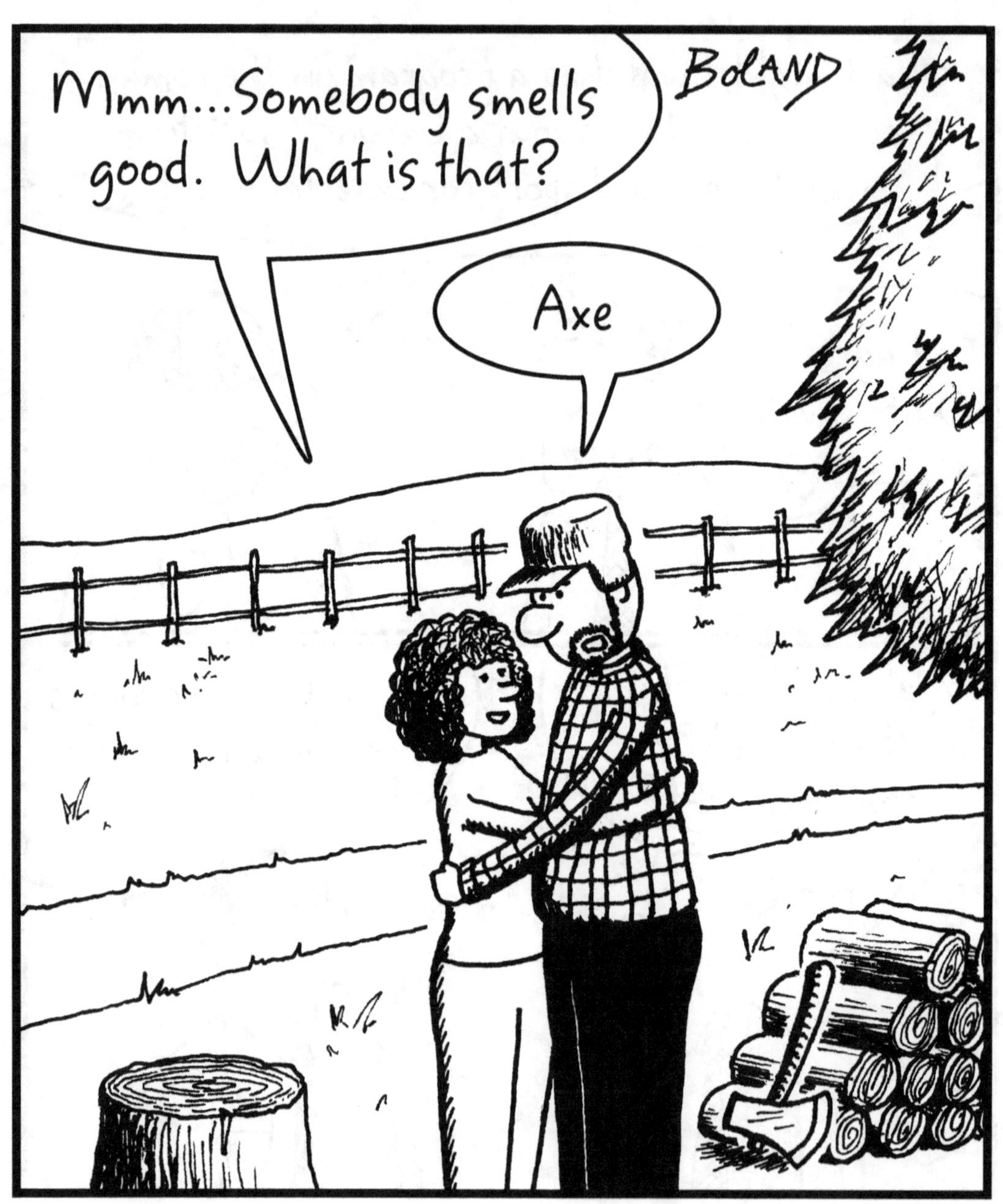
BOLAND
Mmm...Somebody smells good. What is that?
Axe

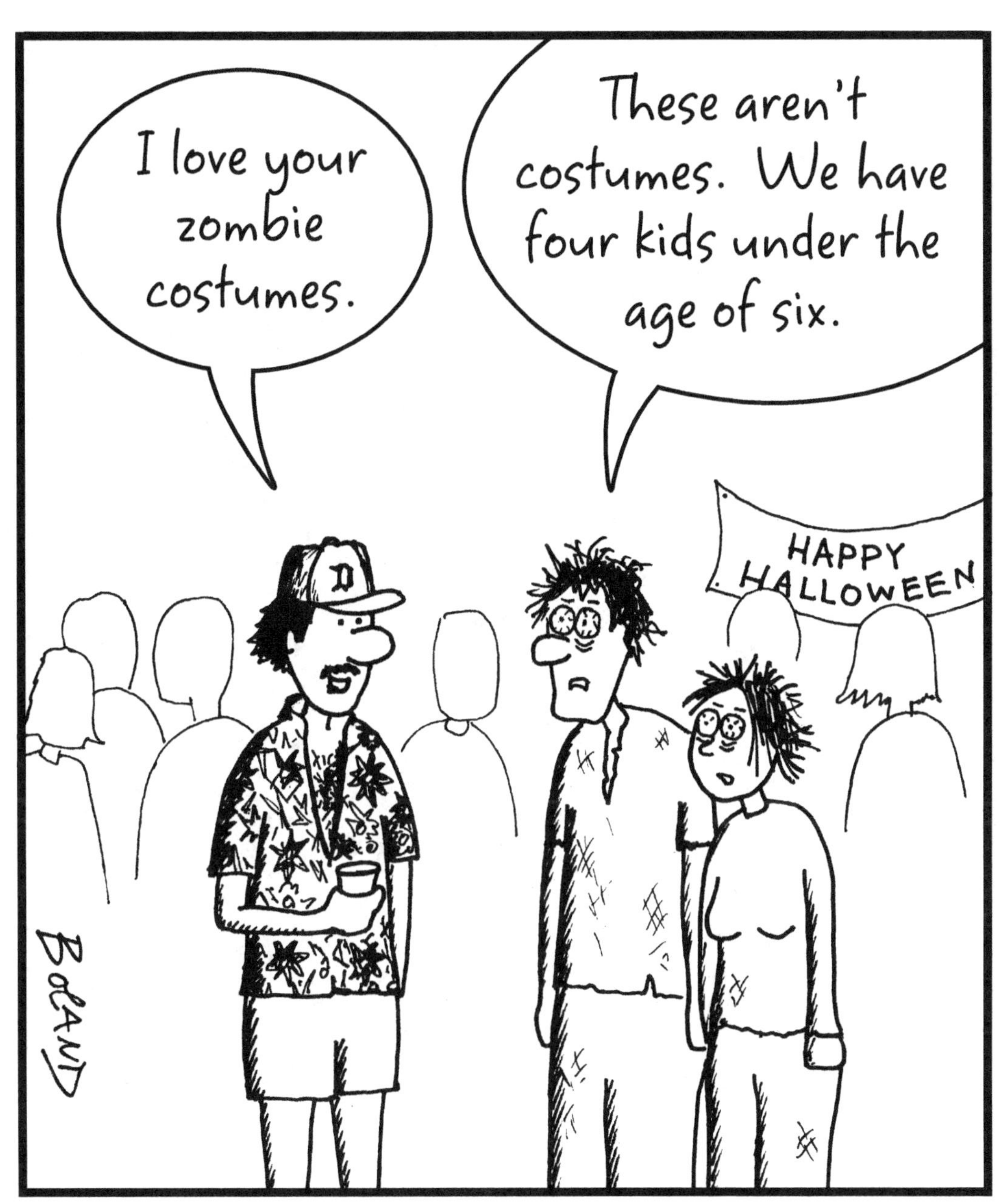
I love your zombie costumes.
These aren't costumes. We have four kids under the age of six.
HAPPY HALLOWEEN
BOLAND

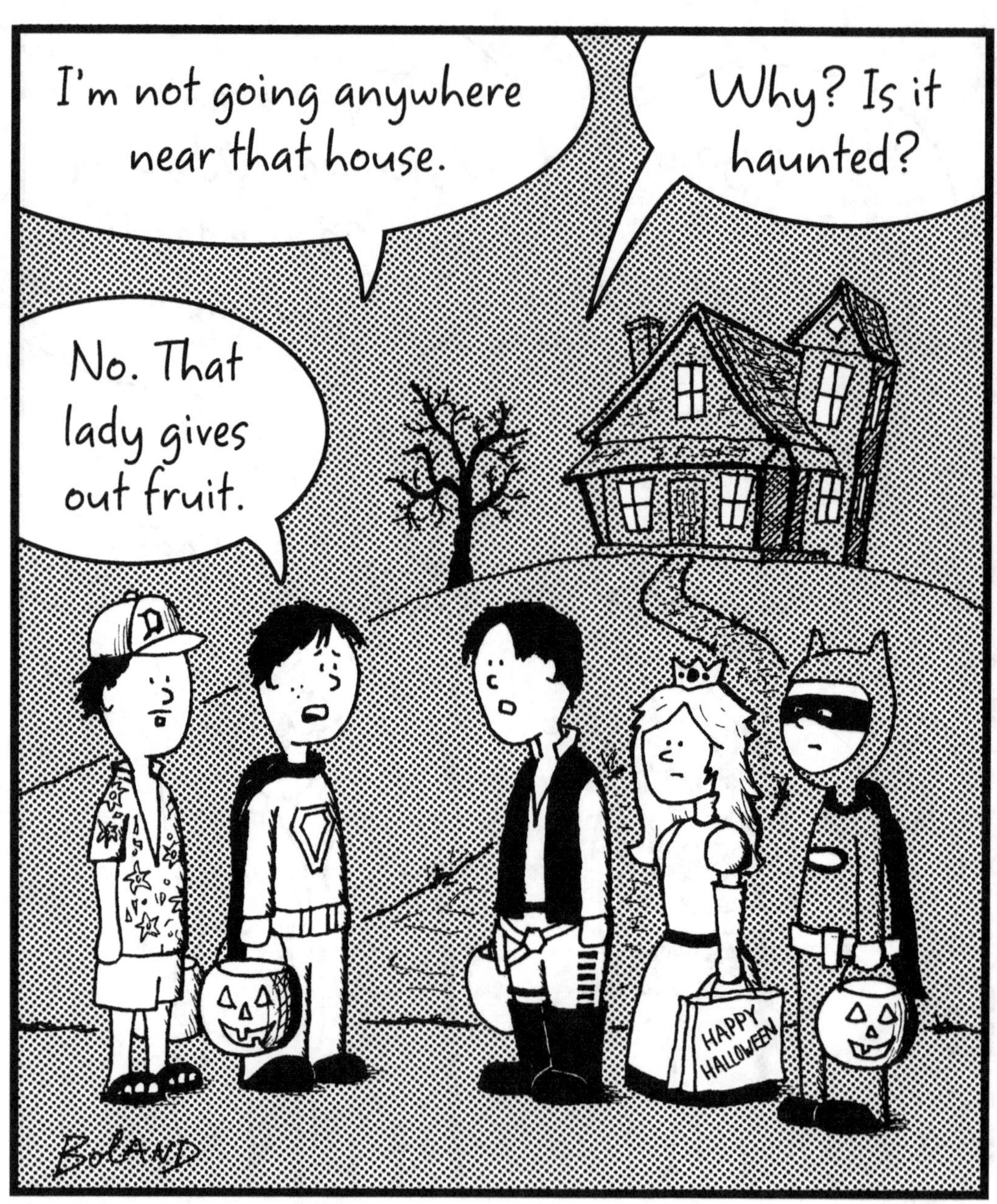
I'm not going anywhere near that house.
Why? Is it haunted?
No. That lady gives out fruit.
HAPPY HALLOWEEN
BOLAND

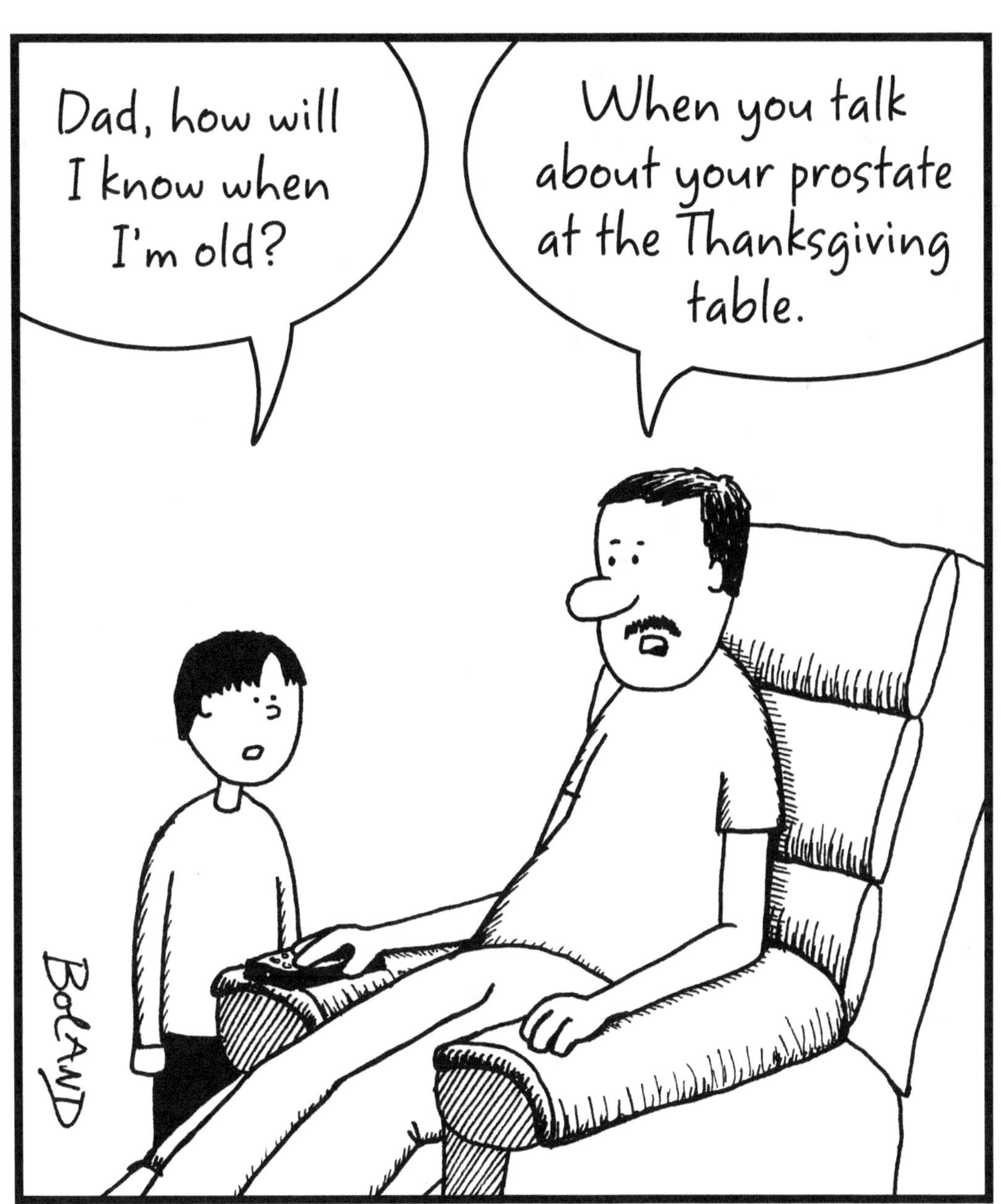
Dad, how will I know when I'm old?
When you talk about your prostate at the Thanksgiving table.
BOLAND

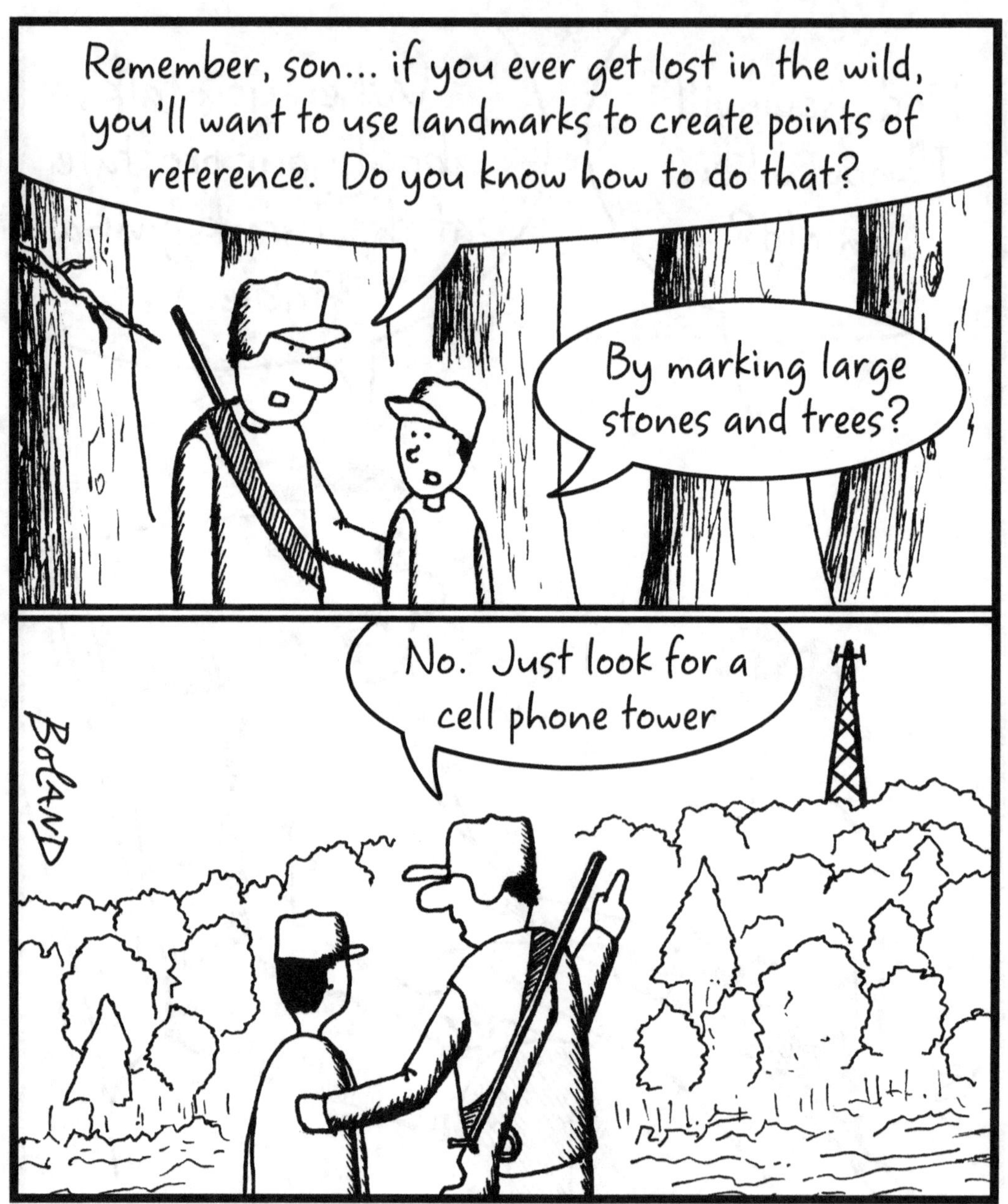
Remember, son... if you ever get lost in the wild, you'll want to use landmarks to create points of reference. Do you know how to do that?
By marking large stones and trees?
No. Just look for a cell phone tower
BOLAND

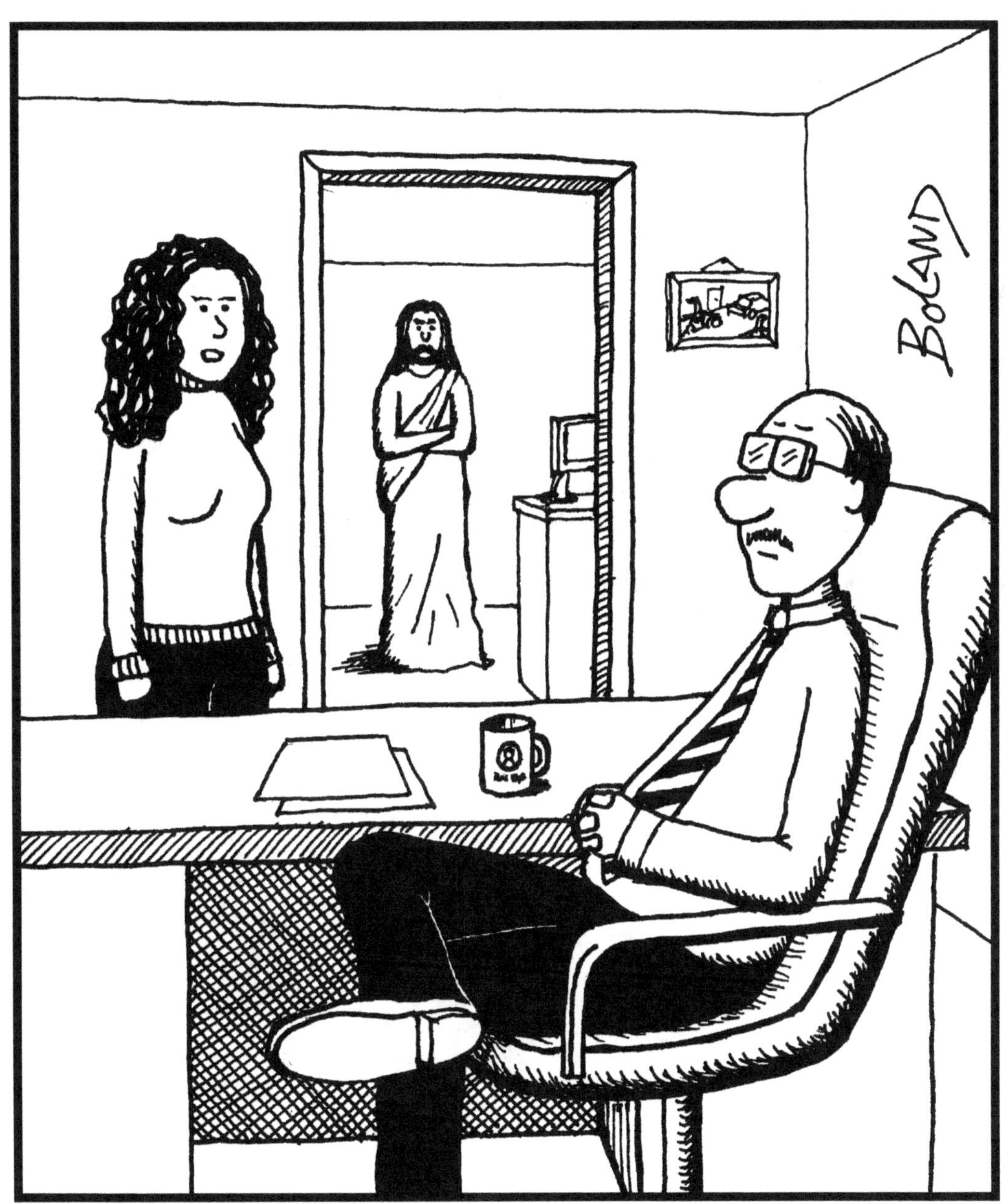

"I'm sorry, Mayor, but there's a man out front insisting that he speak to you. Something about the town changing Christmas to Sparkle Season."

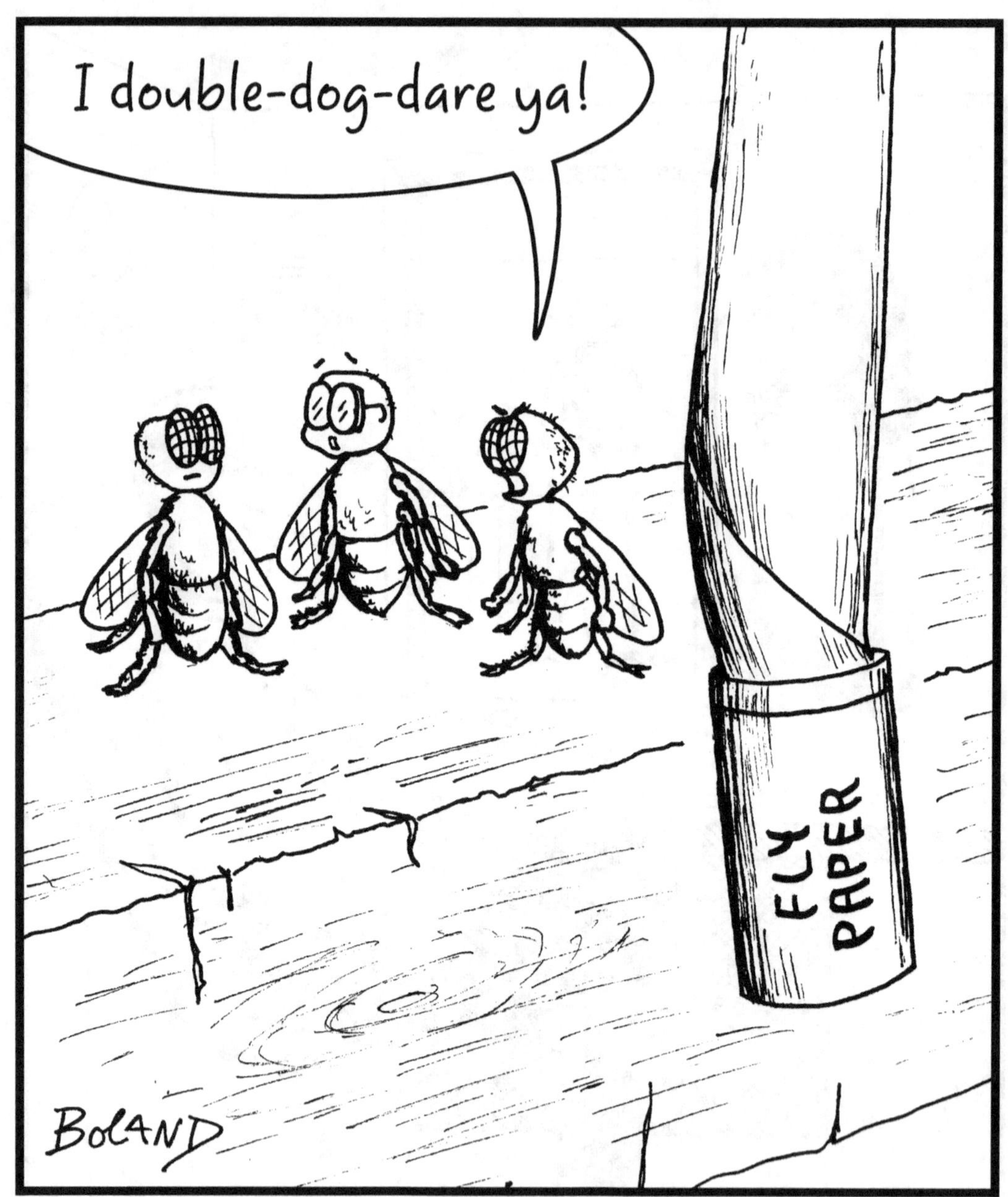
I double-dog-dare ya!
FLY PAPER
BOLAND

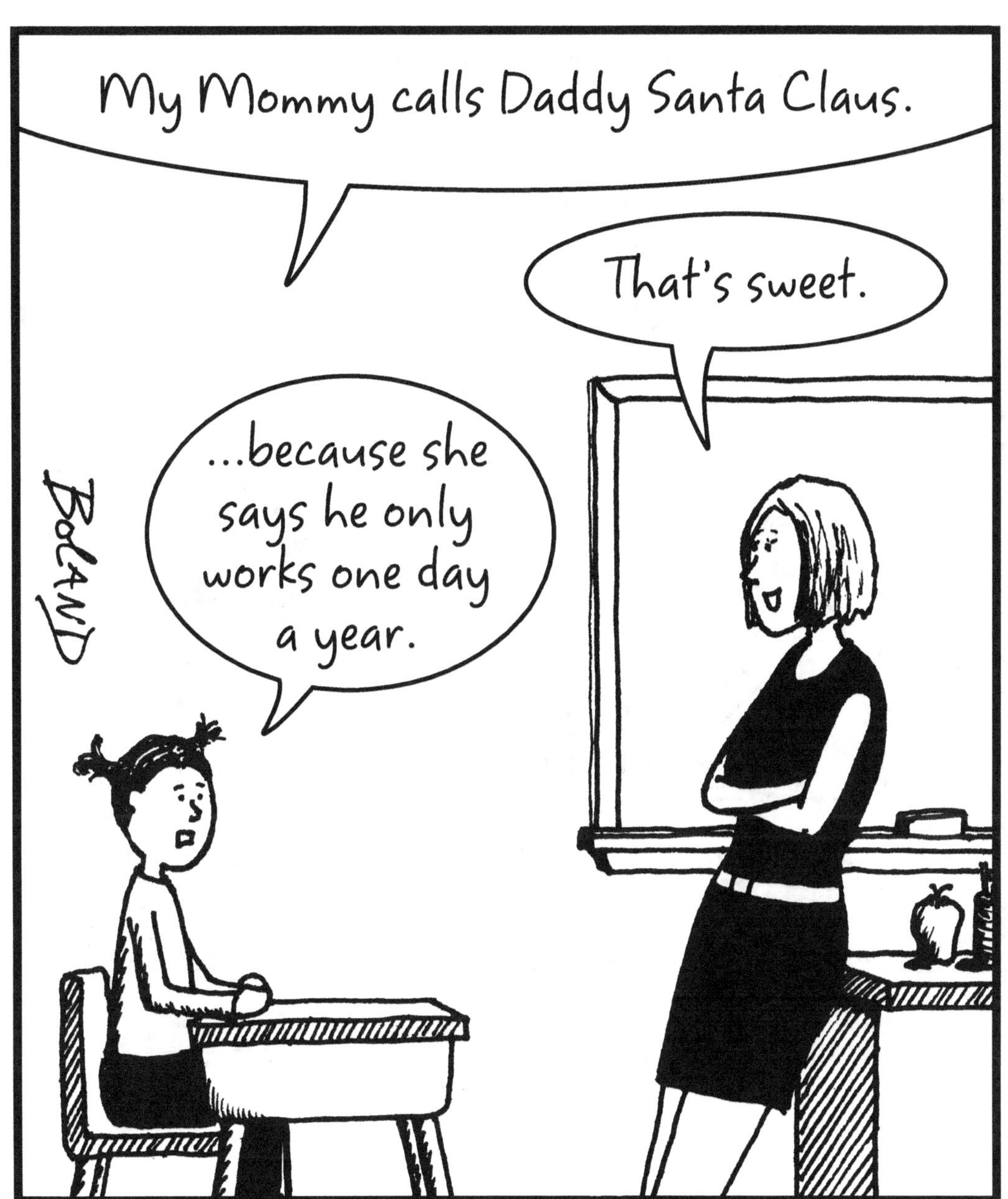
My Mommy calls Daddy Santa Claus.
That's sweet.
...because she says he only works one day a year.
BOLAND

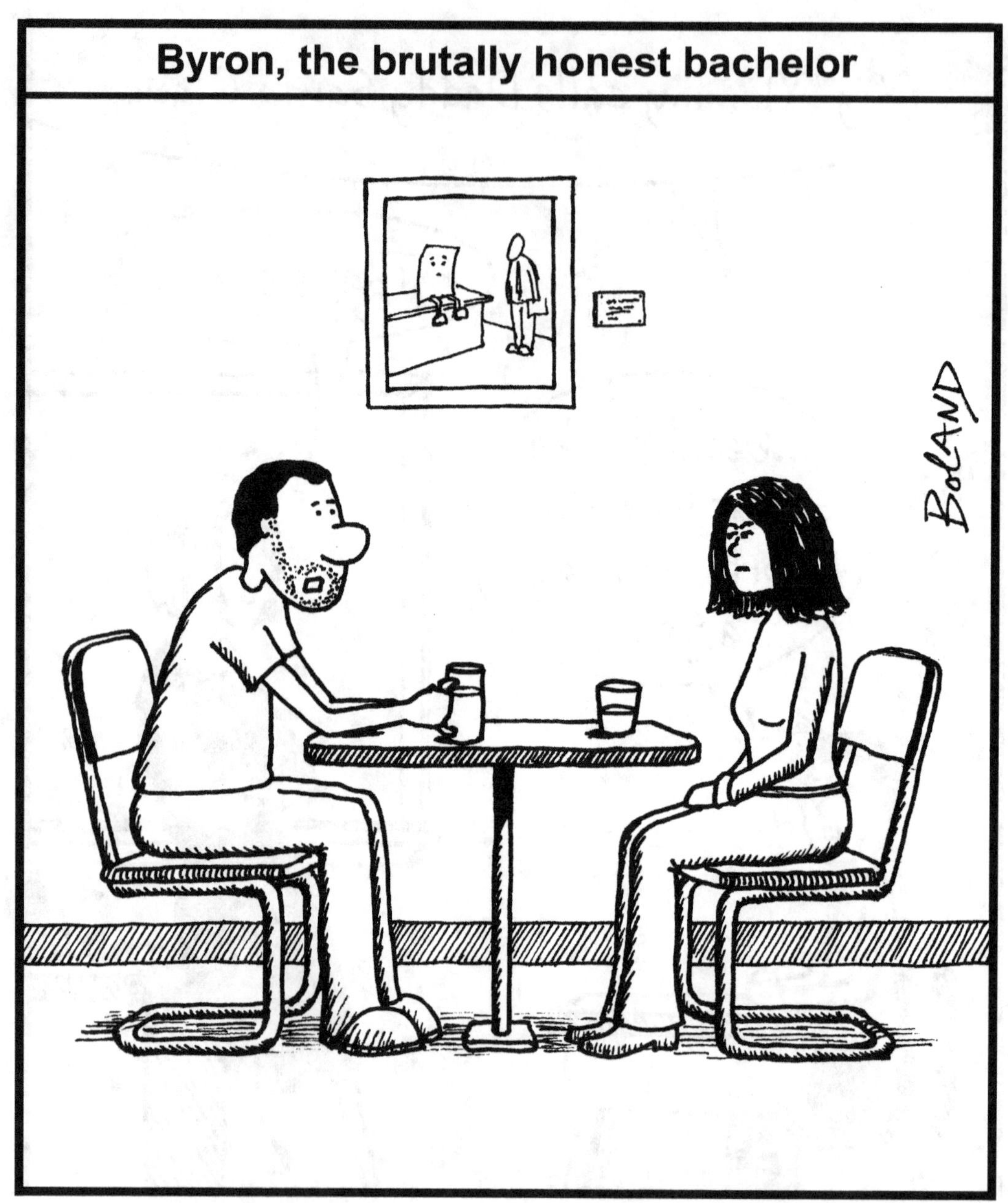

"I'm actually much funnier than this. I just can't take any more of your laugh."

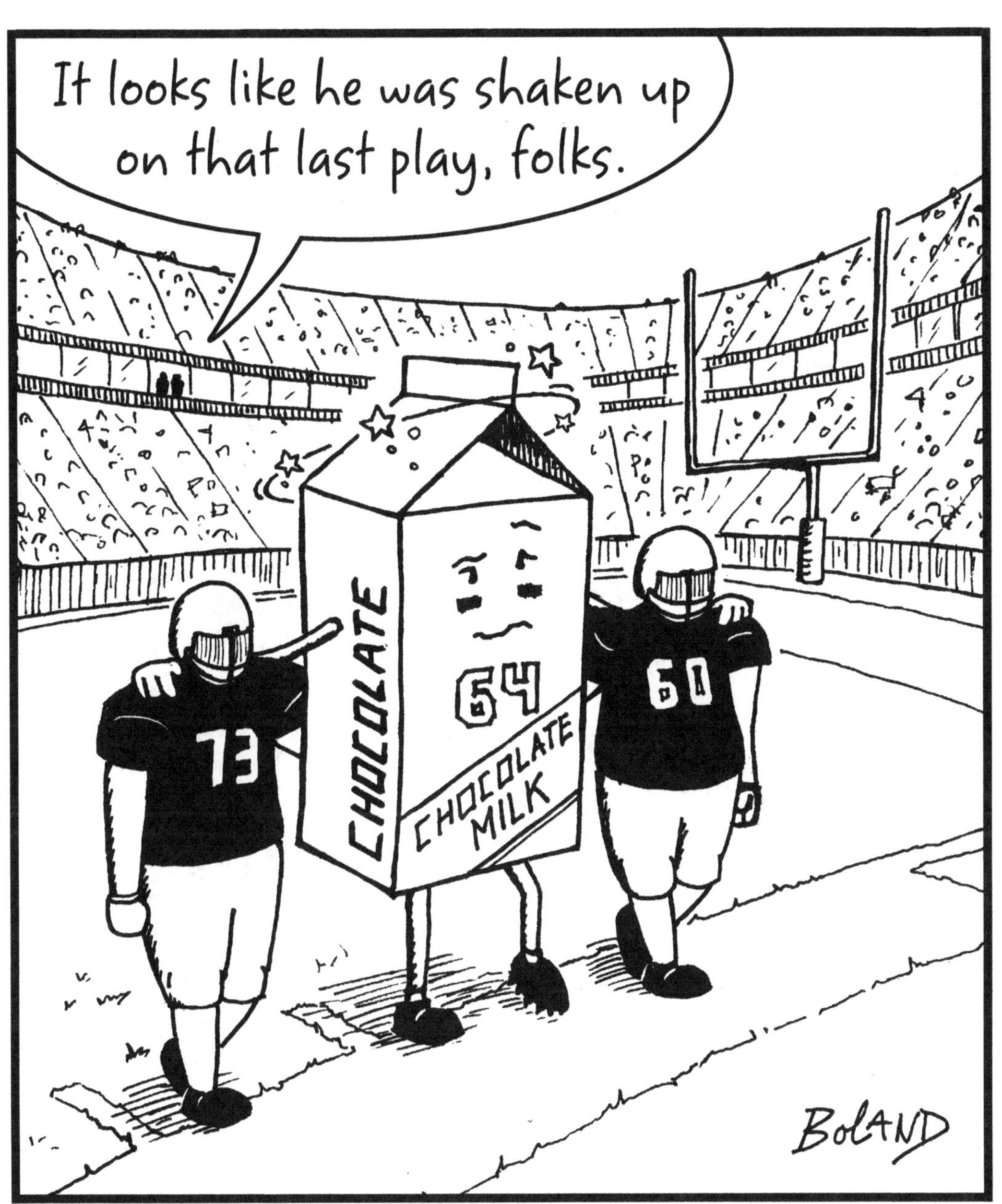
It looks like he was shaken up on that last play, folks.
CHOCOLATE
64
CHOCOLATE MILK
73
60
BOLAND

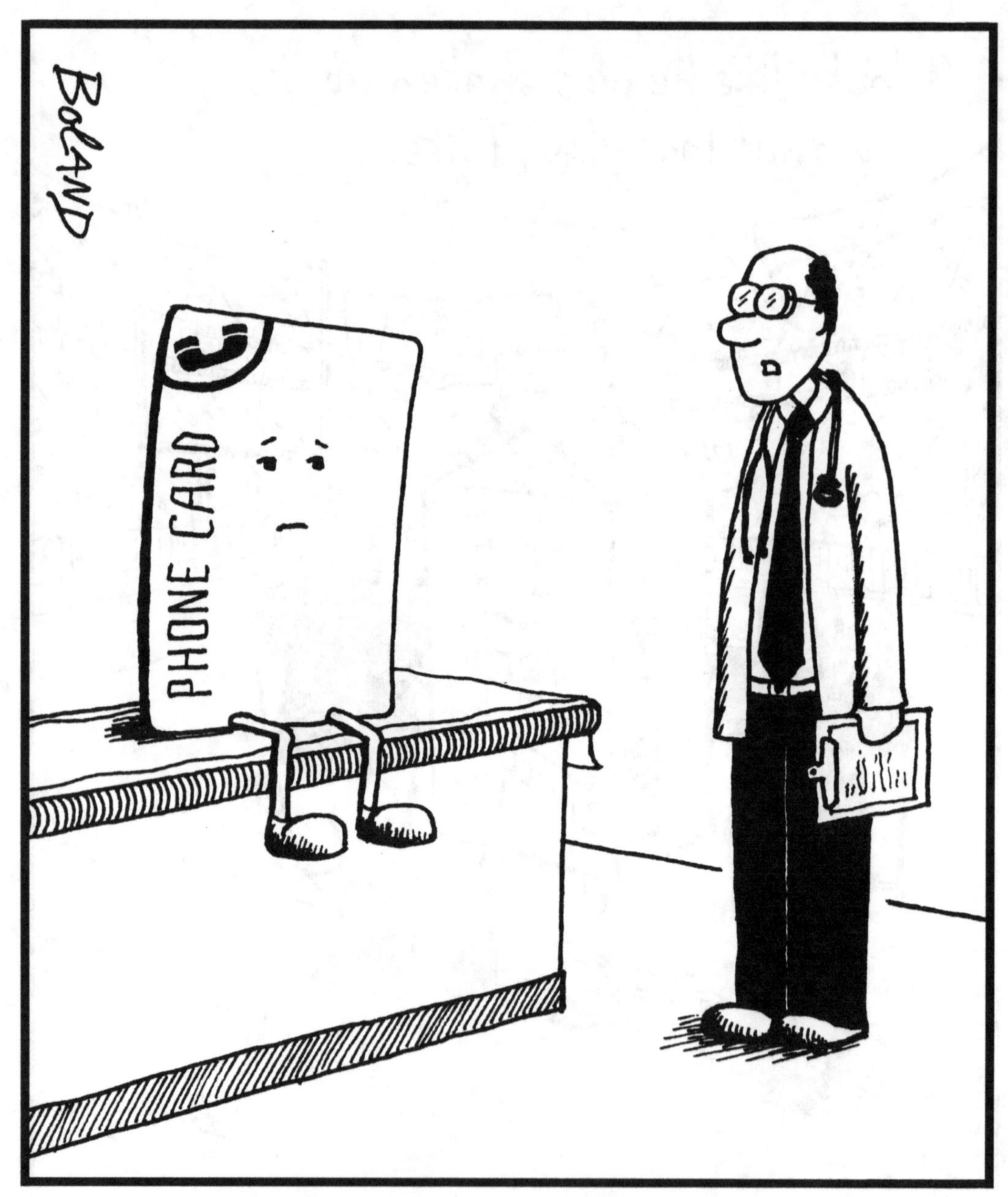

"I'm sorry to say this, but you don't have much time left."

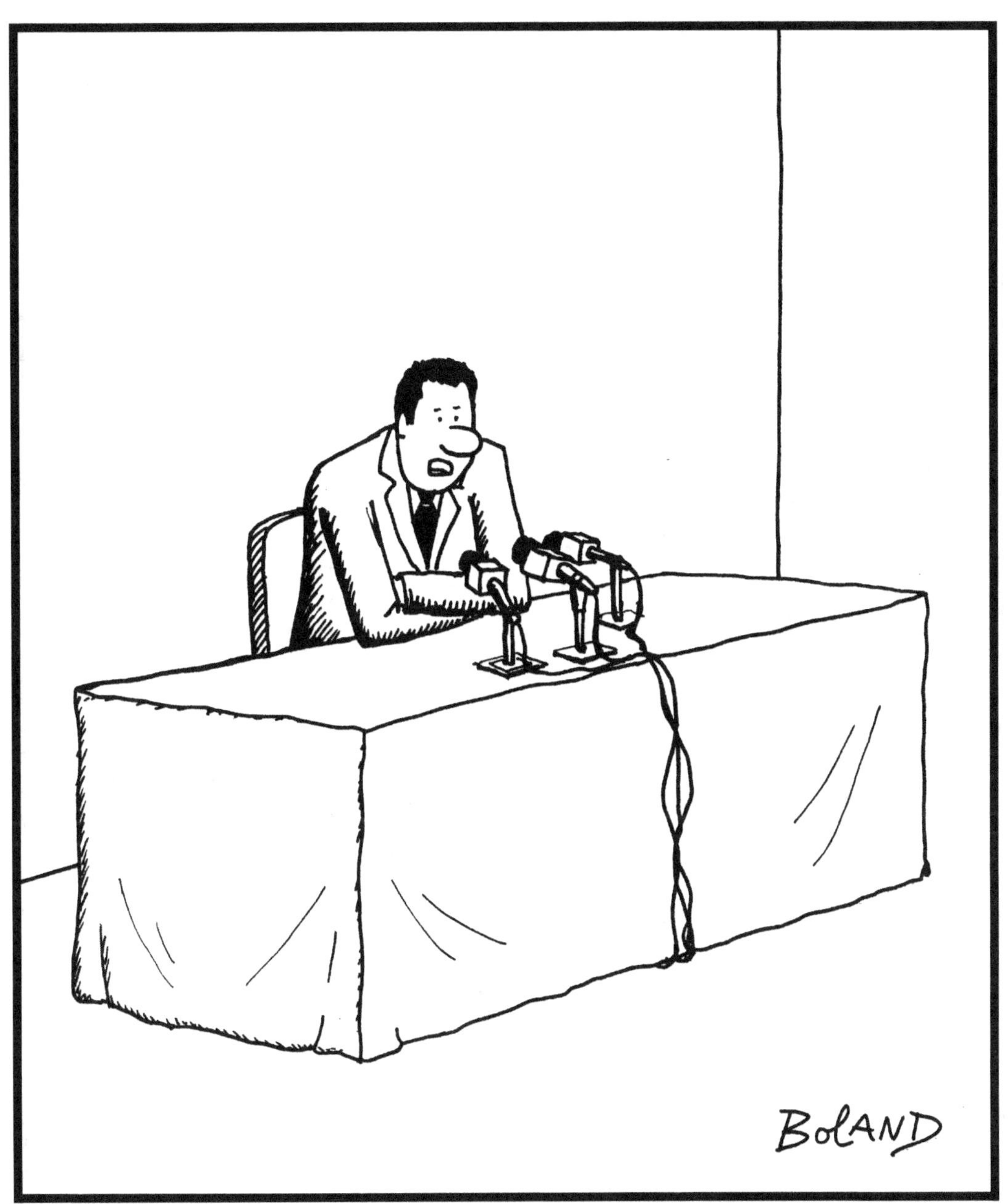

"And finally, I just want to re-emphasize that my playing career is over. I'm done. I'm retired. I'm finished. I'll never compete again. Thank you for coming today. I hope to see you all again at my comeback press conference."

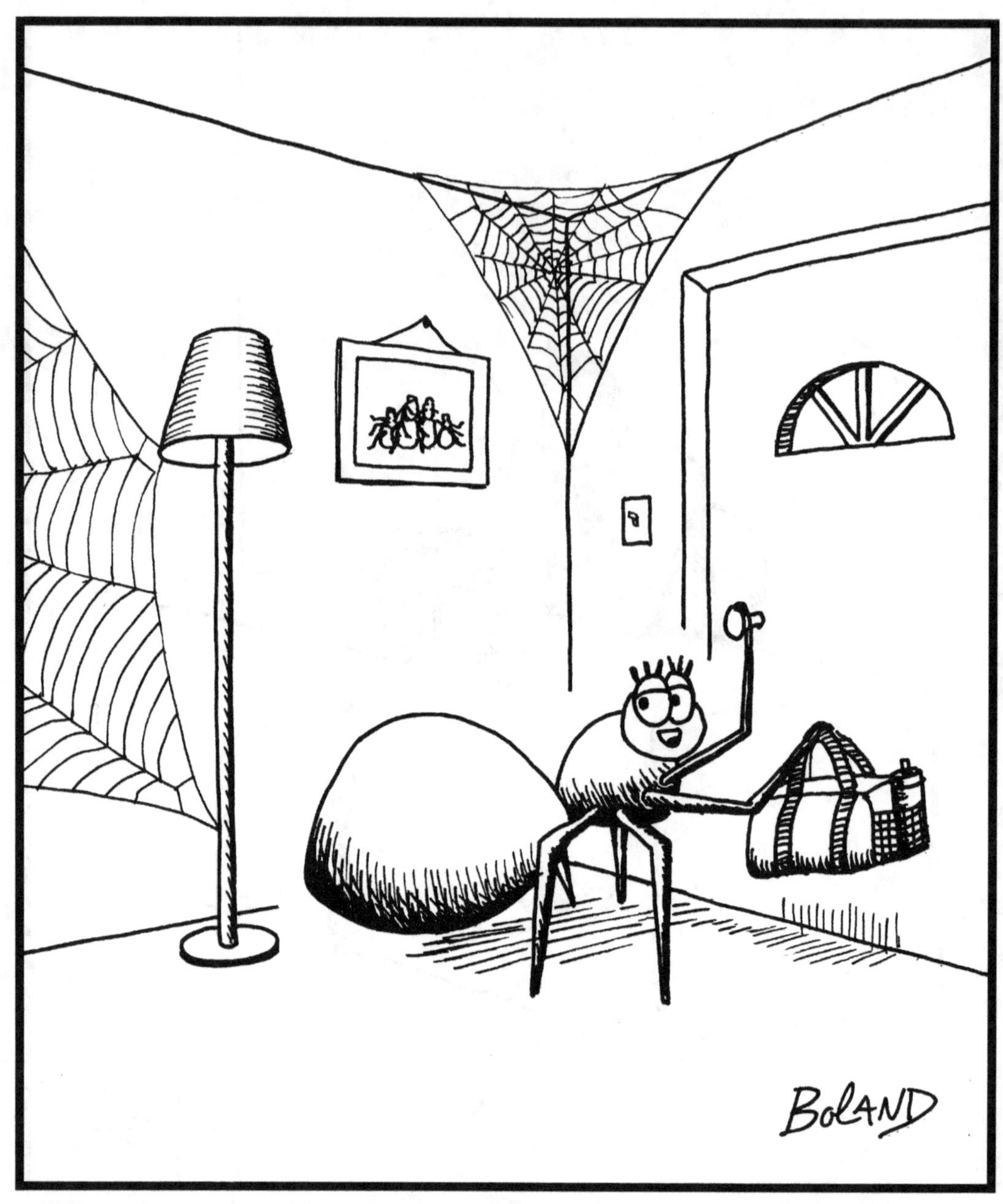

"Bye honey. Bye kids. I'm off to spinning class."

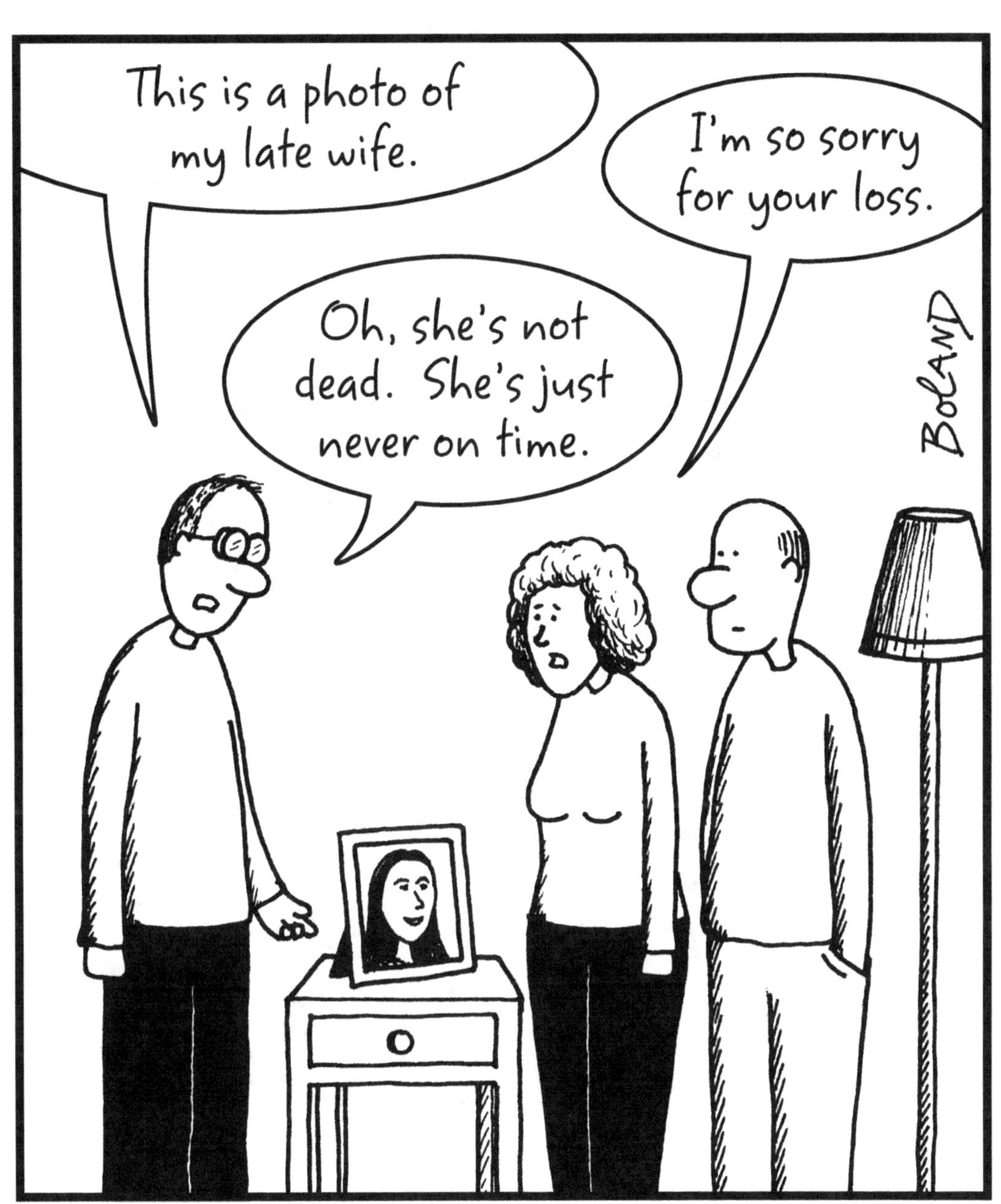
This is a photo of my late wife.
I'm so sorry for your loss.
Oh, she's not dead. She's just never on time.
BOLAND

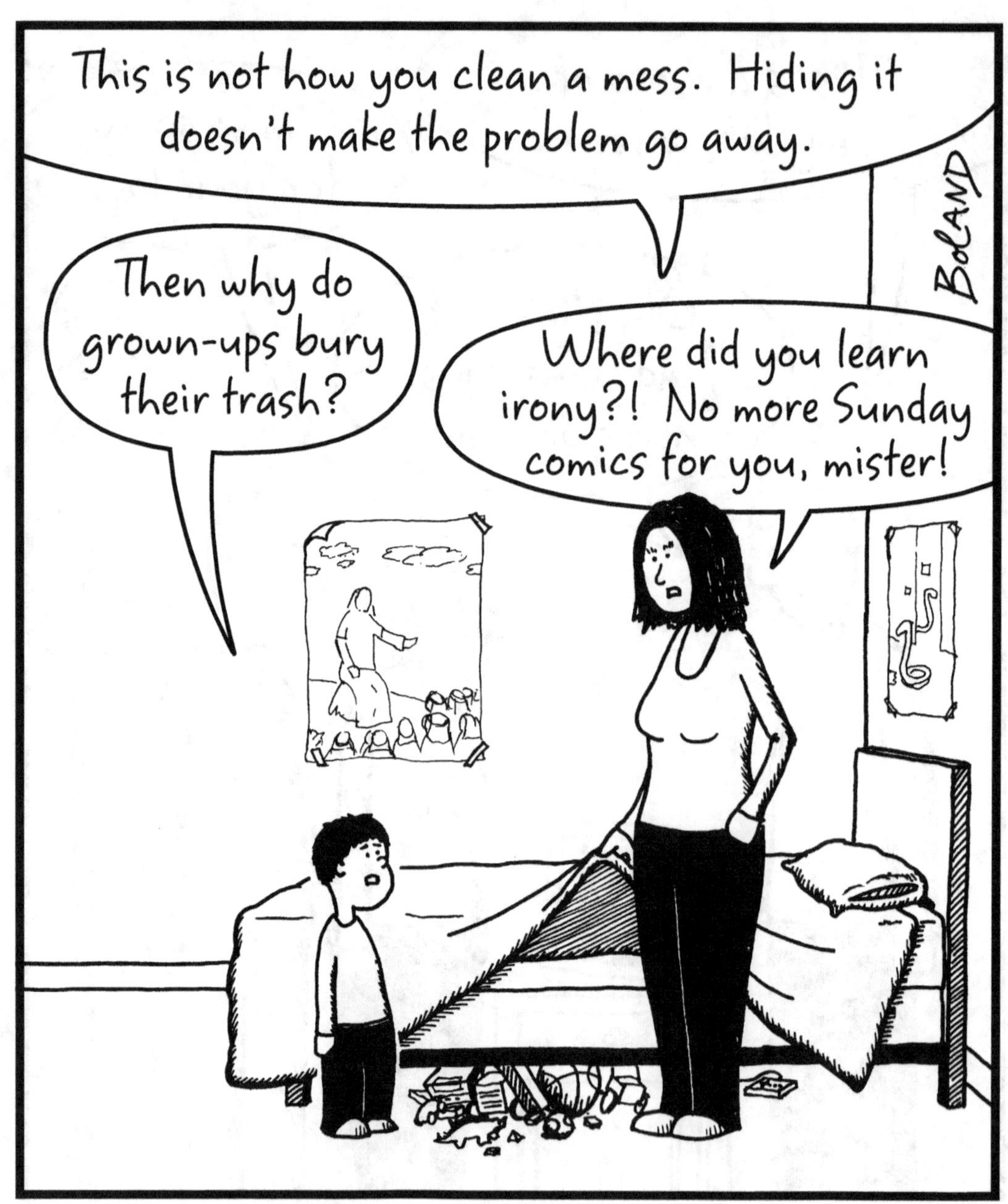
This is not how you clean a mess. Hiding it doesn't make the problem go away.
Then why do grown-ups bury their trash?
Where did you learn irony?! No more Sunday comics for you, mister!
BOLAND

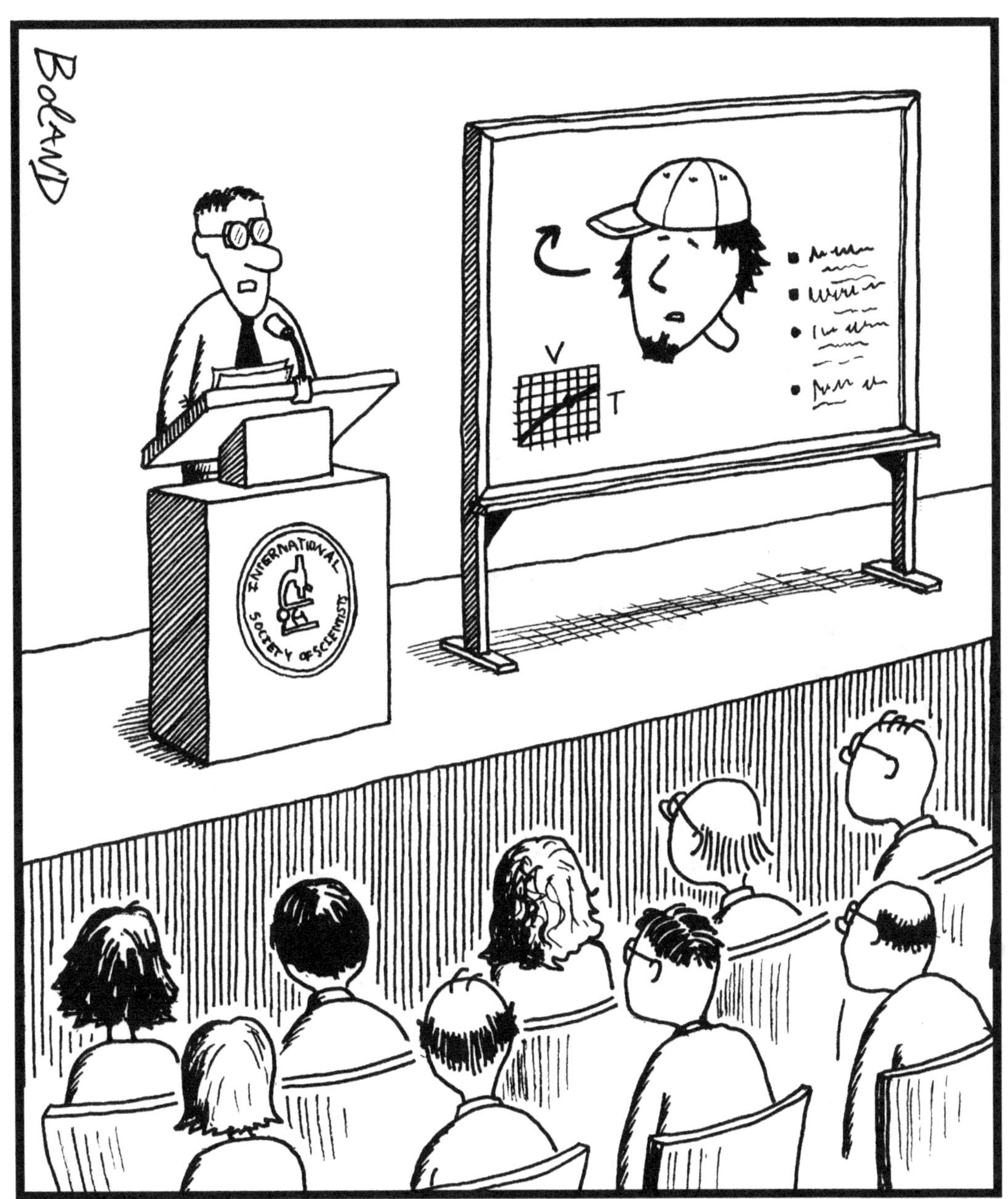

"After extensive examination of rotation rates, trend cycles, and rap music videos, I have calculated that in approximately 13 years, the ball cap will complete a full orbit, allowing us to briefly view it in the front facing position."

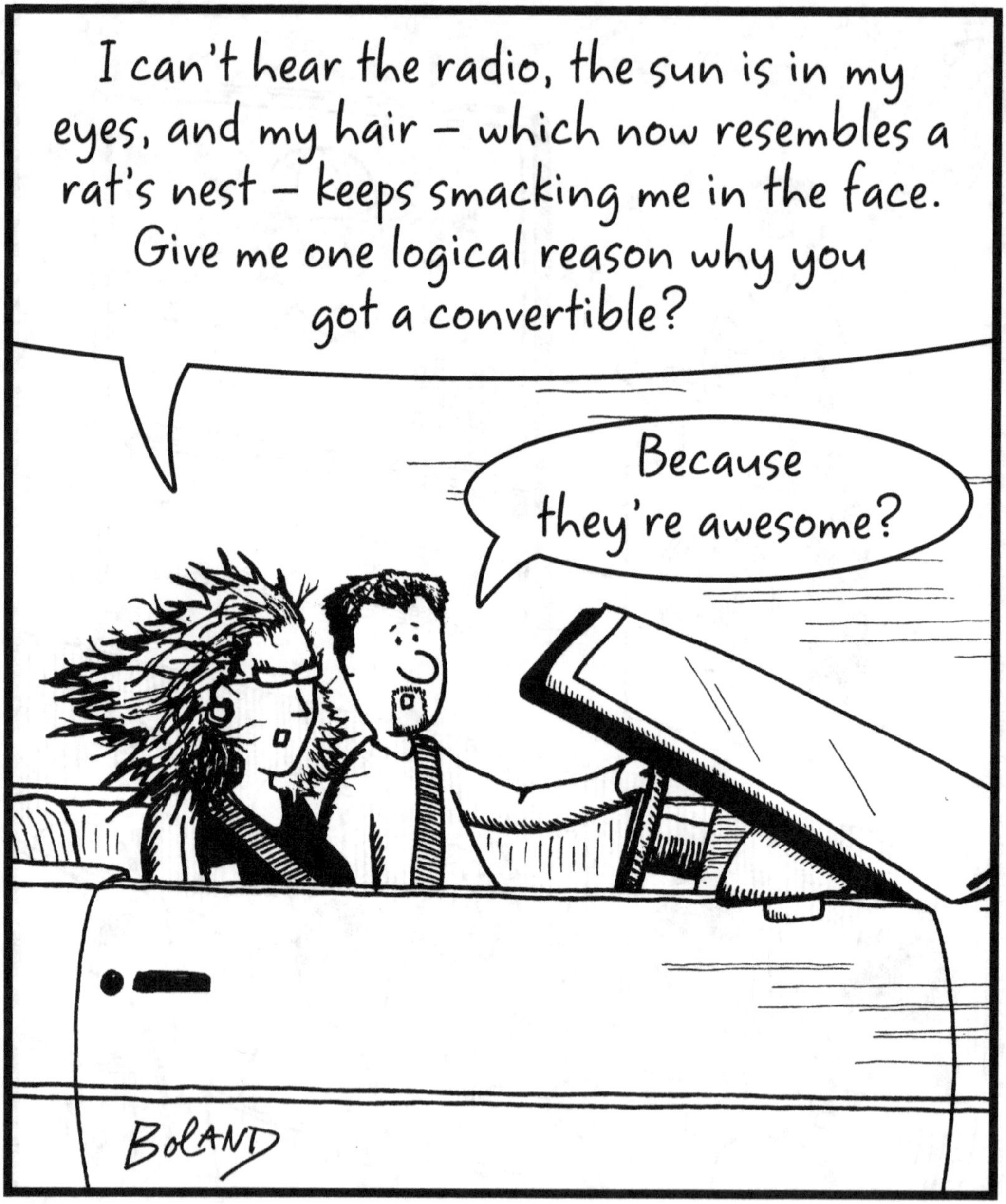

I can't hear the radio, the sun is in my eyes, and my hair – which now resembles a rat's nest – keeps smacking me in the face. Give me one logical reason why you got a convertible?

Because they're awesome?

BOLAND

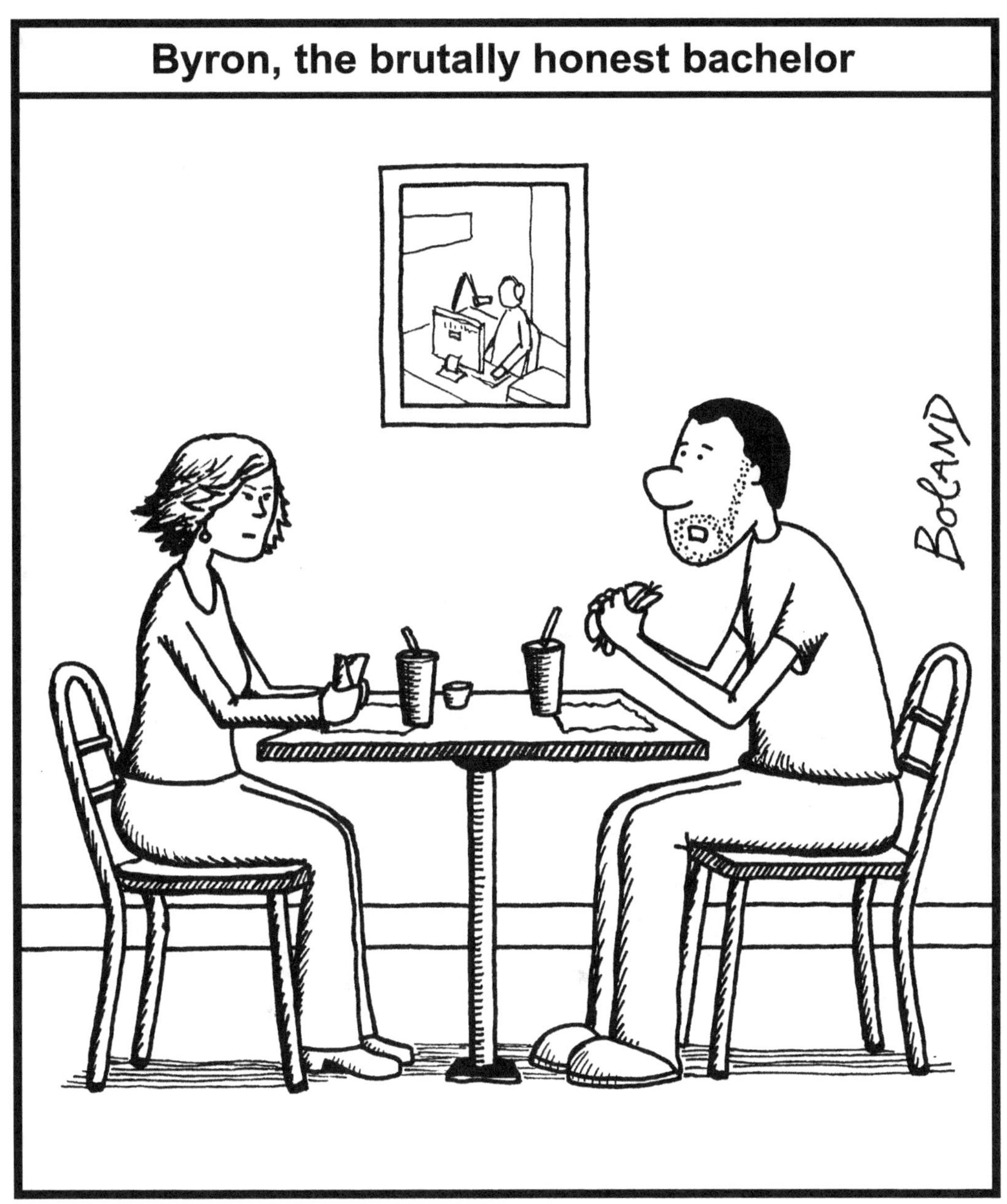

Byron, the brutally honest bachelor

"You're not like the other women I've dated. You're much older."

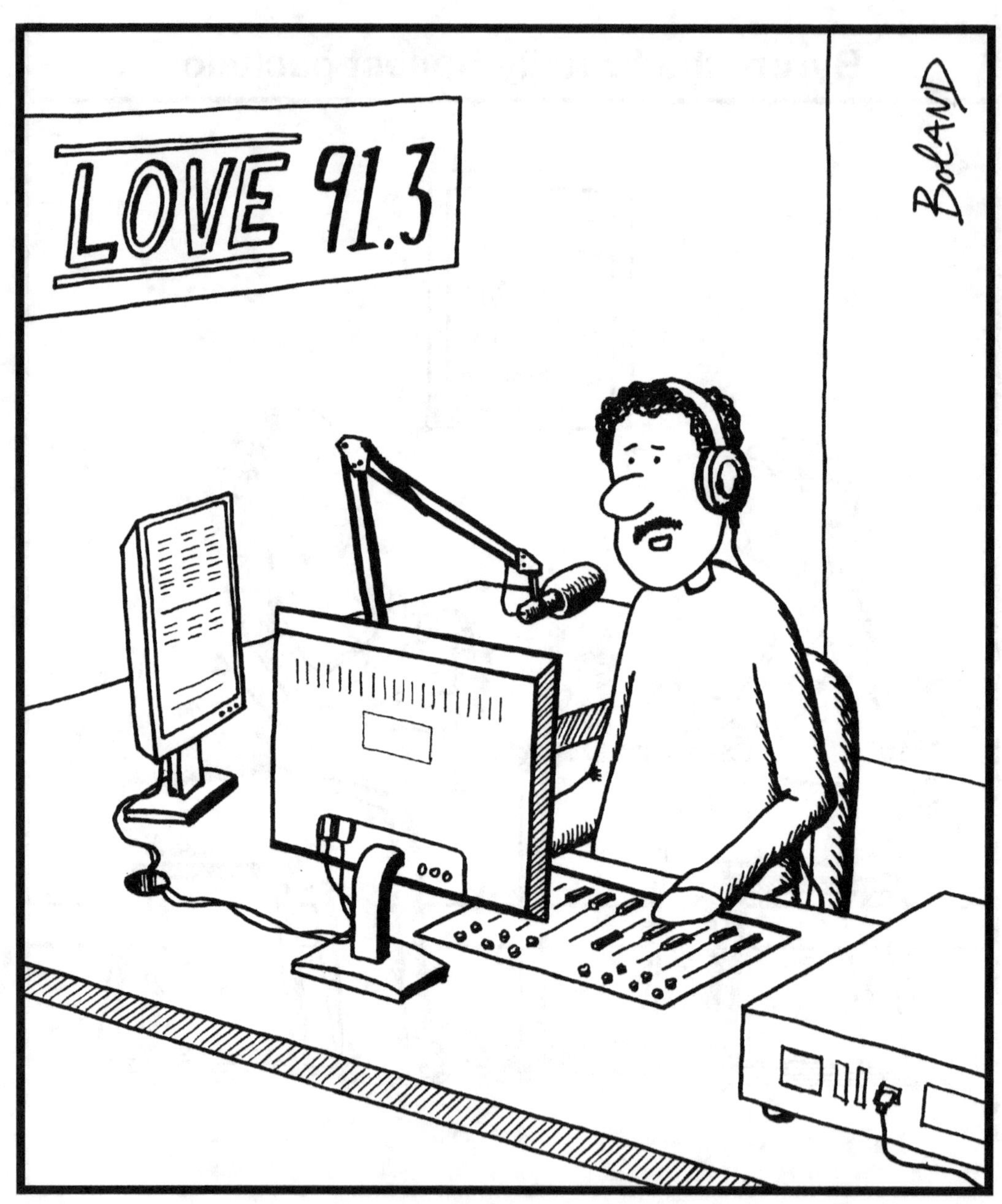

"That was 'Together Forever' by Clint Jackson. Congratulations to Clint on his recent marriage to his fifth wife."

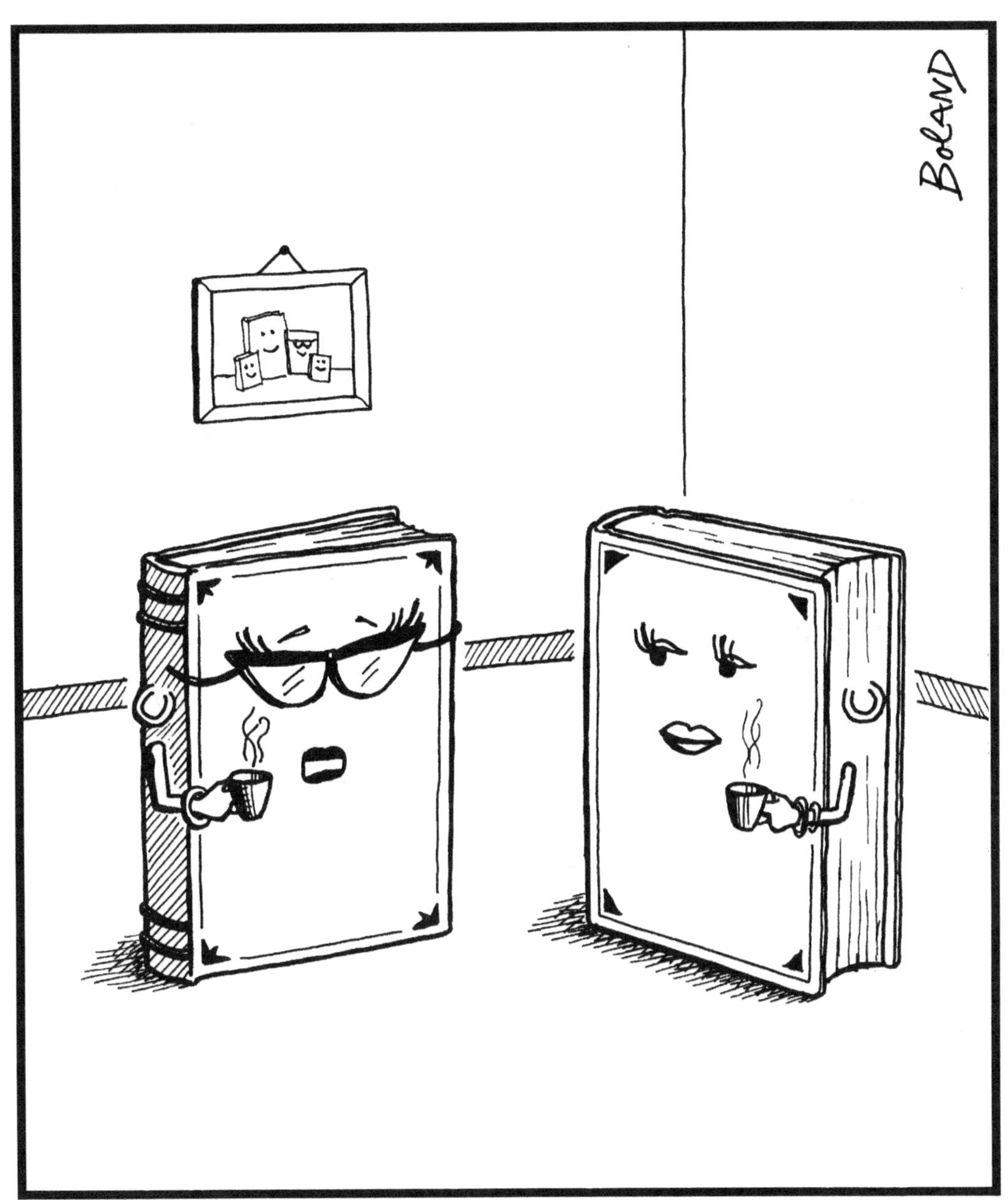

"My husband's company is struggling. He said they're considering chapter eleven."

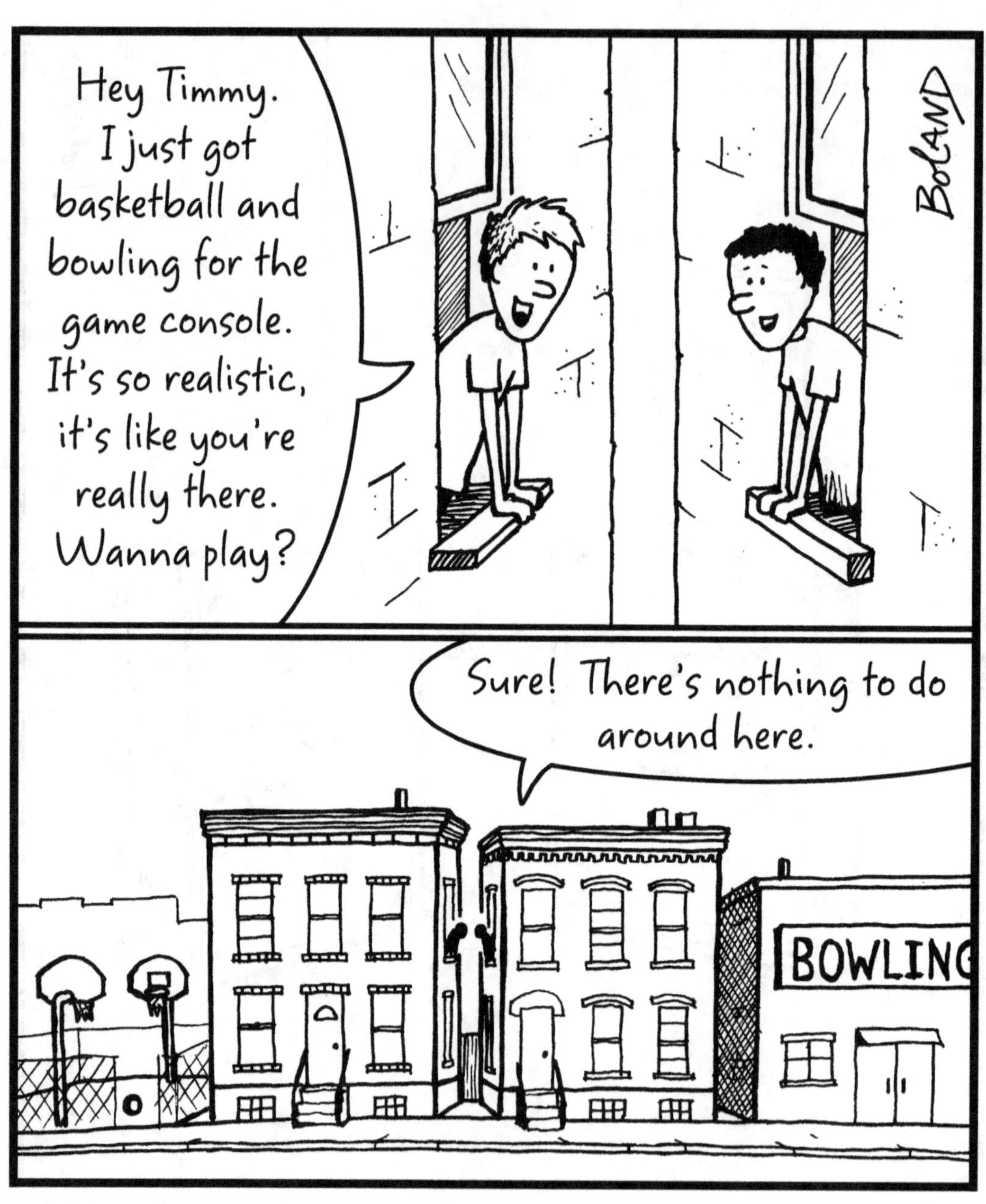
Hey Timmy. I just got basketball and bowling for the game console. It's so realistic, it's like you're really there. Wanna play?
BOLAND
Sure! There's nothing to do around here.
BOWLING

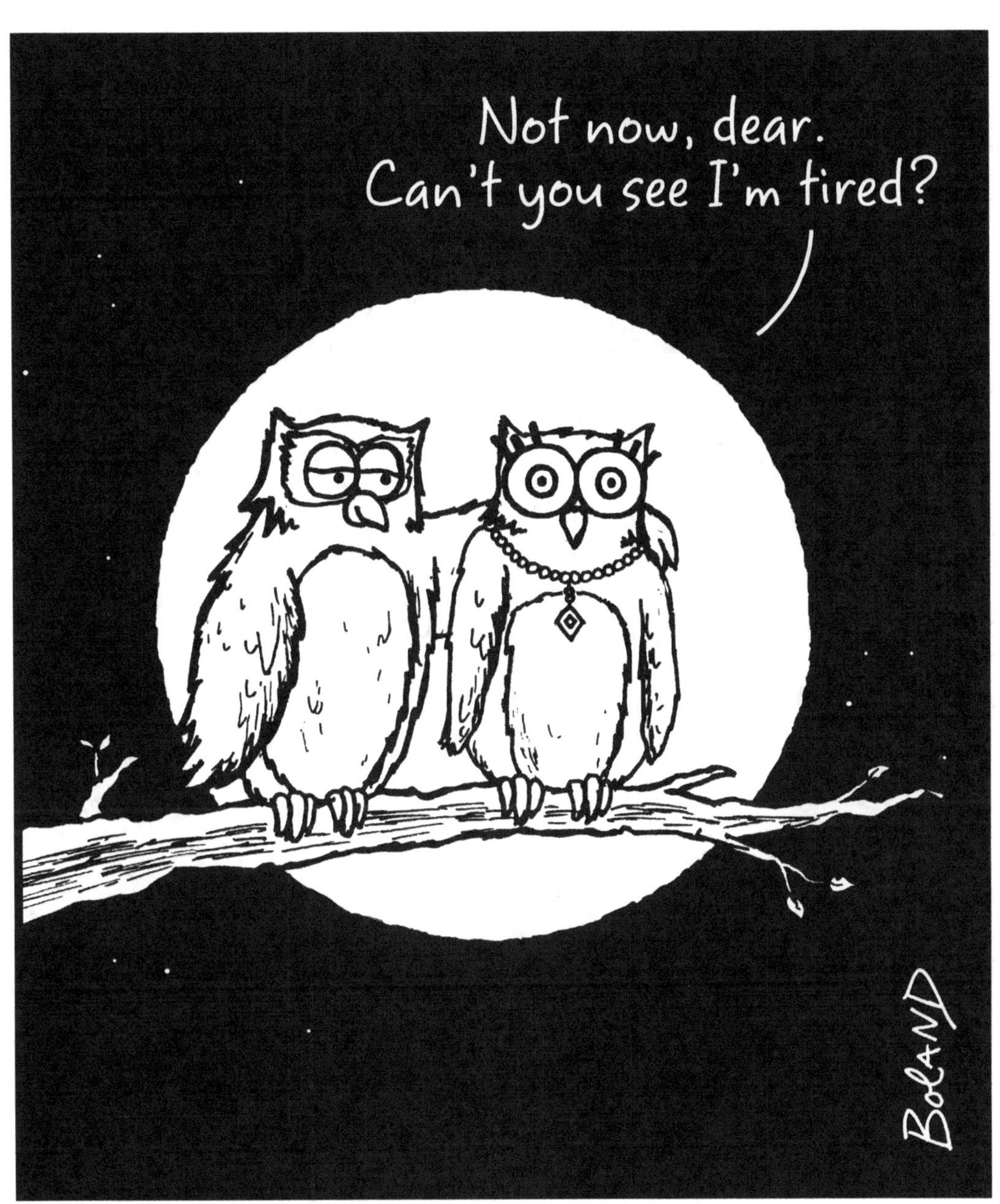
Not now, dear.
Can't you see I'm tired?
BOLAND

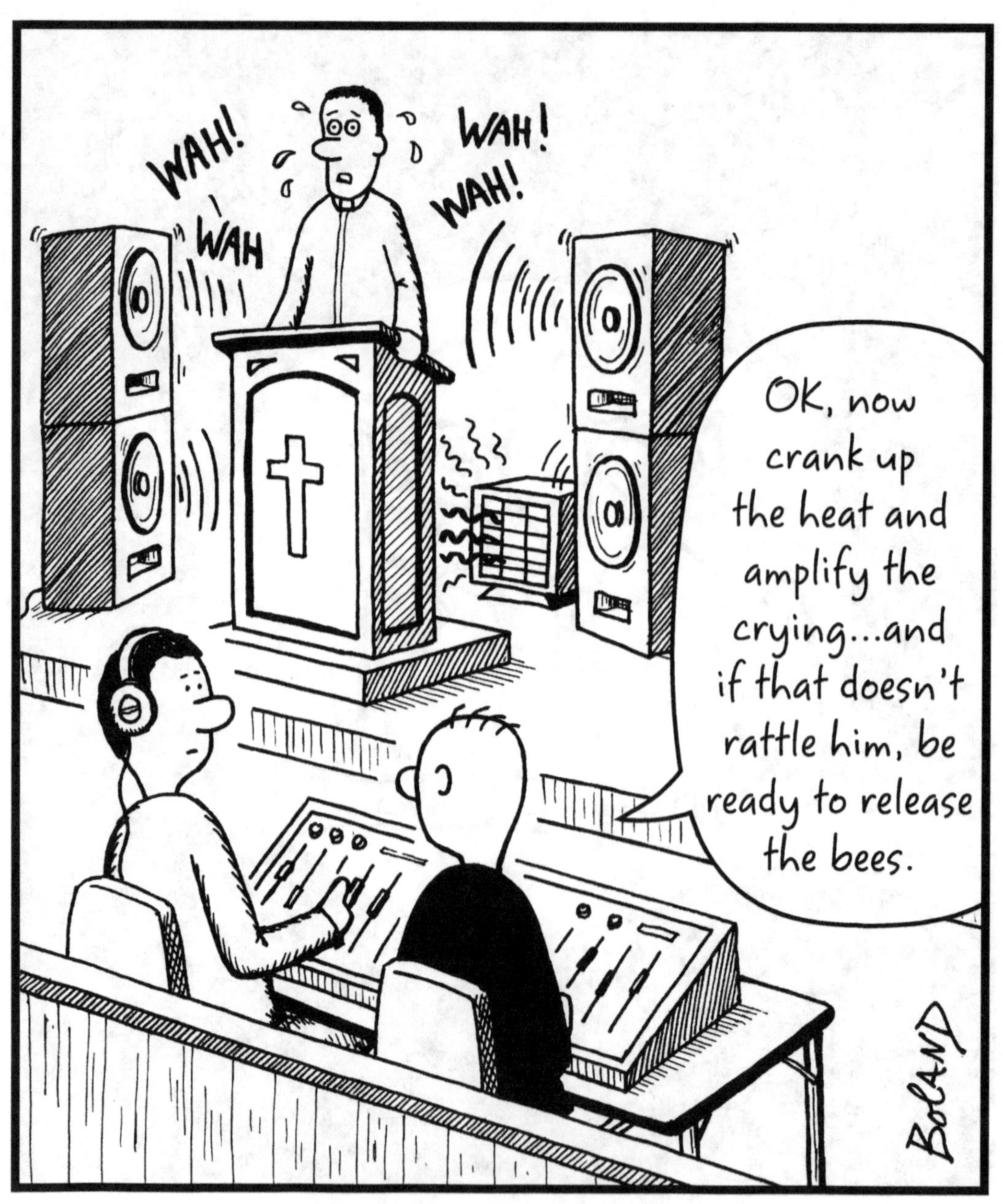

Pastor-in-training

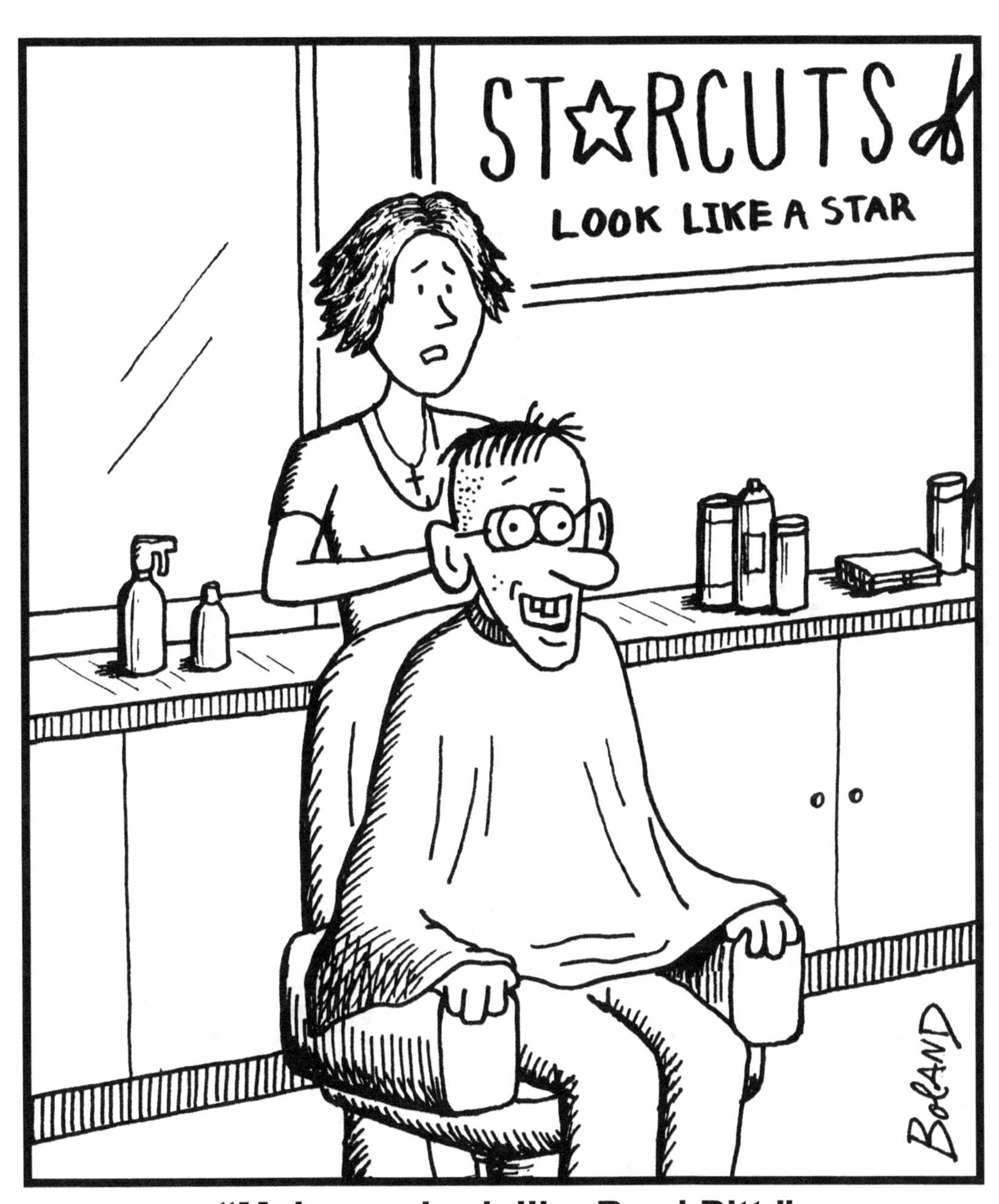

“Make me look like Brad Pitt.”

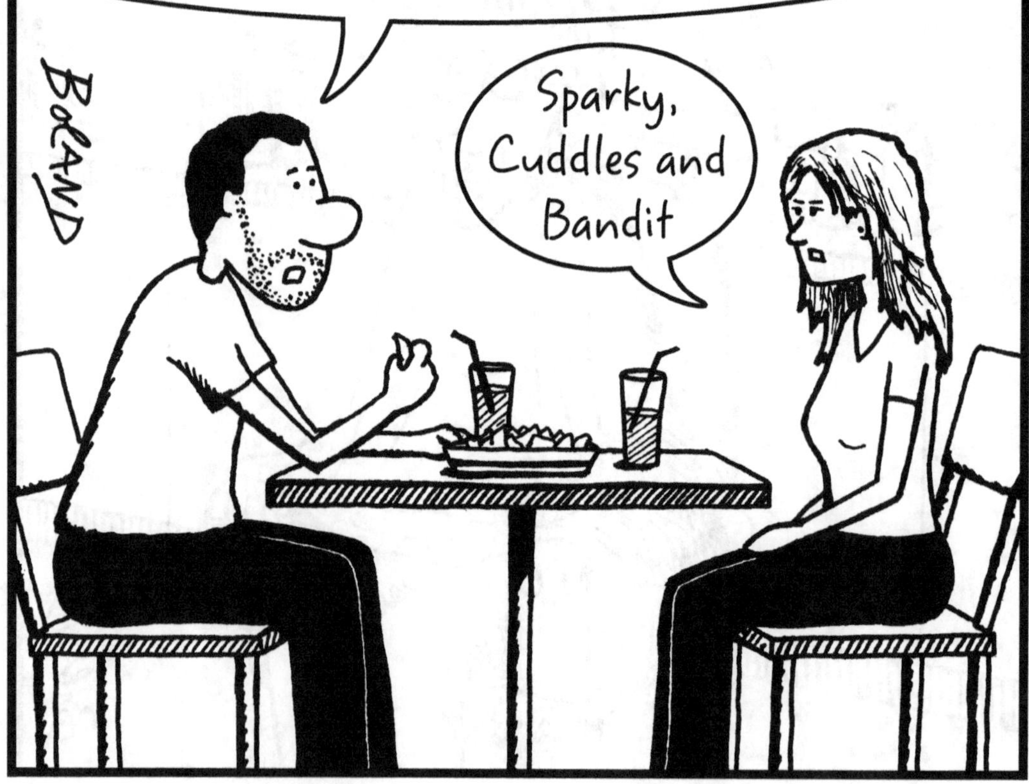
Byron, the brutally honest bachelor
Maybe it's just me, but I think single people with more than one dog scream "needy". Isn't the constant affection from one loving animal enough for them? Anyway... you said you have a dog? What's his name?
Sparky, Cuddles and Bandit
BOLAND

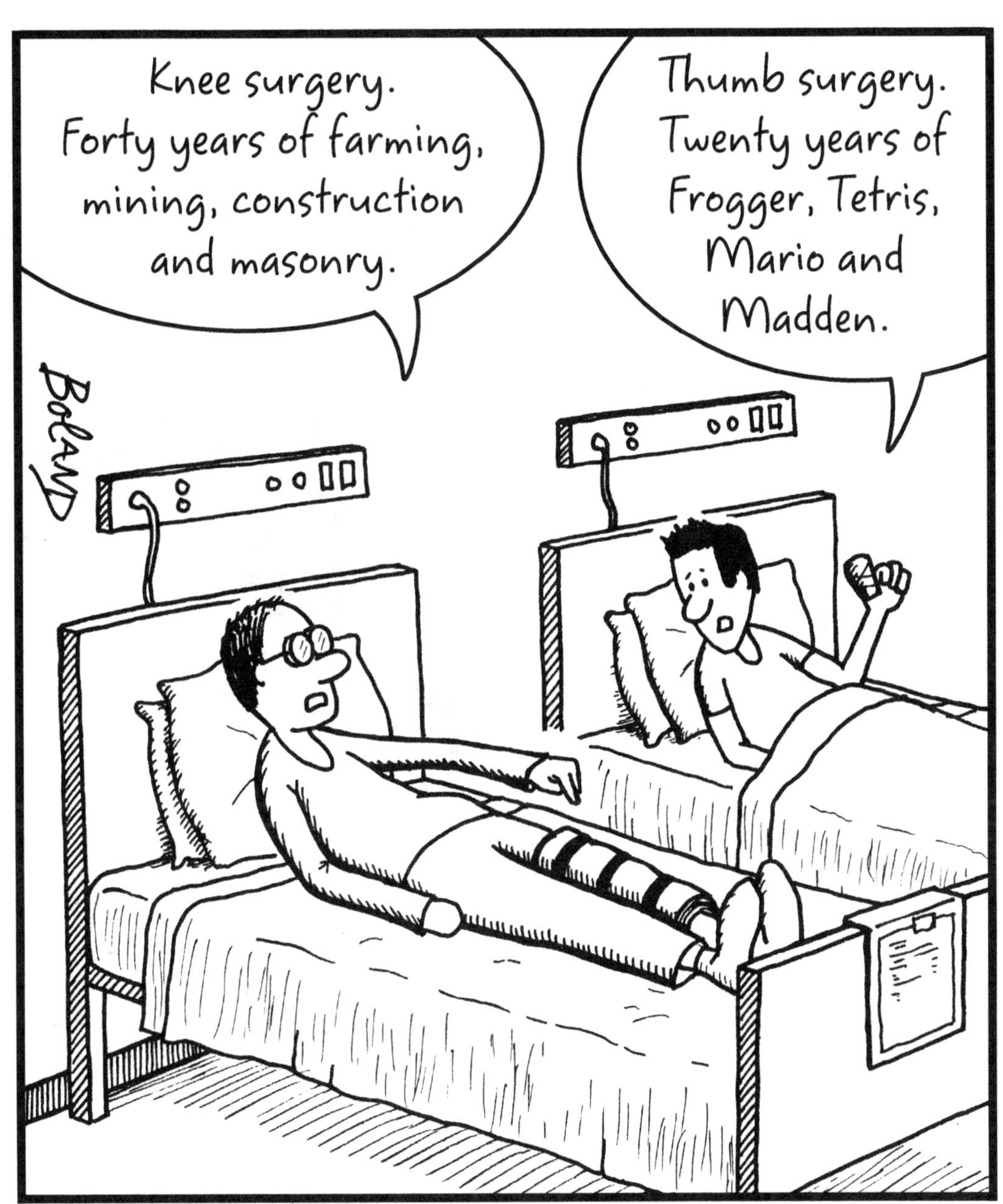
Knee surgery. Forty years of farming, mining, construction and masonry.
Thumb surgery. Twenty years of Frogger, Tetris, Mario and Madden.
BOLAND

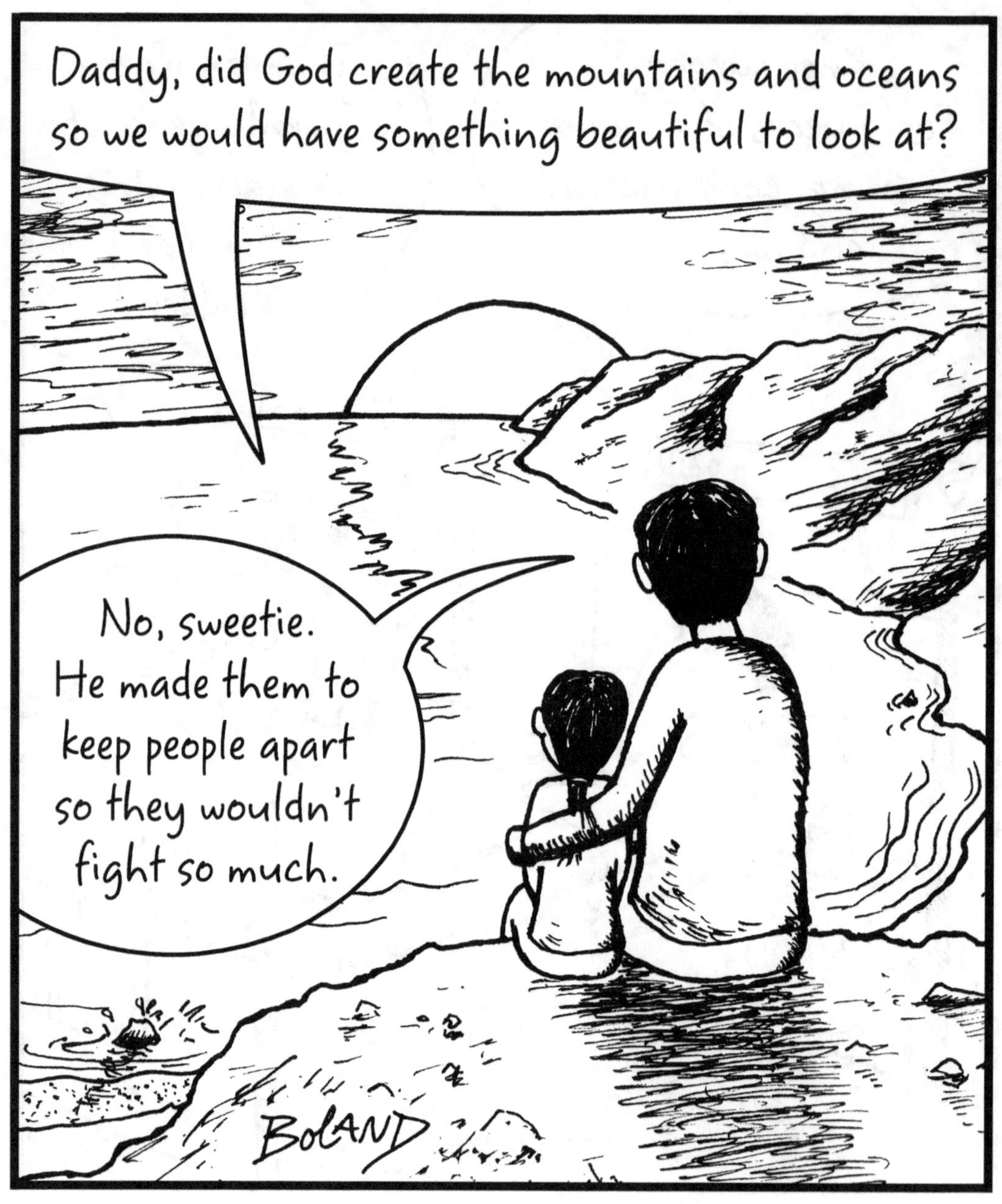
Daddy, did God create the mountains and oceans so we would have something beautiful to look at?
No, sweetie. He made them to keep people apart so they wouldn't fight so much.
BOLAND

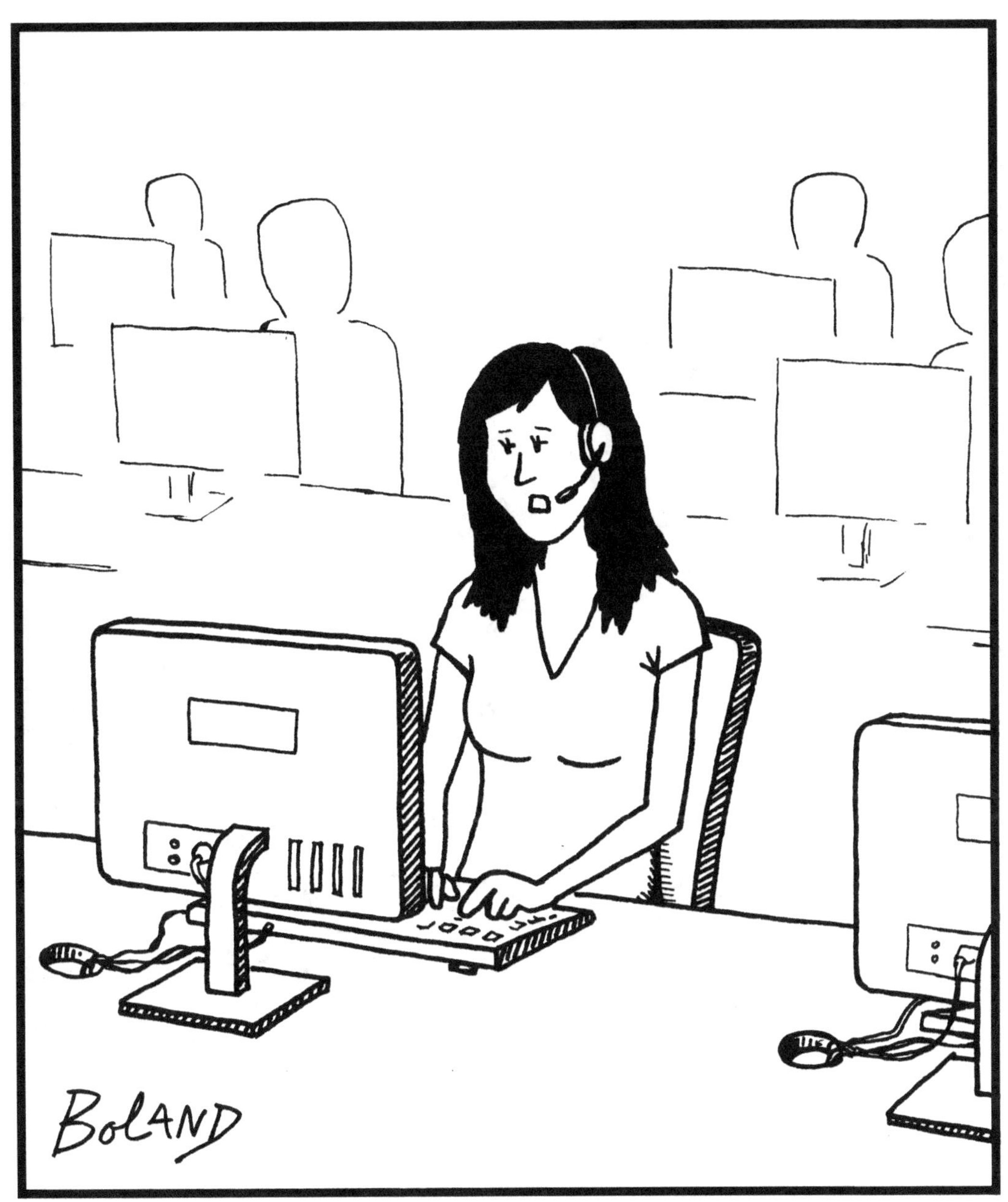

"Urinary disorder hot line. Please hold."

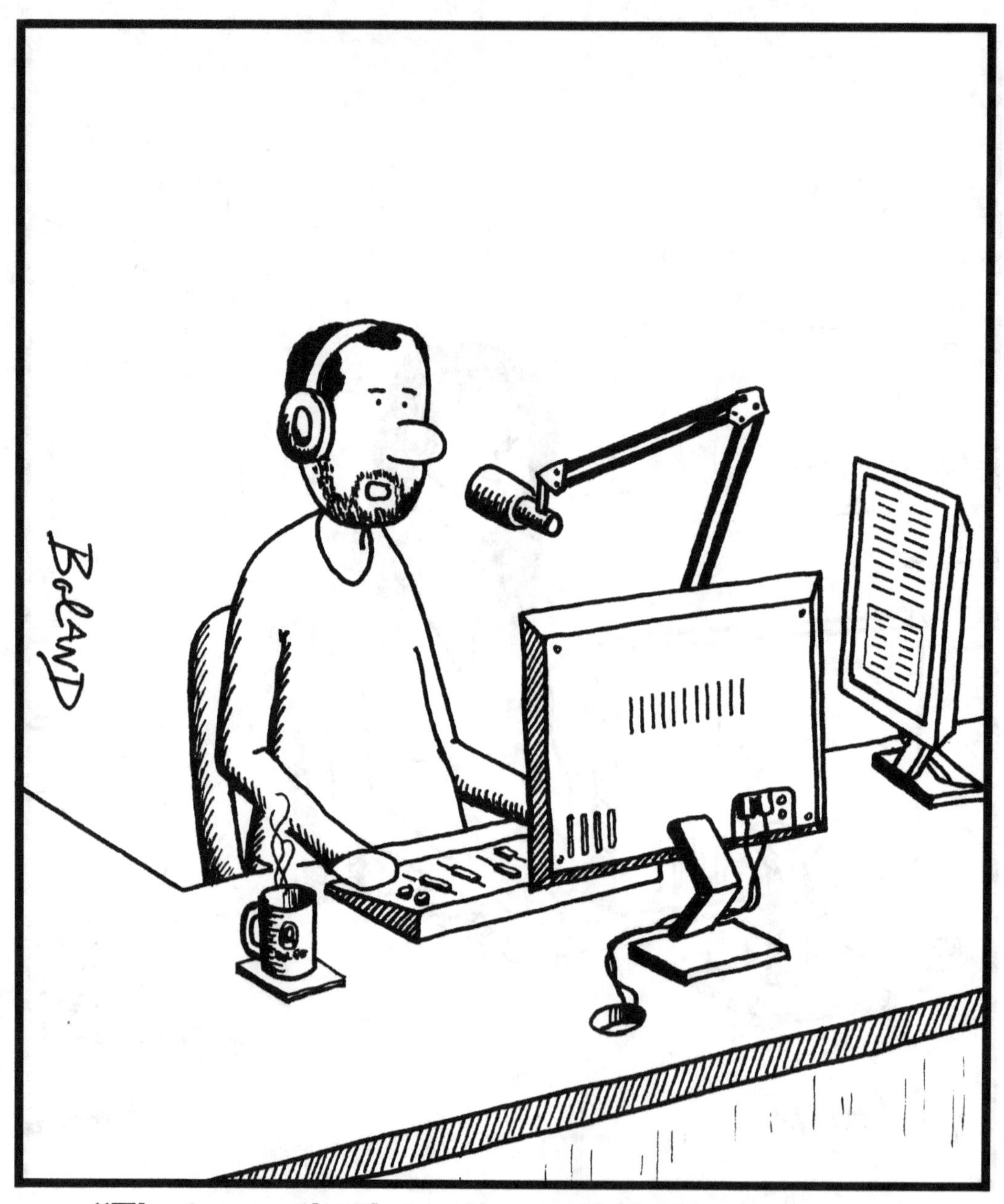

"That was the latest smash hit by request. I'll be doing my best to play that song every ten minutes until you all hate it with a passion."

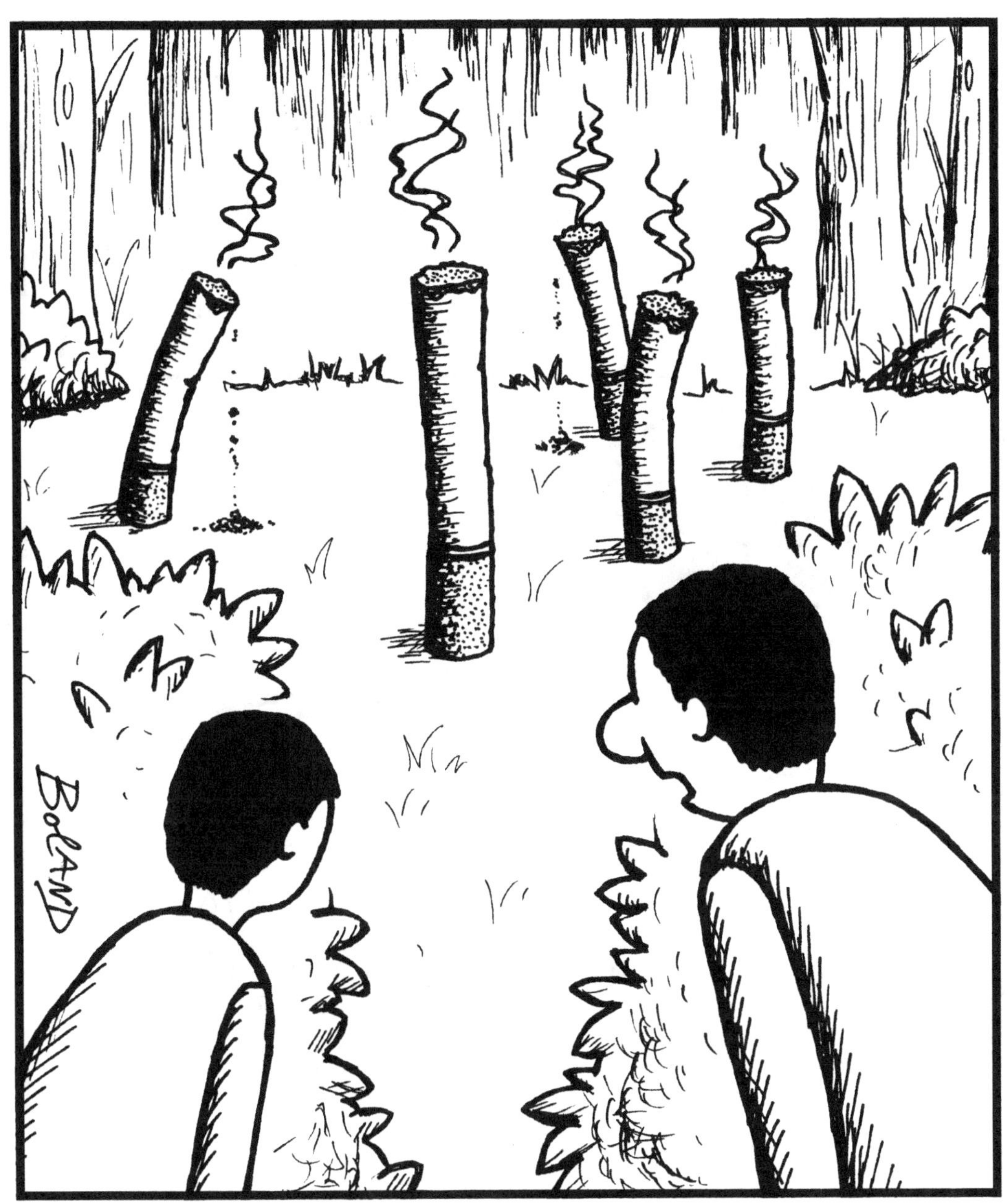

"Always keep your distance, son. They're very dangerous, especially in packs."

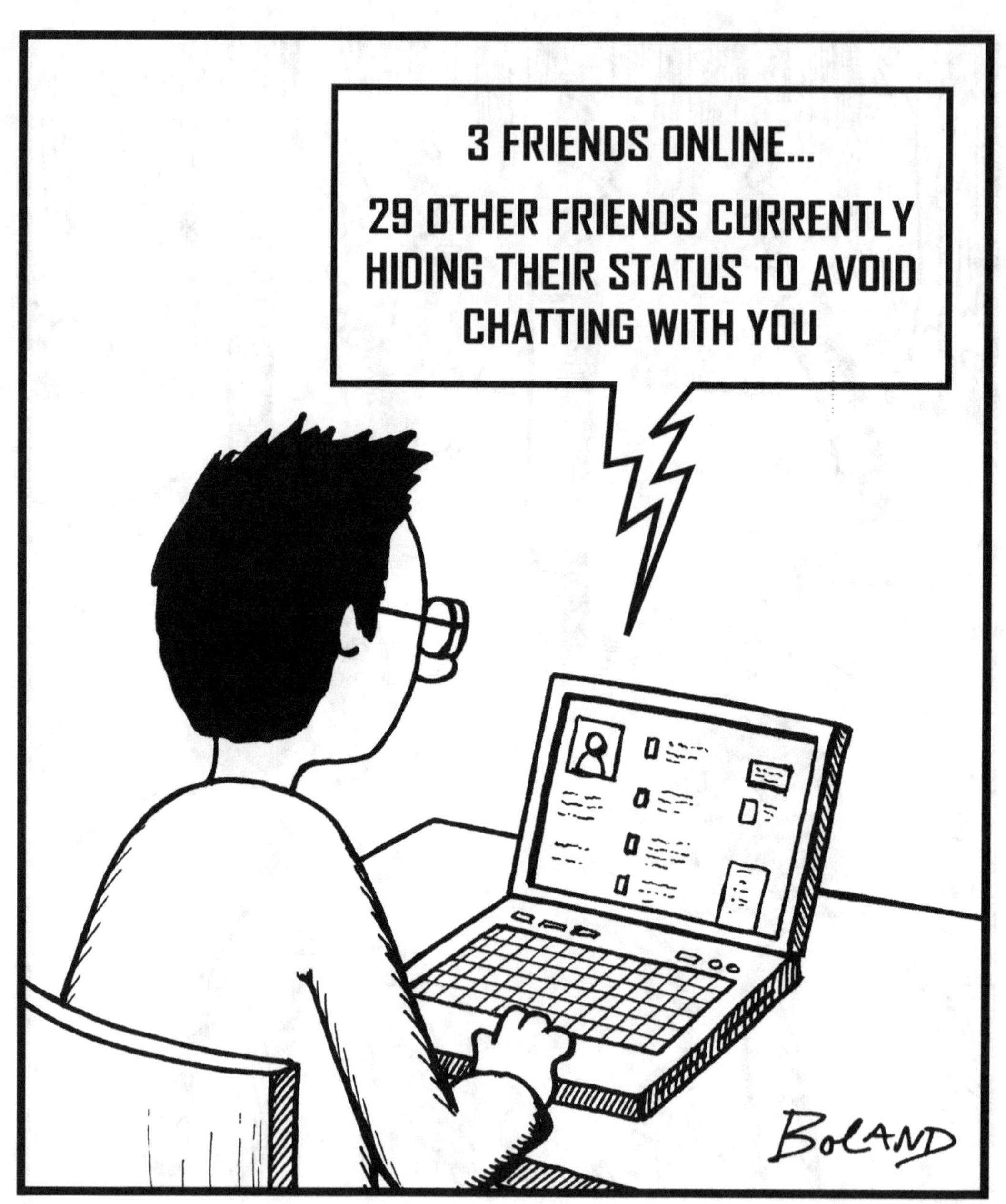
3 FRIENDS ONLINE...
29 OTHER FRIENDS CURRENTLY HIDING THEIR STATUS TO AVOID CHATTING WITH YOU
BOLAND

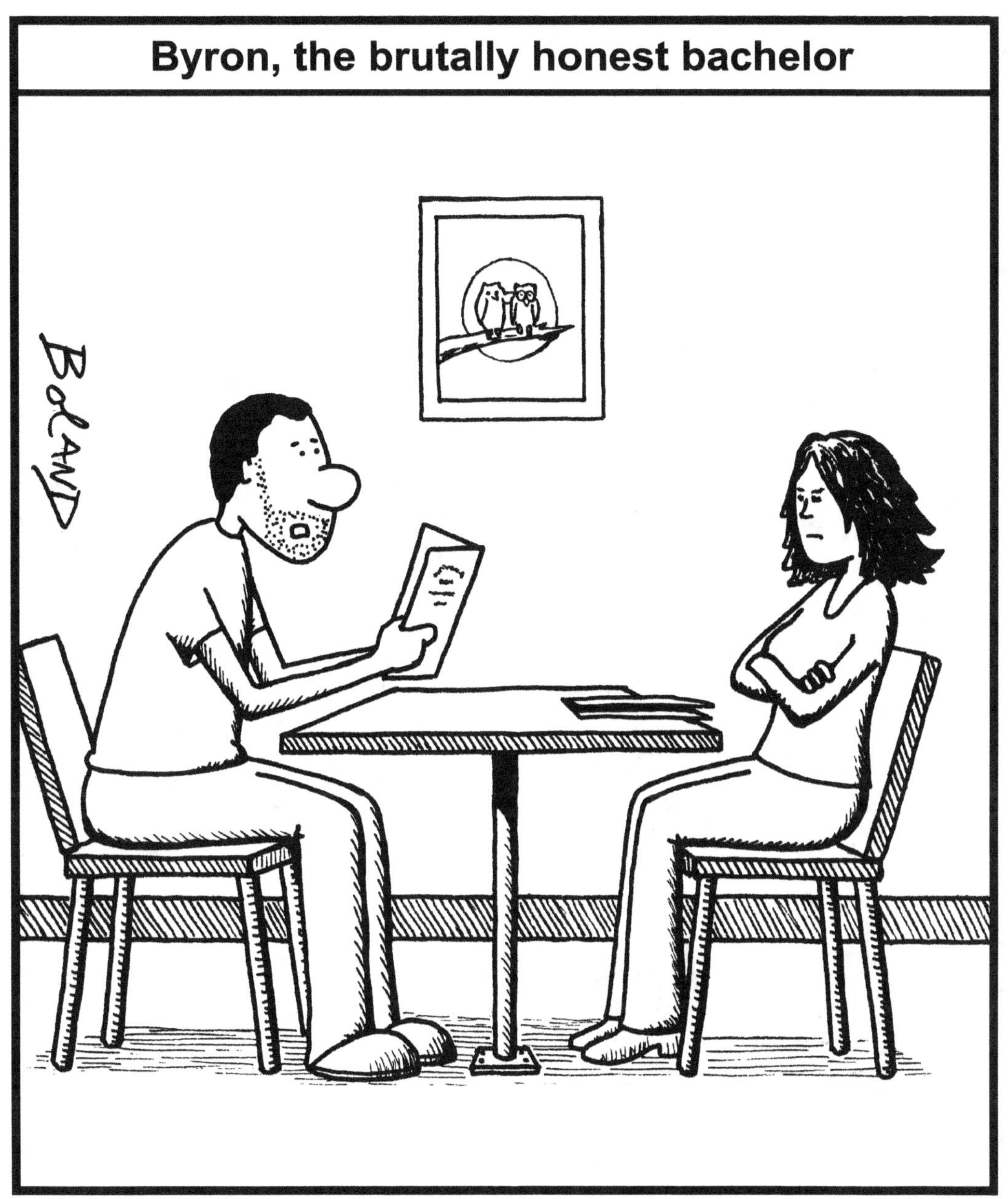

Byron, the brutally honest bachelor

"Yes, I was staring at that waitress... but in my defense, I was only ogling her buffalo wings."

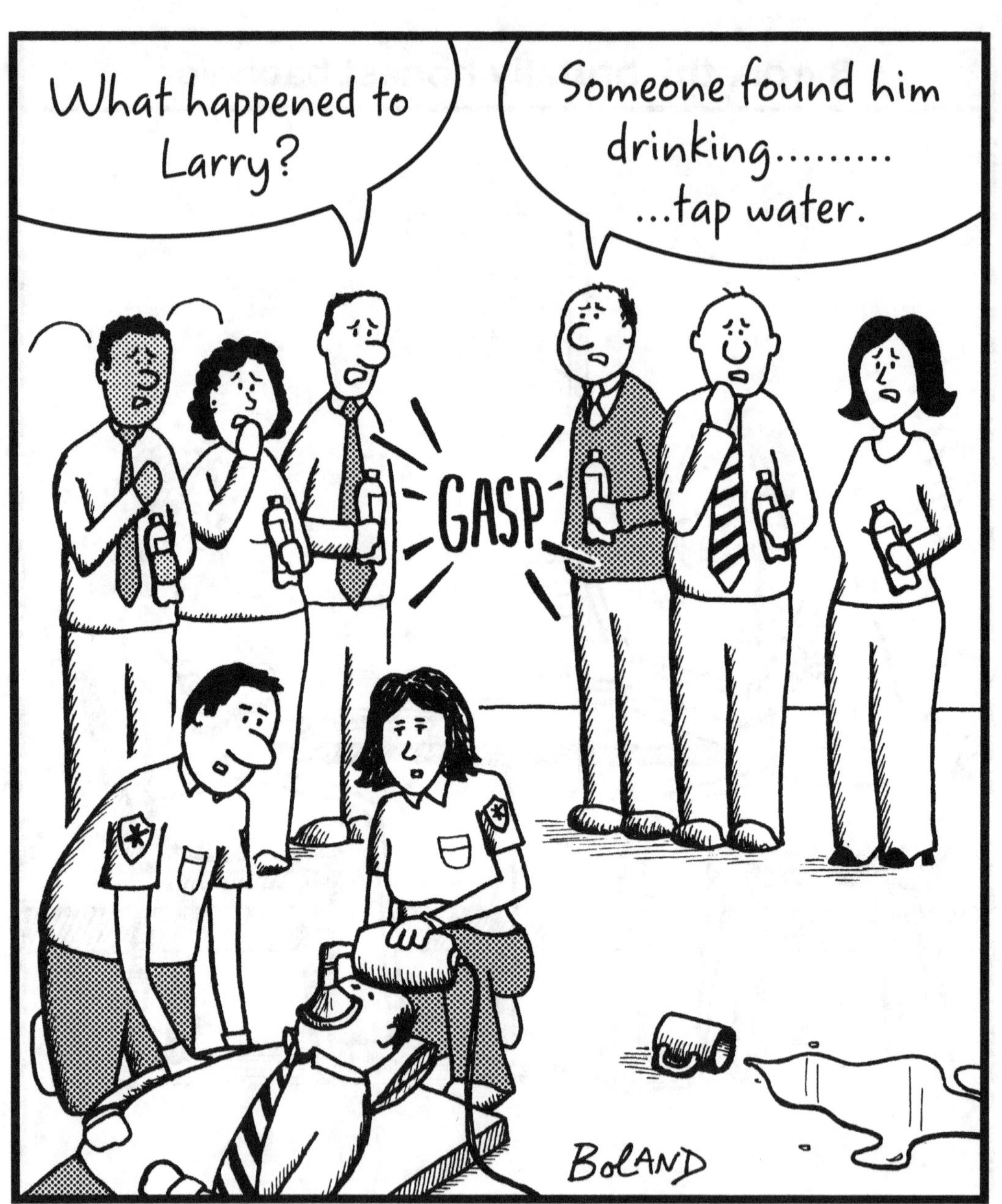
What happened to Larry?
Someone found him drinking.........
...tap water.
GASP
BoLAND

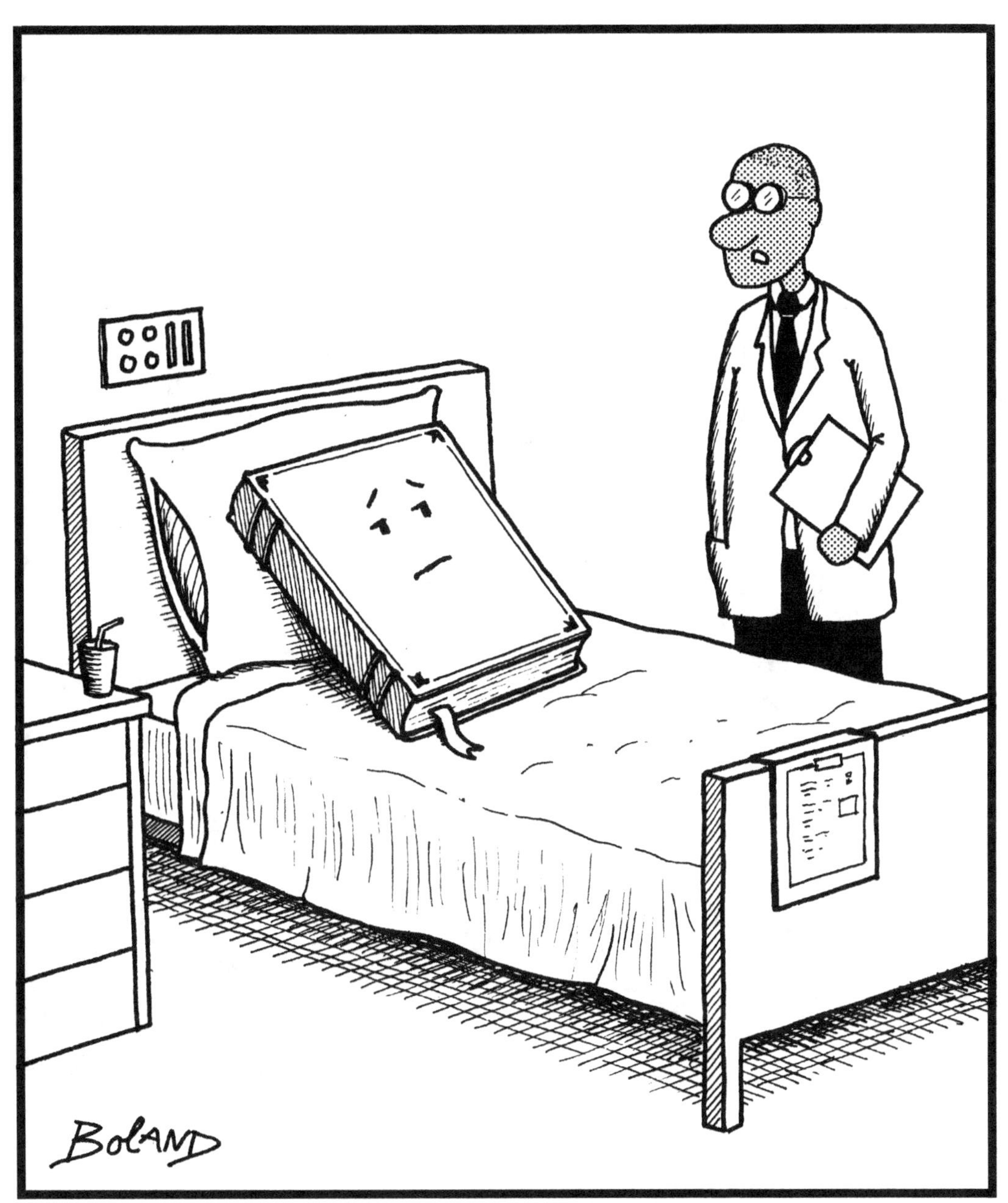

“We need to remove your appendix.”

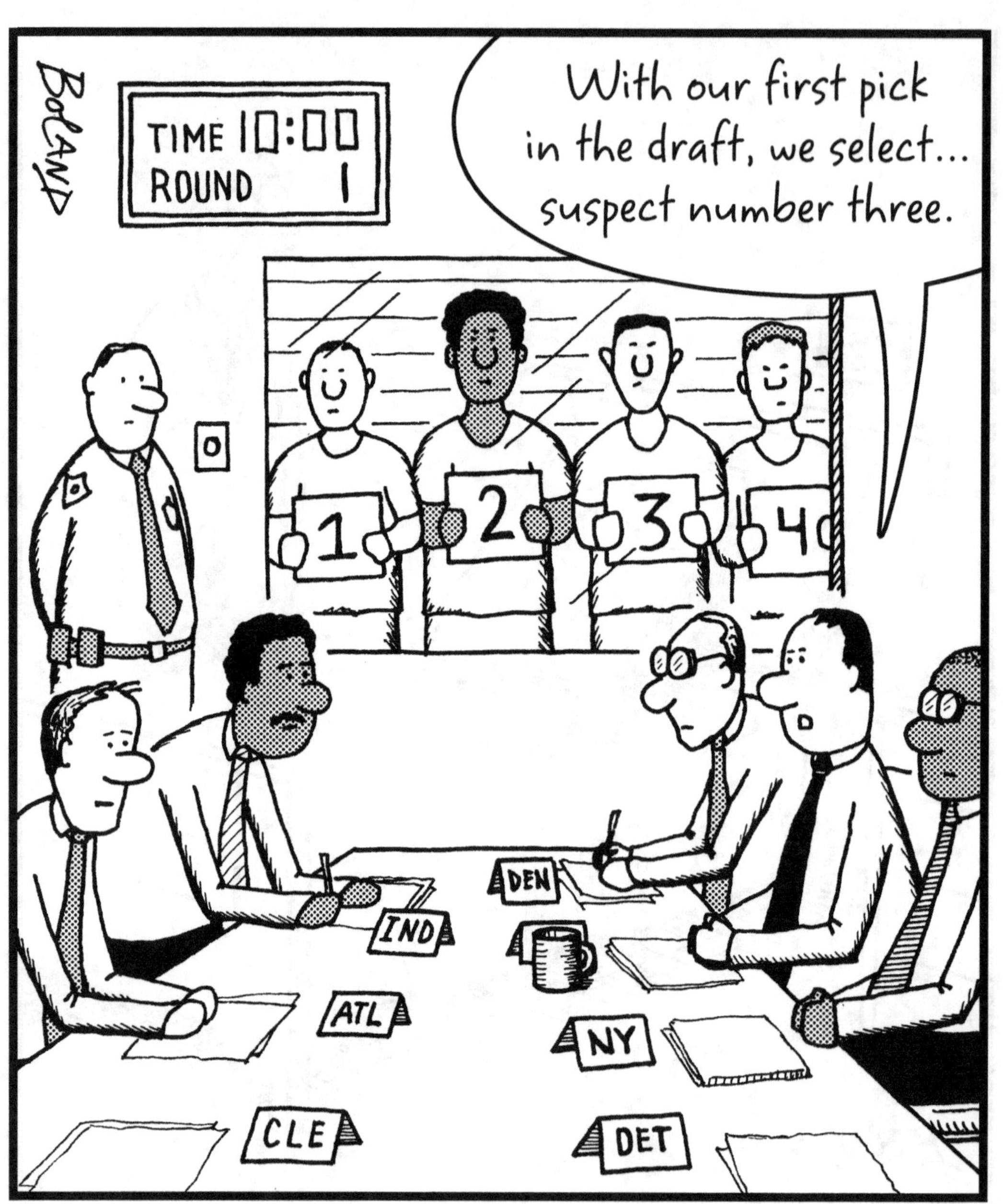
BOLAND
TIME 10:00
ROUND 1
With our first pick
in the draft, we select...
suspect number three.
1
2
3
4
DEN
IND
ATL
NY
CLE
DET

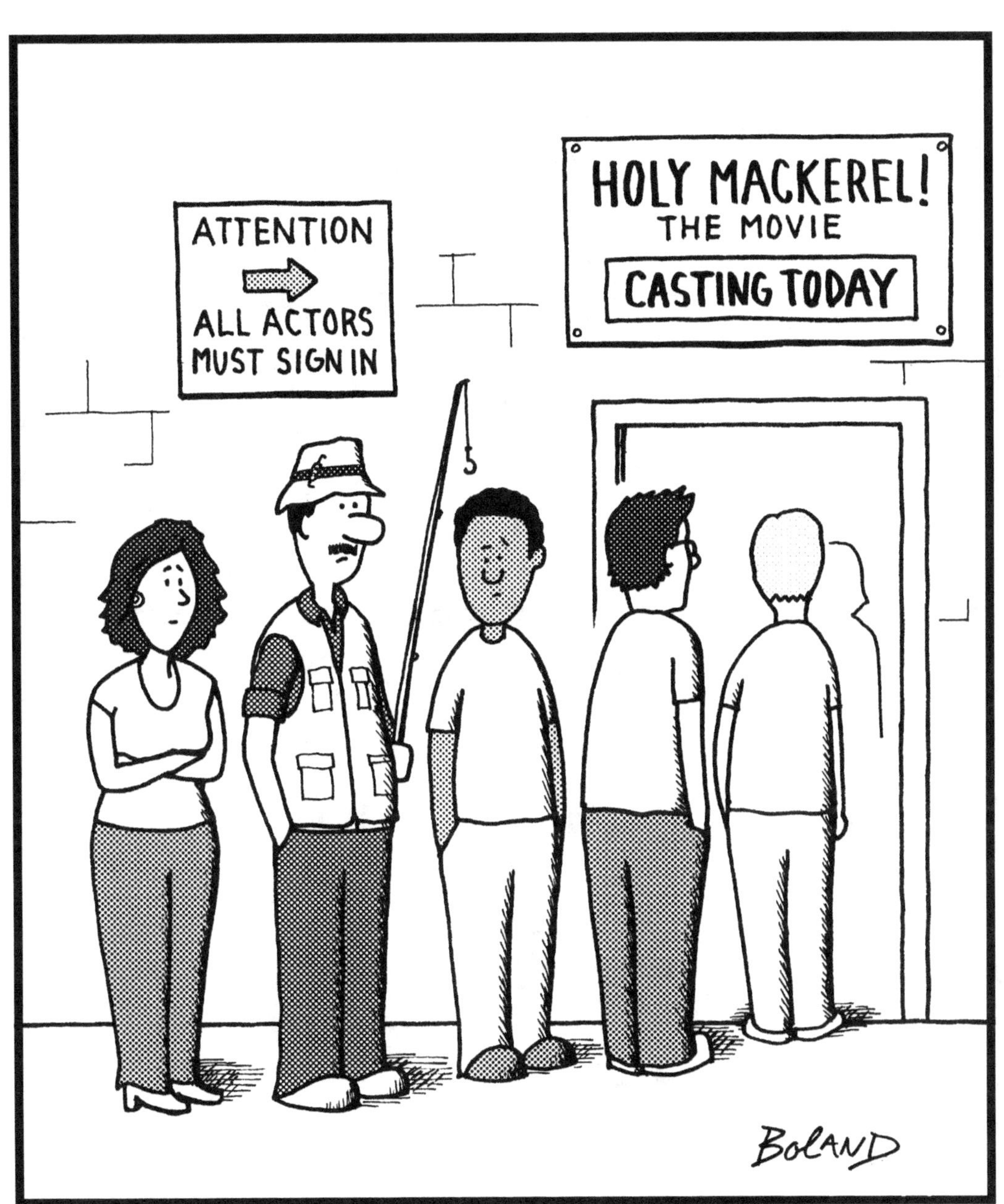
ATTENTION
ALL ACTORS MUST SIGN IN
HOLY MACKEREL!
THE MOVIE
CASTING TODAY
BOLAND

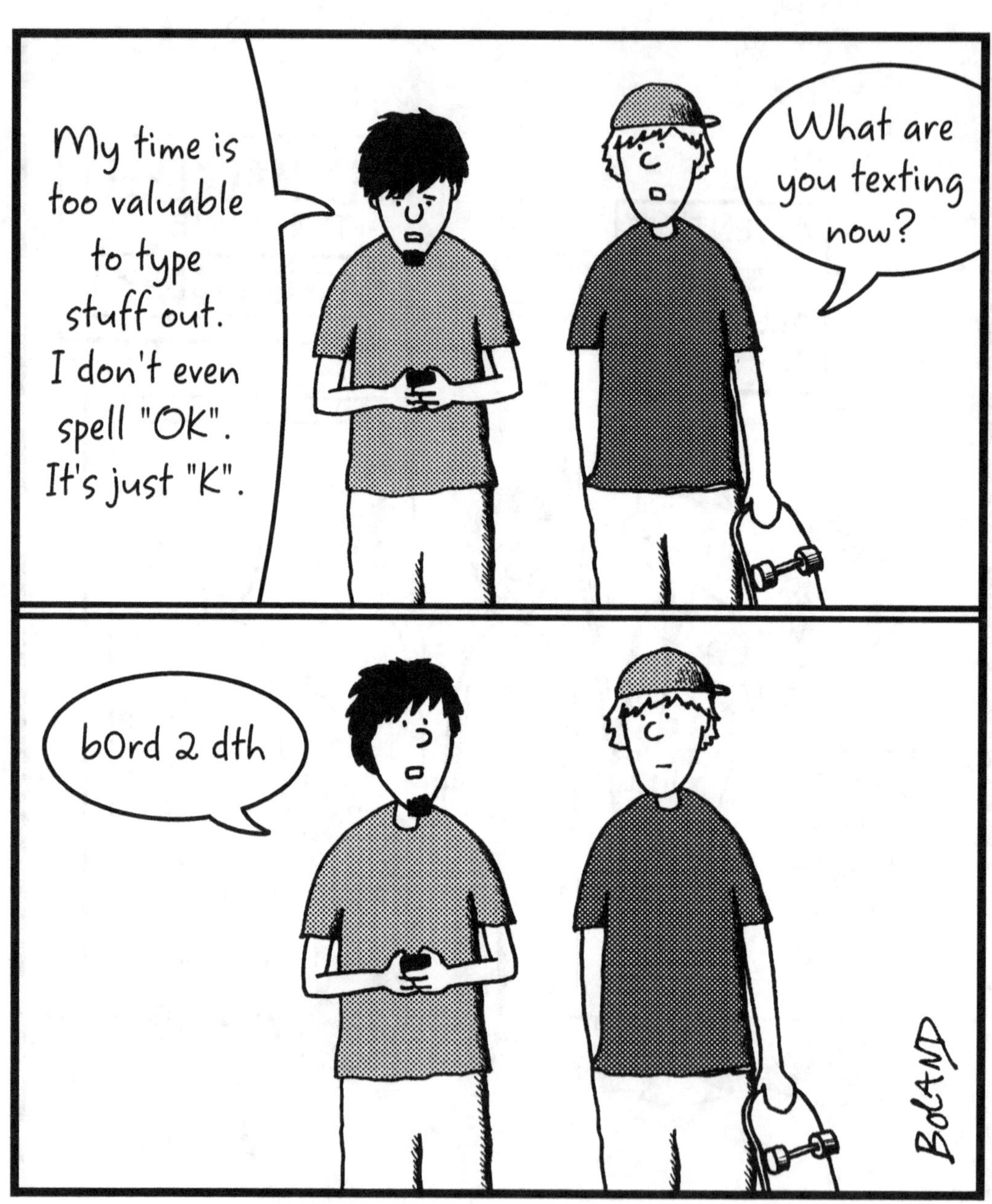
What are you texting now?
My time is too valuable to type stuff out. I don't even spell "OK". It's just "K".
b0rd 2 dth
BOLAND

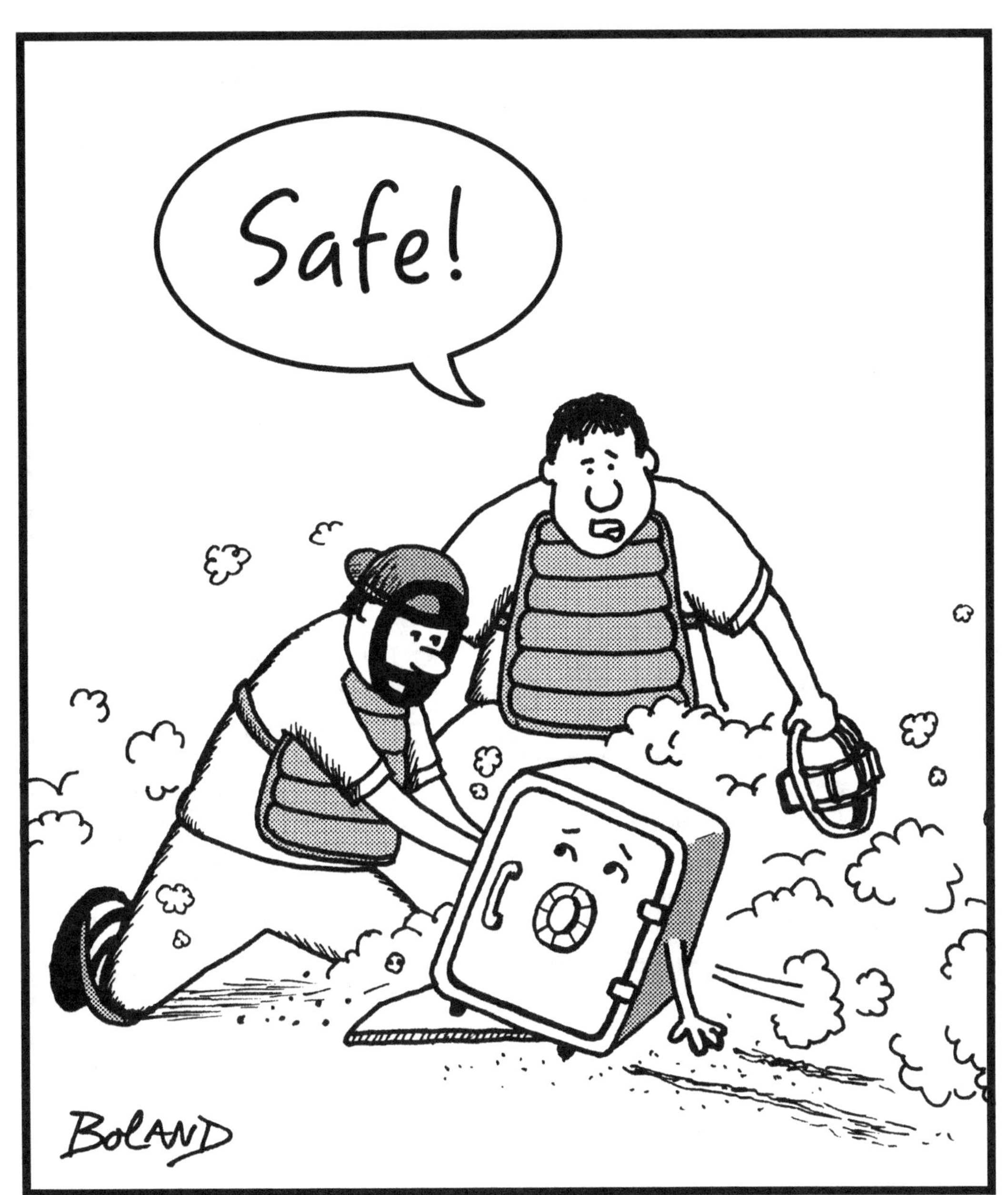
Safe!
BOLAND

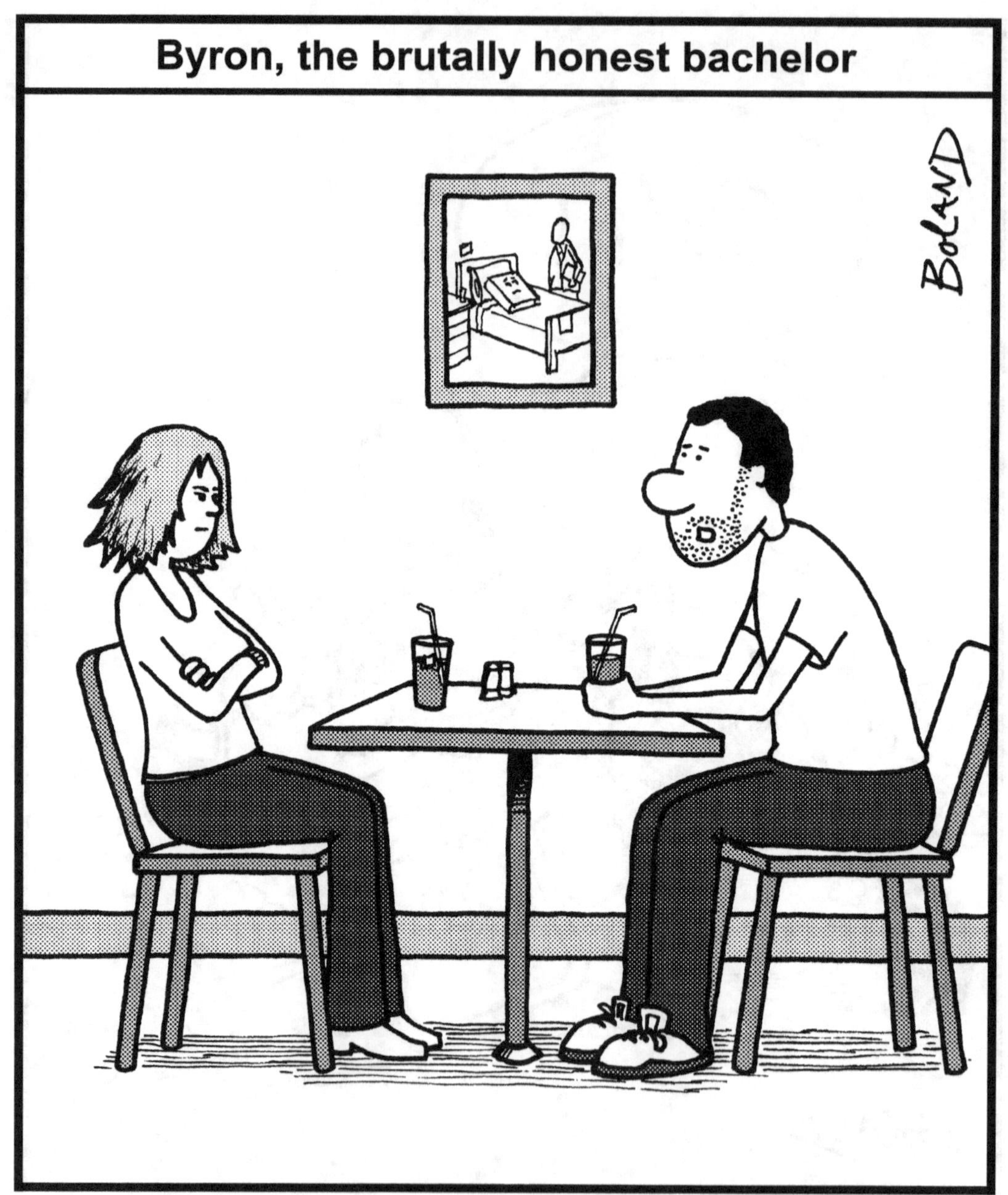

"Sorry about that. I like footsie...I really do... but these are vintage Jordans."

www.ingramcontent.com/pod-product-compliance
Lightning Source LLC
LaVergne TN
LVHW061222100826
845148LV00004B/833

* 9 7 8 0 6 1 5 4 0 6 9 6 1 *